THAILAND: ECONOMIC, POLITICAL AND SOCIAL ISSUES

THAILAND: ECONOMIC, POLITICAL AND SOCIAL ISSUES

RANDLE C. ZEBIOLI
EDITOR

Nova Science Publishers, Inc.
New York

Copyright © 2009 by Nova Science Publishers, Inc.

All rights reserved. No part of this book may be reproduced, stored in a retrieval system or transmitted in any form or by any means: electronic, electrostatic, magnetic, tape, mechanical photocopying, recording or otherwise without the written permission of the Publisher.

For permission to use material from this book please contact us:
Telephone 631-231-7269; Fax 631-231-8175
Web Site: http://www.novapublishers.com

NOTICE TO THE READER

The Publisher has taken reasonable care in the preparation of this book, but makes no expressed or implied warranty of any kind and assumes no responsibility for any errors or omissions. No liability is assumed for incidental or consequential damages in connection with or arising out of information contained in this book. The Publisher shall not be liable for any special, consequential, or exemplary damages resulting, in whole or in part, from the readers' use of, or reliance upon, this material. Any parts of this book based on government reports are so indicated and copyright is claimed for those parts to the extent applicable to compilations of such works.

Independent verification should be sought for any data, advice or recommendations contained in this book. In addition, no responsibility is assumed by the publisher for any injury and/or damage to persons or property arising from any methods, products, instructions, ideas or otherwise contained in this publication.

This publication is designed to provide accurate and authoritative information with regard to the subject matter covered herein. It is sold with the clear understanding that the Publisher is not engaged in rendering legal or any other professional services. If legal or any other expert assistance is required, the services of a competent person should be sought. FROM A DECLARATION OF PARTICIPANTS JOINTLY ADOPTED BY A COMMITTEE OF THE AMERICAN BAR ASSOCIATION AND A COMMITTEE OF PUBLISHERS.

LIBRARY OF CONGRESS CATALOGING-IN-PUBLICATION DATA

Thailand : economics, politics and sociology / Randle C. Zebioli (editor).
   p. cm.
 Includes bibliographical references and index.
 ISBN 978-1-60456-583-6 (hardcover : alk. paper)
 1. Thailand--Social conditions--1986- 2. Thailand--Economic conditions--1945-1986. 3. Thailand--Economic conditions--1986- 4. Thailand--Foreign relations--1988- 5. Thailand--Politics and government--1988- 6. Public health--Thailand. 7. Education--Thailand. I. Zebioli, Randle C.
 HN700.55.A8T45 2008
 306.09593--dc22
                         2008012150

Published by Nova Science Publishers, Inc.,   New York

CONTENTS

Preface		vii
Chapter 1	Thailand: Country Profile and Current Events	1
Chapter 2	The Differential Impact of the Economic Crisis on Thailand, Indonesia and South Korea *Chung Sang-Hwa*	11
Chapter 3	Thailand Trade *Ida M. Conway*	35
Chapter 4	The New International Order in the Asia-Pacific Region: Thailand's Responses and Options *Chookiat Panaspornprasit*	51
Chapter 5	Decision-Making Process and Health-Seeking Patterns of Young Women with Unplanned Pregnancies, Bangkok, Thailand *Wanapa Naravage and Rungpetch C. Sakulbumrungsil*	61
Chapter 6	*Yu Duan* Practices: The Significance and Implications for Women's Health in Northern Thailand *Pranee Liamputtong*	123
Chapter 7	Childrearing Practices among Primary Caregivers of HIV-Infected Children Aged 0-5 Years in Chiang Mai, Thailand *Pimpaporn Klunklin, Prakin Suchaxaya, Chawapornpan Chanprasit and Wichit Srisuphun*	139
Chapter 8	Creating Scales to Measure Reading Comprehension, and Attitude and Behaviour, for Prathom (Grade) 7 Students Taught ESL Through a Genre-Based Method in Thailand *Russell F. Waugh, Margaret H. Bowering and Sanguansri Torok*	151

Chapter 9	Cooperative Learning versus Communicative Thai Teaching of English as a Second Language for Prathom (Grade) 6 Students Taught in Thailand *Russell F. Waugh, Margaret H. Bowering and Sutaporn Chayarathee*	**189**
Index		**201**

PREFACE

A unified Thai kingdom was established in the mid-14th century. Known as Siam until 1939, Thailand is the only Southeast Asian country never to have been taken over by a European power. A bloodless revolution in 1932 led to a constitutional monarchy. In alliance with Japan during World War II, Thailand became a US ally following the conflict. Thailand is currently facing separatist violence in its southern ethnic Malay-Muslim provinces. This new book presents new issues directly connected to Thailand.

Chapter 1 - This chapter briefly outlines the people, history, government and political conditions, economy, foreing relations, U.S.–Thai relations, and trade and investments.

Chapter 2 - Korea began the process of industrialisation in the late 1960's, followed by Thailand and Indonesia in the mid-1970's. Despite variations in resource endowments, all three countries had recorded such impressive records of industrialisation[1] that international society loudly applauded their economic successes. In the late 1990's, however, the Asian economic crisis had entered a totally new phase, spawned by the July 1997 foreign currency crisis in Thailand. 'Currency crisis', defined as a large drop in the value of currency in a short period of time, had spread to Southeast Asia, and eventually reached Korea. Among the victims, Thailand, Indonesia and South Korea (hereafter Korea) asked the International Monetary Fund (IMF) for rescue loans, but Malaysia, which also had been hard hit by the crisis, closed its foreign exchange market instead of requesting the IMF for help.

The three Greater East Asian countries had several characteristics in common when they encountered economic crisis: they relied on trade in the process of economic development; enjoyed high levels of liquidity; had recently introduced financial liberalisation; and had opaque corporate and banking systems.[2] After they accepted the IMF stabilisation programs, they also faced such problems together as the precipitate decline of currency value, the instability of financial sectors, market contractions, decreases in investment, and increases in unemployment. As of early 2001, the economic crisis appears to be contained in Korea, but it still scratches Indonesia with its fingernails, and Thailand is located somewhere between the two.

Although there has been much research on the Asian economic crises, many issues still remain unclear and unanswered. Were the crises unavoidable? What was the decisive cause(s) of the foreign exchange crises? Were the IMF interventions adequate? What were the political

---

[1] Korea had poor natural resources, but it could develop its economy thanks to skilled manpower and the effective governmental policies of the time. Indonesia and Thailand had rich natural endowments and could invite generous foreign investments to encourage speedy industrialisation.

[2] However, it is also true that each country had its own political and economic specificities as will be discussed later in detail.

and economic consequences of the crises? Should and can Asian countries reform their political and economic management styles? Which international political economy approach, for example, the interdependence school, neomercantilism, or structuralism, more adequately explains the crises?

This analysis examines the economic crises of Indonesia, Thailand and Korea in order to understand better their causes, processes and consequences. A comparative study has an advantage in that it clarifies the issue by contrasting similarities and differences. In the next section, the pre-crisis political and economic developments are compared. The following section explores the causes of the three countries' economic crises. Then, IMF programs and each country's reform efforts, and the consequences of the economic crises, are surveyed. The last section critically assesses the nature of the Asian economic crises based on the discussions of the previous parts, and presents theoretical and policy implications.

Chapter 3 - The U.S. goods trade deficit with Thailand was $14.3 billion in 2006, an increase of $1.7 billion from $12.6 billion in 2005. U.S. goods exports in 2006 were $8.2 billion, up 12.4 percent from the previous year. Corresponding U.S. imports from Thailand were $22.5 billion, up 13.0 percent. Thailand is currently the 24th largest export market for U.S. goods.

U.S. exports of private commercial services (i.e., excluding military and government) to Thailand were $1.5 billion in 2005 (latest data available), and U.S. imports were $1.1 billion. Sales of services in Thailand by majority U.S.-owned affiliates were $3.0 billion in 2004 (latest data available), while sales of services in the United States by majority Thailand-owned firms were $3 million.

The stock of U.S. foreign direct investment (FDI) in Thailand in 2005 was $8.6 billion (latest data available), up from $7.6 billion in 2004. U.S. FDI in Thailand is concentrated largely in the manufacturing, finance, professional, scientific, and technical services, and wholesale trade sectors.

Chapter 4 - *Objectives*: This study examined the decision-making process and health-seeking patterns of low-income young women with unplanned pregnancies who opted for abortion, putting baby up for adoption, or keeping the baby.

Methods: Research methodology in this study focused on formative research utilizing qualitative data. The study was conducted covering all five shelters and low-income communities in Bangkok, Thailand. The data collection was through Focus Group Discussions, and in-depth interview. Forty-five cases were purposefully recruited into the study. The data were analyzed using content analysis.

Results: From the qualitative research, the results indicated that the majority of the young women tended to select abortion as their first choice, while a few cases continued their pregnancies to term without any attempt to terminate the pregnancy. These women tended to delay seeking assistance once they found out their pregnancy situation. The majority of the low-income young women were more likely to resort to self-medication as their first alternative, which was sometimes hazardous to their health. Decision on self-medication or abortions with unskilled personnel sometimes resulted in serious and life-threatening complications. Many pregnancy-termination situations resulted from self-medication. While most of these women made the important decision themselves, they still sought advice, guidance, and support from their partners, peers and parents. When the first attempt failed, they would seek a second or third attempt until they felt it was not possible to achieve what they had planned.

Most women with unplanned pregnancies knew that they had options regarding termination of their pregnancies but their main concern was confidentiality. Consequently, the women who wanted to terminate their pregnancies adopted three patterns of action, i.e., 1) visiting drugstores / grocery stores, 2) visiting private clinics or hospitals, and 3) using physical pressure or vigorous actions. Most of the women realized that private clinics provided effective methods for terminating pregnancy, but due to its high cost, they would first resort self-medication or self-management. If they were not successful, they would then visit a private clinic and asked others to support the cost.

Understanding the women's decision-making process and their health-seeking patterns allows us to understand their decision and course of actions. The program managers, implementers, providers, partners, parents/relatives, and friends should do as much as possible to support the decision of the women in order to provide better information and services to reduce the impact, both physical and mental, of their choice.

Chapter 5 - In this chapter, the author addresses traditional confinement beliefs and practices among Thai women in northern Thailand. The chapter is based on qualitative research involving in-depth interviews with 30 women in Chiang Mai province. In northern Thai culture, the period after birth is considered as the most vulnerable period of a new mother and of her life. For a period of 30 days, known as *yu duan* in northern Thailand, she is in a state of vulnerability to ill health and diseases. During this period, a new mother follows many dietary and behavioural proscriptions and prescriptions. It is clear that traditional beliefs and practices are still carried on by the women in this study. It is, therefore, imperative that these traditions need to be taken into account in providing postpartum care to Thai women. The author contends that a serious consideration of traditional beliefs and practices may go a long way in improving women's birthing care in Thailand and elsewhere.

Chapter 6 - HIV has become one of the leading causes of death worldwide in the past two decades. Having no cure, HIV causes more than 13,500 new infections each day. The Joint United Nations Programme on HIV/AIDS (UNAIDS) reported that there were 2.3 millions of children living with HIV and 57,000 of these died by AIDS in 2005 (UNAIDS, 2005). In Thailand, approximately one-seventh of new infections are children. Roughly 4,000 Thai children are being infected with HIV each year. Currently, 24,662 children are living with HIV/AIDS (The Thai Working Group on HIV/AIDS Projection, 2001). Moreover, HIV epidemiology studies in Thailand found that the highest prevalence of the infection occurs in Northern Thailand (Ministry of Public Health, Thailand, 2002). This information could be used to estimate that the number of HIV-infected children would be high around this region as they contracted the disease through their parents.

Children born with HIV infection often display physical impairments, such as a weakened immune system, which makes them vulnerable to various illnesses and opportunistic infections. Infectious causes of death that were often reported included pneumonia, diarrhea, sepsis, and fungal esophageal infections (Chearskul et al., 2002). HIV-infected children require intensive medical and emotional attention as a result of their HIV exposure. Some presented with malnutrition, lack of vaccination, delayed development, and poor hygiene (Kompayack et al., 2002). Further, research on disease progression among HIV-infected Thai children suggests that about half of the children die by the age of 5 years with an estimated 82, 74, 56, 49 and 43 percent survival rate for 1, 2, 3, 5, and 6 year olds, respectively (Chearskul et al., 2002).

HIV-infected children often lose one or both parents to AIDS. Many grow up in traumatic circumstances without the support and care of their parents as they are often moved from one home to another during the duration of their parent's illness. Therefore, grandparents, in particular, grandmothers are often left with the responsibility to serve as the child's primary caregiver (Kespichawattana and VanLandingham, 2002). A study of HIV affected children in northern Thailand indicated that the children experience psychological distress before and after a parent dies. They often express feelings of depression, sadness, loneliness, discrimination, and tend to perceive themselves negatively (Chontawan et al., 2002).

HIV-infected children are at risk of violence, exploitation, abuse, and also mistreatment by their caregivers. Poverty, insufficient food and substandard housing are other problems they face. Moreover, society often views them as a negative stereotype, thus, increasing their sense of isolation. Having a parent with HIV is perceived to be different from having a parent who is affected by other illnesses (Chontawan et al., 2002)

Childrearing is essential to promote the child's health. Many HIV-infected children have lived with the illness and its demands on their bodies most of their life. As such, they often have health problems. Therefore, greater care is needed during childrearing to prevent or control opportunistic infections. Limited research that examines different approaches to childrearing practices from a cultural perspective was available. Further, little is known about how the presence of HIV/AIDS may influence caregivers' idea about childrearing practices, and their beliefs and practices of childrearing.

The purpose of this study was to explore Thai primary caregiver's beliefs and practices about childrearing for HIV infected children aged 0-5 years old. A focus ethnographic approach was used to examine childrearing practices of primary caregivers of those who are affected by HIV/AIDS. The study was conducted in Chiang Mai, the capital city of Northern Thailand, where culture has great influences on childrearing practices of northern Thai people.

Chapter 7 - A questionnaire involving attitudes and behaviour towards genre-based learning of English as a second language (based on text, inter-personal relations, and behavioural controls) was given to 300 prathom 7 (grade 7) students in Thailand. A Rasch analysis was performed to create a linear scale using 18 of the original 48 items (each answered in two perspectives, an ideal and an actual). These data had good reliability and validity, and supported a modified structure of attitudes and behaviour, from which valid and reliable inferences could be made. A Rasch analysis was performed on data from a separate reading comprehension test (based on three kinds of genre texts) with the same 300 prathom 7 students using 18 of an original 60 items. These data fitted the measurement model well, but had a low Index of Separation for these students. Both scales were used in an experiment described in the next chapter on genre-based teaching versus traditional teaching learning of English as a second language.

Chapter 8 - A controlled experiment in teaching English as a second language was implemented. The experiment involved 96 students from three primary schools in Ratchaburi, Thailand. The students from each school were randomly assigned to an experimental group (N=48) and a control group (N=48). The experimental group was taught by using cooperative learning and the control group was taught by the Thai communicative method. Great care was taken to ensure that students were treated the same in all respects, except the method of learning, in both the experimental and control groups. Pretest and posttest measures were administered and significant differences tested using ANOVA (SPSS). There were four main findings. (1) Students improved their English reading comprehension under both the cooperative learning and Thai communicative group methods of teaching. (2) Students improved their English reading comprehension under the cooperative learning method significantly more than under the Thai communicative group method. (3) Students improved their attitude and behaviour towards learning English as a second language under both the cooperative learning and Thai communicative group methods of teaching. (4) Students improved their attitude and behaviour towards learning English as a second language significantly more under the cooperative learning method than under the Thai communicative group method of teaching.

In: Thailand: Economics, Political and Social Issues
Ed: Randle C. Zebioli

ISBN: 978-1-60456-583-0
©2009 Nova Science Publishers, Inc.

Chapter 1

THAILAND: COUNTRY PROFILE AND CURRENT EVENTS

KINGDOM OF THAILAND

Geography

Area: 513,115 sq. km. (198,114 sq. mi.); equivalent to the size of France, or slightly smaller than Texas.
Cities: Capital--Bangkok (population 9,668,854); Nakhon Ratchasima (pop. 437,386 for Muang district and 2,565,685 for the whole province), Chiang Mai (pop. 247,672 for Muang district and 1,595,855 for the whole province).
Terrain: Densely populated central plain; northeastern plateau; mountain range in the west; southern isthmus joins the land mass with Malaysia.
Climate: Tropical monsoon.

People

Nationality: Noun and adjective--Thai.
Population (2006): 65.28 million. (Data based on Bank of Thailand.)
Labor force (2006): 36.43 million.
Annual population growth rate (2006 est.): 0.3%.
Ethnic groups: Thai 89%, other 11%.
Religions: Buddhist 94-95%, Muslim 4-5%, Christian, Hindu, Brahmin, other.
Languages: Thai (official language); English is the second language of the elite; regional dialects.
Education: Years compulsory--12. Literacy--94.9% male, 90.5% female.
Health (2006 est.): Infant mortality rate--19.5/1,000. Life expectancy--68 years male, 75 years female.

Government

Type: Thailand remains a constitutional monarchy. Prime Minister, Cabinet, and National Legislative Assembly were appointed by the leaders of a September 19, 2006 coup d'etat.

Military leaders constitute a Council for National Security. The current structure will remain in place until a democratically elected government takes office.
Constitution: Thailand adopted its current constitution following an August 19, 2007 referendum.
Independence: Never colonized; traditional founding date 1238.
Branches: Executive--King (chief of state), Prime Minister (head of government). Legislative--National Assembly (unicameral, appointed by the military leadership). Judicial--composed of the Constitutional Tribunal, the Courts of Justice, and the Administrative Courts.
Administrative subdivisions: 76 provinces, including Bangkok municipality, subdivided into 796 districts, 81 subdistricts, 7,255 tambon administration, and 74,435 villages.
Political parties: Multi-party system; Communist Party is prohibited.
Suffrage: Universal and compulsory at 18 years of age.

Economy

GDP (2006): $206 billion.
Annual GDP growth rate (2006): 5.0%.
Per capita income (2006): $3,155.
Unemployment rate (2006): 1.5% of total labor force.
Natural resources: Tin, rubber, natural gas, tungsten, tantalum, timber, lead, fish, gypsum, lignite, fluorite.
Agriculture (8.9% of GDP): Products--rice, tapioca, rubber, corn, sugarcane, coconuts, soybeans.
Industry: Types--tourism, textiles, garments, agricultural processing, cement, integrated circuits, jewelry, electronics, and auto assembly.
Trade (2006): Merchandise exports--$128.2 billion: textiles and footwear, fishery products, computers and parts, electronics, electrical appliances, jewelry, rice, tapioca products, integrated circuits, rubber, automobiles. Major markets--ASEAN, U.S., EU, Japan, China, and Singapore. Merchandise imports--$125.9 billion: machinery and parts, petroleum, iron and steel, chemicals, vehicles and parts, jewelry, fish preparations, electrical appliances, fertilizers and pesticides. Major suppliers--Japan, ASEAN, Middle East, China, EU, and U.S.

PEOPLE

Thailand's population is relatively homogeneous. More than 85% speak a dialect of Thai and share a common culture. This core population includes the central Thai (33.7% of the population, including Bangkok), Northeastern Thai (34.2%), northern Thai (18.8%), and southern Thai (13.3%).

The language of the central Thai population is the language taught in schools and used in government. Several other small Thai-speaking groups include the Shan, Lue, and Phutai.

Up to 12% of Thai are of significant Chinese heritage, but the Sino-Thai community is the best integrated in Southeast Asia. Malay-speaking Muslims of the south comprise another significant minority group (2.3%). Other groups include the Khmer; the Mon, who are substantially assimilated with the Thai; and the Vietnamese. Smaller mountain-dwelling tribes, such as the Hmong and Mein, as well as the Karen, number about 788,024.

The population is mostly rural, concentrated in the rice-growing areas of the central, northeastern, and northern regions. However, as Thailand continues to industrialize, its urban population--31.6% of total population, principally in the Bangkok area--is growing.

Thailand's highly successful government-sponsored family planning program has resulted in a dramatic decline in population growth from 3.1% in 1960 to less than 1% today. Life expectancy also has risen, a positive reflection of Thailand's efforts at public health education. However, the AIDS epidemic has had a major impact on the Thai population. Today, over 500,000 Thais live with HIV or AIDS--approximately 1.4% of the adult population. Each year, 25-30,000 Thais die from AIDS-related causes. Ninety percent of them are aged 20-49, the most productive sector of the workforce. The situation could have been worse; an aggressive public education campaign in the early 1990's reduced the number of new HIV infections from over 100,000 annually to around 15,000 annually now.

The constitution mandates 12 years of free education, however, this is not provided universally. Education accounts for 18.0% of total government expenditures.

Theravada Buddhism is the major religion of Thailand and is the religion of about 95% of its people. The government permits religious diversity, and other major religions are represented. Spirit worship and animism are widely practiced.

HISTORY

Southeast Asia has been inhabited for more than half a million years. Archaeological studies suggest that by 4000 BC, communities in what is now Thailand had emerged as centers of early bronze metallurgy. This development, along with the cultivation of wet rice, provided the impetus for social and political organization. Research suggests that these innovations may actually have been transmitted from there to the rest of Asia, including to China.

The Thai are related linguistically to Tai groups originating in southern China. Migrations from southern China to Southeast Asia may have occurred in the 6th and 7th centuries. Malay, Mon, and Khmer civilizations flourished in the region prior to the arrival of the ethnic Tai.

Thais date the founding of their nation to the 13th century. According to tradition, in 1238, Thai chieftains overthrew their Khmer overlords at Sukhothai and established a Thai kingdom. After its decline, a new Thai kingdom emerged in 1350 on the Chao Praya River. At the same time, there was an equally important Tai kingdom of Lanna, centered in Chiang Mai, which rivaled Sukhothai and Ayutthaya for centuries, and which defines northern Thai identity to this day.

The first ruler of the Kingdom of Ayutthaya, King Rama Thibodi, made two important contributions to Thai history: the establishment and promotion of Theravada Buddhism as the official religion--to differentiate his kingdom from the neighboring Hindu kingdom of Angkor--and the compilation of the Dharmashastra, a legal code based on Hindu sources and traditional Thai custom. The Dharmashastra remained a tool of Thai law until late in the 19th century. Beginning with the Portuguese in the 16th century, Ayutthaya had some contact with the West, but until the 1800's, its relations with neighboring kingdoms and principalities, as well as with China, were of primary importance.

After more than 400 years of power, in 1767, the Kingdom of Ayutthaya was brought down by invading Burmese armies and its capital burned. After a single-reign capital established at Thonburi by Taksin, a new capital city was founded in 1782, across the Chao Phraya at the site of present-day Bangkok, by the founder of the Chakri dynasty. The first Chakri king was crowned Rama I. Rama I's heirs became increasingly concerned with the threat of European colonialism after British victories in neighboring Burma in 1826.

The first Thai recognition of Western power in the region was the Treaty of Amity and Commerce with the United Kingdom in 1826. In 1833, the United States began diplomatic exchanges with Siam, as Thailand was called until 1938. However, it was during the later reigns of Rama IV (or King Mongkut, 1851-68), and his son Rama V (King Chulalongkorn (1868-1910), that Thailand established firm rapprochement with Western powers. The Thais believe that the diplomatic skills of these monarchs, combined with the modernizing reforms of the Thai Government, made Siam the only country in South and Southeast Asia to avoid European colonization.

In 1932, a bloodless coup transformed the Government of Thailand from an absolute to a constitutional monarchy. King Prajadhipok (Rama VII) initially accepted this change but later surrendered the kingship to his 10-year-old nephew. Upon his abdication, King Prajadhipok said that the obligation of a ruler was to reign for the good of the whole people, not for a select few.

Although nominally a constitutional monarchy after 1932, Thailand was ruled by a series of military governments interspersed with brief periods of democracy. Following the 1932 revolution that imposed constitutional limits on the monarchy, Thai politics was dominated for a half-century by a military and bureaucratic elite. Changes of government were effected primarily by means of a long series of mostly bloodless coups. Thailand was occupied by the Japanese during the Second World War until Japan's defeat in 1945.

Beginning with a brief experiment in democracy during the mid-1970's, civilian democratic political institutions slowly gained greater authority, culminating in 1988 when Chatichai Choonavan--leader of the Thai Nation Party--assumed office as the country's first democratically elected Prime Minister in more than a decade. Three years later, yet another bloodless coup ended his term.

Shortly afterward, the military appointed Anand Panyarachun, a businessman and former diplomat, to head a largely civilian interim government and promised to hold elections in the near future. However, following inconclusive elections, former army commander Suchinda Kraprayoon was appointed Prime Minister. Thais reacted to the appointment by demanding an end to military influence in government. Demonstrations were violently suppressed by the military; in May 1992, soldiers killed at least 50 protesters.

Domestic and international reaction to the violence forced Suchinda to resign, and the nation once again turned to Anand Panyarachun, who was named interim Prime Minister until new elections in September 1992. In those elections, the political parties that had opposed the military in May 1992 won by a narrow majority, and Chuan Leekpai, a leader of the Democratic Party, became Prime Minister. Chuan dissolved Parliament in May 1995, and the Thai Nation Party won the largest number of parliamentary seats in subsequent elections. Party leader Banharn Silpa-Archa became Prime Minister but held the office only little more than a year. Following elections held in November 1996, Chavalit Youngchaiyudh formed a coalition government and became Prime Minister. The onset of the Asian financial crisis caused a loss of confidence in the Chavalit government and forced him to hand over power to Chuan Leekpai in November 1997. Chuan formed a coalition government based on the themes of prudent economic management and institution of political reforms mandated by Thailand's 1997 constitution.

In January 2001, telecommunications multimillionaire Thaksin Shinawatra and his Thai Rak Thai (TRT) party won a decisive victory on a populist platform of economic growth and development. In the February 2005 elections, Thaksin was re-elected by an even greater majority, sweeping 377 out of 500 parliamentary seats. Soon after Prime Minister Thaksin's second term began, allegations of corruption emerged against his government. Peaceful anti-government mass demonstrations grew, and thousands marched in the streets to demand Thaksin's resignation. Prime Minister Thaksin dissolved the Parliament in February 2006 and declared snap elections in April. The main opposition parties boycotted the polls, and the judiciary subsequently annulled the elections. A new round of elections was anticipated in November 2006.

On September 19, 2006, a group of top military officers overthrew the caretaker administration of Thaksin Shinawatra in a non-violent coup d'etat. Soon thereafter, the coup leaders issued an interim constitution and appointed Surayud Chulanont as interim Prime Minister for the approximately one-year period until a new constitution could be written and ratified and new democratic elections held. On August 19, 2007, Thai voters approved a new constitution in a national referendum. The government subsequently announced that general elections would take place December 23, 2007.

Since the end of the Second World War in 1945, Thailand has had very close relations with the United States. Threatened by communist revolutions in neighboring countries such as Vietnam, Cambodia, and Laos, Thailand actively sought U.S. assistance to contain communist expansion in the region. Thailand also has been an active member in multilateral organizations like the Association of Southeast Asian Nations (ASEAN) and the Asia-Pacific Economic Cooperation (APEC) forum.

GOVERNMENT AND POLITICAL CONDITIONS

Thailand is a constitutional monarchy. From 1992 until the 2006 coup, the country was a functioning democracy with constitutional changes of government. Elections for a democratically elected government are expected in December 2007. The King has been given little direct power under Thailand's constitutions but is a symbol of national identity and unity. King Bhumibol (Rama IX)--who has been on the throne since 1946--commands enormous popular respect and moral authority, which he has used on occasion to resolve political crises that have threatened national stability.

Under the interim constitution in force between the 2006 coup and the enactment of the 2007 constitution, a unicameral National Legislative Assembly was appointed by the military leadership. Under the 1997 constitution, the National Assembly consisted of two chambers-- the Senate and the House of Representatives. The Senate was a non-partisan body with limited legislative powers, composed of 200 directly elected members from constituent districts, with every province having at least one Senator. The House of Representatives had 500 members, 400 of whom were directly elected from constituent districts, and the remainder drawn proportionally from party lists. Under the 2007 constitution, the Senate will have 150 members, 76 of whom will be directly elected (one per district). The remaining 74 will be appointed by a panel comprised of judges and senior independent officials from a list of candidates compiled by the Election Commission. The House will have 480 members, 400 of whom will be directly elected from constituent districts and the remainder drawn proportionally from party lists.

Thailand's legal system blends principles of traditional Thai and Western laws. Under the 1997 constitution, the Constitutional Court was the highest court of appeals, though its jurisdiction was limited to clearly defined constitutional issues. Its members were nominated by the Senate and appointed by the King. The Courts of Justice have jurisdiction over criminal and civil cases and are organized in three tiers: Courts of First Instance, the Court of Appeals, and the Supreme Court of Justice. Administrative courts have jurisdiction over suits between private parties and the government, and cases in which one government entity is suing another. In the current environment, the court system is largely the same, with the exception that the Constitutional Court has been replaced by a Constitutional Tribunal composed of judges from the other high courts. In Thailand's southern border provinces, where Muslims constitute the majority of the population, Provincial Islamic Committees have limited jurisdiction over probate, family, marriage, and divorce cases. Thailand's 76 provinces include the metropolis of greater Bangkok. Bangkok's governor is popularly elected, but those of the remaining provinces are career civil servants appointed by the Ministry of Interior.

Principal Government Officials:

- Chief of State--King Bhumibol Adulyadej
- Interim Prime Minister--Surayud Chulanont
- Interim Minister of Foreign Affairs--Nitya Pibulsongram
- Ambassador to the U.S.--Krit Garnjana-Goonchorn
- Ambassador to the UN--Laxanachantorn Laohaphan

Thailand maintains an embassy in the United States at 1024 Wisconsin Ave. NW, Washington DC 20007 (tel. 202-944-3600). Consulates are located in New York City, Chicago, and Los Angeles.

Economy

The Thai economy is export-dependent, with exports of goods and services accounting for 68.6% of GDP in 2006. Thailand's recovery from the 1997-98 Asian financial crisis relied largely on external demand from the United States and other foreign markets. The Thaksin government took office in February 2001 with the intention of stimulating domestic demand and reducing Thailand's reliance on foreign trade and investment. From 2001-2006, the Thaksin administration embraced a "dual track" economic policy that combined domestic stimulus with Thailand's traditional promotion of open markets and foreign investment. Weak export demand held 2001 GDP growth to 2.2%. Beginning in 2002, however, domestic stimulus and export revival fueled a better performance, with real GDP growth at 7.1% in 2003 and 6.3% in 2004. In 2005, the economy decelerated to a 4.5% annual GDP growth rate due to the tsunami catastrophe, drought, and violence in the three southernmost provinces. For 2006, the rebound of production in agriculture and manufacturing coupled with soaring numbers of tourists increased GDP by 5.0% (year-on-year).

Before the financial crisis, the Thai economy had years of manufacturing-led economic growth--averaging 9.4% for the decade up to 1996. Relatively abundant and inexpensive labor and natural resources, fiscal conservatism, open foreign investment policies, and encouragement of the private sector underlay the economic success in the years up to 1997. The economy is essentially a free-enterprise system. Certain services--such as power generation, transportation, and communications--are state-owned and operated, but the government is considering privatizing them in the wake of the financial crisis. The timetable for privatization of some state-owned enterprises, however, has slipped due to resistance from labor unions and parts of civil society. Despite the resistance, some firms were successfully privatized, such as Airports of Thailand (renamed from Airport Authority of Thailand), PTT Public Company Limited (renamed from the Petroleum Authority of Thailand), and MCOT (renamed from Mass Communication Authority of Thailand).

The Royal Thai Government welcomes foreign investment, and investors who are willing to meet certain requirements can apply for special investment privileges through the Board of Investment. To attract additional foreign investment, the government has modified its investment regulations. In a reaction to former Prime Minister Thaksin's sale of his telecommunications company to foreign investors, the interim Thai government introduced amendments to its Foreign Business Act during 2007 which would apply greater restrictions on the ability of non-Thais to own or control businesses operating in the Thai services sector.

The organized labor movement remains weak and divided in Thailand; less than 2% of the work force is unionized. In 2000, the State Enterprise Labor Relations Act (SELRA) was passed, giving public sector employees similar rights to those of private sector workers, including the right to unionize.

Roughly 40% of Thailand's labor force is employed in agriculture (data based on Bank of Thailand.) Rice is the country's most important crop; Thailand is the largest exporter in the world rice market. Other agricultural commodities produced in significant amounts include fish and fishery products, tapioca, rubber, corn, and sugar. Exports of processed foods such as canned tuna, canned pineapples, and frozen shrimp are on the rise.

Thailand's increasingly diversified manufacturing sector is the largest contributor to growth. Industries registering rapid increases in production included computers and electronics, furniture, wood products, canned food, toys, plastic products, gems, and jewelry. High-technology products such as integrated circuits and parts, hard disc drives, electrical appliances, vehicles, and vehicle parts are now leading Thailand's strong growth in exports. The appreciation of the Thai baht to the U.S. dollar relative to other regional currencies during the 2006-2007 period has dampened some of Thailand's exports, and export sector margins have been affected. To help arrest baht appreciation, the Bank of Thailand applied controls on the import of capital into the country in December 2006. Nevertheless, the baht continued to appreciate.

The United States is Thailand's largest export market and third-largest supplier after Japan and China. While Thailand's traditional major markets have been North America, Japan, and Europe, economic recovery among Thailand's regional trading partners has helped Thai export growth (21.6% in 2004, 15.0% in 2005, and 17.4% in 2006, and 16.6% in the first half of 2007). Due to domestic political uncertainty and concern about government's economic policies, Thai domestic demand and private investment were flat from early 2006 and remained flat at mid-2007.

Machinery and parts, vehicles, electronic integrated circuits, chemicals, crude oil and fuels, and iron and steel are among Thailand's principal imports. The moderation in import levels (7.0% increase in 2006 versus 26.0% in 2005) reflects the low confidence of both consumers and investors.

Thailand is a member of the World Trade Organization (WTO) and the Cairns Group of agricultural exporters. Tourism contributes significantly to the Thai economy (about 6%). Tourist arrivals, which declined in 2005 due to the tsunami catastrophe, recovered strongly in 2006.

Bangkok and its environs are the most prosperous part of Thailand, and the barren northeast is the poorest. An overriding concern of successive Thai Governments, and a particularly strong focus of the Thaksin government, has been to reduce these regional income differentials, which have been exacerbated by rapid economic growth in and around Bangkok and the financial crisis. The government has tried to stimulate provincial economic growth with programs such as the Eastern Seaboard project and the development of an alternate deep-sea port on Thailand's southern peninsula. It also is conducting discussions with Malaysia to focus on economic development along the Thai-Malaysian border.

Although the economy has demonstrated moderate positive growth since 1999, future performance depends on continued reform of the financial sector, corporate debt restructuring, attracting foreign investment, and increasing exports. Telecommunications, transportation networks, and electricity generation showed increasing strain during the period of sustained economic growth and may pose a future challenge. Thailand's growing shortage of engineers and skilled technical personnel may limit its future technological creativity and productivity.

FOREIGN RELATIONS

Thailand's foreign policy includes support for ASEAN in the interest of regional stability and emphasis on a close and longstanding security relationship with the United States.

Thailand participates fully in international and regional organizations. It has developed increasingly close ties with other ASEAN members--Indonesia, Malaysia, the Philippines, Singapore, Brunei, Laos, Cambodia, Burma, and Vietnam--whose foreign and economic ministers hold annual meetings. Regional cooperation is progressing in economic, trade, banking, political, and cultural matters.

Thailand continues to take an active role on the international stage. When East Timor gained independence from Indonesia, Thailand, for the first time in its history, contributed troops to the international peacekeeping effort. As part of its effort to increase international ties, Thailand has reached out to such regional organizations as the Organization of American States (OAS) and the Organization for Security and Cooperation in Europe (OSCE). Thailand has contributed troops to reconstruction efforts in Afghanistan and Iraq.

U.S.-Thai Relations

Since World War II, the United States and Thailand have developed close relations, as reflected in several bilateral treaties and by both countries' participation in UN multilateral activities and agreements. The principal bilateral arrangement is the 1966 Treaty of Amity and Economic Relations, which facilitates U.S. and Thai companies' economic access to one another's markets. Other important agreements address civil uses of atomic energy, sales of agricultural commodities, investment guarantees, and military and economic assistance. In June 2004 the United States and Thailand initiated negotiations on a free trade agreement which, when concluded, will reduce and eliminate barriers to trade and investment between the two countries. These negotiations were placed on hold following the dissolution of the Thai Parliament in February 2006 and the subsequent coup in September.

The United States and Thailand are among the signatories of the 1954 Manila pact of the former Southeast Asia Treaty Organization (SEATO). Article IV(1) of this treaty provides that, in the event of armed attack in the treaty area (which includes Thailand), each member would "act to meet the common danger in accordance with its constitutional processes." Despite the dissolution of the SEATO in 1977, the Manila pact remains in force and, together with the Thanat-Rusk communiqué of 1962, constitutes the basis of U.S. security commitments to Thailand. Thailand continues to be a key security ally in Asia, along with Australia, Japan, the Philippines, and South Korea. In December 2003, Thailand was designated a Major Non-NATO Ally.

Thailand's stability and independence are important to the maintenance of peace in the region. Economic assistance has been extended in various fields, including rural development, health, family planning, education, and science and technology. The formal U.S. Agency for International Development (USAID) program ended in 1995. However, there are a number of targeted assistance programs which continue in areas of mutually defined importance, including: health and HIV/AIDS programming; refugee assistance; and trafficking in persons. The U.S. Peace Corps in Thailand has approximately 100 volunteers, focused on primary education, with an integrated program involving teacher training, health education, and environmental education.

Thailand has received U.S. military equipment, essential supplies, training, and assistance in the construction and improvement of facilities and installations for much of the period since 1950. Over recent decades, U.S. security assistance included military training programs carried out in the United States and elsewhere. A small U.S. military advisory group in Thailand oversaw the delivery of equipment to the Thai Armed Forces and the training of Thai military personnel in its use and maintenance. Funding for the International Military Education and Training and the Foreign Military Financing programs, along with selected other programs totaling $29 million, was suspended following the September 19, 2006 coup d'etat in Thailand. As part of their mutual defense cooperation over the last decade, Thailand and the United States have developed a vigorous joint military exercise program, which engages all the services of each nation and averages 40 joint exercises per year.

Thailand remains a trafficking route for narcotics from the Golden Triangle--the intersection of Burma, Laos, and Thailand--to both the domestic Thai and international markets. The large-scale production and shipment of opium and heroin shipments from Burma of previous years have largely been replaced by widespread smuggling of methamphetamine tablets, although heroin seizures along the border continue to take place with some frequency. The United States and Thailand work closely together and with the United Nations on a broad range of programs to halt illicit drug trafficking and use and other criminal activity. The U.S. supports the International Law Enforcement Academy (ILEA) in Bangkok, which provides counter-narcotics and anti-crime capacity-building programs to law enforcement and judicial officials from a number of regional countries.

Trade and Investment

The United States is Thailand's second largest trading partner after Japan; in 2006 merchandise imports from Thailand totaled $22.5 billion, and merchandise exports totaled $8.2 billion. The U.S., Japan, Taiwan, Singapore, and the European Union are among Thailand's largest foreign investors. American investment, concentrated in the petroleum and chemicals, finance, consumer products, and automobile production sectors, is estimated at $21 billion.

In: Thailand: Economics, Political and Social Issues
Ed: Randle C. Zebioli

ISBN: 978-1-60456-583-6
©2009 Nova Science Publishers, Inc.

Chapter 2

THE DIFFERENTIAL IMPACT OF THE ECONOMIC CRISIS ON THAILAND, INDONESIA AND SOUTH KOREA

Chung Sang-Hwa
Institute of East and West Studies, Yonsei University, Korea

INTRODUCTION

Korea began the process of industrialisation in the late 1960's, followed by Thailand and Indonesia in the mid-1970's. Despite variations in resource endowments, all three countries had recorded such impressive records of industrialisation[3] that international society loudly applauded their economic successes. In the late 1990's, however, the Asian economic crisis had entered a totally new phase, spawned by the July 1997 foreign currency crisis in Thailand. 'Currency crisis', defined as a large drop in the value of currency in a short period of time, had spread to Southeast Asia, and eventually reached Korea. Among the victims, Thailand, Indonesia and South Korea (hereafter Korea) asked the International Monetary Fund (IMF) for rescue loans, but Malaysia, which also had been hard hit by the crisis, closed its foreign exchange market instead of requesting the IMF for help.

The three Greater East Asian countries had several characteristics in common when they encountered economic crisis: they relied on trade in the process of economic development; enjoyed high levels of liquidity; had recently introduced financial liberalisation; and had opaque corporate and banking systems.[4] After they accepted the IMF stabilisation programs, they also faced such problems together as the precipitate decline of currency value, the instability of financial sectors, market contractions, decreases in investment, and increases in unemployment. As of early 2001, the economic crisis appears to be contained in Korea, but it still scratches Indonesia with its fingernails, and Thailand is located somewhere between the two.

---

[3] Korea had poor natural resources, but it could develop its economy thanks to skilled manpower and the effective governmental policies of the time. Indonesia and Thailand had rich natural endowments and could invite generous foreign investments to encourage speedy industrialisation.

[4] However, it is also true that each country had its own political and economic specificities as will be discussed later in detail.

Although there has been much research on the Asian economic crises, many issues still remain unclear and unanswered. Were the crises unavoidable? What was the decisive cause(s) of the foreign exchange crises? Were the IMF interventions adequate? What were the political and economic consequences of the crises? Should and can Asian countries reform their political and economic management styles? Which international political economy approach, for example, the interdependence school, neomercantilism, or structuralism, more adequately explains the crises?

This analysis examines the economic crises of Indonesia, Thailand and Korea in order to understand better their causes, processes and consequences. A comparative study has an advantage in that it clarifies the issue by contrasting similarities and differences. In the next section, the pre-crisis political and economic developments are compared. The following section explores the causes of the three countries' economic crises. Then, IMF programs and each country's reform efforts, and the consequences of the economic crises, are surveyed. The last section critically assesses the nature of the Asian economic crises based on the discussions of the previous parts, and presents theoretical and policy implications.

BEFORE THE ECONOMIC CRISES

1. Politics and Economics

Thailand had recorded spectacular economic growth rates since it implemented export-led industrialisation policies in the mid-1970's. Annual growth rates had been over 8 per cent and new buildings had changed the skyline of Bangkok (Table 1). In the early 1990's, the Anand and the first Chuan Governments had pushed on deregulation and liberalisation in order to attract more foreign investment. In 1996, however, an economic slowdown was expected and the Bank of Thailand revised its estimation of GDP growth rates from 8 per cent at the end of 1995 to 6.7 per cent. Exports were inactive and the current deficit was rising (Table 2). The Banharn Government in 1995 and the new Chavalit Government in 1996 could not handle the situation appropriately. Deregulation and financial liberalisation, along with political reforms, had weakened these governments' discretion and power. The fixed exchange rate system could not respond swiftly to the fast-growing trade deficit.

The Thai economy started to show signs of fading in 1996, and by early 1997 GDP growth rates were not as robust as previously. The GDP growth was sluggish in the third quarter of 1996, and recorded a minus growth rate in the first quarter of 1997. While inflation had been modest (between 4.2 per cent and 7.4 per cent) (www.nso.go.kr/cgi-bin/sws_999.cgi 2001),[5] external debt reached at the end of 1996 was US$108.7 billion (about 60 per cent of GDP) where short-term debts accounted for US$47.7 billion (43.9 per cent of the total external debt) (www.bot.or.th/bothomepage/databank/EconData 2001). In 1997, Thai external debt increased further, and so did the proportion of private debt. The government and the central bank failed to control the excessive borrowings of private financial institutions (Punyaratabandhu 1998, 162).[6] In July, the Thai government adopted a floating exchange system, but foreign investors competed to withdraw their money from the Thai market. The popularity of the Chavalit Government had dropped considerably. In the same month the cornered government asked for a Stand-by Credit Arrangement from IMF.

---

[5] Developing economies usually have higher rates of inflation than those in developed economies.

[6] The Bangkok International Banking Facility, established in 1993 by the central bank, played an intermediary role between foreign lenders and private Thai corporations (Punyaratabandhu 1998, 163).

Table 1. Gross Domestic Product, Q1 1996 - Q3 2000

Year and Quarter	Thailand (mil. of baht)	Indonesia (bil. of Rp)	S. Korea (bil. of won)
1996			
Q1	1,120,089	122,530	94,533
Q2	1,151,915	128,846	102,169
Q3	1,154,597	136,940	104,870
Q4	1,196,231	144,253	116,907
1997			
Q1	1,159,123	145,801	101,061
Q2	1,168,765	149,406	110,337
Q3	1,181,739	163,252	113,227
Q4	1,230,622	169,252	112,865
1998			
Q1	1,211,955	217,654	107,674
Q2	1,118,301	232,387	107,992
Q3	1,112,595	273,463	108,357
Q4	1,185,580	266,108	120,344
1999			
Q1	1,162,112	281,052	107,797
Q2	1,095,676	279,712	116,412
Q3	1,144,423	277,583	121,847
Q4	1,213,177	281,095	137,722
2000			
Q1	1,229,472	301,929	121,240
Q2	1,197,668	317,604	126,123
Q3	1,226,205	329,279	130,426

Data: Indonesia - www.bi.go.id/bank_indonesia2 (2001);
Thailand – www.bot.or.th /bothomepage/databank/EconData (2001);
S. Korea – www.nso.go.kr/cgi-bin/sws_999.cgi (2001).

Until mid-1997, Indonesia under Suharto had healthier macroeconomic indicators than Thailand and Korea. GDP had grown steadily (Table 1) and inflation had been contained under 10 per cent (www.nso.go.kr/cgi-bin/sws_999.cgi 2001). Although current account was in deficit, the trade balance was positive (Table 2). Also, Indonesian external debt had been slightly decreasing in 1996 and in early 1997, from US$64 billion to US$56 billion (about 25 per cent of GDP) (www.bi.go.id/bank_indonesia2 2001). However, the New Order had been eroding the soundness of the Indonesian economy. Mostly Chinese private banks had been spawned by the 1988 deregulation, and many of them had connections with Suharto's family and friends. Foreign investments were wasted in support of prestige national projects such as the construction of a bridge to Malaysia and the tallest building in Jakarta (Bird 1998, 172).

Before the crisis, Bank Indonesia had set the rupiah's exchange rates to be depreciated 4-5 per cent annually. This 'managed' floating foreign exchange system was doomed to collapse when international funds massively flowed out, as occurred in Thailand, and the rupiah was depreciated by 9 per cent in August. The government further eased the 49 per cent limitation of foreign investors' stakes in corporations for holding foreign capital, but even this could not compensate for the short-term borrowings amounting to US$33 billion. In November, the Indonesian government and the IMF agreed on a US$38 billion package loan.

Table 2. National Account Balance / Trade Balance (millions of US$), Q1 1996 - Q2 2000

Year/Quarter	Thailand	Indonesia	S. Korea
1996			
Q1	-3,420 / -2,741	-2,034 / 1,166	-4,358 / -2,383
Q2	-4,888 / -3,032	-2,564 / 910	-5,127 / -3,125
Q3	-3,628 / -2,154	-2,111 / 1,343	-7,249 / -5,528
Q4	-2,756 / -1,561	-954 / 2,529	-6,272 / -3,931
1997			
Q1	-2,098 / -1,492	-2,192 / 1,438	-7,353 / -5,402
Q2	-3,134 / -1,413	-1,103 / 3,482	-2,723 / -806
Q3	-696 / 705	-1,393 / 2,176	-2,053 / -27
Q4	2,907 / 3,773	-201 / 2,979	3,962 / 3,055
1998			
Q1	4,183 / 4,100	1,001 / 4,821	10,712 / 9,717
Q2	2,799 / 3,633	669 / 4,971	11,007 / 11,458
Q3	3,406 / 4,148	1,682 / 5,100	9,745 / 10,596
Q4	3,854 / 4,357	744 / 3,537	8,901 / 9,856
1999			
Q1	3,954 / 3,671	1,512 / 4,039	6,057 / 6,770
Q2	2,220 / 3,274	852 / 4,457	6,146 / 7,902
Q3	3,003 / 3,597	1,886 / 6,344	6,597 / 6,923
Q4	3,251 / 3,471	1,535 / 5,804	5,676 / 6,776
2000			
Q1	3,188 / 3,350	1,898 / 6,264	-
Q2	1,484 / 2,408	-	-

Data: www.nso.go.kr/cgi-bin/sws_999.cgi (2001).

Korea was economically different from Indonesia and Thailand.[7] It was a member of the OECD and the eleventh largest economy in the world, and its per capita income was US$13,269 in 1995.[8] The history of Korea's economic development also had been considerably more seasoned than those of Thailand and Indonesia. Moreover, the country's development was mainly owing to the internal savings gained from export, although foreign capital had had its share. Korean GDP growth was set back in early 1997 (Table 1), but not many seriously worried about it because macroeconomic indicators such as inflation, the unemployment rate, and fiscal balance appeared to be sound.[9] The foreign currency market

---

[7] Korea was a creditor and an investor in Southeast Asia.

[8] When the IMF prepared the draft of its conditionality, the IMF, the US Treasury, Wall Street and major European bankers, as well as the American Chamber of Commerce in Korea, acted in coordination. The IMF introduced a new loan system for Korea, the Supplemental Reserve Facility, in order to circumvent the quarter option. Korea received a rescue loan that was 20-fold larger than its quarter (Focus on the Global South and CAFOD 1998, 54-56).

[9] The issue of currencies seems tricky because there is no agreed standard for judging a currency's overvaluation. According to Park (2000), exchange rates of the three countries before the crises were not seriously overvalued if the currency value is analysed based on the evaluation of their purchasing powers. However, if the currency value is tested based on the equilibrium of real exchange rates considered in terms of trade, the difference of productivity between domestic and international industries, capital accounts, and the ratios of governmental expenditure on national product, all three countries had had considerably overvalued currencies for one or two years before the crises.

had maintained stability until October 1997, despite the Southeast Asian countries' foreign currency crises.

However, several interrelated factors had eroded the robustness of the Korean economy. First of all, trade had been under continuous stress in the 1990's. The US, suspecting Korea to be another Japan, had pressed heavily on the Korean government to reduce its trade surplus. In 1992, Korea started to record a trade deficit with the US.[10] Meanwhile, other East Asian countries, notably China, had emerged as competitors in international markets. Thanks to the democratisation in the latter half of the 1980's, labour unions and strikes had appeared, and wages had increased at unprecedented levels. In the presence of deteriorating businesses, Korean corporate owners tried in 1996 to trim their sizes by legalising lay-offs. However, the relevant bill could not pass the legislature because of strong opposition from both the unions and the opposition party. Korean companies were obliged to rely on borrowing to cope with decreasing profits.[11] Taking advantage of the recently introduced liberalisation and deregulation,[12] financial institutions, especially the newly established secondary (non-bank) financial institutions, competitively invited short-term loans from foreign financial institutions.[13] The result was growing national debt; external debt had increased from US$127.5 billion in 1995 to US$163.5 billion (about 32 per cent of GDP) in 1996.

Making things worse, the ratio of short-term borrowing in total foreign debt had been increasing and rose to 59 per cent at the end of 1997, while the foreign exchange reserves usable during this period had been reduced to approximately US$33 billion (www.nso.go.kr/cgi-bin/sws_999.cgi 2001). In addition to this, business accounts of major firms and banks were deteriorating due both to the bankruptcies of some big companies like Hanbo and to the foreign exchange crises in Southeast Asian countries.[14] Foreign creditors refused to roll over their loans, and the lame duck of the Kim Young Sam Government prevented Korea from steering clear of economic instability. In December 1997, the won slumped and foreign currency reserves dropped from US$22.5 billion in October to the value of US$3.9 billion. The Korean government, afraid of a moratorium, urgently requested help from the IMF, and a relief loan of US$55 billion was agreed between the IMF and Korean government on 3 December.

To summarise, macroeconomic statistics reveal that the Thai economy was the worst among the three countries before their crises. Its production looked worse than that of Korea, and, above all, its debt was too heavy compared to its GDP. If we look at just macroeconomic data, it is not easy to understand why Indonesia had fallen into an economic crisis.[15] Above all, the political leaderships of Indonesia and Korea had been without serious threats, although Thai governments had been short-term as usual. However, all three countries'

---

[10] The US asked for voluntary restrictions on exports such as cars and steel, and strongly protested along with the EU at the Korean government's boycott campaigns against importation of luxury goods.

[11] In early 1997, chaebols like Hanbo, Sammi, and Kia were on the verge of bankruptcy. It is also true that chaebols, the long-served engines of Korean economic development, had sunk into moral hazards; they had neglected efforts in RandD when their businesses were doing well. Many of them, instead, sought to make profits in real estate and portfolio investments.

[12] Korea was not prepared for the opening of its financial market. Without appropriate regulatory, supervisory, and legal provisions, Korea hastily permitted financial liberalisation in order to acquire OECD membership, which was encouraged by the US Treasury Department, on the basis that Korean financial liberalisation would serve US financial interests (*Joongang Ilbo* 1997).

[13] Korean financial institutions played a dangerous game; they borrowed short-term loans for long-term lending.

[14] In 1997 Korea had lent a total of US$173 million to Thailand, and 34 per cent of export was destined to Southeast Asian countries (*Digital Chosunilbo* 1997; 1998b).

[15] However, this judgement should be weighed against the consideration that there are no clear or agreed standards to judge a country's economic conditions based on statistical figures.

governments could not effectively control their economies because of recent deregulation and liberalisation.

2. International Perspectives

It is not difficult to explain an event after it took place; more illuminating is an examination of what the international society had in mind when the crisis was in progress. The IMF claimed that it had given the Thai government continuous warnings for the 18 months preceding the foreign exchange crisis. However, according to Gohama (1999, 128), it was nothing but an *ex post facto* excuse. Although the Thai financial industry had shown signs of unhealthiness, there is little evidence indicating that the IMF as well as individual governments did in fact realise the formidable seriousness of the problem. On the contrary, the IMF and the World Bank reports continuously praised Thailand as a model country of sound macroeconomic management and open economy. Even foreign debt, the lion's share of which belonged in private hands instead of being the direct responsibility of the government, was regarded as a sign of Thailand's favorable business environment for foreign investors (Focus on the Global South and CAFOD 1998, 12-16). Thailand's 1996 economic inactivity was regarded by the other East Asian governments and international institutions as a sign of tuning up its overheated growth (*Joongang Ilbo* 1997). It is not surprising that Thai governments and financial institutions failed to respond accordingly. Like Thailand, Indonesia was also praised by international financial institutions as a country of successful macroeconomic management, deregulation and liberalisation, as was Korea. Korean president Kim Young Sam argued just several days before his country's asking for rescue that Korea was different from Southeast Asian countries.

In short, it would be reasonable to say that Asian countries and international agents, with the exception of speculative investors, did not take the situation seriously before the crises became apparent.

CAUSES OF THE ECONOMIC CRISES

There are many analyses that address the causes of the Asian crises (see Goldstein 1998; Delhaise 1998, 11-32; Yoo and Moon 1999; Warne 1998; Demetriades and Fattough 1999). The causes presented range widely from a simple liquidity bottleneck, a US conspiracy, and so on, to the defects of Confucian state and corporate governances.[16] Now there seems a general agreement that all of these factors are interwoven.

1. Internal Factors

Among the explanations focusing on internal factors, the negativity (or out-of-datedness) of the East Asian development model or Confucian capitalism are prominent. The so-called

---

[16] If we talk about the cause of the 'exchange rate' crises, this can be understood simply as the combined force of the withdrawal of foreign funds and the shortages of an individual country's liquidity. According to a report of the McKinsey consulting company, the Thai exchange rate crisis was initiated by the loan collecting of Japanese, French, and German banks, not by either stock or foreign exchange withdrawing (*Digital Chosunilbo* 1998a). However, when we say the Asian 'economic' crises, we comprehend them in a broader conceptual framework comprising major macroeconomic instabilities.

East Asian development model[17] is characterised by the close formal and informal relationship between government, business and finance sectors. It sometimes means the patriarchal character of governmental leadership and the protection of domestic industries, and, in an extreme expression, crony capitalism where human networks play a much more important role than institutional provisions. Of the three countries, Korea seems to fit the first type, and Suharto's Indonesia can be labelled as the last type. Thailand is located somewhere between the two.

According to critics, the East Asian model of development has produced moral hazards and market inefficiency, and eventually hurt the soundness of the market economy, resulting in the crises (Delhaise 1998, 33-35). The crony relations among governments, banks and corporations have developed weaknesses in financial institutions and inadequacies in bank regulation and supervision (Fischer 1998). Large corporations had relied on lending to fuel their expansions. It is also true that capital for investments had been inefficiently used in real estate and money games leading to bubble economies (Corsetti, et al. 1999; Bird and Milne 1999). However, there is evidence that modifies this argument. First, it is not clear why the problem bulged out at that time. The government-led development strategy had been long embedded in East Asia, and many developmentalists had praised it when the regional economy looked good.[18] Also, the argument *per se* cannot explain why China, where the government was heavily involved in economic management, was immune from crisis when the others were not.

It is not clear, moreover, what proportion of bankers' and businessmen's moral hazards can be explained by the East Asian development model. Their moral hazards may simply be the result of protracted economic growth and generous investment. East Asian business and financial actors with limited experience could be too optimistic about their futures to respect risks. In fact, most East Asian countries except Hong Kong and, controversially, Singapore, have adopted state-led developmental strategies, and the countries devastated by the crises were ironically the model students of deregulation and liberalisation.[19] As we will see later, especially in the case of Indonesia, the negativity of politico-economic coalitions is prominent in the process of coping with the crises, not in the introductory phase of the crises.

Another explanation focusing on internal factors is the argument of governmental failure. It cannot be denied that Thailand, Indonesia and Korea had liberalised and deregulated their financial industries without adequate provision of supervisory and auditing institutions.[20] Although contemporary international financial transactions are very speedy and grow at rates well over those of objective economies, the governments can not avoid being blamed for their negligence. However, as mentioned before, the exchange rate crises and the economic crises should be distinguished from each other. Governmental agents were surely responsible for the occurrences of the exchange rate crises, but the ensuing economic crises included many other factors beyond that.

---

[17] For discussion of the Asian model, see Chun (2000).

[18] Many developmentalists recommend developing countries appropriate governmental interventions for their economic development. They argue that it is necessary in the presence of, among other elements, capital shortage (Rosenstein-Rodan 1989).

[19] Some may argue that the East Asian developmental state is out of date because corporations now can access the global capital market. However, the Asian crises have shown that states still can exert their wills to tame corporations. Moreover, the crises had stemmed from the lack of governmental regulation, not from regulation. Thus, East Asian states require changes in regulation not the removal of regulation itself.

[20] In Korea the policy confusion had been partly due to the reorganisation of government. In December 1994 the Korean government had merged the Economic Planning Board and the Ministry of Finance into the Board of Finance and Economy, which later in February 1998 changed its name to the Department of Finance and Economy, transferring some rights to other governmental agencies.

2. International Factors

If we turn to the explanations focusing on external causes, a series of factors can be named. Firstly, the conspiracy hypothesis claims that the crises were intended by Western economic powers that were feeling threats from the rising Asian economies. According to this argument, the Western interests concerned had agreed to discipline Asian countries to follow 'international' market principles. It is true that the essence of the so-called Washington consensus in the early 1990's was liberalisation and deregulation. Accordingly, one of the major objectives of IMF programs is the realisation of transparent and freer business activities. It is in a sense a compulsory program for making recipient countries assimilate into the US-led global market system. Although this argument seems persuasive, it might be implying a more complicated reasoning than is actually the case.

According to Sachs (1998, 17), the IMF's imposing of conditionality on troubled economies had made the international financial market aware of the looming crises. The IMF had encouraged rather than subdued the crises in East Asia. To normalise the foreign exchange crisis, investors' confidence needed to be restored as soon as possible. However, the investors equipped with electronic transaction instruments respected uncertainty above other indicators. Hedge funds and credit rating companies have also been blamed for contributing to the situation. Although hedge funds did not account for great volumes, they could have played the role of pilot in the international financial market. In Thailand, hedge funds sold baht in May and strengthened the confidence of those concerned about the Thai economic crisis (*Economist* 1998a). In a similar vein, the downgrading of country and corporation credits by such international credit rating companies as Moody's Investor's Service and Standard and Poor had driven foreign investors to retreat from risky businesses. Although the empirical causality between the prophecy effect and the economic crisis is not easy to trace, this argument seems logically robust.

Thirdly, some argue that the Asian crises were rooted in the changed international politico-business environment. In the post-Cold War era the US was not sufficiently concerned with protecting its strategic partners. Its hegemony had more interest in maintaining system-level stability than in helping individual needs. When the shocks shattered Asian economies, the victims were individual countries, not the international financial system itself.[21] Since the 1980's, China, with plenty of cheap labour, has risen as a competitor of the other Asian countries in export markets. The growth rates of Chinese exports of goods and services in GDP were 17.5 per cent in 1990 and 24.0 per cent in 1995 respectively, while its GDP growth rates during the equivalent years were each 4.0 per cent and 10.5 per cent (World Bank 2001). What these statistics show is that Chinese exports had grown at a very fast rate. Behind this development lay the 40 per cent depreciation of Chinese currency in 1994. Thai and Indonesian goods, therefore, lost their competitiveness in the presence of cheap Chinese products. Moreover, wages in manufacturing had risen rapidly in Thailand and Indonesia because of an insufficient pool of experienced workers.

The Japanese economic slump has been also blamed. When real estate and stock prices fell after the bursting of the bubble, Japanese financial institutions began to look for new international markets. They had increased their investments in Southeast Asia to a great degree; in 1994, Japan's investment in that region was US$40 billion, but by 1996 it was US$260 billion (*Businesshankyung* 1998, 52). The massive inflow of capital into Southeast Asian countries had raised real estate prices, encouraging speculative investment in real estate that eventually led to the bubble economies. Moreover, the low yen since the mid-1990's had

---

[21] The socially disadvantaged in the victim countries were hurt most and the international capital investors fared best.

weakened the competitive powers of the other East Asian countries, especially Korea, which had entered a technological upgrading process.[22] In addition to this, the Japanese trade surplus could not efficiently provide liquidity to East Asian countries because of the troubles and backwardness of its own financial institutions. Most trade surplus had been either kept inside Japan or invested in US Treasury bonds.

The boom of the US economy has also been named as a cause of the Asian economic crises. When the exchange rate crises took place, opportunistic international investors were not obliged to remain on risky East Asian capital markets. They regarded the US capital market that had prospered for nearly 10 years as a safe refuge. The economic boom of the US in the latter 1990's has sucked in considerable foreign direct investment (FDI), providing a shelter for the capital flowing from Asia. The total amount of the world FDI had been US$320.4 billion in 1995, and increased to US$884.5 billion in 1999, but during this period the FDI flowing into the US amounted to US$57.8 billion and US$275.5 billion, respectively (World Bank 2001). While the world FDI grew 2.8 times, the US equivalent increased 4.8 times, accounting for 31.1 per cent of the total world FDI in 1999. These international factors can partially, although not completely, explain the occurrence of the crises.

Lastly, the 'contagion effect' needs to be mentioned. When the Thai crisis had become apparent, international investors suspected the soundness of the other East Asian countries' economies. A country's vulnerability to the contagion of economic crisis is conditioned by both the visible similarities of economic behaviour and the proximity of geographical location between the country under crisis and the other countries (Pavan 2000). The strategic behaviour of foreign investors is understandable in two senses. One is rooted in the nature of money games. When selling is the common strategy of players, the faster player is less damaged in stock markets. Even banks competitively collect their lendings to make sure they receive their money back. The other driving factor is uncertainty and risk. If a country's business operations lack transparency, foreign investors cannot secure sufficient information in making decisions and generally choose safety over risk (as was claimed to be the case in East Asia). However, this argument refers to a catalyst factor and cannot explain the crises *per se*.

In brief, there were numerous factors in the Asian economic crises. If we concentrate on actors for the convenience of discussion, three groups seem prominent. The first is the group of international investors who made speculative or strategic choices of withdrawal. The second is the IMF that amplified the exchange crises. The third is the group of Asian governmental officials who neglected their roles in supervising dangerous financial games, and businessmen who engage in them. It was possible to cope with some changes in the international business environment in advance, but not all. The crisis-hit countries could have prepared for the intensification of international competition, but a shock like the sudden depreciation of the Chinese currency was purely, at least in the short run, external. Above all, it is noteworthy that the contemporary international financial market is not a perfect market in that, while demand exists everywhere, supply rests with the limited number of wealthy countries' financial institutions and funds (see Radelet and Sachs 1998, 70-71). This oligopolistic supplier market can be unstable in the short run and the occasional instability can hurt individual economies seriously, although it may seek an equilibrium in the long run.

---

[22] Some argue that Japan should increase its imports from the troubled countries; the US already has trade deficits with East Asian countries, and Europe is busy both preparing for further economic integration and supporting former communist neighbours. Thus Japan, which has close production networks with Southeast Asia, should play a leading role as export market. However, we have to admit that Japan's economy itself has long been in recess.

COPING WITH THE ECONOMIC CRISES

1. IMF Conditionalities

IMF conditionality prescribes in general fiscal balance, price stability, restructuring of corporate governance, and free trade and capital/foreign exchange transactions. While these neoliberal prescriptions have positive effects in augmenting the transparency of economic activities and market efficiency, they may bring about unemployment, tax increases, and high interest rates (Choi 1999). However, the recipient countries that desperately need IMF money usually cannot make their own voices heard in arranging the loan conditions.

In Thailand, the Chavalit Government was replaced in early November 1997 by the Chuan-led coalition government on the excuse of its failure to handle economic disturbances. Although the new cabinet was not a cohesive body, Thai economic ministers could devote themselves to implementing IMF-recommended programs. Indonesia under Suharto admitted the IMF's assistance reluctantly, unlike Thailand and Korea. To this old dictator, Indonesia was a regional hegemony and a big country in terms of population and natural resources. The conflict between the IMF and Suharto, however, had caused enormous pain to the Indonesian people. Post-IMF Indonesia had fallen into confusion; Suharto's health was in doubt; his family and ministers had continued their old-style practices; and the IMF was embarrassed in the presence of the discrepancies between governmental announcements and actions. Later on, Indonesia had to negotiate with the IMF twice to gain the relief loans.

Although President Kim Dae Jung's party was not the first major party in the National Assembly, he could concentrate on rebuilding Korea's economy thanks to his coalition with the third party. The opposition party, the former government party responsible for the economic crisis, could not influence the new government at its disposal. Kim, who was elected just before the occurrence of the crisis, managed to implement the IMF package consistently.

The total amount of the rescue loans agreed to be given to Thailand was US$17.2 billion, and the equivalents to Indonesia and Korea were US$42.3 and US$58.4 billion, respectively (Gohama 1999, 122). Although the IMF was the main donor, the World Bank, the Asian Development Bank, and individual countries also contributed to these funds. Despite the IMF's announcements of rescue, there had been a continuous exodus of foreign investment from all three countries. As the Fund later painfully admitted, Thai, Indonesian and Korean markets failed to regain foreign investors' confidence.

It has been said that the IMF committed some critical mistakes in the early phase of the crises (Madrick 1998). The first was tight monetary policy, that is, maintaining high interest rates in the framework of a floating exchange system. In the three countries, the sharp increases in interest rates were associated with the flight, not holding or invitation, of foreign investments. Investors suspected that higher levels of interest rates would bring about the bankruptcy of companies. As a result, risk levels in these countries had increased, and speculative investors had turned their faces away (Basurto and Ghosh 2000).[23] Moreover,

---

[23] Although there were other factors that conditioned country risk, it cannot be said that this tight monetary policy was irrelevant to the decreasing country risk ratings of Thailand and Indonesia. The Thai foreign currency rating could not recover until early 1999, and that of Indonesia, in late 2000 (www.standardandpoors.com/ratings/sovereigns/index.htm 2001). Korea, however, has increased its equivalent rating ever since the occurrence of the foreign exchange crisis.

even if interest rates were set at high levels, they could not invite foreign investments if the levels were not high enough to compensate the decrease in exchange rate.[24]

It is conventionally believed that an external impact or shock is absorbed in the exchange rate regime under a floating exchange system. However, it did not happen in any of these three countries.[25] The depreciation of their currencies had failed not only to restore market confidence, but also to boost exports. The economies of the three countries, especially Thailand and Korea, are heavily dependent on their exports (about 30 per cent). In the presence of the contracted domestic markets, exports should have led their economic recoveries. Exports, however, were sluggish, at least in the early phase of the crises. The Thai baht, Indonesian rupiah, and Korean won dropped by about half their value after the crises, but these countries' exports had recorded only one digit rates of increase, unlike that of Mexico in the mid-1990's that recorded over 30 per cent. The currency values of the other competing exporters also dropped, while the prices of imported raw materials and parts increased. Moreover, following the IMF guidelines, the banks of these countries sharply raised interest rates (about 20-30 per cent) and became more prudent in their lending activities in order to meet the international Bank for International Settlements (BIS) standard.[26] One of the main outcomes was a kind of liquidity trap and severe credit crunch. The three Asian countries could not secure the raw materials and parts necessary for their exports because of their foreign currency shortage and domestic credit crunch. What made things worse was that the Asian market had shrunk[27] because of the member countries' tight fiscal policies and high interest rates, and Japan's economic stagnation. The IMF's prescription for recovering trade balance worked in the end, but it owed more to import contraction than to export growth, and above all it led to the costly extension of the economic disaster.

The IMF also made strong requests for the restructuring of corporate governance and bank activities. Many of the Thai, Indonesian and Korean business and financial sectors had high levels of moral hazard from their long associations with the financial and business conglomerates, *chaebols*,[28] which had dominated markets. As mentioned earlier, the IMF imposed the BIS capital ratio on banks, and, in order to maintain their reserve and capital adequacy ratios, banks were very prudential in their lending. As governments guaranteed deposits and investors did not have other viable alternatives, banks could accumulate deposits. However, the high interest rates resulted in a credit crunch, which in turn led to the contraction of business and to the increase in non-performing loans. Although the IMF programs have positively contributed to the transparency of business activities and to the decrease in moral hazards, they had led to business contraction and a tightening of liquidity. After this early post-IMF period, the East Asian governments lowered interest rates but their economies already had deep scars.

What were urgently needed in troubled Thailand, Indonesia and Korea were not austerity programs but agreeable expansionist policies that would have made up for the decreases in

---

[24] If an interest rate increases by 10 per cent and an exchange rate decreases by 10 per cent, there are no offsetting effects from which foreign investors benefit.

[25] Indonesia and Korea had had floating foreign exchange systems before their crises, although the former had 'managed' the system. Thailand changed its foreign exchange system just before the crisis from a managed floating to a floating system.

[26] The Bank of International Settlements is located in Switzerland. Established after the First World War to take care of German reparation, the bank now mainly deals with European central banks' foreign currency exchanges. The bank proposed in 1988 an international standard of banks' capital ratio (the BIS standard) in order to cope with risk.

[27] The Asian market explains about 30-40 per cent of the total exports of Indonesia, Thailand and Korea (Lee 1998).

[28] The US and other developed countries worried about the Korean chaebols' aggressive building of semi-conductors, steel, and car producing facilities.

foreign investment. The government finances of the three countries had been healthy before the crises. The tight fiscal policies 'recommended' by the IMF in the early stage of the foreign exchange crises had driven these countries near to a state of economic depression. The fiscal adjustment requested by the IMF was 3 per cent of GDP for Thailand, 1 per cent for Indonesia, and 1.5 per cent for Korea, reflecting the sizes of their current account deficits (Fischer 1998). The IMF later agreed to ease the tightness of the targets but they had badly hurt the economies already.

2. Post-IMF Intervention Development

Since the first half of 1999 the three East Asian countries have shown healthier economic indicators than right after the crises. However, the improvements of these indicators are mainly due to such Keynesian credit creations as the expansion of fiscal expenditure, generous monetary policies, and international rescue funds. Their real economies have not recovered fully to the pre-crises level. Although the trade balances of the three countries have been positive (Table 2), such surpluses were, as previously mentioned, owed more to the decrease in imports than to the increases in export.

The Thai GDP has recovered since the latter half of 1999 (Table 1). Inflation also has been reduced from the mid-1998 double digits to lower one-digit levels since early 1999. The exchange rate, which plunged by 77 per cent in December 1997, has become stable in the range of around Bt40 per US$1 since the latter half of 1998. As the Thai economy has become healthy, so has its stock market. The Stock Market Exchange of Thailand (SET) increased by 29.8 per cent in mid-June 1999 (*Hanguk Ilbo* 1999). In 1999, the Bank of Thailand, the Ministry of Finance, the National Economic and Social Development Board, and international agencies such as the World Bank and the IMF agreed that the Thai economy has recovered steadily, although slowly (Bowornwathana 2000, 88-89). Although Thai businesses have shown clear signs of recovery since the latter half of 1999, thanks to the improvements in consumption, manufacturing output, export (cars and electronics), and construction, the country still has a huge sum of bad loans. The ratio of non-performing loans to the total bank loans was over 46 per cent in the first half of 1999 (*Far Eastern Economic Review* 1999, 63). Thus, the clearance of bank debts has become an urgent agenda for the Thai government.

Unlike the situation in Thailand, the Indonesian economy has taken a jagged way. It was only since late 1999 that Indonesia has shown signs of the restoration of economic stability. Indonesia was hit worse by the crisis than Korea or Thailand. Right after the crisis of 1997, the Indonesian rupiah plunged to Rp5,000 per US$1; the stock market index dropped from 734 to 335; inflation recorded double digits; and numerous small companies in Java closed their doors (Bird 1998, 175). In November 1997, Indonesia closed 16 private banks by the direction of the IMF,[29] but the closure of banks made people rush to withdraw their deposits, and Chinese capital started flying out to Singapore and Hong Kong looking for safe refuge. The Indonesian financial crisis had deepened, and the internal and international confidence in the Indonesian economy had weakened. Thus, in January 1998, the value of the rupiah dropped further to Rp11,200 per US$1. Of the 282 companies listed in the stock market, 260 were put into a state of default. The inconsistent attitudes of Suharto towards reform had made things worse. Sometimes he cooperated with, but sometimes resisted, the IMF. The Fund detailed the dismantling of the cartel, monopoly, and preferential treatment, and the

---

[29] Also, four national banks were merged into one.

cancellation of national projects where Suharto and his family had their vested interests (*Economist* 1998b).

In early 1998, unlike its Thai and Korean equivalents, the Indonesian financial system had not yet restored stability. As living expenses went up (inflation had increased by 250-500 per cent since July 1997),[30] attacks on ethnic Chinese and other social disturbances proliferated. In May, riots and violent demonstrations by not only students, but also by the middle class, took place. The sudden rise in food prices further led to the paralysis of food trading because many decided to secure foodstuffs at home. Importers could not fulfil their jobs because foreign banks refused to issue letters of credit, and the prices of importing goods were doubled or trebled. The exchange rate plunged beyond Rp10,000 per US$1, even lower than that of the foreign exchange crisis period in 1997. The central bank raised interest rates by 58 per cent making it impossible for many borrowers to pay back their interest. The number of unemployed reached around 8 million in May. Eventually the government dispatched soldiers to control the social disturbances. The then president Habibi and the IMF, realising the seriousness of the Indonesian economic situation, agreed with the third revision of the original IMF program. As a result, fiscal tightness was eased and macroeconomic targets were rearranged.[31]

The Indonesian GDP has shown signs of recovery since the end of 1999 (Table 1). From that time on, official inflation also declined considerably to less than 2 per cent, but it has increased again to more than 5 per cent since August 2000 (www.nso.go.kr/cgi-bin/sws_999.cgi 2001). The exchange rate had become stable since October 1998 at less than Rp9,000 per US$1, but has slightly increased again since May 2000 (www.nso.go.kr/cgi-bin/sws-999.cgi 2001). Also, the Indonesian composite stock price index rebounded in the latter half of 1999 but has dropped again since May 2000 (www.bi.go.id/bank_indonesia2 2001). Indonesian macroeconomic indicators such as inflation, exchange rate, and stock index, have deteriorated since the latter half of 2000, albeit not as seriously as before. The leadership crisis of Wahid is named as one of the main reasons.[32]

The recovery of the Korean economy has been relatively smooth compared to those of Thailand and Indonesia. The foreign currency reserve increased to US$30 billion in May 1998, US$64.3 billion in October 1999, and to over US$90 billion in 2000. International investors have started to reinvest in Korea since 1998. Exchange rates have been stable from the end of 1998 at under 1,300 won per US$1. GDP, National Account and the Balance of Trade all have shown robust signs of improvement (Tables 1 and 2). In 1999, some even worried about the possibility of business overheating. The recovery was owed largely to the increase in exports, thanks to the robust US economy and to the government's pump-priming policies. Consumption and major internal businesses like construction, however, were not yet so active. In 1999, the investments in manufacturing machines and equipment reached only 77 per cent of the pre-crisis level. Korea then encountered, in the latter half of 2000, another, although less serious, economic setback when the stock market deteriorated and the Daewoo, the then third greatest *chaebol*, became insolvent. As a result, the exchange rate increased to

---

[30] The IMF asked for the dismantling of the *Bulog*, a monopolistic importing organisation aided by the government and responsible for providing food such as rice, sugar, cooking oil, and the like at lower prices than international levels. This led to an abrupt rise in cost of basic necessities.

[31] They agreed to lower their expectations as follows: GDP growth rate, from -5 per cent to over -10 per cent; inflation, from 45 per cent to 80 per cent; and the end-year exchange rate, from Rp6,000 to Rp10,000 per US$1 (Ko 1998, 119).

[32] On Wahid's announcement in spring 2000 of the legalisation of the communist party, Islamic parties threatened to leave the coalition government. In spring, Indonesia also suffered from the independence movements of Sulawesi and Aceh.

about 1,300 won per US$1 in early 2001 but there have been no apparent signs of serious economic setback.

Although Thailand and Korea have suffered from the crises, Indonesia has been most damaged of the three. In Indonesia, politics and economics have amplified each other's negativities. Political leadership has been unstable, and Indonesian business activities, which have long been explained by human networks rather than market principles, have been in turmoil. The Indonesian government also traditionally has been involved in the country's resource allocation to a greater degree than Thai and Korean governments. Indonesian society experienced much greater social disintegration than the other two countries. These factors together have aggravated the country's efforts to restore economic stability, and distorted the effects of reform programs (*Far Eastern Economic Review* 1999).

CONSEQUENCES OF THE ECONOMIC CRISES

1. Political Aspects

Thai, Indonesian and Korean governments all launched campaigns against corruption, clientism and cronyism in order to enhance efficiency and invite foreign investment. It has been said that their crises in part had stemmed from the opaque relationship between political and business sectors. As a byproduct of the economic crises, these countries could in some degree promote political development.

However, behind this façade, the political developments of individual countries show divergent paths. While the Korean political situation has been relatively stable compared to Thailand and Indonesia, the latter two countries' political situations have not settled down. The Thai general election of 6 January 2001, the first small-district election in Thai history, and the re-election of 26 January (held because 109 of those elected were nullified on the accusation of dishonest campaigns by the newly established Election Commission), showed enormous evidence of electoral irregularities, as did the 1998 Senate election. Apparent vote-buying and even bloody shootings contaminated the elections. The leader of the Thai Rak Thai (TRT, Thai Love Thai) party and a telecommunications tycoon, Thaksin Shinawatra, could secure the support of more than half of the 500-member Lower House. However, Thaksin himself is still under the investigation of the National Anti-Corruption Commission because of his intentional omission of millions of US dollars worth of stocks when he was inaugurated as deputy Prime Minister in 1997. His commitment to writing off farmers' and banks' debts would also be a political burden in the future. Further, one major reason for the defeat of the Chuan-led Democratic Party was the popular criticism of his government's selling-off of national banks and companies to foreigners. In order to perform economic reform successfully, Thaksin needs to convert the Thai people's nationalism to positive means of economic recovery. If he fails to handle it (and returns to protectionism), Thailand may invite further trouble.

Indonesia has experienced political instability ever since the crisis. Because of this political, and thus social, instability, Indonesia could not attract its previous levels of tourism, despite its depreciation of currency, although traditionally it has been a famous sightseeing country. In 1997, the number of tourists to Indonesia was 5.2 million, but it dropped to 4.6 million in 1998 and to 4.7 million in 1999 (www.bps.go.is/statbysector/tourism 2001).

Suharto, whose 32 years' dictatorship[33] had been blamed for the economic crisis, stepped down on 21 May 1998, leaving his country near a state of default. Habibi, the then Vice-President, replaced Suharto, but gave his position to Wahid in October 1999. Wahid's democratisation programs (such as the legalisation of the communist party) have provoked internal disputes in his government. As a coalition, Wahid's government could not exert its power effectively, and, as a byproduct of democratisation, some Indonesian provinces have asked for their independence. Moreover, Wahid himself has been suspected of embezzlement, and the powerful military and students still have strong voices in Indonesian politics. In early 2001, street demonstrations both for and against Wahid have covered the front pages of the press, and Wahid's cabinet has continued to experience internal disputes.

Korea has been under the leadership of President Kim Dae Jung from the crisis until now. Although there was a general election in 2000, the political landscape of Korea has changed little. What has been lucky for Korea is its relative political stability compared to the other two countries after their crises.

In brief, the crisis has changed government in Thailand, and a more nationalistic and, in a sense, populist Thaksin and his party replaced the old coalition government. Indonesian politics has been beleaguered by government change and instability, troubling its economics and shaking its role as the leader of ASEAN. The present Korean government that took its power right after the crisis has managed to get along with economic difficulty.

2. Economic Aspects

The three countries have partially trimmed their economies. In Thailand, 56 of the total of 89 financial companies closed permanently because of bad loans. In Indonesia and Korea, 16 and 5 commercial banks were closed, respectively. In Thailand and Korea, corporate restructuring has proceeded in some degree, and parts of non-core businesses have been sold off through asset auctions aimed at lowering debt. Also, many Chinese family business networks in Thailand have disintegrated.

In Korea, many *chaebols*, such as Daewoo, Kia, Donga and Hanla, have disappeared. Although some bigger *chaebols* regarded their groups as too big (and thus too important to the economy) to be discarded, the Daewoo Group, the then third biggest conglomerate, could not continue its existence. The Daewoo case appeared to show that, if *chaebols* refuse to change their old-style business practices, they would, without exception, be restructured.[34] In August 1999 President Kim reconfirmed his government's will to reform corporate governance in order to enhance transparency. Regulations imposed on *chaebols* include the prohibition of cross-share holding, unfair internal transactions, and mutual assurance of payment. Mandatory framing of combined (consolidated) balance sheets has been codified also. As a result, the transparency of business has been enhanced considerably, and the financial soundness of the *chaebols* has become robust at the level of an approximately 200 per cent debt-equity ratio. However, this record of Korean restructuring should not be exaggerated. Many corporations had been marginal before their bankruptcy, and restructuring has been more successful in promise than in action.

---

[33] Suharto had made political parties powerless by the forcible merging of opposite parties and by organising a de facto ruling party, *Golkar* (a coalition of vocational representatives). Moreover, all parties had to adopt *Pancasila* (nationalism, democracy, internationalism, socialism, and monotheism) as their party ideology.

[34] However, the relief of the near bankrupt Hyundai construction company in spring 2001 shows that there can be an exception.

The ratio of short-term loans in the total debt has significantly fallen in all three countries. In Thailand, it dropped from US$44.1 billion in 1995 to US$23.4 billion in 1999 (World Bank 2001). The equivalent figures for Indonesia and Korea are each from US$26.0 billion to US$20.0 billion, and from US$46.6 billion to US$34.7 billion (World Bank 2001). All countries have introduced safeguard systems and early warning systems. For example, in Korea, the Fair Trade Commission and the Financial Supervisory Service were established in 1999 for the supervision, examination and enforcement of the business activities of financial institutions.

Among the three East Asian countries, the Thai FDI had fallen from US$2.4 billion in 1990 to US$2.1 billion in 1995, but recovered to US$6.2 billion in 1999 (World Bank 2001). Korea has shown a continuous increase in inviting FDI after its foreign exchange crisis; from US$0.8 billion in 1990, to US$1.8 billion in 1995, and to US$9.3 billion in 1999 (World Bank 2001). Unlike these two countries, Indonesian FDI has dropped from US$4.3 billion in 1995 to US$2.8 billion in 1999 (World Bank 2001). This difference in inviting FDI is the reflection of the country's difference in economic recovery.

Certainly there have been negative effects of the crises. Public debt has increased in the East Asian countries because their governments have pursued expansionist fiscal policies during the last two or so years for the purpose of stimulating their economies. While tax collection, which may contract business again, cannot be activated, governmental expenditures either for bailing out troubled major corporations (Korea) or for supporting public corporations and activities (Thailand and Indonesia) have increased considerably.

In addition to this, the Thai external debt recorded in 1999 was US$94.3 billion, and it still cast a murky prospect on Thai economic recovery considering its GDP (US$124.4 billion in 1999) (World Bank 2001). The external debt is also too great considering its GDP. As of 1999, the external debt is US$149.7 billion, whereas that of GDP is US$142.5 billion (World Bank 2001). Korean external debt in 1999 was US$124.3 billion, a little over one fourth of its GDP (US$406.9 billion) (World Bank 2001). This external debt is a considerable amount, even if it indicates a much better performance than exists in Thailand and Indonesia, and the country can avoid foreign exchange crisis thanks to its provision of over US$90 billion foreign reserve.

There have been growing numbers of foreign investors in the economies of these countries, especially in their stock markets. After the crises foreign investors could increase their shares in many business and financial institutions when entry restrictions were lifted. Foreign hands took over some of the major banking and finance industries.[35] Also, much real estate has been sold to foreign investors.

The ratios of trade in national production have increased in all three countries, helping the recovery of their economies (World Bank 2001). The world averages of the trade ratio to GDP have been 19.4 per cent in 1990, 21.4 per cent in 1995, and 26.0 per cent in 1999 (World Bank 2001). However, the equivalent ratios of Thailand's trade are 37.9 per cent in 1990, 45.2 per cent in 1995, and 51.1 per cent in 1999, and those of Korea, 29.7 per cent in 1990, 31.0 per cent in 1995, and 38.7 per cent in 1999, respectively (World Bank 2001). Indonesian trade ratios in GDP have shown relatively sluggish growth rates (24.5 per cent in 1990, 27.0 per cent in 1995, and 30.9 per cent in 1999) compared to those of Thailand and Korea, reflecting its economic instability. Although trade *per se* can not be assumed to have negative effects on the economy, and it is true that trade growth is an international phenomenon, these figures imply that the three countries' economies have become increasingly sensitive to outside influences, and other outer shocks could interfere with policy

---

[35] For the Thai case, see Bowornwathana (2000, 18).

efforts to revive their troubled economies. For firm economic restoration, domestic consumption needs to be revived.

There have been resistances and delays in reforming as well.[36] In Thailand, where many cabinet members are former businessmen, politicians and other vested interests have slowed the pace of restructuring (*Far Eastern Economic Review* 2000, 76-79). One typical example is Siam Cement, the largest Thai business group which is also partially owned by the royal family. The company was funded in the early crisis period by international investors who believed the announcement of restructuring. Many believed that the group could play a role as the model for Thailand's corporate restructuring. However, the group's selling-off of non-core branch companies and slashing of debt seem to have failed to show any progress (*Far Eastern Economic Review* 2000, 81). According to a foreign entrepreneur in Bangkok, Thai companies do not yet quite understand why they should change their managerial practices, which traditionally have stressed total assets and gross outputs, into those emphasising net assets and profits (*Far Eastern Economic Review* 2000, 82). Lack of legal provisions, as well as political interventions, mean that punishment of economic criminals has not been very visible. Moreover, the estimated non-performing loans as of July 1999 are still 46.1 per cent of the total loans (Limskull 2000).

In Indonesia, financial scandals have been more frequent than restructuring stories. The Bank Indonesia, the Ministry of Finance, and even the Indonesian Bank Restructuring Agency (IBRA), which was established after the 1998 banking collapse to assume the function of financial restructuring, have been riddled with scandals (Liddle 2000, 40-41). Also, populist styles of policy have continued, for example, bus fares were frozen and the rice and sugar industries have been protected. Politicians have resumed their interventions in market functioning, too. President Wahid claimed that four large, but financially troubled, Indonesian business groups, the Texmaco Group, Barito Pacific, the Gajah Tungal Group, and the Slaim Group, must be saved in order to keep up their exports (*Far Eastern Economic Review* 2000, 76).[37] Many major companies are still under the influence of a small group of Chinese families who have intimate relationships with politicians. Moreover, Indonesian restructuring has been focused on debt-to-equity swaps, loan extensions, and debt discounts rather than the introduction of new accounting and management systems and corporate culture. In Indonesia corporate restructuring has failed to show visible outcomes.

In Korea, lay-off has turned out to be the first and highest hurdle in the restructuring process. While the cosmetic accounting practice of corporations is finally being wiped out thanks to strengthened auditing, many public corporations are still believed to have excess labour (*Digital Chosunilbo* 2001). The resistance of workers and labour unions against layoff have intensified also. As the term of President Kim Dae Jung will end in 2002, the government will encounter increasingly difficult obstacles.

In brief, the signs of economic recovery vary across countries. While Korea has shown the most robust outcomes of recovery, Indonesia has fared worst, reflecting its political and social instability. What the restructuring efforts in the three countries have revealed in common is that old practices stubbornly remain in place. Moreover, as economic liberalisation proceeds, governments are losing their policy leverages *vis-à-vis* private financial institutions and corporations. Restructuring has a trade-off nature; while the benefit may be given to the society in general, the immediate cost is likely to be borne by certain social groups, especially workers and small investors; and the government enthusiasm for

---

[36] For detail, see Sikorski (1999); *Economist* (1999).

[37] These groups have accounted about 41.6 per cent of the total amount owed to the Indonesian Bank Restructuring Agency (IBRA). Of major concern, however, is that, rather than being punished, the owners are still controlling their groups without inviting new management partners.

driving restructuring may hurt either democratic or market values. Although restructuring is a worthy pursuit, its structural complexity requires strenuous policy efforts and time.

3. Social Aspects

The crises have yielded enormous impacts on Thai, Indonesian and Korean societies. Because of restructuring and bankruptcy many people had fallen into a state of poverty. In all three countries a considerable proportion of the middle classes has disappeared. In the absence of social safety nets for the unemployed, and of flexible labour markets, lay-offs have brought serious social problems.[38]

The unemployment rates of these countries, however, have shown different patterns. In Thailand, the official unemployment rate at one time reached 10 per cent (3 million), and many unemployed had to go to the countryside where the situation was by no means better than in the cities. However, the unemployment rate has fallen from 4.6 per cent in February 1998 to 3.7 per cent in November 2000 (www.bot.or.th/bothomepage/databank/EconData 2001). In Indonesia, the unemployment rate increased to 10 per cent (20 million) and over 40 per cent of 220 million had been put into a state of absolute poverty (*Chosun Ilbo* 1998a). Even after the initial stage of the crisis, the situation has not improved significantly; even the official data reveals the rise of unemployment from 4.7 per cent in 1997, 5.5 per cent in 1998, to 6.4 per cent in 1999 (www.bps.go.id/statbysector/employ 2001). Thailand and Indonesia have numerous unofficial and provisional labourers, and the official statistics may not represent adequately their abject situations.

In Korea, the income of the middle class (those between the upper 20 per cent and lower 20 per cent) decreased on average by 5.5-5.8 per cent in 1998, and, as of June 1998, 64.9 per cent of Koreans thought they belonged to the lower class while only 34.8 per cent responded that they belong to the middle class (*Chosun Ilbo* 1998b).[39] A year ago those figures were 44.5 per cent and 53.1 per cent, respectively. The unemployment rate reached 6.8 per cent in 1998, and, moreover, among the unemployed, the ratio of the structural unemployed had increased to 20 per cent. In 1998, the real wage considering inflation dropped by 9.3 per cent, while the upper 10 per cent of urban households raised their annual income by 4 per cent thanks to their increased banking and portfolio incomes. But, in the same year, the lower 20 per cent, mainly relying on wage income, had experienced a 17.2 per cent decrease in their incomes.[40] However, the recent data shows an improvement; the unemployment rate has dropped to 6.3 per cent in 1999 and to 4.1 per cent in 2000 (www.nso.go.kr/eindex 2001).

The resistance of the workers in these three countries has been stronger and more effective than before thanks to the rise of their union powers and activities. Korean trade unions, which have developed through the democratisation movements in the 1980's, seem to be much stronger than their Thai and Indonesian counterparts. In Thailand two factors have suppressed labour union movements; one is the segregation of labour by region, gender, age, skill, and the like, and the other, submissive attitudes owing to the Buddhist culture (Yoon 1997; 83-84). Thai civil organisations have initiated many protests and demonstrations for the poor, and union strikes also have increased since the crisis. In Indonesia, thanks to the

---

[38] Thailand and Indonesia still have traditional sectors. Fortunately, the effects of the crises in the modern sector did not reach into the more remote areas, which consequently avoided significant economic hardship.

[39] For the detailed discussion of the Korean unemployment issue, see Yoon (1998).

[40] Although the Korean job market recently has been generous, many of the jobs offered are part-time. It is not surprising that many workers, who have witnessed their discharged colleagues' tragedies, stubbornly resist being dismissed.

democratisation pursued by Wahid, trade unions have been spawned and labour movements have expanded since early 1998. Before that, Indonesian trade union movements had been heavily suppressed by the strong authoritarian state. According to a foreign businessman in Indonesia, the lack of experience with labour movements has encouraged the unorganised labour campaigns by workers (*Digital Chosunilbo* 1998b).

Another social issue stemming from the crises is racial conflict. Although Chinese hold economic power both in Thailand and Indonesia, Thai Chinese have had good relationships with the indigenous Thai. Their immigration history can be traced farther than that of Indonesian Chinese, and many of them have been incorporated into the Thai nation. In Indonesia, however, the indigenous Indonesians often have attacked Chinese in the presence of economic difficulties.

Since the economic crises, all three countries have curtailed expenditure on health, education, social development and welfare. Social vices gain secondary consideration in relation to economic recovery in these countries. Poverty, disease, crime and child abuse, all of which have long-term negative effects, have increased enormously. The neglect of these issues may cost them dearly in the future.

4. International Aspects

The East Asian crises reminded the international society of the predominance of the US in the region. Although Japan contributed significant funds to help the three Asian countries, its role has not been so conspicuous.[41] The United States sponsored, either directly or via international organisations, the post-crisis economic management.

While the crises have proceeded, the need for regional cooperation has gained attention. The Asian Monetary Fund (AMF) was proposed by Japan at the annual meeting of the IMF, in September 1997, to prevent another crisis and to enhance the region's financial stability.[42] At first the US and China, afraid of lowering their voices and concerned by the rise of Japan's influence,[43] opposed the proposal; later, at the APEC Conference in November 1998, they indicated positive attitudes towards its institutionalisation. In a separate arrangement, Korea, China, Japan and ten ASEAN countries agreed in May 1998 to establish a collective foreign exchange swap system. Already Korea-Japan and Japan-Malaysia had organised reciprocal foreign currency swap systems after the crises.

CONCLUSIONS - SUMMARY AND POLICY IMPLICATIONS

The East Asian crises, originating in Thailand, spread quickly to other countries. Not many predicted the occurrence of the crises. Among those countries affected by the crises, Thailand, Indonesia and Korea requested IMF rescue loans. These countries had open economic systems heavily reliant on export and foreign investment, and all three countries had weak, underdeveloped financial sectors. Numerous factors, which are to some degree or another inter-related, explain the crises. Although the three countries' foreign exchange crises

---

[41] Japan provided US$44 billion to help the three troubled Asian countries (Gohama 1999). Kim (1998) argues that Japan's role has been neither enough nor appropriate. Because of its lack of initiative, Japan seemed to fail to gain international respect. However, considering that the total amount given to the three countries was US$117.9 billion, Japan's monetary contribution should be appreciated.

[42] For a discussion of new international rescue systems, see Wesley (1999); Kumar *et al.* (2000).

[43] See Feng and Choo (1998).

are unlikely to be repeated (except, perhaps, in Indonesia), the economic crises are not over yet, especially if one considers consumption, investment, and the normalisation of the banking system.

From a theoretical perspective, the development of the Asian crises strongly supports the argument of structuralism rather than liberal or realism traditions. US hegemony fails to provide regional stability, or, at best, it could contain the spread of economic instability beyond the region. Mutual transactions between Western investors and East Asian countries turn out to be structured for the interests of the former. The deeply vulnerable position of the borrowers casts doubt on the universal application of the interdependence thesis. The economic philosophy of neoliberalism and its practical program of globalism appear to downplay the difference in size and strength of transaction partners. Moreover, the beneficiaries of the crises have not been national entities, as the argument of neomercantilism would have it. Although the US Treasury and the IMF have initiated the post-crisis treatments, capital interests, not the states in general, have benefited most. Such structural approaches as Wallerstein's world-system argument (Wallerstein 1974; 1989) and Galtung's international structuralism (Galtung 1971) provide robust explanations of the Asian economic crises.[44] While Western investors, who had long enjoyed lucrative businesses in Asia, were exempted from paying the cost, the socially disadvantaged in the victim countries encountered most of the backwash. Foreign investors could successfully collect their shares from the crises, while many East Asian citizens paid the prices and donor countries' citizens contributed to the funds through their taxes.[45]

The conditionality of the IMF propelled the damaged economies into a vicious chain reaction of economic troubles that eventually led to economic contraction. In order to be flexible, the IMF should consider both the particular conditions of individual countries and the long-term stability of the regional economy. Thanks to the effects of the crises themselves as well as the policy prescriptions of the IMF, the three countries could somehow or other tune up their economies to varying degrees. However, the old practices have strongly resisted reform. The crises have had great impact on political and social fields, too. While democratisation has been enhanced to some extent, social problems have been generated by the crises. The most conspicuous costs of reform and restructuring have been the sharp increase in the number of the unemployed and the poor, and the contraction of the middle class. Along with economic difficulties, both class and ethnic conflicts have intensified. The shadow of the crises will long linger in the three countries.

The policy prescriptions of the IMF have centred on securing investment and institutionalising neoliberal economic order, rather than promoting healthy and smooth economic development. The general feature of the Asian economic crises clearly shows that the present international financial system is of advantage to investors rather than to investment recipients.

International financial institutions should take responsibility for their imprudent investments. The amount of international money transacted overnight is known to be more than US$1 trillion. If financial big hands play a game of 'casino' capitalism, small open countries are easily exposed to economic turmoil. Although individual investors and traders are rational, the contemporary international economic system is neither perfect nor rational in nature, considering both the imbalance of power between participants and the high mobility of information and transaction. Foreign exchange crisis can take place in any weak economy,

---

[44] Although both macrohistoric approaches pay attention to the inequality of international and internal structures, Wallerstein emphasises the exchange structure, while Galtung stresses the actors.

[45] Unlike Latin American foreign currency crises in the early 1980's, foreign investors were exempted from accountability in the East Asian crises.

especially in fast developing countries where capital is short, generating serious negative externalities that are very likely to develop into serious financial and economic crises. In order to prevent this inhumane misfortune, both national and international safeguarding arrangements should be introduced.

REFERENCES

Basurto, Gabriela and Atish Ghosh (2000) 'The Interest Rate-Exchange Rate Nexus in the Asian Crisis Countries'. *IMF Working Paper WP/00/19*.
Bird, Judith (1998) 'Indonesia in 1997: The Tinderbox Year'. *Asian Survey* 38: 2.
Bird, Graham and Alistair Milne (1999) 'Miracle to Meltdown: A Pathology of the East Asian Financial Crisis'. *Third World Quarterly* 20: 2.
Bowornwathana, Bidhya (2000) 'Thailand in 1999: A Royal Jubilee, Economic Recovery, and Political Reform'. *Asian Survey* 40: 1.
Businesshankyung (1998) 'Special Report: Asian Economic Crisis (Korean)'. March 3.
Chosun Ilbo (Korean Newspaper) (1998a) August 14.
—— (1998b) September 26.
Choi, Kwang (1999) 'Korean Financial Crisis and Fiscal Policy'. *International Area Review* 2: 2.
Chun, Jin-Hwan (2000) 'East Asian Economic Development and Confucian Tradition'. A Paper at the 8th International Regional Cooperation in Northeast Asia, Cheju, Korea.
Corsetti, Giancarlo, Paolo Pesenti and Nouriel Roubini (1999) 'Paper Tigers? A Model of the Asian Crisis'. *European Economic Review* 43.
Delhaise, Philippe F. (1998) *Asia in Crisis: The Implication of the Banking and Finance Systems*. Singapore: John Wiley and Sons.
Demetriades, O. Panicos, and Bassam A. Fattough (1999) 'The Korean Financial Crisis: Competing Explanations and Policy Lessons for Financial Liberalization'. *International Affairs* 75: 4.
Digital Chosunilbo (Korean Newspaper) (1997) October 1.
—— (1998a) April 3.
—— (1998b) April 10.
—— (2001) March 6.
Economist (1998a) June 13-19. 'A Hitchhiker's Guide to Hedge Funds'.
—— (1998b) January 17-23. 'And Now the Political Fall Out'.
—— (1999) August 21-27. 'On their Feet Again?'
Far Eastern Economic Review (1998) October 15.
—— (1999) August 19.
—— (2000) October 19.
Feng, Zhu and Jaewoo Choo (1998) 'Asian Financial Crisis and East Asian Economic Cooperation: A Chinese View'. *Global Economic Review* 27: 4.
Fischer, Stanley (1998) 'The Asian Crisis, the IMF, and the Japanese Economy'. *www.imf.org/external/np/speeches/1998/040898.htm*. April 8.
Focus on the Global South and CAFOD (1998) *IMF's Taming of Asian Tigers: The Economic Crises of Korea, Thailand, and Indonesia* (Korean). Seoul: Munhwagwagaksa.
Galtung, Johan (1971) 'A Structural Theory of Imperialism'. *Journal of Peace Research* 8: 1.
Gohama, Hirohisa (1999) 'The East Asian Economic Crises and Japan's Cooperation (Korean)'. *Wolganataejiyukdinghyang* 88.
Goldstein, Morris (1998) *International Policy Brief*. Washington, D.C.: Institute for International Economics.

Hanguk Ilbo (Korean Newspaper) (1999) June 9.
Joongang Ilbo (Korean Newspaper) (1997) March 10.
Kim, Gyu-ryun (1998) 'Financial Crises and Asian International Relations (Korean)'. *Sinasea* 5: 1.
Ko, Woo-sung (1998) 'The Influence of Southeast Asian Politico-Economic Instability on Korea (Korean)'. *Ataefocus* 9.
Kumar, Manmohan S., Paul Masson and Marcus Miller (2000) 'Global Financial Crises: Institutions and Incentives'. *IMF Working Paper WP/00/105*.
Lee, Kyung-Sook (1998) 'The Three Countries' Exports are Less Lively than Expected (Korean)'. *KIET Silmukyngje*.
Liddle, R. William (2000) 'Indonesia: Democracy Restored'. *Asian Survey* 40: 1.
Limskull, Kitti (2000) 'The Financial and Economic Crisis in Thailand: Dynamics of the Crisis-Root and Process'. *Economic Crisis in Southeast Asia and Korea: Its Economic, Social, Political and Cultural Impacts*. Seoul: Tradition and Modernity.
Madrick, Jeff (1998) 'The IMF Approach: The Half-Learned Lessons of History'. *World Policy Journal* 15: 3.
Park, Dae-Geun (2000) 'Looking for the Indicators of Overestimated Exchange Rate during the Asian Foreign Exchange Crisis (Korean)'. *Daedoekyungjejongchaekyongu* 4: 1.
Pavan, Ahluwalia (2000) 'Discriminating Contagion: An Alternative Explanation of Contagious Currency Crisis in Emerging Markets'. *IMF Working Paper WP/00/14*.
Punyaratabandhu, Suchitra (1998) 'Thailand in 1997: Financial Crisis and Constitutional Reform'. *Asian Survey* 38: 2.
Radelet, Steven and Jeffrey D. Sachs (1998) 'The East Asian Financial Crisis: Diagnosis, Remedies, Prospects'. *Brookings Papers on Economic Activity* 1.
Rosenstein-Rodan, Paul N. (1989) 'External Economies and Industrialization'. In Gerald M. Meier, ed., *Leading Issues in Economic Development*. New York: Oxford University Press.
Sachs, Jeffrey (1998) 'The IMF and the Asian Flu'. *The American Prospect* March-April.
Sikorski, Douglas (1999) 'The Financial Crisis in Southeast Asia and Korea: Issues of Political Economy. *Global Economic Review* 28: 1.
Wallerstein, Immanuel M. (1974) *The Modern World System I: Capitalist Agriculture and the Origin of the European World-Economy in the Sixteenth Century*. New York: Academy Press.
—— (1989) *The Modern World System III: The Second Era of Great Expansion of the Capitalist World-Economy, 1730-1840's*. New York: Academy Press.
Warne, W. Robert (1998) 'Washington's Perceptions on Korea's Financial Crisis'. *Korea Observer* 29: 3.
Wesley, Michael (1999) 'The Asian Crisis and the Adequacy of Regional Institutions'. *Contemporary Southeast Asia* 21: 1.
World Bank (2001) May 3. 'Country Data'. *www.worldbank.org/data/countrydata*.
Yoo, Jang-Hee and Chul Woo Moon. 'Korean Financial Crisis during the 1997-1998: Causes and Challenges'. *Journal of Asian Economics* 10: 2.
Yoon, Jin-ho (1998) 'IMF Regime and the Unemployment Crisis'. *Korea Focus* 6: 2.
Yoon, Jin-Pyo (1997) 'Changing State-Market Relations: The Case of Thailand (Korean)'. *Dongnamasiayongu* 5.
www.bi.go.id/bank_indonesia2 (2001) February 4.
www.bot.or.th/bothomepage/databank/EconData (2001) Feburuary 4.
www.bps.go.id/statbysector/employ (2001) May 3.
www.bps.go.is/statbysector/tourism (2001) May 3.
www.nso.go.kr/cgi-bin/sws_999.cgi (2001) February 7.

www.nso.go.kr/eindex (2001) May 5.
www.standardand poors.com/ratings/sovereigns/index.htm (2001)

In: Thailand: Economics, Political and Social Issues
Ed: Randle C. Zebioli
ISBN: 978-1-60456-583-6
©2009 Nova Science Publishers, Inc.

Chapter 3

THAILAND TRADE

Ida M. Conway

TRADE SUMMARY

The U.S. goods trade deficit with Thailand was $14.3 billion in 2006, an increase of $1.7 billion from $12.6 billion in 2005. U.S. goods exports in 2006 were $8.2 billion, up 12.4 percent from the previous year. Corresponding U.S. imports from Thailand were $22.5 billion, up 13.0 percent. Thailand is currently the 24th largest export market for U.S. goods.

U.S. exports of private commercial services (i.e., excluding military and government) to Thailand were $1.5 billion in 2005 (latest data available), and U.S. imports were $1.1 billion. Sales of services in Thailand by majority U.S.-owned affiliates were $3.0 billion in 2004 (latest data available), while sales of services in the United States by majority Thailand-owned firms were $3 million.

The stock of U.S. foreign direct investment (FDI) in Thailand in 2005 was $8.6 billion (latest data available), up from $7.6 billion in 2004. U.S. FDI in Thailand is concentrated largely in the manufacturing, finance, professional, scientific, and technical services, and wholesale trade sectors.

FREE TRADE AGREEMENT (FTA) NEGOTIATIONS

The U.S. Government began FTA negotiations with Thailand in June 2004, and conducted seven rounds of discussions through 2006. The negotiations were suspended indefinitely following a military-led coup against the Thaksin government in September 2006. The United States is prepared to continue FTA negotiations with Thailand once democracy is restored, and will continue to strongly urge Thailand to lift martial law, restore civil liberties and maintain its current timeline regarding constitutional reform and elections.

IMPORT POLICIES

Thailand's tariff structure remains an impediment to market access in many sectors. The country's average applied MFN tariff rate is 10.9 percent, but some tariffs are as high as 80 percent. The highest tariff rates apply to imports competing with locally-produced goods, including agricultural products, automobiles and automotive parts, motorcycles, alcoholic beverages, fabrics, paper and paperboard products, and restaurant equipment. The Thai government is in the process of unilaterally streamlining its tariff schedule. Tariffs are being reduced to zero or to one of three rates: 1 percent for raw materials; 5 percent for intermediate goods; and 10 percent for finished goods. The Thai government has so far completed restructuring approximately 70 percent of the tariff lines, and plans to restructure another 10 percent soon. In 2006 the government eliminated tariffs on 768 items related to electronics and electrical appliances and 105 products in the printing industry. Further tariff reductions on some automobile and food products are also planned. Tariffs remaining to be restructured are primarily agricultural and luxury products.

Taxation

Thailand's tax administration generally is complicated and non-transparent. Excise taxes are high on some items, such as unleaded gasoline, beer, wine, and distilled spirits. When import duties, excise taxes, and other surcharges are calculated, the cumulative tax burden on most imported spirits is approximately 284 percent. In 1999, as part of an economic stimulus package, the value-added tax (VAT) was temporarily reduced from 10 percent to 7 percent and the excise tax on fuel oil was reduced from 17.5 percent to 5 percent. The Thai government frequently has announced its intention to restore the VAT to 10 percent, but has not yet done so. The most recent effort to restore the VAT to 10 percent was delayed until September 30, 2007.

Agriculture and Food Products

High duties on agriculture and food products and arbitrary management of import licenses and application of sanitary and phytosanitary (SPS) measures (see section below on Standards, Testing, Labeling, and Certification) remain the primary impediments to U.S. exports of high-value fresh and processed foods. Under its WTO Uruguay Round agriculture obligations, Thailand committed to reduce its import duties, but agriculture is scheduled to be among the last sectors targeted under the Thai government's plan.

Duties on imported consumer-ready food products typically range between 30 percent and 50 percent – the highest in the ASEAN region – with some as high as 90 percent (*e.g.*, coffee). Tariffs on meats, fresh fruits (including citrus fruit and table grapes) and vegetables, fresh cheese and pulses (*e.g.*, dry peas, lentils, and chickpeas) are similarly high, even for products for which there is little domestic production. Frozen french fries, for example, are not produced in Thailand, yet face a tariff of 30 percent. When import duties, excise taxes, and other surcharges are calculated, imported wines face a total tax of nearly 400 percent. The excise tax on wine (made of grapes) is 60 percent of value or 100 baht per liter of pure alcohol, whichever is higher. Fermented spirits made from fruits other than grapes, *e.g.*, mangosteen, are subject to an excise tax of 25 percent of value or 70 baht per liter of pure alcohol, whichever is higher.

With the exception of wine and spirits, Thailand no longer applies "specific" duties on most agricultural and food products, and *ad valorem* rates are declining in accordance with Thailand's WTO commitments. Nevertheless, import duties on some agricultural and processed food goods have an average tariff rate of

25.4 percent. Moreover, bound duties on many high-value fresh and processed food products will remain high, from 30 percent to 40 percent, even after Thailand implements reductions required under its WTO commitments. Tariffs on apples are at 10 percent, while duties on pears and cherries remain as high as 30 percent to 40 percent. U.S. fruit growers estimate lost sales of up to $25 million annually from the combined effect of Thailand's high tariffs, surcharges, and a customs reference price system that often disregards the declared transaction price of these products (see "Customs Barriers" section below).

Thailand's overall import policy is directed at protecting domestic producers, and the Thai government has implemented non-transparent price controls on some products and maintains significant quantitative restrictions that impede market access. The United States is concerned that access to tariff-rate quotas for agricultural products is often managed in an arbitrary and non-transparent manner. Although Thailand has been relatively open to imports of feed ingredients, including corn, soybeans, and soymeal, in recent years, the Thai government maintains excessively burdensome requirements associated with the issuance of import permits for feed ingredients. For example, corn imports enjoy liberalized tariff rates, but the benefit of this tariff reduction has been offset by a Thai government requirement that corn imports arrive between March and June, a seasonal limitation not provided for in Thailand's WTO schedule. This requirement places U.S. suppliers at a disadvantage and gives most of the market to corn from the southern hemisphere. Corn is also subject to a tariff-rate quota (TRQ); in-quota corn imports (54,700 mt) are subject to a 20 percent tariff rate, while out-of-quota corn imports are subject to a 73 percent tariff. There are import quotas for soybeans, for which the import duty is 5 percent. However, Thailand requires that importers purchase a certain amount of domestically-produced product before being granted licenses for imported products. Importers of skim milk powder report that import quota allocations are often released late, which sometimes causes interruptions in trade flows.

In addition, the Thai government requires import license fees for meat products of approximately $114 per ton on beef and pork, $227 per ton for poultry, and $114 per ton on offal that do not appear to reflect the costs of import administration. SPS standards for certain agricultural products also often appear to be applied arbitrarily and without prior notification. The Thai government is implementing a long-dormant requirement of inspecting individual slaughterhouse or farm facilities that export animals and animal products into Thailand. Efforts have been made to negotiate a system audit, as opposed to a plant by plant audit the Thai government is seeking.

U.S. agricultural exports to Thailand, including fish and forestry products, which dropped dramatically in the aftermath of the 1997 financial crisis to $440 million in 1998, have recovered and approached $750 million for the past three years. According to U.S. industry estimates, potential exports to Thailand could reach as much as $1.5 billion annually if Thailand's tariffs and other trade-distorting measures are substantially reduced or eliminated and the economy recovers to pre-crisis levels.

Automotive Sector

Thailand's import duties and taxes on vehicles are among the highest in ASEAN. In response to the 1997 financial crisis, the Thai government raised tariffs on Completely Built Up (CBU) passenger cars and sport utility vehicles to 80 percent, up from 42 percent and 68 percent, respectively and they remain at that level today. Thailand negotiated an FTA with Japan during 2005, but it remains unsigned. If ratified among other tariff cuts, the agreement will phase in over four years a reduction of tariffs to 60 percent on Japanese vehicles with engines greater than 3000 cc.

Excise taxes in Thailand are based on various vehicle characteristics, such as engine size, weight and wheelbase. In July 2004, Thailand revised its excise tax structure, but it remains complex and heavily favors domestically manufactured vehicles. Taxes on passenger vehicles range from 30 percent to 50 percent, while pickup trucks are taxed at a rate of 3 percent. As a result, pickups account for more than 50 percent of total vehicle sales in Thailand.

The Thai government administers several incentive measures that benefit automotive exports. These include tax reimbursements on imported materials for export production; tax redemption on exported parts and vehicles; tax reduction on imported materials. Additionally, Thailand has established a Free Trade Zone Area (FTZ) in order to support export-related investments. In the FTZ area, the Thai government provides services to facilitate customs processing and production.

Customs valuation issues have been particularly acute in the automotive sector (see "Customs Barriers" section below).

Textiles

Thailand's tariff rates for U.S. textile exports are high, ranging from 20 percent to 30 percent for most fabrics and 30 percent for most clothing and other made-up textile products. In addition, Thailand applies specific unit duties on more than one-third of all textile tariff lines, which make effective rates even higher. Furthermore, on the APEC website, Thailand's applied tariffs for certain clothing are incorrectly listed as 60 percent. Thailand has not yet addressed United States' concerns that these higher published tariffs could be misleading and discourage potential United States exporters.

Quantitative Restrictions and Import Licensing

Thailand is still in the process of changing its import licensing procedures to comply with its WTO obligations. Import licenses are required for at least 26 categories of items, including many raw materials, petroleum, industrial materials, textiles, pharmaceuticals, and agricultural items. Import procedures for jute and marble will soon be brought into line with WTO requirements.

Imports of used motorcycles and parts and gaming machines are prohibited. Imports of other products must meet burdensome regulatory requirements, including extra fees and certificate-of-origin requirements. Thailand does not have specific measures of general application relating to non-preferential rules of origin.

Imports of food, pharmaceuticals, certain minerals, arms and ammunition, and art objects require special permits from relevant ministries. Thailand requires that detailed and often proprietary business information about the manufacturing process and composition of food be provided in applications for food product registration.

Customs Barriers

Thailand continues to take steps to improve its customs practices, building on the U.S.-Thai bilateral dialogue held over the past five years. While the international business community maintains that some positive customs policy changes are slow in filtering down through the bureaucracy, most acknowledge the progress to date.

The lack of transparency and efficiency of the Thai customs regime remain a concern. In July 2003, Thailand formally notified the WTO of legislation passed in 2000 implementing the WTO Customs Valuation Agreement. Meanwhile, Thailand has drafted, but not yet submitted to Parliament, legislation limiting the discretion of the Customs Director General to arbitrarily increase the customs value of imports (though in practice, the Director General has not made use of that discretion). Some industry representatives continue to report inconsistent application of the WTO transaction valuation methodology and repeated use of arbitrary values. Industry representatives have asked that Thai Customs publish proposals for changes in customs laws, regulations, and notifications and allow time for comments on these proposals. They have also requested that Customs impose a time limit on the issuance of rulings, respond to appeals within an established time period, provide a full explanation of its decisions regarding appeals, establish a reasonable time period at the beginning of an audit or an investigation for their completion and provide a written report of the findings of the audit or investigation.

In addition, as is the case with some Thai agencies, Customs has an incentives program rewarding officials for identifying violators based on a percentage of the recovered revenues. This practice encourages revenue maximization rather than compliance with legal requirements. Corruption in the Customs Department reportedly remains a serious problem.

STANDARDS, TESTING, LABELING AND CERTIFICATION

Thailand's Food and Drug Administration (TFDA) imposes standards, testing, and labeling requirements, and requires certification permits for the importation of all food and pharmaceutical products, as well as certain medical devices. Many U.S. companies have raised concerns that the cost, duration, and complexity of the permitting processes are overly burdensome and are concerned about the periodic demands for disclosure of proprietary information. TFDA has streamlined its procedures somewhat, but

U.S. companies still report delays of up to a year. All processed foods must be accompanied by a detailed list of ingredients and a manufacturing process description, disclosure of which could potentially jeopardize an applicant's trade secrets. A labeling regime for foods derived by the use of biotechnology, modeled on the Japanese system, was put into effect in May 2003. In 2004, the Ministry of Public Health (MOPH) introduced new regulations on food safety testing, known as Ministerial Decree 11, requiring that many imported food products undergo testing and certification for a number of chemical additives. Decree 11's implementation has been delayed as MOPH has undertaken revisions of the guidelines but these guidelines have yet to be finalized.

In August 2006, the Department of Agriculture in the Ministry of Agriculture and Cooperatives, notified the WTO of its proposed new rules on Thai quarantine practices on certain imported fruits and vegetables from all exporting countries. Under these rules, all imported relevant commodities will be subject to pest risk assessment (PRA) prior to importation. While commodities that have a record of export can be allowed to ship during the PRA review, other products will be prohibited.

The Thailand Industrial Standards Institute (TISI) is the national standards organization under the Ministry of Industry. TISI is empowered to provide product certifications according to established Thai standards and is an accredited body for International Standards Organization (ISO) and other certifications in Thailand. The Thai government requires the certification of 60 products in ten sectors, including agriculture, construction materials, consumer goods, electrical appliances and accessories, PVC pipe, medical equipment, LPG gas containers, surface coatings, and vehicles. In the case of medical equipment, Thailand requires product approval in the country of origin before it can be registered, which disadvantages products that have already received regulatory approval in other countries (usually the EU) before receiving U.S. FDA approval. Uninterruptible power supply product imports must meet a more stringent radio signal emissions standard that appears to favor local suppliers.

Thailand prohibits motorcycle traffic from its expressways, including large-engine motorcycles that are sufficiently powerful and intended for expressways and do not pose the same safety risk to other travelers as underpowered motorcycles. Thailand's motorcycle emissions regulations are an amalgamation of standards and tests used elsewhere in the world, resulting in standards that reportedly are among the most stringent in the world. Enforcement of these standards has been non-transparent so that even producers utilizing advanced low-emission technology have difficulty meeting these standards.

GOVERNMENT PROCUREMENT

Thailand is not a signatory to the WTO Agreement on Government Procurement. A specific set of rules, commonly referred to as the Prime Minister's Procurement Regulations, governs public-sector procurement for ministries and state-owned enterprises. While these regulations require that nondiscriminatory treatment and open competition be accorded to all potential bidders, different state enterprises and ministries typically have their own individual procurement policies and practices. Preferential treatment is provided to domestic suppliers (including subsidiaries of U.S. firms registered as Thai companies), which receive an automatic 7 percent price advantage over foreign bidders in initial bid round evaluations.

A "Buy Thai" directive from the Prime Minister's office issued in 2001 has raised additional concerns about the Thai government procurement policies. While Thailand denies that the "Buy Thai" policy discriminates against foreign producers, specific language used in government instructions on some procurement tenders explicitly excludes foreign-made, non-Thai products from the bidding process.

Government agencies and state enterprises reserve the right to accept or reject any or all bids at any time and may also modify the technical requirements during the bidding process. The latter provision allows considerable leeway to government agencies and state-owned enterprises in managing tenders, while denying bidders any recourse to challenge procedures. Allegations that changes are made for special considerations frequently surface, including charges of bias on major procurements. Despite an official commitment to transparency in government procurement, U.S. companies and Thai media have reported allegations of irregularities. In addition, private sector representatives have expressed concern regarding a Thai government decision to no longer include arbitration clauses in concessions and government contracts.

Regulations promulgated in May 2000 formalized a Thai government practice requiring a countertrade transaction on government procurement contracts valued at more than 300 million baht, on a case-by-case basis. A counterpurchase of Thai commodities valued at not less than 50 percent of the value of the principal contract may be required. As part of a countertrade deal, the Thai government also may specify markets into which commodities may not be sold; these are usually markets where Thai commodities already enjoy significant access. From 1994 through August 2006, 309 countertrade agreements were signed, resulting in exports valued at over 74 billion baht. The Thai government is reviewing its countertrade policies due to concerns about delays and the management of these transactions. The United States is monitoring this issue.

EXPORT SUBSIDIES

Thailand maintains programs to support trade in certain manufactured products and processed agricultural products, which may constitute export subsidies. These include various tax benefits, import duty reductions, credit at below-market rates on some government-to-government sales of Thai rice (established on a case-by-case basis), and preferential financing for exporters. The Thai government terminated its packing credit program in compliance with WTO commitments but received an extension of its WTO exemption period for the Industrial Estate Authority of Thailand and the Board of Investment. Low interest loans provided under the Export Market Diversification Promotion Program to exporters targeting new markets ended in December 2003.

INTELLECTUAL PROPERTY RIGHTS (IPR) PROTECTION

Widespread commercial IPR counterfeiting and piracy continue. U.S. copyright industries reported an estimated annual trade loss of more than $308 million in 2005 from IPR infringement in Thailand. An increasing volume of pirated and counterfeited products manufactured in Thailand is exported. Thailand has been on the U.S. Special 301 Watch List since November 1994.

The United States and Thailand held extensive consultations on IPR issues under the TIFA and during the FTA negotiations aimed at strengthening Thailand's regime. During the FTA negotiations, Thailand enacted optical disc legislation but it lacked many key elements, and U.S. officials continue to press Thailand to address these deficiencies. The Copyright Act amendments have not been enacted and lack of sustained, aggressive, and coordinated enforcement remains a substantial problem.

On January 30, the Ministry of Public Health issued implementing regulations for the 2002 Trade Secrets Act. The regulations restrict the government from releasing protected data for a period of five years, but do not provide data exclusivity that would prevent unfair commercial use.

The Geographical Indications Act was passed by the Thai Parliament in September 2003 and went into effect in April 2004. This legislation allows rights holders to seek protection for indications which identify a good as originating in the territory of a member or a region or locality in that territory, where a given quality, reputation, or other characteristic of the good is essentially attributable to its geographic origin.

Registration of new plant varieties under the Plant Variety Protection Act began in April 2006. Private sector representatives have expressed concern about the implementation and enforcement of the Act, noting the wide availability of pirated counterfeit seeds and other products in Thailand. The United States urged Thailand to strengthen the 1999 Act to make it consistent with the 1991 International Convention for the Protection of New Varieties of Plants (UPOV) and to accede to this convention.

Thailand's IPR enforcement efforts have been inconsistent. Although conviction rates are high, corruption and a cultural climate of leniency can complicate prosecution of cases. The frequency of raids compromised by leaks from police sources remains a concern. Pirates, including those associated with transnational crime syndicates, have responded to intensified levels of enforcement with intimidation against rights holders' representatives and enforcement authorities. The Ministry of Commerce has the lead in promoting interagency cooperation on IPR enforcement issues. In August 2006, the Ministry concluded a Memorandum of Understanding (MOU) between enforcement authorities, retail establishments and rights holders to better coordinate operations. While the MOU is an important step, the Thai government has yet to ensure sustained enforcement actions against retailers, distributors, and manufacturers of pirated and counterfeit goods.

The Department of Special Investigations (DSI) was established in 2004 and took on an IPR enforcement role, focusing on major infringing production, warehousing and trafficking operations, as well as those activities associated with organized crime. In January 2006, the threshold for cases to be referred to DSI was lowered to 500,000 baht ($13,400), promising stronger investigative action into more cases. In December 2003, the Thai Cabinet approved in principle draft amendments to the Anti-Money Laundering Act, one of which makes IPR crimes a "predicate" offense. These amendments would allow police and other law enforcement officials to seize and investigate funds and suspected bank accounts. However, in July 2004, the Council of State, which reviews pending legislation, rejected the inclusion of IPR crimes as a predicate offense, citing concerns that IPR violations are "commercial disputes."

The Thai government established a specialized intellectual property court in 1997, which has improved judicial procedures and imposed tougher penalties. Criminal cases generally are disposed of within 6 months to 12 months from the time of a raid to the rendering of a conviction. However, courts frequently hand down light sentences that are not considered a deterrent to criminal behavior. Thai officials generally lack sufficient resources to undertake enforcement actions apart from those initiated by rights holders. Effective prosecutions can be labor intensive for rights holders, who often investigate, participate in raids, and assist in the preparation of documentation for prosecution.

Patents

Thailand's patent regime generally provides adequate protection for most innovations. However, U.S. industry has expressed concerns that the legislation that Thailand enacted to implement its data protection obligations under the TRIPS Agreement would not provide adequate protection of confidential information from disclosure. U.S. industry is also concerned that Thailand does not have a formal patent linkage system to prevent the regulatory approval of copies of pharmaceuticals that are still patented. There has been a recent increase in the number of such copies receiving Thai FDA approval while the original product is still under patent. Thailand's patent office lacks sufficient resources to keep up with the volume of applications, and patent examinations can take more than five years. The Department of Intellectual Property is seeking to contract out to academic institutions some parts of patent search for novelty and preparation of applications in order to speed up the registration process. In 2005 Thailand began preparations to accede to the Paris Convention and the Patent Cooperation Treaty.

Thailand's Ministry of Public Health has pursued the issuance of compulsory licenses on certain patented drugs and has indicated it may consider using compulsory licensing with respect to drugs for treating a broad range of medical conditions. The United States acknowledges Thailand's ability to issue compulsory licenses to address public health emergencies, subject to its own law and its obligations as a member of the WTO. At the same time, the United States has expressed concern regarding a lack of transparency and consultation in the Thai government's pursuit of this policy and about the potentially expansive use of compulsory licenses. The United States has also raised concerns about the potential impact of this and other recent actions by the Thai government on the broader trade and investment climate in Thailand. The United States has urged Thailand to address judiciously the complex intersection between health and intellectual property policy, and to do so in ways that recognize the role of intellectual property in the development of new drugs.

Copyrights

Thailand's copyright law, intended to bring Thailand into conformity with international standards under TRIPS and the Berne Convention, became effective in March 1995. Despite efforts by Thai police at the retail, distribution, and production levels and by corporate end users, piracy remains a serious concern. The Copyright Law is ambiguous regarding decompilation and regulations for enforcement procedures leave loopholes that frustrate effective enforcement.

The Thai government is in the process of amending the Copyright Law in order to bring it in line with two 1996 World Intellectual Property Organization (WIPO) treaties, the WIPO Copyright Treaty and the WIPO Performances and Phonograms Treaty. The draft amendments to the Copyright Law have been approved by the Cabinet, but await legislative consideration.

Cable piracy continues to be a major problem throughout Thailand, as pirate providers expand their reach in the provinces. In December 2003, the Thai government initiated a new policy offering amnesty to operators who agree to cease infringing actions under threat of legal action. This policy is intended as a temporary measure pending the establishment of a National Broadcasting Commission and new regulations for cable operators. However, the Thai government has failed to initiate enforcement operations.

U.S. copyright industries continue to express serious concerns over the rapid and unchecked growth of optical media piracy in Thailand. In August 2005, the Optical Disk Manufacturing Control Act went into force. This Act is designed to enhance the authority and capabilities of the Thai government to act against operators of illicit optical disc factories and to control the production materials and machines of legal producers. U.S. copyright industries are concerned that the Optical Disk Act is deficient in several respects, including that penalties are not high enough to deter pirates and do not enhance the Thai government's enforcement and oversight powers sufficiently.

Book publishers have raised concerns that the existing copyright law is being interpreted in a manner that is allowing extensive book piracy, especially in the form of illegal photocopying, to go unchecked. According to industry, annual losses are estimated at about approximately $30 million.

Trademarks

The Thai government amended its trademark law in 1992, increasing penalties for infringement and extending protection to service, certification, and collective marks. The Thai government also streamlined trademark application procedures, addressing issues raised by the U.S. Government. Additional amendments designed to bring Thailand's trademark law into compliance with the TRIPS Agreement were enacted in June 2000, broadening the legal definition of a mark. While these developments have created a viable legal framework and have led to some improvements in enforcement, especially for clothing, accessories, and plush toys, trademark infringement remains a serious problem.

U.S. companies with an established presence in Thailand and a record of sustained cooperation with Thai law enforcement officials have had some success in defending trademarks, but the process remains time-consuming and costly. Penalties for proven trademark violations are insufficiently high to have a deterrent effect.

SERVICES BARRIERS

Telecommunications Services

Thailand has made substantial progress toward reforming its telecommunications regulatory regime during the past year, but several controversial issues remain unresolved and significant obstacles to foreign investment in the sector remain in place. While Thailand is still working to liberalize its basic telecommunications services, new technologies such as mobile telephony and broadband Internet services have transformed the telecommunications sector in the intervening period.

The seven-member National Telecommunications Commission (NTC) -- the independent regulator mandated by the 1997 constitution responsible for licensing, spectrum management, and supervision of telecommunications operators — began its operations in November 2004. The creation of the NTC follows reorganization with respect to ministerial oversight of the telecommunications sector in 2002. While the new Ministry of Information and Communication Technology (MICT) is responsible for overall telecommunications policy, including such major initiatives as privatization of the state-owned telecommunications firms, the initiative for liberalization of the sector clearly rests with the industry regulator, the NTC.

The NTC formulated a Telecom Master Plan for 2005-2007, to guide the development of the telecommunications sector. It established licensing criteria for the three types of telecommunications licenses it may issue: Type I (without network); Type II (with or without network for specific groups or users); and Type III (with network for public telecommunication services). The NTC has set criteria for the allocation of telephone numbers. It has set temporary measures for radio and frequency allocation. The NTC has issued six Type I and Type III telecommunications licenses to state-owned telecommunications providers TOT and CAT. The licenses granted cover the existing telecommunications services operated by the two incumbent operators.

Since the NTC began its work in November 2004, a clearer regulatory framework for the operation of Internet Service Providers (ISPs) has emerged. The NTC has established licensing criteria, license fees, and interconnection charges for ISPs. The NTC issued the first Type I telecommunications license (for an operator without its own network) in June 2005. As of this writing, the NTC has issued Type I licenses to a total of 44 ISPs.

A March 2006 study by the World Bank noted complaints by many local ISPs that "prices charged for international bandwidth and access to international Internet gateway services are extremely high; there is a critical shortage of international data capacity; and the quality of service, including the lack of redundancy is very poor, leading to frequent, long and unplanned service outages."

The NTC has also begun to move forward with licenses for satellite services. The three types of licenses will be: Type I for Satellite Operators (the licensing principles for Type III telecommunications licenses will apply); Type II for Earth-station Operators (the licensing principles for Type II telecommunications licenses will apply); and Type III for Satellite Service Re-Sellers (the licensing principles for Type I telecommunications licenses will apply).

NTC plans to issue licenses for third-generation (3G) mobile telephone services have been delayed. By law, allocation of frequencies requires participation by both the NTC and a

National Broadcast Commission (NBC), which is still not yet operational. It remains unclear how frequencies will be allocated and whether allocation must await the formation of the NBC.

An amendment to the Telecommunications Business Law went into effect in December 2005 that raised the limit of allowable foreign ownership from 25 percent to 49 percent. State-owned enterprises continue to control large segments of the market, particularly in fixed-line and international long-distance services. With the growth of new markets such as mobile phone and satellite services in recent years, however, the role of private companies in this dynamic sector has grown accordingly. The two largest mobile service operators have pursued controversial tie-ups with foreign telecommunications firms. In January 2006, Singapore-based Temasek bought a controlling interest in Shin Corporation, the parent of mobile provider AIS, and in October 2005, Norway's Telenor AS bought out both TAC and its parent company UCOM. The Ministry of Commerce initiated an investigation into foreign ownership of Shin Corporation that may force Temasek to divest some of its ownership to comply with the law.

Thailand's telecommunications operators have historically operated as state-owned enterprises and the legacy of state ownership continues to affect the business environment in this sector. The two outstanding issues are concession conversion and privatization. Beginning in the mid-1980's, the Thai government introduced competition into the telecommunications sector to increase capacity so as to meet the booming economy's demand for telecommunications services. The state-owned telecommunications companies, now TOT and CAT Telecom, granted several concessions to private companies on a Build-Transfer-Operate (BTO) contract basis. Under the BTO contracts, the private contracting party established telecommunications networks at their own expense. Upon completion of the concession period, all assets are to be transferred to the concession grantor. Revenue sharing payments for each concession have differed. A dual structure in the sector resulted, where the concessionaires both compete with TOT and CAT Telecom while at the same time submitting to their regulation and making revenue sharing payments to them. While early plans for reform of the sector called for concession conversion, the NTC decided not to interfere in the concessions but to begin issuing licenses to provide telecommunications services. Concessions are thus expected to expire gradually as the private operators migrate subscribers for mobile services from 2G to 3G services, which will bring their operations under the purview of the NTC and free them from revenue sharing payments.

The Thai government is also planning to partially privatize TOT and CAT Telecom, but the privatization has met resistance. Regulatory uncertainty on such issues as interconnection charges complicates the task of determining the companies' market value.

Legal Services

Current Thai law prohibits foreign equity participation in Thai law firms in excess of 49 percent, and foreign nationals are prohibited from practicing law in Thailand. However, under the U.S.-Thailand Treaty of Amity and Economic Relations (AER Treaty), U.S. investments are exempted from the general restriction on foreign equity participation in law firms. U.S. investors may own law firms in Thailand; but U.S. citizens and other foreign nationals (with the exception of "grandfathered" non-citizens) may not provide legal services. In certain circumstances, foreign attorneys may act in a consultative capacity.

Financial Services

After the 1997-98 financial crisis, the Thai government liberalized foreign firms' access to the financial sector. However, significant restrictions remain on foreign participation in the sector. While aliens have been allowed to engage in brokerage services since 1997, for example, foreign firms are allowed to own shares greater than 49 percent of Thai securities firms only on a case-by-case basis.

Foreigners are permitted to hold a maximum of 25 percent of the equity in Thai banks. Within the "Financial Sector Master Plan" drafted by the Bank of Thailand and approved by Parliament, this percentage may be increased to 49 percent at such time as the Central Bank deems appropriate. The Master Plan requires all Thai deposit-taking institutions to become either a retail or commercial bank with differing minimum capital requirements. The Bank of Thailand has indicated that no new banking licenses will be issued until "economic conditions" permit greater competition in the Thai banking market.

Foreign banks currently operating in Thailand are disadvantaged in their ability to compete. Most notably, they are limited to one branch, and are not permitted to operate off-site ATM machines, which are considered as branches. Foreign banks must maintain minimum capital funds of 125 million baht ($3.1 million) invested in government or state-enterprise securities or deposited directly with the Bank of Thailand. Expatriate management personnel are limited to six professionals in full branches and two professionals in Bangkok International Banking Facility operations, although exceptions are often granted.

Charged with helping to restructure the financial sectors' non-performing loans, the government-owned Thai Asset Management Corporation gives priority to Thai nationals when contracting for management, technical, and advisory services. Foreigners may be hired, however, in the absence of qualified Thai nationals.

Construction, Architecture, and Engineering

Foreigners are prohibited from working as engineers or architects, but in practice, they can work as consultants in these fields. Construction firms must also be registered in Thailand (*i.e.*, establish a commercial presence). Under the U.S.-Thailand AER Treaty, American firms may establish companies in Thailand that provide construction, architectural, and engineering services. The Thai government regulates the billing rates of foreign construction, architectural, and engineering firms. Current practice places a ceiling on billing for these services by foreign firms.

Accounting Services

Foreigners cannot be licensed as Certified Public Accountants and therefore cannot practice accounting in Thailand. Foreign accountants may only serve as business consultants.

Transport Services, Including Express Delivery Services

The passage of the Multimodal Transport Act of July 2005 represents a new barrier to trade in the transport services sector. While the full impact of the law remains unclear, it introduces new uncertainty into the treatment of operations of foreign shipping companies. Political difficulties in 2006 delayed approval of implementing regulations. While the text of the law itself appears to require foreign shipping companies performing multimodal services in Thailand to either incorporate in Thailand or appoint a Thai agent (as opposed to operating out of their branch offices in Thailand as they have to date), the draft ministerial regulations implementing the law provide that the law shall not apply to foreign shipping companies transporting goods under bills of lading governed by international convention. In view of the severe penalties for non-compliance (including a retroactive fine of Baht 50,000 per contract), international shipping firms have sought to contain their downside risk by either incorporating in Thailand or appointing an agent, passing the attendant costs on to customers. In addition, private express companies must pay postal "fines" and penalties in Thailand that can amount to an average of 37 baht per item.

The 49 percent limit on foreign ownership in land transport (trucking) hampers investment in the growth of express delivery services. Express delivery firms prefer to have the option to control items throughout the supply of the service, including both air and ground-based operations in order to speed the movement of goods.

The United States and Thailand signed a comprehensive bilateral Open Skies Agreement in September 2005 that provides for full liberalization by 2010. The agreement includes phase-in periods with respect to pricing and fifth freedom rights.

Healthcare Services

Thai government policy is highly restrictive in the healthcare services sector (*e.g.*, hospital, dental, physician services), particularly regarding the lack of transparency relating to hospitals and the possibility of foreign ownership, administration, and equity shares in treatment facilities. Thailand has offered no medical services commitments in the current General Agreement on Trade in Services (GATS) negotiations.

Retail Services

The Ministry of Commerce is finalizing a draft Retail Act that will regulate retail business. In September, the Thai government requested major foreign and domestic retailers to voluntarily freeze their expansion plans while regulations were drawn up to protect smaller retailers. In October 2006, the Thai government issued guidelines, under the Trade Competition Act (1999) to prevent retailers from setting "unfair practices" such as: pricing goods lower than costs; requesting discounts from suppliers; charging high introduction fees for new products; and returning products to the supplier without valid reasons.

Advertising

The Ministry of Public Health proposed a new law in October 2006 that would ban advertising for alcohol products in all media. Thai law prohibits advertising on pay television. There are no regulations on foreign participation in the advertising sector.

INVESTMENT BARRIERS

The Alien Business Act lays out the overall framework governing foreign investment and employment in Thailand. Although the Act prohibits foreign investment in most sectors, Thailand makes an exception for U.S. investors pursuant to the AER Treaty. Under the AER Treaty, Thailand may discriminate against U.S. investors only in the following sectors: communications, transportation, fiduciary functions, banking involving depository functions, the exploitation of land or other natural resources, and domestic trade in indigenous agricultural products. Moreover, Thailand's obligation to accord national treatment to U.S. investors in all other sectors does not extend to "the practice of professions, or callings reserved for [Thai] nationals."

The Alien Business Act's prohibitions on foreign investment generally do not affect projects established by Board of Investment promotion privileges or export businesses authorized under the Industrial Estate Authority of Thailand law.

In January 2006, the Thai Cabinet approved amendments to the Foreign Business Act. The United States has expressed serious concerns to the Thai government about the restrictions that these amendments would impose on certain investments in Thailand and about the implications that these amendments would have for Thailand's international legal obligations and for the investment environment in Thailand. These amendments were sent to the Council of State for legal review. When this review is completed, the Thai Cabinet is expected to send the proposed amendments to the National Legislative Assembly. In response to the strong interest expressed in this proposed legislation by the foreign business community and foreign governments, the Thai government has indicated its willingness to engage in a dialogue with all interested parties and consider changes to these amendments.

Trade-Related Investment Measures

In 1995, pursuant to the WTO Agreement on Trade-Related Investment Measures (TRIMS), Thailand notified the WTO that it would maintain local content requirements to promote investment in a variety of sectors, including milk and dairy processing, and the motor vehicle assembly and parts industries. Thailand eliminated the measures in the automotive sector by the January 1, 2000, deadline established by the TRIMS Agreement. In 2001, along with several other developing countries, Thailand received an extension for its milk and dairy processing measures. It eliminated those measures at the end of 2003.

ELECTRONIC COMMERCE

Thailand lacks a complete legal framework to support electronic commerce, and the business community has been unable to fully take advantage of electronic commerce opportunities. Most electronic commerce takes place business-to-business. Internet penetration and computer usage are still relatively low but have increased markedly in recent years. A survey by the National Statistics Office in 2005 found that 14.5 million Thais (25 percent) over the age of six used computers, and seven million (12 percent) use the Internet.

The Thai government enacted the Electronic Transactions Act (ETA) in April 2002 to govern civil and commercial transactions made electronically. A royal decree on transactions excluded from enforcement of the Electronic Transactions Act became effective in March 2006. Three other decrees necessary to fully implement the ETA have been approved in principle but await final Cabinet approval and submission to the King. Four pieces of legislation relating to electronic commerce are nearing final stages. A cyber-crime bill, an electronic funds transfer bill, and a national information infrastructure bill to facilitate universal service are expected to be enacted in 2007. A data protection bill is still under review by the Council of State and will require Cabinet and parliament approval. An undeveloped legal framework nevertheless continues to constrain the development of electronic commerce.

OTHER BARRIERS

Several government firms are protected from foreign competition in Thailand. In the pharmaceutical sector, the Government Pharmaceutical Organization is not subject to requirements faced by the private sector on registration. In addition, it can produce and market generic formulations of drugs marketed in foreign countries irrespective of safety monitoring program protection. Thai government requirements limiting government hospitals' procurement and dispensing of drugs not on the national list of essential drugs significantly constrain the availability of many imported products.

The Thai government retains authority to set *de facto* price ceilings for 33 goods and two services, including staple agricultural outputs, liquefied petroleum gas, medicines, sound recordings and student uniforms. Under the 1999 "Act Relating to Price of Merchandise and Service" a government committee headed by the Minister of Commerce has the authority to "Prescribe the purchase price or distribution price of merchandise or service...", "prescribe maximum profit per unit..." and set the terms and conditions – including maximum permissible volumes – of any goods and service in the Kingdom. The law was amended in 1999 with the advent of a Competition Law and was meant to be phased out. However, with several critical aspects of Competition Law still undefined, the old law continues in place with no expiration under current consideration by the Thai government. Price control review mechanisms are non-transparent. Price control determinations are sometimes based on outdated assumptions, including with respect to exchange rates, and go for long periods without review, even upon repeated petition for review by affected parties. Only sugar currently is subject to a retail price ceiling. In practice, the Thai government also uses its control of major suppliers of products and services under state monopoly, such as the petroleum, aviation, and telecommunication sectors, to influence prices in the local market.

The Thai government has made some efforts to counter official corruption. The Thai Constitution of 1997 contains provisions to combat corruption, including enhancement of the status and powers of the Office of the Counter Corruption Commission (OCCC), which is independent from other branches of government. Persons holding high political office and members of their immediate families now are required to disclose their assets and liabilities before assuming and upon leaving office. Moreover, a law regulating the bidding process for government contracts both clarifies actionable anti-corruption offenses and increases penalties for violations. Nonetheless, counter-corruption mechanisms continue to be employed unevenly. The lack of transparency in administrative procedures also contributes to perceptions of corruption in Thailand. Prescribed comment periods for new legislation and regulations are sometimes not honored, and implementing regulations can be unclear, causing uncertainty among companies about the interpretation of the provisions.

In: Thailand: Economics, Political and Social Issues
Ed: Randle C. Zebioli
ISBN: 978-1-60456-583-6
©2009 Nova Science Publishers, Inc.

Chapter 4

THE NEW INTERNATIONAL ORDER IN THE ASIA-PACIFIC REGION: THAILAND'S RESPONSES AND OPTIONS

Chookiat Panaspornprasit

INTRODUCTION

There is no denying that the post-Cold War security challenges which confront numerous policymakers and scholars have moved beyond the decades-old traditional security paradigm. Currently, in parallel with many traditional security issues which remain unresolved in many sub-regions of Asia-Pacific, the re-emergence of multi-dimensional, non-traditional security issues is likely to pose a graver challenge than initially speculated. For instance, the 1997 financial crisis and its subsequent political, social and economic implications underscored the necessity for policymakers to focus on non-military security threats as well. Added to this are cultural, sectarian, ethnic and religious conflicts, as well as a number of multi-faceted transnational crimes (for example, cyber crimes and drug, human and small arms trafficking).

With the dawn of the twenty-first century, the international community has come under largely unforeseen pressure to deal with one of the most pressing non-traditional security issues—terrorism, especially in the aftermath of 9 September 2001 (hereafter referred to as the 9/11 attacks). Determined to highlight the importance of this threat, the Bush administration maintains a stance that, ironically, politicises this issue at the international level. In seeking as many allies as possible to fight the 'War on Terror' on a global basis, the Bush government coopted most countries of the Asia-Pacific region into the US-led global strategy. As a result, prospects for any new, viable international order in Asia-Pacific have not been bright. At the same time, some developments in the region are reconfiguring the ways in which any new international order in Asia-Pacific should be formulated. The rises of both China and India, together with the existing role of Japan, make up crucial variables for regional policymakers. On the Thai domestic front, the issue of political violence in the south, apparently linked to terrorism, also poses a grave challenge to the Thai administration's leadership.

Against the background of the changing international environment portrayed above, the question is how Thailand, under Prime Minister Thaksin Shinawatra (the business tycoon-cum-political leader), is to adopt and implement any options for responding to the dynamic of the region. The basic contention here is that a 'marriage of expediency' will probably win out.

WAR ON TERROR: SYMBOLIC ENGAGEMENT

Launched with determination and a confidence in its military superiority, the Bush administration quickly toppled Afghanistan's Taliban regime in October 2001. This was in response to the Taliban allegedly providing a safe haven for Osama bin Laden, the mastermind behind the 9/11 attacks (Morgan, 2004). The Bush administration's objectives in Afghanistan included both getting rid of the oppressive rule of the fanatical regime in Kabul, and bringing bin Laden to justice. Although the Taliban regime was toppled and a large number of bin Laden-led Al Qaeda fighters were detained indefinitely at Guantanamo Bay, the Bush administration still cannot achieve its other major objective: Bin Laden is still at large in late 2005. Thus, the Bush administration's 'War on Terror' in Afghanistan, one can argue, has not been a great success. Worse still is the increasing prominence of Jemaah Islamiyah (JI), the Al Qaeda-linked terrorist offshoot. Southeast Asian countries have been profoundly traumatised by JI's activities. Indonesia has been the most directly affected target in the region. The Bali attack in October 2002, the attack on JW Marriott hotel in Jakarta in 2003, the attack on the Australian embassy compound in Jakarta in 2004 and the second Bali bombing in October 2005 confirm the Indonesian state's consistent vulnerability to terrorist groups. Though not directly affected by the JI-planned attacks themselves, other ASEAN members, especially Malaysia, the Philippines, Singapore and Thailand, cannot feel immune from the JI terrorist operations (Tan and Ramakrishna, 2002: 142).

It is noteworthy that the Thai government has always regarded acts of international terrorism as direct threats to its own national security. Before the 9/11 attacks, the Thai National Security Council (NSC) had, in August 2001, organised a three-day workshop in Phuket on combating international terrorism (*Bangkok Post*, 29 August 2001: 4). The principal purpose was to streamline and strengthen efforts by relevant agencies in fighting terrorism. On a more practical front, the workshop was also aimed at enhancing the security training drills at the Phuket International Airport and Phuket's deep-sea port. Despite such measures, the 9/11 attacks rocked Thailand's sense of security, and tested the very foundations of the Thai-US security relationship. The issue of Islamic terrorists being globally politicised by the US administration's actions could create dilemmas for the Thai government; the government's close cooperation with the US risked antagonising Thailand's own Muslim population. Despite the fact that Thailand as a whole condemned without reservation such terrorist attacks, it nonetheless found it hard to accept the US's grand strategy for dealing with the new challenge. Thailand was not alone in this sense of unease, as the pronouncement of 'either you are with us or against us' caused a high degree of discontent amongst many of the US's close allies, both in Europe and the Asia-Pacific region (Fuller, 2001: 5).

The Thai government was taken by surprise by the 9/11 attacks, but perhaps even more so by the Bush ultimatum. The Central Islamic Committee of Thailand immediately urged Thai leaders to refrain from permitting military bases on Thai soil to be used for any US reprisals on Afghanistan (*Bangkok Post*, 3 October 2001: 4). Prime Minister Thaksin's initial neutral position at first seemed incompatible with Bush's expectations. As in the 1991 Gulf War, the US government sought from its Thai counterpart not only general political and diplomatic support, but also direct logistical, non-combat aid (out of the U-Tapao airbase in the eastern province of Chon Buri) (Panaspornprasit, 2004: 264). However, the complications implicit in the US's Afhganistan operation compelled the Thai government to approach the matter with considerable caution. Any explicit and unequivocal Thai military support for the US military operations in Afghanistan would, the Thai government felt, trigger widespread disenchantment among the Thai Muslims. This point appeared to be reinforced by a number of the anti-war protests and demonstrations organised by the Thai Muslim communities in Thailand. These protests were non-violent, and posed no major direct threat to the stability of the Thai government; in fact, no major outbreaks of violence took place even after it was revealed (some time later) that US military personnel were given access to the U-Tapao base for purely non-combat operations during the US military campaign in Afghanistan.

In order to assure Bush that Thailand was 'with him', the Thai government made gestures of political and diplomatic support for the War on Terror. For example, the Thai Finance Ministry (together with eighteen other countries worldwide), complied with the US Treasury Department's request to order financial institutions to freeze assets allegedly linked to any terrorist groups (*Bangkok Post*, 3 October 2001: 7). Furthermore, and aided by strong US pressure to do so, the Thai government revised its immigration checks and entry visa guidelines. The latter included seriously re-evaluating the so-called 'visa privileges' policy, first implemented in 1986 to boost Thailand's tourism industry.[1]

No sooner had the major US military engagement in Afghanistan come to an end than the Bush administration planned to shift its target to one of the so-called 'axis of evil' countries: Iraq (*Bangkok Post*, 31 January 2002: 8). From March 2002, the clouds of war over Iraq grew distinctly darker as the Bush administration produced its allegations of Iraq possessing, and indeed developing, weapons of mass destruction (WMDs). It is perhaps telling of the pressure that Thailand found itself under that it was not one of the close US allies who opposed the war against Iraq.

On the diplomatic front, the White House had claimed that it could mobilise a 'coalition of the willing', comprising two groups of thirty countries, thereby demonstrating strong and explicit support for the invasion of Iraq. In addition to these, fifteen other supporters were conscripted that wanted their inclusion to remain secret. Thailand, although part of the latter group, was widely rumoured to have contributed directly to the action in Iraq. The Thai government granted permission for covert US military use of its U-Tapao military base to assist against Iraq. Thaksin preferred to keep this cooperation very low profile—a decision that caused considerable discomfort to the Bush administration. During an 'unofficial' visit to Washington in June 2003, the Thai prime minister reportedly explained his position to Bush, although Thaksin himself denied this (Morrison, 2004: 179-80). The Thai leader is said to have reassured President Bush of the appropriateness of US forward-positioning rights for its anti-terrorism campaign in Southeast Asia. As a result, Bush officially designated Thailand a 'major Non-NATO Ally' (MNNA) in December 2003 (*Bangkok Post*, 1 January 2004: 1). Although this was regarded as only a symbolic designation, it still drew the criticism of a former foreign minister, Surin Pitsuwan, who opposed such a close alliance for security reasons (*Bangkok Post*, 13 June 2003: 4). With the post-war US-led rehabilitation and reconstruction in Iraq in operation, 448 non-combatant Thai troops were deployed in Iraq for humanitarian purposes. To date, only two Thai deaths have resulted from this involvement, and these casualties have not been enough to force a withdrawal of non-combat personnel (*Bangkok Post*, 3 December 2003: 7). Suffice it to say, the Thai government's response to the US-led War on Terror is mainly symbolic.

---

[1] This policy legally permits citizens from 57 countries to stay in Thailand for a month without a visa; and citizens of another 96 countries are allowed to apply for a 15-day visa upon the arrival in Thailand.

The threat of terrorism, especially that posed by the Al Qaeda group, remains high on the US government's security agenda. Recently, the US Central Intelligence Agency (CIA) has warned that the Al Qaeda network is fully capable of building a radioactive dirty bomb for use against the US and/or other Western nations, as well as having crude procedures for producing chemical weapons (*Bangkok Post*, 25 November 2004: 11). Even before issuing this warning, however, the Bush administration had approved two major experimental projects for the creation of advanced weaponry that ostensibly targeted the Al Qaeda threat. First, a large amount of the US's defence budget was allocated to the development of a so-called 'bunker-busting' nuclear weapon (*Bangkok Post*, 3 December 2003: 1). Second, a clandestine project was initiated at the National Biodefence Analysis and Countermeasures Centre, experimenting with bio-defence weaponry (*Bangkok Post*, 23 May 2004: 5). Against this background, there is still no confirmation of any imminent attacks by either Iran or North Korea, the two other members of the 'Axis of Evil'.

THE ROLES OF CHINA, INDIA AND JAPAN: PARTNERS OR COMPETITORS?

There has been long-standing speculation as to whether China's rise has been borne out by its increased economic and political momentum. Along with its economic liberalisation and reform campaign, the combination of China's other economic advantages has placed it in a better position to pursue its own economic growth strategy. The abundance of cheap (but increasingly skilled) labour, access to advanced technology for small- to medium-sized enterprises and the controlled deflation rate of its currency are attracting increased trade and investment-relocation. There is no denying that China's share of total global trade has expanded at a dramatic rate (Snitwongse, 2003: 38). In the last decade, it has clearly become a major trading partner with ASEAN and with Thailand in particular. Its entry to the World Trade Organization (WTO) formed a catalyst for ASEAN countries to consider forming a China-ASEAN free trade area by 2010. Moreover, Thailand is also keen to conclude its own Free Trade Agreement (FTA) with Beijing on a bilateral basis. Expectations of securing benefits from this free trade area scheme are even greater in the more developed ASEAN countries (Singapore and Thailand) than the new members of ASEAN including the so-called 'CLMV' (Cambodia, Laos, Myanmar and Vietnam). Moreover, the Chinese proposal in June 2003 of a strategic partnership with ASEAN, and its accession to the ASEAN Treaty of Amity and Cooperation (TAC), demonstrated its increased political engagement with Southeast Asian countries, a move which alarms China's main rival in the region's strategic sphere—the US.

With the rise of India, it cannot be denied that Thailand also brings to the equation a 'Look West' policy. It is imparting more significance than before to the Indian Ocean region in general and dovetailing with India's adoption of a 'Look East' policy. Thailand aims not only to maintain close political, cultural and economic relationships with India, but also advocates a peaceful solution to the Kashmir conflict. The combination of the confrontation between the two nuclear-armed arch rivals in this dispute, together with the Indo-Pakistani stand-off over long-standing religious and sectarian conflicts, plus the rise of terrorism on the subcontinent as a whole, causes major concern to countries such as Thailand who are worried about the impact of these issues on the peace, stability and order of the region in general. Significantly, the refusal of both India and Pakistan to be signatories to the Nuclear Non-Proliferation Treaty (NPT), and the missile testing conducted by both sides, led to serious doubts as to the possibility of placing the proliferation of the WMDs in South Asia under tight control.

The traditional and non-traditional security issues on the subcontinent are directly linked to the shifting configuration of power, especially in the aftermath of the 9/11 attacks. The Indian Defence Minister George Fernandes, for example, announced that India plans to buy more military hardware from the US after both sides agreed to boost cooperation on counter-terrorism initiatives (*Bangkok Post*, 10 February 2002: 4). These closer military ties appear not to be at the expense of ties with the Pakistani and Russian governments. The Bush administration and Pakistan's Musharraf government signed a new defence pact to consolidate their mutual defence needs (*Bangkok Post*, 10 February 2002: 4). As for the Indo-Russian military ties, the Indian arms procurement programme still relies heavily on its Russian suppliers. In 2002, for example, India concluded a defence deal with Russia that involved the acquisition of a Russian aircraft carrier and TU-22M supersonic bombers (*Bangkok Post*, 9 February 2002: 5).

India's bid to be a dialogue partner with ASEAN yielded fruit when it became the organisation's sectoral dialogue partner in 1993, and, three years later, a full dialogue partner. Most recently, in Vientianne, the Indian Prime Minister Manmohan Singh signed a historic partnership agreement on the ASEAN-India Partnership for Peace, Progress and Shared Prosperity Pact (*Bangkok Post*, 1 December 2004: 7). In trade relations, Thailand is India's third largest ASEAN investor, lagging behind only Malaysia and Singapore. The 2002 total of bilateral trade was $US 1,184 million, an increase of 2.6 per cent over 2001 figures. Thaksin's official visits to India in November 2001 and February 2002, together with the return visit of the former Indian Prime Minister Vajpayee in October 2003, paved the way for both countries to conclude an FTA that was intended to double the total volume of bilateral trade to $US 2 billion per year (*Bangkok Post*, 12 October 2003: 3).

In the case of Japan, leaders in Tokyo and their counterparts in Southeast Asia deem the re-evaluation of how to maintain, re-assert and perhaps even increase Japan's role in the region as timely and necessary, especially in relation to Japan's contribution to the maximisation of 'international public goods' there. This refers to the means or instruments, both tangible and non-tangible, which are utilised to enhance international peace, security, stability and mutual understanding in the international community through non-violent approaches and mechanisms.

Japan's national interests are closely linked to both the existence of some traditional security issues, and the proliferation of various non-traditional security issues in the present international system. The tension on the Korean Peninsula, the ongoing confrontation between the two nuclear rivals on the subcontinent, and the Cross-Strait relations between China and Taiwan remain vital issues (both directly or indirectly) for Japan's national strategic outlook (Haller, 1995: 118). Since 2002, the renewed North Korean crisis, when the Pyongyang government admitted that it has an active nuclear enrichment programme, and the subsequent stand-off between the neo-conservative government in Washington and North Korea's reclusive regime, have led to a major political impasse, resulting in tension for the north Pacific region. A series of the Six-Party Talks, aimed at peacefully defusing the crisis on the peninsula, has still achieved no major breakthrough. Compared with the Chinese government's role, one can argue that the Japanese role in these talks is a relatively indistinct one. Posing the same level of threat to policymakers in Japan is the tension between the Beijing government and the pro-independence ruling party in Taipei. The Chinese government's deployment of large numbers of missiles along the east coast of China has resulted—with the latter's strong resistance—in the decision of Taipei's government to procure more sophisticated weaponry from the US. For Japan, these two crises—one to its very near west and the other to its near south—pose very direct security threats.

The ongoing traditional security threats aside, Japanese and Southeast Asian national leaders expect to come up with long-term and effective solutions to the non-traditional security issues as well. For example, the horizontal and vertical networks of illegal human and drug trafficking in the Asia-Pacific region have become so transnational in their character that they have come to affect members of its societies at a number of different levels. The recent news reports on cracking down on the illegal trafficking of women into Japan have served as a further reminder of these problems. Japan and its neighbours also share a rising awareness of the significance of terrorist activities in their region. Japan's own experience of terrorism began with the Aum Cult bio-terrorism in 1995, and this has helped to establish very strong policies for pre-empting bio-terrorism in that country (*Japan Times*, 2005).

An already uncertain world becomes even more so for Japan after the spate of violent terrorist attacks in various parts of the world, especially those in the Asia-Pacific region itself. The secure sea-lanes of communication, both regionally and internationally, have formed a major lifeline for Japan's economic and financial well-being. Any unforeseen disruption to these lanes is likely to have adverse consequences not only for Japan's domestic economy, but also for its close economic ties with Southeast Asian countries, including Thailand. Under the current Thaksin government, the bilateral FTA scheme with Japan is also high on the economic agenda, and so the security dimension looms somewhat larger still in that relationship.

As mentioned earlier, it may be reasonably expected that Japan play a leading role in providing public goods in various fields in the future, and does so at both regional and broader international levels. Functional contributions by the Japanese government in these areas could ensure mutual goodwill, mutual confidence and long-term prosperity in many regions around the world. Japan's foreign direct investment (FDI) and its Overseas Development Assistance (ODA) schemes would, of course, become more effective by being shaped into forms that are more complementary to other instruments, such as Japan's cultural exchange and humanitarian assistance programmes. While such clear-cut and enhanced measures are not being adopted, Japan's currently passive foreign policy is probably running the risk of seeing Japan's status decline in the eyes of Southeast Asian states. Hence, bilateral FTA negotiations between Japan and many Southeast Asian countries, including Thailand, serve the purpose of reasserting Japan's role in the region, even if this is in response to the ongoing FTA plans pursued by both the Chinese and Indian governments.

The domestic debate in Thailand centres on whether or not the conclusion of the FTAs with the three Asian powers would really benefit its business sector. There is some concern over the possibility that only a few narrow sectors in Thailand would reap benefits from the FTAs, while Thai society as a whole would have to live with the geopolitical uncertainties deriving from them.

MULTILATERALISM AND A NEW ORDER: MYTH OR REALITY?

Apart from joining a number of multilateral cooperation frameworks like ASEAN, Thailand has become a member state of other less well-known multilateral bodies: for example, the Indian Ocean Rim Association for Regional Cooperation (IOR-ARC) and the Asian Cooperation Dialogue (ACD). Most states of the Indian Ocean region are signatories to the IOR-ARC. First launched in 1995 with seven founding-member states (Australia, India, South Africa, Kenya, Singapore, Oman and Mauritius), the prime purpose of this relatively new alliance is to enhance and uphold economic cooperation among the littoral states of the Indian Ocean region. The approach is tripartite, involving the private sector, governments and academic communities. At the Council of Ministers' meeting in March 1999, the original members reached consensus on the expansion of the organisation, with up to 19 new members being allowed for.[2]

The Thai government applied for full membership of the IOR-ARC in June 1997. Under the umbrella of the organisation, three working groups were set up in order to coordinate, facilitate and maximise opportunities for trade cooperation among the member states.[3] Unfortunately, the outbreak of the July 1997 financial crisis in the Southeast Asian region overshadowed the attractiveness of this new forum.

It is important to note that progress in building up economic cooperation under this multilateral scheme remains limited for a number of reasons. First, the leading roles of Australia and India in launching any new project always receive a lukewarm reception from other countries of the region. Second, there is a lack of well-structured coordination among the three working groups, resulting in the overlapping of various projects. Third, in the short-term, ASEAN countries Indonesia, Malaysia, Singapore and Thailand are more likely to promote trade within the ASEAN Free Trade Area (AFTA) than under IOR-ARC.[4]

Added to the existing, complicated network of multilateral frameworks in the Asia-Pacific region is Prime Minister Thaksin's initiative of the Asian Cooperation Dialogue (ACD). The fundamental objective of the ACD is to link the sub-regions of the entire Asian region. Through the ACD, the Northeast Asian countries (China, Japan and South Korea) will be closely integrated with the nine ASEAN member states (minus Myanmar), three South Asian countries (India, Pakistan and Bangladesh), and two oil-rich Persian Gulf states (Bahrain and Qatar).[5] Ideally, the ACD will be instrumental in upgrading the standard of living of the population of Asia, developing and integrating solidarity among Asian communities, and forming the basis for strategic partnerships with other parts of the world. The evolving process of this initiative emphasises the inculcation of positive thinking in areas of cooperation, and that this should be based on channels of informal and non-institutional discussion. To this end, two ministerial meetings, intended for consultative discussion, have already been convened in Thailand (in June 2002 and June 2003).

Considered by many as the 'mega-idea' for the whole Asian region, it is often argued that the ultimate motive behind this Thaksin initiative is for Thailand to take on a leading role in the region, and to allow it to further its broader geostrategic ambitions. However, this initiative brings with it many loopholes and drawbacks. First, a major (and somewhat controversial) defect of the ACD lies in the general argument that it is first and foremost meant to enhance Thailand's own modest diplomatic history, but, even more, to confirm Thaksin's political slogan of 'think anew, act anew' (Panaspornprasit, 2004: 261). Second, the framework proposed is so multi-layered that most member countries are likely to see greater benefit in consolidating the existing sub-regional cooperation in their own regions.

Putting the two multilateral schemes in the Thai political context, it is evident that the Thaksin administration pays only lip service to the IOR-ARC, especially in comparison to its attention to the ACD. For example, the former Thai Foreign Minister Surakiart Sathirathai (under the first Thaksin administration) did not attend the two IOR-ARC Council of the

---

[2] The nineteen full members of IOR-ARC are: Australia, Bangladesh, India, Indonesia, Iran, Kenya, Madagasgar, Malaysia, Mauritius, Mozambique, Oman, Seychelles, Singapore, South Africa, Sri Lanka, Tanzania, Thailand, United Arab Emirates and Yemen. The four dialogue partners are China, Egypt, Japan and the United Kingdom. (See the official documents prepared by the Division of International Economics, Department of Economic Affairs, the Ministry of Foreign Affairs, Thailand, April 2002

[3] They are Working Groups on Trade and Investment (WGTI), Indian Ocean Rim Business Forum (IORBF) and Indian Ocean Rim Academic Group (IORAG).

[4] In an interview with a senior officer of the Ministry of Foreign Affairs, Thailand, 29 July 2003.

[5] See the official documents prepared by the Policy and Planning Office, the Ministry of Foreign Affairs, Thailand, 20 May 2003.

Ministers meetings in Muscat in 2002 and Colombo in 2004. Conversely, the same foreign minister hosted two ACD ministerial meetings in Bangkok in 2002 and 2003.

The discussion above mainly involves the changing international components that could effect the new order in Asia-Pacific confronting the Thaksin administration. In addition, Thaksin's government is now being challenged by another pressing political issue on the domestic front.

VIOLENCE IN THE SOUTH: THE RE-EMERGENCE OF TERRORISM

The security situation in southern Thailand has been a thorny long-term national issue for successive Thai governments. It is a problem that is multi-dimensional in nature, bringing to the fore historical, political, territorial, cultural and religious concerns. The separatist movement's operations, based mainly on guerrilla warfare and terrorism, have been conducted under the leadership of the Pattani United Liberation Organization (PULO), formed in 1968 and aimed at separating the southern Muslim provinces from the rest of Thailand. Although the situation was brought under some control in the 1980's through the strategy of accommodation adopted by former Prime Minister Prem Tinsulanonda, the Muslim radicals still persist in fighting for separation because of their ethno-religious differences with the Buddhist majority. As a result, only small-scale, intermittent acts of violence were reported.

On 4 January 2004, however, the central government in Bangkok was taken by surprise by the well-planned armed attacks on the army camp in Narathiwat, the deliberate looting of 400 firearms from an army depot, and the death of four military officers (*Bangkok Post*, 5 January 2004: 1). At the same time, about twenty high schools were set ablaze. These attacks were a major blow to the reputation of the government's state-of-the-art intelligence capabilities, to the extent that the actual identity of the perpetrators still cannot be substantiated (*Bangkok Post*, 7 January 2004: 1). The lack of coordination among Thai government security agencies can be confirmed by the different explanations classing the perpetrators as local bandits, home-grown terrorists or suspected links with the JI operatives in other countries (*Bangkok Post*, 8 January 2004: 1).

Thaksin himself first vehemently denied any foreign terrorists operating on Thai territory (*Bangkok Post*, 7 January 2004: 1). Be that as it may, it is widely believed the 4 January 2004 incident flew in the face of Thaksin's official claim at the October 2003 APEC summit in Bangkok that Thailand is immune from terrorist attacks. While most of the perpetrators are still at large, the government has adopted a heavy-handed, top-down strategy for clamping down on the violence in the three southernmost provinces of Pattani, Narathiwat and Yala. To the Thai Muslim communities in these areas, the imposition of martial law and the deployment of para-military troops in the provinces do not make for a satisfactory solution to the problems there (*Bangkok Post*, 8 March 2004: 1). As a result, there emerged among the Thai Muslim populace a sense of social injustice, discrimination, alienation, frustration and mistrust. Worse still, violent and malicious attacks on civilians and public property are so commonplace that the general public has lost faith in the government's strategy and policies in the south. The disappearance since March 2004 of the Muslim human rights lawyer, Somchai Neelahphaiji, who stood firm in his defence of some Muslim suspects apprehended earlier, and the lip service of the government in probing into the case, reinforces the general perspective that respect for human rights is not on the government's agenda. This can be confirmed by two more tragic events: the April 2004 Krue Se Mosque tragedy and the October 2004 Tak Bai incidents. These events resulted in the deaths of 32 and 84 Muslims, respectively. Both tragic incidents resulted from the government's use of the armed forces in cracking down on the lightly-armed Muslims protesting against the government's strategy of handling the violence in the region.

Not only has the ongoing violence in the south of Thailand complicated the country's security agenda and planning, but also, one can argue, the overall security outlook of other ASEAN countries (such as Malaysia, Indonesia and the Philippines) as well. Some high-ranking government officials firmly believe that the current cooperation among ASEAN countries in various anti-terrorism projects could be counter-productive, if each individual country fails to put its own house in order first. In addition, the Thai government, as the argument goes, must have a real sense of urgency about regaining its people's confidence, trust and, finally, cooperation in rooting out terrorism (*Bangkok Post*, 8 February 2004: 1). The last general election, held on 6 February 2005, was expected to be a major political barometer to gauge the current Thai government's political popularity (and attitudes to its controversial policies) in the south. As the official election results showed, the ruling TRT party could secure only one constituency seat in the south, while the opposition Democrat party won 52 seats (out of its total of 70 constituency seats) there (*Bangkok Post*, 9 February 2005: 1). In order to handle the situation in the south and to 'save face' for its failure to do so thus far, the government supported the establishment of the National Reconciliation Commission (NRC), headed by former Prime Minister Anand Panyarachun. The hope is that this commission will restore peace and stability, and lead to reconciliation in southern Thailand (*Bangkok Post*, 1 March 2005: 1). Whether this commission is successful in its mission remains to be seen.

CONCLUSION

During the first Thaksin administration (2001-2004), new challenges have emerged in domestic, regional and broader international arenas to test the Thaksin government. Claiming the authority stemming from being the first democratic civilian government in Thai political history to complete a four-year term, the second Thaksin administration aims to consolidate its authority in a predictable fashion. With no credible opposition (either from formal opposition parties or the civil society groups) to Thaksin's political authority in domestic politics, it is very likely that the TRT will lead the new government with more confidence, and cast into oblivion any dissenting voices. Without a clear programme or effective opposition, the government will, both domestically and internationally, continue to be reactive and launch policies of expediency.

REFERENCES

Bangkok Post (2001) 29 August: 4.
—— (2001) 'Islamic Committee Urges Neutral Stance'. 3 October: 4.
—— (2002) 31 January: 8.
—— (2002) 1 February: 6-7.
—— (2002) 2 February: 8.
—— (2002) 'Delhi to Acquire Russian Aircraft Carrier'. 9 February: 5.
—— (2002) 'India Looks to US for Hi-Tech Arms Systems'. 10 February: 4.
—— (2002) 20 February: 6.
—— (2002) 27 February: 8.

―――― (2002) 17 March: 6.
―――― (2002) 13 July: 6.
―――― (2003) 13 June: 4.
―――― (2003) 'Africa Next on Agenda, Says Thaksin'. 12 October: 3.
―――― (2003) 'Bush Signs Bill for Bunker Buster Nukes'. 3 December: 1.
―――― (2003) 'Safety the Deciding Criteria in Considering Withdrawal'. 3 December: 7.
―――― (2004) 'Bush Confers Ally Status', 1 January: 1.
―――― (2004) 'Soldiers Die, School Burns', 5 January: 1.
―――― (2004) 'Deadline: 7 Days to Catch Raiders', 7 January: 1.
―――― (2004) 'Kitti: Separatists, Not Bandits', 8 January: 1.
―――― (2004) 'Open Up the Bottleneck'. (Perspective), 8 February: 1.
―――― (2004) 'Government Advised to Lift Martial Law', 8 March: 1.
―――― (2004) 'Experts Warn Against Plans on Biodefence'. 23 May: 5.
―――― (2004) 'CIA Warns of Terror Threats'. 25 November: 11.
―――― (2004) 'Indian, ASEAN Leaders Sign pact for Peace, Progress, Prosperity'. 1 December: 7.
―――― (2005) 'Thaksin Gets Total Control'. 9 February: 1.
―――― (2005) 'Anand Heads Up Peace Panel'. 1 March: 1.
Fuller, Graham E. (2001) 'Anti-Terrorism Coalition Fatally Flawed'. Perspectives, 30 September: 5.
Haller, Kenneth J. (ed.) (1995) *Japanese International Responsibility and Contribution to Peace and Prosperity in the Asia-Pacific Region*, Bangkok: Japanese Studies Center, Institute of East Asian Studies, Thammasat University.
International Herald Tribune (2002) 11 March.
Japan Times (2005) 'Warning to Japan and the World'. Editorial, 27 March, http://www.japantimes.co.jp/cgi-bin/getarticle.pl5?ed20050327a1.htm
Morgan, Matthew J. (2004) 'The Origins of the New Terrorism'. *Parameters*, Spring: 29-43.
Morrison, Charles E. (ed.) (2004) *Asia-Pacific Security Outlook 2004*, Tokyo: Japan Center for International Exchange.
Panaspornprasit, Chookiat (2004) 'Thailand: Politicized Thanksinization'. *Southeast Asian Affairs 2004*, Singapore: Institute of Southeast Asian Studies.
Snitwongse, Kusuma (2003) 'New World Order in East Asia?' *Asia-Pacific Review*, 10(2).
Tan, Andrew and Ramakrishna, Kumar (eds) (2002) *The New Terrorism: Anatomy, Trends and Counter-Strategies*, Singapore: Eastern Universities Press.
Washington Post (2002) 18 March: A10.

In: Thailand: Economics, Political and Social Issues
Ed: Randle C. Zebioli

ISBN: 978-1-60456-583-6
©2009 Nova Science Publishers, Inc.

Chapter 5

DECISION MAKING PROCESS AND HEALTH-SEEKING PATTERNS OF YOUNG WOMEN WITH UNPLANNED PREGNANCIES, BANGKOK, THAILAND

Wanapa Naravage[1] and Rungpetch C. Sakulbumrungsil[2]
[1]Program Manager, Contraceptive Technologies, Concept Foundation, Thailand
[2]Faculty of Pharmaceutical Sciences, Chulalongkorn University, Thailand

ABSTRACT

Objectives: This study examined the decision-making process and health-seeking patterns of low-income young women with unplanned pregnancies who opted for abortion, putting baby up for adoption, or keeping the baby.

Methods: Research methodology in this study focused on formative research utilizing qualitative data. The study was conducted covering all five shelters and low-income communities in Bangkok, Thailand. The data collection was through Focus Group Discussions, and in-depth interview. Forty-five cases were purposefully recruited into the study. The data were analyzed using content analysis.

Results: From the qualitative research, the results indicated that the majority of the young women tended to select abortion as their first choice, while a few cases continued their pregnancies to term without any attempt to terminate the pregnancy. These women tended to delay seeking assistance once they found out their pregnancy situation. The majority of the low-income young women were more likely to resort to self-medication as their first alternative, which was sometimes hazardous to their health. Decision on self-medication or abortions with unskilled personnel sometimes resulted in serious and life-threatening complications. Many pregnancy-termination situations resulted from self-medication. While most of these women made the important decision themselves, they still sought advice, guidance, and support from their partners, peers and parents. When the first attempt failed, they would seek a second or third attempt until they felt it was not possible to achieve what they had planned.

Most women with unplanned pregnancies knew that they had options regarding termination of their pregnancies but their main concern was confidentiality. Consequently, the women who wanted to terminate their pregnancies adopted three patterns of action, i.e., 1) visiting drugstores / grocery stores, 2) visiting private clinics or hospitals, and 3) using physical pressure or vigorous actions. Most of the women realized that private clinics provided effective methods for terminating pregnancy, but due to its high cost, they would first resort self-medication or self-management. If they were not successful, they would then visit a private clinic and asked others to support the cost.

Understanding the women's decisions-making process and their health-seeking patterns allows us to understand their decision and course of actions. The program managers, implementers, providers, partners, parents/relatives, and friends should do as much as possible to support the decision of the women in order to provide better information and services to reduce the impact, both physical and mental, of their choice.

1. BACKGROUND AND RATIONALE

1.1. Situation of Unplanned Pregnancy Among Young Women

Worldwide, there is an estimated 15 million adolescents age 15 to 19 who give birth, approximately for up to one-fifth of all births each year. Furthermore, each year 1 million to 4.4 million adolescents in developing countries undergo abortion, and most of these procedures are performed under unsafe conditions (RHO, 2002) due to unplanned pregnancies. These pregnancies lead to their health problems in two ways: first, many unplanned pregnancies can threaten the young women's health or well being; they may face a medical, psychological, social problem and lack of resources to support themselves during pregnancy and raise a child. Second, if young women do not have access to or cannot afford safe abortion services, many unplanned pregnancies are terminated using unsafe procedures that can lead to the women's death or disability.

Legal Situation of Abortion in Thailand

Induced abortion is a crime under the Articles 301-305 of the 1957 Penal Code of Thailand. Both the women and the person terminating the pregnancy are subject to legal penalty. The women can be sentenced to three years in prison and a fine of 6,000 baht (US$ = 171; 1US$ = 35 baht). Heavier prison sentences and fines are prescribed for the person who conducts the pregnancy termination. However, attempted but unsuccessful termination of pregnancy is not punishable under some circumstance, which allows women who have had the operations to be treated in hospital. The other major exception to the law is that medical practitioners are permitted to terminate pregnancies in case of rape or if continuation of pregnancy will endanger the health of the women. During the last few decades' abortion law was debated worldwide, as well as in Thailand. At present, there are some movements of many non-government organizations (NGOs) especially those working in women issues. Some groups of people from governmental organization are calling in for reform abortion law. Until now, nothing in the law has been changed (Gray et al., 1999).

However, changing law takes a long period of time. Prevention and care for long and short-term plan can help solve the problem of the unplanned pregnancies.

Sexual Health and Risk of Unplanned Pregnancy

Along with increase exposure to unplanned pregnancy, Sexually Transmitted Infection, and Human Immunodeficiency Virus (STI/HIV), young women who engage in sexual activity outside of marriage may face stigmas, family conflicts, problems with school and the potential need for unsafe abortion. Married adolescents and youth who become pregnant may not encounter the same social risk as the unmarried women, but they may face the same complications from STI/HIV and the health risk of early pregnancy, which will cause both physical and psychosocial problems.

Among Thai youth who are sexually active, the median age at first sexual encounter is between 16 to 18 years. The median age for girls was higher compared to that of boys. More than half of those who have had sex had unprotected first sexual intercourse. Moreover, it was found that a relatively small proportion of males had commercial sex workers (CSWs) as their first partner. This behaviour has been changed as compared with the period before the HIV/AIDS epidemic when men tended to go to CSWs more (UNESCO/Thailand, 2001). Now their partner has changed to their girl friend(s). There is clear evidence from many studies showing that sex is initiated at a younger age and sex partner are either friends or lovers of similar age (Boonmongkon et al., 2000). Thus, this situation puts their girlfriend(s) at a high risk of unplanned pregnancies, and STI/HIV.

Among female adolescents, they revealed that unplanned pregnancy was a major problem (Boonmongkon et. al., 2000; Porapakkham et al., 1985 and Deemar, 1980 as cited in Soonthornthada, 1996). Findings from a study of sexual experience of school adolescents in Bangkok showed that 35 percent of sexually active male adolescents stated that their girlfriends become pregnant and 4 out of 5 pregnancies ended with abortion. Moreover, 30 percent of sexually active girls stated that they had had abortion (Porapakkham et al., 1985 and Deemar, 1980, as cited in Soonthornthada, 1996). A study by Soonthornthada (1996) found that out of school adolescents (factory workers) were more likely to accept abortion when compare with school adolescents. Thus from reviewing many studies, it is found that female out of school youth is more vulnerable to unplanned pregnancy, unsafe abortion, and STI/HIV than school adolescents.

Furthermore, studies estimated that one out of three pregnancies are unplanned (Chayowan and Nodel, 1992) and 200,000-300,000 women at the reproductive age terminated their pregnancies each year (Koetsawang, 1993). Adolescents are more likely than adults to hide a pregnancy, seeking late term abortions, and having a procedure performed by untrained providers under unsafe conditions, often leading to permanent disability or death (Sertthapongkul et al., 1993; Koetsawang, 1993).

Psychological Consequences

Major and Gramzow (1999) found that apart from physical consequences, women who feel stigmatized about their pregnancy are more likely to feel a need to keep it hidden from family and friend. Secrecy was related positively to suppressing thoughts of abortion and negatively to disclosing related emotion to others. More importantly, suppression was associated with experiencing intrusive thoughts and distress. Both suppression and intrusive thoughts, in turn, were positively related to psychological distress over time.

Impact on Health Services

Spontaneous abortion or uncomplicated case is rarely a fatal and seldom presents complications. It may require up to 3 days of hospitalization, complicated cases may need a stay of up to 5 times longer. The treatment of abortion complications in hospital uses a disproportionate share of resources, including hospital beds, blood supply, medication, as well as access to operating theatres, anesthesia and medical specialists. Thus, consequences of unsafe abortion place great clinical, material and financial demands on the scarce hospital resources of many developing countries (WHO, 1997). In Thailand, it is calculated that cost per case of severe complication per abortion is 21,024 baht (Warakamin and Boonthai, 2001) where as the first trimester abortion is about 3,000-5,000 baht.

1.2. Causes of Unplanned Pregnancy

Unplanned pregnancies are caused by several factors including the nature of transition from childhood to adulthood; lack of knowledge, moral, values, and education at home and in school; relationship with parents; gender inequalities situation; inadequate reproductive health resources for providing information, education, and communication to the young people. Moreover, all these factors intern effect on health seeking patterns and access to health care of the young women. Details are as follows:

Transitional from Childhood to Adulthood Especially Physical and Emotional Development

Adolescence is a transitional phase from childhood to adulthood. While becoming physiologically mature during this transitional period, they become less dependent on their parents and more involved with peers. They begin to form identities as individuals and develop further capacity for interpersonal relationships with others. Moreover, it is a critical period that lays the foundation for reproductive health of the individual's lifetime. It is also a period when *"sexuality"* emerges in the form of physical body changes. Feeling, psychological changes including emotions and consciousness about one's sexuality and these of the opposite sex also occur at this time. It is also a phase of life where one searches for self-identity, is vulnerability to sexual risk behavioral including unplanned pregnancy (AIDC, 1999).

Lack of Knowledge, Moral and Values, Education at Home and in School

Many young people lack accurate knowledge of reproductive health anatomy, physiology and the pregnancy process including the consequences of unprotected sex. Also, they might lack knowledge of pregnancy prevention and access to family planning methods due to several factors, such as, social taboo on unmarried young women seeking for contraceptive methods.

A large-scale study by Maungman et al. (1983) in Bangkok found that schooled females had different knowledge and attitude about sex than out of school female youth. School adolescent had higher level of basic knowledge about reproductive biology, conception, and awareness of sexuality than out of school adolescents. A subsequent study in 1996, conducted among in and out of school youth revealed that among the sexually active out of school youth, less than half used contraceptives while having sex. Among the non-users, some of them reported that they did not use any method of birth control due to lack of adequate knowledge while some of them feared side effects (Soonthornthada, 1996).

Another source of information revealed that parents and teachers rarely talk and openly discuss sexual knowledge, values, and moral with their children. This may lead youth to lack of concern for the outcome of irresponsible sexual behavior and to seek information from many unreliable and harmful sources such as pornography, magazine, Internet sites and etc. to educate themselves. Although, some issues on sexual health have begun to be taught in some school effective sex education requires trained personnel which is lacking at the present time.

Gender Inequality

In Thailand, young women are more restricted than men in their personal movements because of concerns over their virginity and chastity. After puberty, daughters are not allowed to go out alone. Daughters are kept under strict supervision, while brothers take advantage of their social and sexual freedom. Young men gain status if their peers believe they have seduced many women, whereas young women lose their reputation if people hear that she slept with a man (Boonmongkon et al., 2000; Gray and Pungpuing, 1999; Sainsbury, 1997; Ford and Kittisuksathit, 1996).

This inequality situation puts young women at a disadvantage in controlling sexual relations and contraceptive use. Social experiences and pressures define what is or is not acceptable for a young woman to do. These make it difficult for them to protect themselves from unplanned pregnancy. The inequality among man and woman include social taboos and power over women often prevents her from using contraceptives. Opposition from their partners/lovers is one of the most common reasons women give for not using barrier contraception.

Stigmatizing Young Women in Utilizing Reproductive Health Resources

In Thailand, there are limited reproductive health service resources for young people. In the last decade, the existing government health services were for adults, which their operations based on the assumption that the adolescent group did not require reproductive and sexual health services. The use of health care services is complicated and stigmatizes adolescents who come to use the services for their sexual health problems (Limsampan, 1997 and Pracharat, 1990 as cited in Boonmongkok et al., 2000).

Health Seeking and Access to Reproductive Health Care

The main obstacle for women in Thailand in seeking abortion once they are faced with unplanned pregnancies is that it is illegal. There are no public health facilities that provide abortion if the pregnancy does not result from specific conditions as stated in the law. There are some private professionals who provide such services, but the cost is high. Prohibitively most young women cannot afford it, thus, they will seek alternative services from other sources, such as, traditional healers, and drugstore personnel. Drugstore personnel are more popular than traditional healers among young people because they do not need to answer questions nor reveal their identity but the most important is easy access to products that young women believe can terminate their unplanned pregnancy (PATH, 2001).

Drugstores are an important source of health services for Thai communities. When faced with mild illness, most of people tend to go to a drugstore as their first choice. In the Northern part of Thailand, a study revealed that 66 percent visited drugstores (Chuamanocharn et al., 2000), where as 80 percent in Bangkok (Punyawuthikrai et al., 2001) and 97.7 percent in the Northeastern part of Thailand respectively (Kanchanaraj et al., 2001). Young people also share the same pattern of health seeking that is they will seek services from drugstores as their primary resource especially when they have to seek for sexual health products; abortifacient for terminating pregnancy; or when faced with any sexual health problems.

Another study in 1998 by PATH/Thailand in Had Yai, Songkla province, revealed that vocational school students utilizing drugstores as the common place to seek health services; particularly in regard to sexual and reproductive health issues. The research showed that youth prefer to seek reproductive health advice from drugstores rather than from the government health care service, because they cannot be identified by medical record showing name, marital status, etc. Youth also wish to avoid confronting sometime-negative attitudes of healthcare providers towards unmarried adolescents, particularly females, seeking family planning services, diagnosis and treatment of Sexually Transmitted Diseases (STDs), pregnancy tests, etc.

Peers also influence young people to seek services. When young women missed their menstruation, they usually consult their female friends who would recommend that they get a pregnancy test from the drugstore or private clinic in town. No young women utilize the government health services for a pregnancy test because they were afraid that their secrecy about their sexual relations would be revealed to the public (Boonmongkon et al., 2000).

1.3. Ways to Solve Problem

Unplanned pregnancy is one of the most difficult life experiences among young women. Women are often confused, and then seek for help and support. When the problem occurs, the woman has three choices including parenting the baby, make a plan for adoption, or terminate the pregnancy. However, to choose one of the options, it is hard for the young women to make a decision.

Thus, to implement or initiate any strategies to help solve the unplanned pregnancy problem, it is important to understand thoroughly how young women making decision, and seeking for help - or health services; when, where, how and why they decide in that ways.

Based on the existing evidences on this issue, so far, there is not a single study that addressed, in a holistic manner, health-seeking patterns among young women on unplanned pregnancy. Moreover, research on abortion failed to take into account the role of unplanned pregnancy, which is an important determinant of abortion. The aim of this study is to formulate a theoretical model of health seeking patterns of service utilization among young women with unplanned pregnancy. Findings are expected to support policy and decision makers in designing interventions and services to help young women to make the transition from adolescent to adulthood without physical and psychosocial trauma from unintended pregnancy. Moreover, this explanatory model will help implementers and providers understand the decision making process, why and how women made decision to solve their problems which in turn can provide more appropriate interventions and services that serve the needs for young women.

1.4. Conceptual Framework of the Study

There are many theoretical models on health seeking behavior that attempt to explain utilization of health services. Furthermore, there are many determinants that affect the decision- making options of women with unplanned pregnancies, and their health seeking behavior. However, there has been no definitive conclusion about which factors or variables influence their decision-making options, or their seeking of health care utilization. This is because health behavior involves a number of social and behavioral factors including attitude, perception, beliefs and interpersonal relationships with peers, partners, and family members, as well as the influences of culture, norms, law, and health delivery systems and policies.

Thus, the study conceptual framework of this study is derived from a combination of factors recognized to be important determinants for the decision-making process of options for women with unplanned pregnancies from Ratchukoon (1998) *"A Model on Decision-making Process for Terminating Pregnancy"*.

In addition, the *"Symbolic Interaction Theory"* plays special attention to the symbols individuals use to interpret and define themselves, the actions of other people, and all other things and events. This theory helps us understand how young women interact with themselves when facing the problem of unplanned pregnancy. Moreover, Kleinman's theoretical framework (1980) called *"The Health Care System"*. According to Kleinman, the health care system is a type of cultural system, which integrates all health related components of a society. These components can include the patterns of belief about what causes health problems; the norms that govern choice and the evaluation of treatment and care; power of relationship; interaction settings, and institutions. Kleinman also proposed structural components of the health care system; he divides his model into three overlapping parts: the popular, the professional, and the folk sectors. Moreover, the study's conceptual framework also takes into account some selected sexual and reproductive health variables of the young people. In addition to services characteristics, indicators that are used for measuring the youth friendly services are selected from Nelson's study (2000).

In conclusion, based on the theoretical models, the study of Naravage et al. (2005) on factors affecting decision making of low income young women with unplanned pregnancies, this study classifies determinants of health service utilization into three sets of factors. These sets of factors are including: *1) personal history.* The variables include age at latest unplanned pregnancy; *2) individual psychosocial factors.* The variables used are attitude towards contraception, attitude towards unplanned pregnancy, and making decision without consultation; and *3) relationship factors.* The relationship variables used are relationship with partner, and consulting partner while having problem.

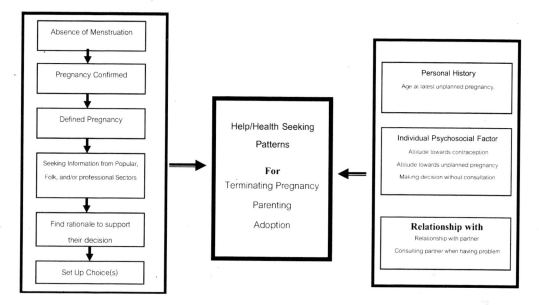

Figure 1.1. Conceptual Frame Work of the Study.

1.5. Purpose of the Study

This study is intents to understand when, where, why and how women with unplanned pregnancies seeking for health services, and patterns of health seeking behavior, their access to health care, and their reasons for using or not using available health services. These results provide valuable insights regarding how best to improve the utilization of existing interventions by influencing health behavior and care seeking choices. The study employs qualitative methods to answer the research questions. The qualitative approaches are employed to provide in-depth information to explain a woman's decision-making process to utilize the service facilities to ultimately formulate a theoretical model of help- or health-seeking patterns of women with unplanned pregnancies.

Research Objectives
1. To explore decision-making processes of the young women with unplanned pregnancy who choose for abortion, parenting, or adoption.
2. To explore health-seeking patterns of the unplanned pregnancy women who choose for abortion, for birth, or adoption.

3. To explore the characteristics of service facilities that influence utilization of unplanned pregnancy services among young people.

1.6. Key Themes and Main Issues for the Study

The main part of this study focused on the collection and analysis of qualitative information to understand when, where, how and why women with unplanned pregnancies making decision and seeking for health and social services, their patterns of seeking services, and the gaps between their needs and the services available. However, key themes and main issues are proposed as follows:

1.6.1. Definition of Pregnancy and their Interaction
- Definition of unplanned/unwanted pregnancy by women.
- What will happen if women keep the baby to full term?
- Interaction and feelings among women and their significant others, when facing unplanned/unwanted pregnancies.
- Feeling towards the fetus, and pregnancy.

1.6.2. Process of Decision-Making, Seeking for Services and their Interaction
- When and why women define the pregnancy as unplanned/ unwanted.
- Sources of information and person that women go for consulting.
- Process of decision making of women who opt for abortion, adoption, or parenting and feeling towards the choice.
- Rationale behind the selected choices
- Choice of services and care seeking patterns of women who select each option.
- Rationale behind the choice of services
- Interaction and feeling towards themselves and service providers.

1.6.3. Social Culture and Stigmatization on Sex, Sexuality, and Culture
- Reaction of others towards sex, sexuality and pregnancies of young women with unplanned pregnancies and ways the women response to the reactions.

1.7. Expected Outcomes

The Specific Outcomes of the Study are Expected as Follows:
- To understand woman's decision – making process and her utilization of services and patterns in order to provide information for policy development, program managers, service providers, teachers, family, and adolescences.
- To provide more in-depth understanding of the relevant factors which facilitate or obstruct the use of certain types of health services by women with unplanned pregnancy. The results also help understanding the low utilization of the government health care facilities.

- To provide valuable insights regarding how best to improve the utilization of existing interventions by influencing help/health seeking choices care, which may lead to danger for women's health.
- Results use as case study to advocate policy development, decision makers, women's NGOs for revision of abortion law, unfair regulation in school and labor force, and decrease in restrictions criteria for doctors to perform induced abortion.

2. RESEARCH METHODOLOGY

2.1. Research Design

Research methodology in this study focused on formative research utilizing qualitative data. The study was conducted covering all five shelters and low-income communities in Bangkok, Thailand. The data collection was through Focus Group Discussions, and in-depth interview. Forty-five cases were purposively recruited into the study. The interview guides important for the formative research because it relies entirely on the spontaneous generating of questions as they come out naturally from the free –flowing discussion between researcher and respondents. So, a researcher concentrates on guiding the discussion around the themes. The data were analyzed using content analysis

2.2. Sites Selected and Sampling Technique

The study conducted in Bangkok which most of the shelters are located. Listed of all the five active government and non-government shelters, and a foster home both located in Bangkok and outskirt in the women networks' bulletin were purposively selected. A foster home was selected for recruiting unplanned pregnancy women during they visited the home for putting the baby for adoption, or for temporary cares. Moreover, some low-income communities were purposively drawn based on voluntary participating.

2.3. Study Samples

The women with unplanned pregnancies were recruited from women who utilized the five government and private (NGO) shelters, a foster home, and women who lived in low-income communities. Verbal reports by the social workers at the shelters disclosed that women with unplanned pregnancies were aged 13 years and more, and 13 was the youngest age of those temporarily staying in the shelters. Thus, this study selected women aged 13-24 who volunteered to participate. Also, young women aged between 13-24, who had experienced unplanned pregnancies at least once, or women currently experiencing unplanned pregnancies, were selected, including young women in and out of school, and married and unmarried.

Inclusion Criteria for the Women's Group
To meet the study objectives, the selection criteria for the young women with unplanned pregnancies were as follows:
Experience of unplanned pregnancy.

Willing to participate in the study.
Total family incomes less than 10,000 bath per month.

Number of Samples
There were no fixed figures for the number of young women with unplanned pregnancies. The numbers of the study sample were elicited until information related to the objectives became saturated.

Data Collection
It took six months, after getting permission from the directors of the shelters to collect the data.

2.4. Study Instruments

Data collection for the formative research included group discussions, and in-depth interviews. Details of each method are as follows:

Focus Group Discussion (FGDs)
FGDs guidelines were constructed to understand the group attitudes and perceptions towards series of themes which they expressed in the public, commencing with the more neutral subjects of group's expectations towards the family and pregnancy; feelings and concerns about unexpected pregnancy; the meaning of unplanned pregnancy; choices for women concerning unplanned pregnancy; social reactions towards women who terminated pregnancy, parenting, or adoption; and expectations of services for young women.

Data collection began with introductory group discussions in order to get to know each other and build understanding and a sense of trust between the researcher (a moderator in the FGDs) and the study group. Moreover, they helped to promote, discuss, and foster a friendly atmosphere between the researcher and the sample population prior to in-depth one-on-one discussions. The results of the FGDs were analyzed to identify key issues that needed further investigation in the in-depth interviews. More important, the results of the FGDs provided an independent cross-check on the validity of the in-depth interviews among the samples. After the group discussion, the researcher met with the women who were willing to participate in the in-depth interviews to make next appointments for the interviews. The tapes were sent to research assistants for transcription. The tapes were transcribed in Thai and entered into computer files to facilitate further analysis.

In-Depth Interview
In-depth interviews with the women were developed to assess the women's experiences of unplanned pregnancy, interaction with their significant persons, the community and providers, the patterns of help- or health-seeking behaviors, and the reasons behind the choice(s) regarding the unplanned pregnancy. In-depth interviews were employed for both the young women with unplanned pregnancy at the shelters and the women who lived in the low-income communities in Bangkok. Details of themes in the guideline are as follows:

Key Themes for Data Collection
The study focused collecting and analyzing qualitative information, to understand when, where, how and why women with unplanned pregnancies sought health and social services, their service-seeking patterns, and the gaps between their needs and the services available.

Key themes and issues included the definition of unplanned pregnancy and their interaction with themselves once they faced the problem; interactions and feelings among the women towards their significant persons; sources of information and the persons the women consulted; the processes and patterns of decision making of the women who opted for abortion, adoption, or parenting, and their feelings about their choice; interactions and feelings between themselves and service providers; social culture and stigmatization of sex, sexuality, and their pregnancy; and the reactions of others towards their sex, sexuality and pregnancy, and the ways the women responded to these reactions. The information was a foundation for constructing a grounded theory on the decision-making process, and health-seeking patterns of young women with unplanned pregnancies.

Process of Instrument Development and Pre-Testing

After the research guidelines had been constructed based on information obtained through the reviewed literature, some ideas and suggestions were obtained through consultation with the researchers, and experts in adolescent health. The constructed guidelines and interview forms were pre-tested using face-to-face interviewing with women who complied with the same inclusion criteria of the study sample. The pre-testing and the sample group were different groups so that it was confident that the instruments could be used with the study group. Pre-testing allowed the researchers to crosscheck appropriate translation of the questions, the appropriateness of the order, the thoroughness of the response, and assessment of the reliability and validity of the interviewees' responses (for the attitudinal section). Moreover, pre-testing was conducted to permit the researcher to know how much time was required to conduct the interview, and the most appropriate place to conduct the interview. Pre-testing was part of the interviewer training process, to gain more skills before the actual data collection. The women who were exposed to pre-testing were excluded from the study.

The in-depth interview and FGD guidelines were pre-tested. Participants were elicited for the pre-testing until the researchers felt confident about the quality of the instruments, questions, responses, and the interviewers' skill levels. Participants who completed the pre-testing had similar characteristics to the intended study participants.

2.5. Definition of Terms

a) **Young women or young people** refer to women aged 13-24 years. However, there are different words, definitions, and age ranges used to describe the transition from childhood to adulthood among this age group. Thus in this study, the terms "Adolescents", "Youth", "Young Adults" and "Young People" are interchangeable.

b) **Health-seeking patterns** refers to young, low-income women with unplanned pregnancies utilizing the services of both the formal and/or informal sectors (popular, professional, and folk sectors), to seek care, support, or treatment once they have decided to opt for abortion, birth and adoption, or birth and keeping the baby. Health-seeking patterns are influenced by several factors, including socio-demographic characteristics, individual psychosocial factors, significant others, and environmental factors of the service facilities.

c) **Patterns** refers to the regularity (similarity, commonality) in what women with unplanned pregnancies disclose about their processes of seeking help and/or utilizing services based on selecting choice(s).

d) Popular sector is a matrix with several levels, including the individual, the family, social network, and community beliefs and activities. It is the lay, non-professional, non-specialist, popular culture arena in which illness is first defined and healthcare activities are initiated based on beliefs, attitudes, relationships, interactional settings, and institutions (Kleinman, 1980).

e) Professional sector is composed of professional physical and mental healing personnel. They have completed training in modern scientific medicine, and comprise trained drugstore personnel, nurses, doctors, social workers, and paramedics (Kleinman, 1980).

f) Folk sector is composed of non-professional healing personnel; traditional birth attendants (TBA), and traditional healers (TH) are in this sector. Folk medicine is a mixture of many different components; some are closely related to the professional sector, but most are related to the popular sector (Kleinman, 1980).

g) Low-income is defined as a total family income of less than 10,000 Baht per month (Pisalbutr, 1997).

h) Choices is defined as options available for young women to solve unplanned pregnancies, including abortion, parenting, or adoption.

i) Decision making process is adapted from Rutchukul (1998) which defined as a process that young women with unplanned pregnancies use to solve the problem by 1) seeking information; 2) arranging their choices; 3) finding rationales to support their choice; and 4) performing as planned. Women who made their decisions might seek services from the formal and informal sectors for abortion, birth and adoption, or birth and keeping the baby. Decisions were influenced by various factors, including socio-demographic characteristics, individual psychosocial factors, relationships with significant others, and environmental factors.

2.6. Data Collection and Management

Data collection took 6 months, from the first week of October 2002 to the end of March 2003, at the five shelters, and in the communities through peers in Bangkok. The researcher interviewed all the study women individually because the questions and discussion concerned premarital sex, pregnancy, and pregnancy termination, and were very sensitive and illegal in Thai culture, and also because the qualitative research had not targeted a sample size number. For this reason, it was important that it was the researcher who made the decision on when the data were saturated and when to stop further recruitment. In addition, most of the women did not disclose their experiences to anyone they were not familiar with. Moreover, by collecting data alone the researcher could ask for and probe in-depth information about each woman's experiences. At the beginning of data collection, the researcher visited each shelter to join their routine activities and assist the social worker teach how to prepare to be a healthy mother. At the session, the social worker introduced the researcher and let her share experiences of pregnancy with the women in the shelters. Thus, a sense of trust was gained from the women, which made it easier to get collaboration from the women. The steps of data collection and management were as follows:

1) Preparation

Prior to data collection, we as the researchers coordinated with peers, social workers, and the directors of all the shelters to make appointments to ask for permission to conduct the study. After receiving permission from the directors and commitment from the peers, the study sites and logistics were prepared, and the data collection tools were developed and pre-tested.

2) Training Research Assistants

The roles of the research assistants were to be note-takers while conducting the FGDs, transcribing tapes, and recruiting and screening the study participants for the researcher. Having the research assistants as the note-taker is important in case the samples do not give the verbal expression in response to the specific issues; then the note-taker can make a note on the fieldnotes. The inclusion criteria for the research assistants were that all of them had the opportunity to contact the potential study group, and had positive attitudes towards premarital sex, sexuality, and abortion. The training content included the sexuality in the Thai context, socio-political values and norms of pregnancy among young unmarried women, unplanned pregnancy and choices. Moreover, the research assistants were briefed about the how to take note in the qualitative ways. The pre-test guidelines were used as a training tool to reinforce the research assistants' skills.

3) Steps in Data Collection

The young women with unplanned pregnancies who complied with the inclusion criteria were elicited for the study. The researcher explained the purpose of the study and read the consent form to the participants in order to get permission to gather information according to the guidelines and the interview forms.

The main concerns at this stage were confidentiality and breaking the ice so that the respondents trusted and felt confident about disclosing their problems freely. The process maintained respondent confidentiality at all times. Information collected through interviews and observation was made permanent by removing the names and other identifying information from the data, to ensure that the names of the participants did not appear on any paper, in any circumstance. A signed consented form was utilized with all of the cases. All data were kept in a secure place to protect them from the authorities.

Tape recordings were used with all cases, if permitted. If any case did not permit tape recording, the researcher used short notes, key words and expanded the notes after returning from the field. The recorded tapes were transcribed and prepared for data analysis. Apart from the notes, comments about the appearance and reactions of the respondents were observed and noted.

4) Performing Quality Control Checks

All of the data were checked in the field to ensure that all the information was properly collected and recorded. Before and during data processing, the data and tapes were checked again for completeness and internal consistency before being sent to the research assistants for transcription. After the tapes had been transcribed, a hardcopy of the transcription results were rechecked again for data consistency. Moreover, the results were cross-checked with other sources of information, including observation, FGDs, and in-depth interviews.

5) Data Processing: Categorizing and Coding

For the qualitative data, preliminary analysis identified the key themes and issues for further analysis. The preliminary data analysis was processed by hand on a master tally sheet, then content analysis was employed for data analysis.

2.7. Data Analysis

During data collection, the researcher analyzed information case-by-case and built a set of basic key issues for further study and investigations in subsequent interviews, which formed the basis for the grounded theory. The accumulation of information with each case was gradually adjusted and the theory clarified until it had reached a stage of theoretical saturation. At this point, the researcher stopped recruiting new participants. Primary data analysis took place immediately after collecting the data for each case, so that the researcher could complete the information while it was still fresh in memory.

Content analysis was used for analyzing the total data. The choice of options by the young women with unplanned pregnancies (abortion, parenting, or adoption) were constantly compared to identify commonality or difference for each choice that the women made to solve the unplanned pregnancy, factors that related to the options considered by the young women, their decision-making processes, their health-seeking patterns, and factors affecting their health-seeking behaviors. Using this method, the researcher could make inductive conclusions from the findings into a larger theoretical picture, or theory, of unplanned pregnancy.

2.8. Ethics and Confidentiality

This study had been reviewed and approved by the ethical committee under the Medical Sciences Faculty, Chulalongkorn University, Bangkok, Thailand. During and after data collection, the maintenance of privacy and confidentiality was very strict. These issues are important because it is a sensitive topic that deals with sexuality, abortion, and political issues. The interviews were conducted where questions and responses could not be overheard. Thus, all of the sample population was informed about confidentiality. In addition, all information was kept confidential according to human subject protection guidelines. Anonymity was employed and maintained during the study. No full names or other information that could identify participants were recorded during any portion of the study. Field notes, tape transcripts, and any other field data collection forms used during the research were collected and stored in a secure location where unauthorized persons could not access them. More importantly, all of the participants in the study were voluntary. The voluntary nature of the study was stressed at the time of recruitment and again at the start of the in-depth interviews. Also, at any time during an interview, a participant was free to leave or terminate the session.

According to the ethics committee standards in Thailand, for women aged under 15 years, the representative of the shelters is the one who is authorized to sign the consent form on behalf of these girls, while women aged 15 years or older were authorized to sign the consent form themselves.

3. Findings

Results of the study present the analysis of focus group discussions and in-depth interviews undertaken among young women. Thus, the main discussion focuses on individuals, partner, family, environment, and socio-demographic characteristics that affect the options considered by young women and their health-seeking patterns--abortion, parenting, or adoption.

3.1. Profile of Samples

3.1.1. Focus Group Discussions (FGDs)

Five Focus Group Discussions (FGDs) were conducted among the women with unplanned pregnancies, between October to December, 2002. The participants were recruited from women who lived in the five selected shelters in Bangkok. Since the discussion topics were sensitive, dealing with feelings towards unplanned pregnancy and sexual health, and the participants were in this situation, discussion initially was difficult and it took time to "open up".

The focus group discussions were held in a room where strict privacy and a lack of interruptions could be assured. The general atmosphere in the group discussion was informal, in order to get to know each other and gain more trust among the participants. Snacks and soft drinks were served at the beginning of the group discussion. The researcher conducted the group discussion as a moderator with an assistant who was a note-taker, and was also a social worker. The number of participants in each group generally ranged from 6-10, although there was one group comprising 4 participants, which was too few due to a small number of women who fall under the inclusion criteria were limited. There were a total of 37 participants aged 14-24 years.

3.1.2. In-depth Interviews

In-depth interviews were conducted among young women with unplanned pregnancies who stayed at the shelters, and women in low-income communities in Bangkok. A total of 45 cases participated in the study during the period October 2002-end March 2003 (Table 3.1). The women who decided to raise the baby were the majority in this group, and the remainders were adoption and abortion, which were 28, 11, and 6, respectively. It was found that the proportion of the middle adolescent and late adolescence was equal (22:22), whereas one case was 14 year old with mean age of 19.7 years of the total sample. More than half (28 participants) was recruited from shelters, whereas 5 cases used the snowball technique, and the remainder was recruited through community health centers' record. Regarding the participants' status, 28 were single, while 17 participants were married. Thirteen participants had completed only primary education (grades 1-6), whereas 32 participants had studied beyond grade six. For living status, 14 of the participants lived in a dormitory, and 16 lived with their parents or caretakers. The remainder or 15 lived with their partners.

3.2. Experiences of Young Women with Unplanned Pregnancies

In Thai culture, men and women are not treated equally. The biases start from when the baby is born. Gender biases are clearly shown regarding sexuality. For men, pre-marital sex is socially accepted, but it is not for women. Only sex among married women is socially accepted. Moreover, as mothers, women are expected to raise, care, and feed the baby. They must not only care for the baby, but it is socially expected that women should care for all family members. In addition, if women want to terminate their pregnancy they will incur the blame of society. Furthermore, it is illegal to do so in Thailand. This situation puts young women in a crisis situation once they are faced with an unplanned pregnancy.

Table 3.1. General Characteristics of Study Women with Unplanned Pregnancy

General Characterstics	Number	Percentage
Adolescence Stages (Mean age =19.7 years)		
Early adolescence (13-14 years)	1	2.2
Middle adolescence (15-19 years)	22	48.9
Late adolescence (20-24 years)	22	48.9
Total	**45**	**100**
Women Recruited from		
Shelters	28	62.2
Communities/Snowball technique	17	37.8
Total	**45**	**100**
Marital Status		
Single	28	62.2
Married	17	37.8
Total	**45**	**100**
Educational Level		
Primary education (grade 1-6)	13	28.9
Beyond grade 6	32	71.1
Total	**45**	**100**
Living Status		
Alone (Dormitory)	14	31.1
With parents/care taker	16	35.6
With partner	15	33.3
Total	**45**	**100**

3.2. Experiences of Young Women with Unplanned Pregnancies

In Thai culture, men and women are not treated equally. The biases start from when the baby is born. Gender biases are clearly shown regarding sexuality. For men, pre-marital sex is socially accepted, but it is not for women. Only sex among married women is socially accepted. Moreover, as mothers, women are expected to raise, care, and feed the baby. They must not only care for the baby, but it is socially expected that women should care for all family members. In addition, if women want to terminate their pregnancy they will incur the blame of society. Furthermore, it is illegal to do so in Thailand. This situation puts young women in a crisis situation once they are faced with an unplanned pregnancy.

If women have sex before marriage, or while they are students, their parents, family members, teachers, friends, and other people in their community will blame them. Moreover, if a woman gets pregnant without a responsible man, society judges her as being promiscuous. Thus, most of the young women with unplanned pregnancies are afraid and want to hide themselves once they face trouble. They do not dare to confront anyone they know. The most important factor is that these women want to avoid seeing the reactions of these people, especially their parents. Thus, this section presents the interactions and meanings of the young women while they are having trouble with their significant persons, including their partners, parents, peers, themselves, and their providers, and the reasons for unplanned pregnancy. These results help us understand the young women's experiences, their thinking and to find opportunities to assist those who have unplanned pregnancies endure and cope with the critical situation with physical and mental well-being.

3.2.1. Terms and Meaning of Unplanned Pregnancy

The meanings and terms for unwanted pregnancy respond to individual situations during pregnancy and after delivery. Most important is the relationship of the women and their sexual partners. If the relationship is good, the terms are more positive, while if the relationship is bad or there is no relationship, the terms are negative. The following are the terms raised by participants during the FGDs:

The participants mentioned "Thong mai prom" and "Thong mai thang jai" most frequently. These two terms reflected similar situations for the women faced with an unplanned pregnancy. Some of the participants were still loyal to their partners even though they had left them. However, the women felt unprepared for raising the baby because some of them were studying, unemployed, or their parents did not accept the pregnancy. The majority of them raised the baby by themselves, whereas some of them put the baby up for adoption.

"The reason it was "mai prom" was because I intended to have a baby, but I had this problem (partner leaving with another woman). Thus, I felt lost" (Lee, married, 21 year-old factory worker, put the baby up for adoption).

Table 3.2. Local Terms for Unplanned Pregnancy

Local Terms	English	Meanings
"Thong mai thong karn"	Unwanted pregnancy	The woman did not want to have a baby at all. She attempted to terminate the pregnancy using various methods, with negative attitudes towards the man.

Table 3.2. (Continued).

Local Terms	English	Meanings
"Thon mai thang jai"	Unintended pregnancy	The baby is wanted but the woman is not ready to have the baby at that time, because of study, work, or unemployment. It reflects a positive relationship with the sexual partner.
"Thong mai prom"	Unplanned pregnancy	In some situations, the baby is wanted, while in others, not. The woman's relationship with the partner is positive.
Thong mai kadkit	Unexpected pregnancy	The woman did not want to have the baby at that time because of a lack of mental and physical preparedness.

"Thong mai thong karn" was mentioned among the women who had negative relationships with the men, because some of them were raped by both known and unknown men. Some of the women had very negative impressions of the man, or felt the enormous burden of having a new baby. Women in these situations tended to put the baby up for adoption, whereas some of them raised the baby by themselves because they became attached to the baby during pregnancy and/or after delivery and after having raised the baby for a while. During these periods, attachments bonded subtly.

"The reason for "Thong mai thong karn" is because I was raped and I couldn't stand for it" (Pia, single, 17 years old, school student, parents raising the baby).

3.2.2. Feelings and Concerns of Women Facing Unexpected Pregnancy

The results from the focus group discussions with the women in the shelters revealed that most of the young women who had faced this situation recently felt anxiety immediately after suspecting pregnancy. They felt concerned because premarital sex, sex while studying, or pregnancy, without a responsible man, were not socially acceptable. Thus, they were afraid that their parents were angry and disappointed in them. Other more minor issues included acceptance by their relatives, friends, and people in the community. Many women felt that these people would look down on them. Some women disclosed that they cared about their parents' concerns the most. However, if their parents accepted their pregnancy, they would feel relieved and calmer. Also, most of them did not want anyone to know that their partner was an unfaithful man, irresponsible, and had abandoned them. Some women were afraid because their parents would not accept their partner's behavior. The concern about parental worry was due to the women feeling that they cared for their parents the most, and did not want to disappoint them.

With urbanization, the relationships between women and their friends or their communities are bonded weakly. The women who stayed at the shelter for longer periods were not much concerned about the reactions or thinking of society towards unplanned pregnancy. This was because, after the women had passed this crisis situation of unplanned pregnancy that was related to their parents, friends and community, the major concerns were the baby and the future. The most important was the situation in the shelter. They had the opportunity to meet women in the same situation. After the newcomers had interacted with others, they felt that there were many women who were falling into a worse situation than themselves. Thus, they felt more relaxed and happier than staying outside. However, at the shelters they were worried about how to manage their lives with the baby, and what the future would be. Most of them revealed that, as a single mother, they were afraid that they could not raise the baby or provide it with a good future. During pregnancy, some of the young women at the shelter could not make definite decisions to raise the baby or put the baby for adoption. This was because many of them relied on their partner's, parents' or relatives' support to raise the baby. Some of them could make a decision once the baby was born, and they gave the reason that it was because the baby's face looked like them. Moreover, many of the women who took several abortifacient products were afraid of the baby being abnormal. The majority of the women made decisions by themselves about options for solving unplanned pregnancy, which was due to the most-mentioned factors, their partners' responsibility, and support from their parents/relatives. They revealed that if their partner agreed to be responsible for the baby, most would raise the baby instead of putting it up for adoption.

As time passed, most of the participants adjusted themselves and felt more relaxed and comfortable with the situation, especially, women who stayed at the shelter, who were protected from stigmatization because they were among friends faced with the same situation. However, most of the women who kept and raised their baby would worry about it, and this issue would not be easily resolved because of economic problems. The women really needed financial and other supports to raise and adapt themselves to the baby, especially when they went back to their communities. If women lacked the support of their parents, relatives or partners, they would feel reluctant to raise the baby. At the same time, the connectedness between mother and baby from pregnancy made them feel that they should raise the baby instead of putting it up for adoption. These feelings put them into a crisis situation for making decisions about the future.

3.2.3. Choices of the Young Women with Unplanned Pregnancies

Once the participants had realized that they were pregnant, most of them tried to terminate the pregnancy by self-medication, not only to avoid stigmatization, but also because of the convenience, low cost, and because it was easy to do. The reasons for terminating the pregnancy included: starting a new family life; financial problems; having just started a new job or being unemployed; studying; parents/relatives disappointed; premarital sex. Drugstores/grocery stores were the most-mentioned places for purchasing abortifacient products. Most of the women would try as hard as they could to terminate the pregnancy. If some of them failed to terminate the pregnancy themselves, they would visit private clinics. However, many of them took time utilizing abortifacient products and waiting for the results. When the women realized that self-medication was unsuccessful, it was too late for them to have a modern medical practitioner manage an abortion, because the pregnancy term was beyond the medical criteria. So, many of them sought a place to hide themselves and support them during their pregnancy. They maintained the pregnancy to full term because they had no choice. Thus, after delivery, some of them raised the baby by themselves, if they got support from their partners, parents or relatives. In contrast, if there was no support from anyone, the women tended to put the baby up for adoption.

3.2.4. Details of Findings for the Reasons of Unplanned Pregnancy and Interactions:
1. Individual. The in-depth interview results showed that many issues caused unplanned pregnancies among young women, including:

1.1. Lack of contraceptive knowledge. Comparing married and unmarried young women, it was found that the knowledge of both groups regarding contraception, and improper utilization of contraception, were not different. Both groups had inadequate knowledge of how to use contraceptive methods properly. Some women lacked knowledge of contraceptive methods. It was surprising that some married women revealed that they did not use any contraceptive methods because they did not know any.

"At that time, I did not protect by using any contraception. I do not know any contraceptive methods. I really knew nothing" (Yam, 19 years old, married).

Some married women indicated that they experienced side effects from using contraceptives, so they decided to stop using them. Subsequently, many of them became pregnant because of discontinuing, or intermittently using, contraceptive pills.

"I know the contraceptive methods. My partner buys them for me, but I cannot take them. When I take them, I get nausea and vomiting" (Pung, 18 years old, married).

"I feel afraid to take contraceptives. I am not sure what will happen if I take it incorrectly" (Air, 20 years old, single).

"When I completed the oral contraceptive course, I thought that it would be OK if I missed it for a while. I felt that missing only one month would not cause pregnancy. So, I would buy it and take it next month. No longer, my belly is getting bigger" (Ploy, single, 17 years old).

"I do not use them (oral contraceptives) continuously. I use them and then stop. As a result, I get pregnant" (Nok, 23 years old, single).

1.2. No time to receive contraceptive services. One reason for unplanned pregnancies was that the women had no time to receive services. Most of the services that they visited were under government authority and operated only during official office hours. Some women said the reason that they could not go was because, if they went, their employers would deduct their daily wages. Some women worked in the factory, and if they could get more work, they could get more money, as well. Thus, they did not really get contraceptives regularly.

"At first I planned to get an injection, but I could not go because I had to work until 10pm. In the morning, I go to work on the factory bus. Everyone needs to get the bus on time. I work as a daily worker, so if I leave I will lose the daily salary" (Kwan, 19 years old, married).

1.3. Inconvenient using contraception. Some married women revealed that they could not choose contraception as they wished because they had no time to get an injection or other form of contraception at government health facilities. If they went to get services from private facilities, it would cost more money, which they did not want to spend. So they ignored using it.

"We used to use natural contraception. He used to use withdrawal, but he does not want to do so lately. I have condoms that I ask him to use, but he does not want to comply" (Pla, 19 years old, married).

1.4. Beliefs and attitudes towards sex. It was found that some unmarried young women believed that having sex only once could not cause pregnancy. Moreover, some single young women acted like their peers, and if their peers did not use contraceptives, they did the same.

Some women revealed that they studied at a women-only school, and had not previously learnt about contraception. However, the married women were more independent from their peers and had more experience of sexual intercourse, so their attitudes were different, as mentioned above. The results reflected a lack of inappropriate sex education in school, and peer pressure. Moreover, if they worked in an environment that did not support information, education, or communication about sexual health education, the women had no opportunity to learn about these issues. Thus, having sex once, they did not know how to protect themselves from unplanned pregnancy.

> "I never had regular sex with anyone, so I did not realize that I was pregnant. I thought that having sex only once could not cause pregnancy. But one day, my colleague said that I looked fat, which made me aware of my pregnancy" (Oam, single, 18 years old, school student).

> "I just pretended to ask my friend whether she used contraception. She told me that she did not use any. Thus, I followed her" (Lek, single, 18 years old, unemployed).

2. Partner relationship. The most important reason that caused the young women to feel that they were not ready for pregnancy or to care for the baby was their partner. Many young women revealed that their partners just abandoned them and did not show any responsibility for their pregnancy. Some men left after they had sex without knowing that the woman had become pregnant. Some men abandoned them and left for a new woman. Some men already had wives, so, when the pregnant women knew, they were disappointed and separated from them. However, if the men showed responsibility, the majority of the respondents said that they were willing to reunite. Thus, many women kept the baby to make a new decision, which depended on their partner.

Among the participants who faced violence, some women were beaten by the men because they used drugs, such as amphetamines or alcohol. Once they had taken it, they could not control their behavior or emotions. Many participants were beaten; the married women were more seriously beaten by their partners, while the single women were less seriously beaten, because among the unmarried there was no social bond. So, they just ran away after they were beaten. Some married women accepted the violence with no choice because they needed financial support from the man. Moreover, if they wanted to separate, their parents or relatives did not allow it, and asked them to come back because they did not want anyone to gossip about their family.

2.1. The men used drugs, and/or alcohol and lost control. When the men used drugs, they lost of control and did not take responsibility for the family.

> "I did not know that I was pregnant. I am thinking about separating from him because I knew that he is a drug addict. I tried to run away from him; I escaped and went to stay with my friend. However, my parents knew and asked me to come back. I agreed to do so" (Jum, married, 24 years old).

> "If he did not beat me, I would live with him. When he beat me the third time, I told him that I would leave him. Then, I ran away from him" (Fon, single, 19 years old, housewife).

> "At the beginning of pregnancy, we did not separate; I felt ready for the pregnancy. When he used amphetamines and had another partner, I felt that I did not want the baby" (Fon, single, 19 years old, unemployed).

3. Unintentional. Some women were not sure whether to settle with the man as a permanent partner. Because they lived away from parents, they had more freedom in their life. Some of them just wanted to try to have sex like their peers without loving each other. Some of them wanted someone to be their friend because they lived away from home and felt lonely. Thus, when they spent more time together, they quarreled and finally separated because the relationship was bonded weakly (Gay, single, 20 years old).

3.1. Having sex by accident. The lifestyle of single young people has more freedom than in the past, which was controlled by their parents or relatives. There are also more places to go out and spend time together. In addition, some of them mentioned that they had more opportunity to have sex without love but by chance.

> "He asked me to go to his house to see his parents. I decided to go with him. At his house, there was no one. Then, he forced me to have sex with him" (Pia, 17 years old, school student).

> "I like him as an older brother, not like a boyfriend. It is not possible to live together. If I lived with him, our family life may collapse soon" (Oil, single, 20 years old, vocational school student).

4. Parents and close relatives

4.1. Living away from parents or relatives. Many of the women with unplanned pregnancies lived alone or with their friend(s). They had more freedom without the control of their parents or relatives. Nowadays, sex among young people is more accepted than in the past. With peer pressure, many of the participants had premarital sex. However, once they got pregnant, they could not hide it because the symptoms and physical signs started to show. Many of them gave the reason that they were afraid that their loved ones would be disappointed, since they were still students.

> "I was desperately depressed. I was so afraid when the provider put the strip into the urine. I wished that I would not be pregnant. I thought my future would disappear because of my pregnancy. All of the efforts of my parents sending me to school would vanish because I got pregnant. I hated the baby very much" (Oam, vocational school student, 18 years old).

> "When I knew, I felt very worried. My father would not accept me. Now, he knows and accepts" (Pu, single, 23 years old, unemployed).

4.2. Family problems. Nearly half of the single young women were from broken homes. Some of them lived with a single parent or together with their father or mother-in-law. Some of them could adjust to the new family but some could not. Some of them left their new father or mother-in-law because they disliked them, or their parents disliked the women's partner, or they could not accept the way the women behaved. Among the married women, many lived separately, so they had fewer family problems.

> "There are many reasons. One reason is that I ran away from my mother. I do not want a baby. I only want to work and collect all the money. If I raise the baby, I will have no money left. Then, people I know will look down on me because I cannot survive by myself" (On, single, 20 years old).

4.3. Having relatives with experiences of unplanned pregnancy. Some women had relatives with experiences of unplanned pregnancy. Hence, they tended to have an unplanned pregnancy.

One example was the two young sisters Lek and Nu, who were 20 and 18 years old, respectively, living with their parents. They had a younger brother and sister who were studying at school. After graduating in grade six, both of them worked together at a small factory in Bangkok. They worked for a few periods of time and then quit after that. When the researcher interviewed them, they were both unemployed. Their father was a taxi driver, while their mother was a house worker. Last year, the eldest sister, Lek, got pregnant but her boyfriend who was 4 years younger ran away. She decided to tell her younger sister, Nu. The younger sister decided to tell their mother. After her mother recovered from the shock, she asked her daughter to terminate the pregnancy and she agreed to do so. She took her daughter, who was two months pregnant, to the abortion clinic and signed for her. Nu was very afraid while she was at the clinic because she was afraid of side effects, such as bleeding and pain. However, she was successfully terminated and was happy. The following year, her younger sister, Nu, became pregnant. She kept it a secret from their parents. She was aware of the pregnancy at the second month, because she went shopping at the Mall and fainted. Nu went to check at the clinic and knew that she was pregnant. Her boyfriend put pressure on her to terminate the pregnancy because he was not ready to have a family. She did not want to do so because she realized that her older sister was suffering from guilt after terminating her own pregnancy. Her boyfriend pressed her again and took her to the abortion clinic. Finally, on the day, she decided to tell her grandmother about the pregnancy because she was closer to her grandmother than her mother. Then, her grandmother told her mother. Her mother forgave for the past and continues to support her.

> "If I terminated pregnancy, it might come to bother me. Like my elder sister, she terminated pregnancy. Then, she had a bad dream…the baby came into her dream and it wanted to live with her" (Nu, single, 18 years old).

5. Peer pressure. The women who had friends with experience of premarital sex and/or unplanned pregnancy tended to behave in the same ways as their peers, since the young people spent more time with their peers than their parents. Some of them lived together with friends to save money while they were working or studying. So, the relationships among them were closer.

As one example of a young factory worker with unplanned pregnancy, the researcher interviewed "Nid", who was 21 years old. Her parents separated when she was young. Her mother remarried, so Nid lived with her grandmother until she moved to work in a factory in Samut Prakan, adjacent to Bangkok. She lived in a room together with 2 other young women who worked at the same place. They all had premarital sex with their boyfriends. "Nid" met a man who became her partner at the age of 17 years. They had one child but they sent the child to her mother-in-law upcountry. Three years later, she fell pregnant again. She felt very disappointed because she took oral contraceptive pills every day. She thought that the pills might have expired. Both of them were unhappy because they did not have enough income to support the second baby. At the sixth month of pregnancy, her partner disappeared. Her belly was getting big and she was laid off from the factory. Her savings were running short, so she decided to go to the hospital near her apartment to request termination of her pregnancy. The social worker referred her to a shelter because the hospital did not provide abortion services. She disclosed not only her own miserable memoirs, but also a sad story about her roommate who came from the same province in "Isan" (northeastern part of Thailand), and from a broken home. Her parents had separated. Later, her father passed away and her mother remarried. She came to work in the same factory as Nid. During the economic crisis of the past five years, the factory laid off many workers and she was one of them. Later, she went to work as a waitress in a restaurant and had sex with the customers to earn more income. She fell pregnant later without knowing who the baby's father was. She was very depressed and committed suicide later, using a high dose of pesticide. After the police examined the dead body, Nid and the other roommate took her body to the temple for cremation. They sent her bones back to her mother in her hometown.

Nid was more stressed after her roommate passed away. She was waiting for her partner to return, but it seemed hopeless. Thus, she decided to seek an abortion during the sixth month of pregnancy, but it was not successful because the providers refused to terminate any pregnancy when the term was more than three months. However, it was fortunate that she was referred to the shelter; otherwise she would have suffered very much.

6. Family income. All of the participants in this study were selected based on their incomes as well as other criteria, which were lower than 10,000 Baht per month. Having this condition, it was found that the greatest concern for the participants was dealing with economic problems. Some of them did not go to government health facilities because they found it was not convenient. They had no money to buy oral contraceptive pills or condoms, so they did not use any contraceptive methods, especially married women who had sexual intercourse regularly. Thus, when they were pregnant, many of the young participants were concerned about the baby's future. Both the married and unmarried women were concerned about the same issue, because some of the young people had no job, were studying, or had been laid off because of their pregnancy. In addition, some married women had the baby more than one. Thus, the married women needed more income to afford the expenses of the whole family. However, it was found that they earned the same or less income, but had increased expenditures.

> "I was concerned after the second baby was born. How will I raise them both? When the elder and the little one are crying at the same time, what will I do?" (Maew, 18 years old, married, housewife).

> "I do not know how to manage it. I just started working less than a month ago. My salary is only 1,500 Baht per month. I do not know what to do" (Lek, single, 23 years old).

> "I plan to have an abortion, taking the baby out of my womb. I really do not want to keep it as a burden for my parents, because I have another younger sister who is 11 years old and still studying" (Kwang, single, 15 years old).

7. Rape. A few of the cases staying at the shelters had been raped. The proportions of the single women, who had been raped by a man they knew, and by a stranger, were equal. Some women did not know that they had a chance of falling pregnant after being raped, and when they knew of the pregnancy, it was too late to terminate it. However, if they knew earlier, in the first trimester, they could have terminated the pregnancy legally at either public or private health facilities. Most of the women who were raped realized they were pregnant when it was too late, because they had no signs and symptoms of pregnancy. When the pregnancy was confirmed, most of the cases kept it secret because they were ashamed to disclose it to anyone. They waited until there were physical changes, which was too late to solve the problem.

"When I was raped, I felt disgusted because I did not want to have sex with him. If I was willing, it would be another story. So, I decided to be a nun" (Oam, single, 18 years old, school student, raped by a known person).

"At the beginning, the man said he would be responsible if I had sex with him. After he had sex with me, he told me that he needed another two years to complete his education" (Daw, single, 24 years old, raped by a known person).

"I was stressed because my aunt knew. Then, all my relatives at home would know, and they would yell at me and ask me who the father of the baby was. It made me scared. I did not dare to tell them what was happening to me" (Pae, single, 16 years old, out-of-school youth, raped by a stranger).

3.3. Decision-Making Process

The in-depth interview results were used to explain the decision-making processes of the young women with unplanned pregnancies. It starts by examining the interaction process of the women when knowing of pregnancy, their decision towards unplanned pregnancies whether to terminate or continue their pregnancy upon missing menstruation, the definition of pregnancy, consulting popular sector, compromising with self-conflict, and making choices (Figure 3.1).

3.3.1. Knowing of Pregnancy, Feelings, and Defining Pregnancy

Knowing of Their Pregnancy. The results of the in-depth interviews showed that the women knew their pregnancy and interacted with themselves in the followings ways (please see figure 3.1):

1. Knowledge and experiences based on signs and symptoms. The knowledge and experience of pregnancy made the women aware that they were pregnant. Most of the participants recognized their pregnancy because they knew the signs and symptoms. The most popular sign of pregnancy was missing menstruation. Many of them revealed that if they had sex and then missed menstruation, it was certain that they were pregnant.

"Since missing my menstruation, I did not take a urine pregnancy test because I used to have a baby. I felt confident one hundred percent" (Pla, married, 19 years old, housewife)

To confirm the pregnancy, most of the primigravida visited private clinics, whereas the same proportion visited drugstores/grocery stores to purchase a pregnancy test kit to perform on their own, to confirm the pregnancy. However, some cases did not trust the self-test and would visit a private clinic for final confirmation. A few cases did not make any confirmation because they had experienced pregnancy before. A few cases visited government hospitals or community health centers for pregnancy tests, because they planned to come back again for antenatal care, delivery, and/or post-natal care.

"I missed my menstruation until the third month, when I decided to ask my friend to buy a urine pregnancy test from a convenience store (7-Eleven)" (Pia, single, 17-years old, high school student).

"I tested (urine pregnancy test) myself but I was not sure, so I decided to borrow my friends' money to visit a private clinic to confirm the pregnancy" (Aui, single, 19 years old, vocational student).

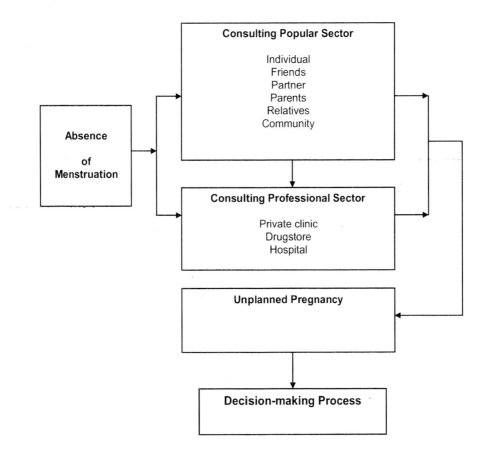

Figure 3.1. Seeking Patterns of Pregnancy Confirmation among Low-income Young Women with Unplanned Pregnancy.

2. Fetal movement. Some knew that they were pregnant because of the movement of the fetus and physical changes. Some of the young women had had irregular menstruation periods since the onset of puberty, and thus did not realize when they were missing menstruation. They realized when they felt something moving in their belly before others suspected that they were pregnant.

"I felt that there was something moving in my belly. In addition, my relatives suspected, so they took me to the clinic. The results showed that I was pregnant" (Pae, single, 16 years old).

3. Physical changes. A few participants did not realize that they were pregnant because they had irregular menstruation patterns since the onset of puberty. One example was a 14-year-old school student who participated in a school camp and overnighted at the school. Someone she did not know raped her that night. She did not realize that it could lead to pregnancy. At the sixth month of pregnancy, her body had changed and was larger. Her mother asked her why she was getting bigger and took her to the clinic.

"My mother asked 'why I am so fat'. Then, she took me to a clinic. The results showed that I was in the sixth month of pregnancy" (Noi, single, 14 years old, school student).

Feelings and Concerns of Women Facing Unexpected Pregnancy

The results of the focus group discussions and in-depth interviews of the samples revealed that most of them experienced anxiety immediately after they suspected that they were pregnant. They felt concerned because premarital sex, sex while studying, and being abandoned by one's partner, were socially unacceptable. Many women revealed that people would look down on them and their parents. Thus, they were afraid that their parents were angry and disappointed in them. Some women disclosed that they cared about their parents' concerns the most. However, if their parents accepted their pregnancy they would feel relieved and calmer. Other minor issues included acceptance by their relatives, friends and people in the community.

Self-Defining Pregnancy

After the women had passed the "shock period", they were thinking about the pregnancy and trying to define it. Although they were all in the same situation, with unplanned pregnancies, there were variations in the degree of pregnancy acceptance, which was due to differences in the individuals, partners, parents/relatives, peers, and communities. As described earlier, "Thong mai thong karn", "Thong mai thang jai", "Thong mai prom", or "Thong mai kadkit" meant unwanted, unintended, unplanned, and unexpected, respectively, as the women mentioned during the FGDs and in-depth interviews. The results revealed that all of the women reflected on being physically and psychologically unprepared for pregnancy, because most of them had an ideal husband and/or family. The main reason was that, in Thai culture, premarital sex, or pregnancy before marriage, are unacceptable. Moreover, pregnancy without a responsible man is a shameful situation for a woman and her family. On the other hand, social norms put the pregnant woman into the role of a mother who should be responsible for the baby in the womb. Thus, when the pregnancy situation did not ensue as they expected, most of them intended to terminate their pregnancy. They did not want to keep the baby because most of them were afraid that their parents and people in the community would know that they had had premarital sex with a consequent pregnancy. The more they loved and respected their parents, the more secretly they kept their pregnancy, to avoid their disappointment.

3.3.2. Consulting Popular Sector (Other People)

Most of the unplanned pregnancies were caused by the women's partners, e.g., partner leaving them, having another woman, or using drugs. Thus, most of the participants would consult friends at school or at work, or relatives they trusted. They would select the person who could make them feel better or give them some advice. They preferred to consult people with similar experiences who were older or in the same age group, because they could understand their situation easily.

> "I was shaking. Then, I ran to see my friend immediately (after knowing of the pregnancy result)" (Rat, single, 22 years old, college student).

Some women who lived alone tended to make decisions by themselves. Many women revealed that they felt stressed because they could not let anyone know about their situation. After they disclosed to someone they trusted, they felt better. To release tension, some of the women who wanted to keep it secret moved away to live in a new place, to avoid questions from close friends or people in the community before their belly started to get big. Some of them moved during the first or second trimester because their bellies were not too big and it was difficult to see from outside. The women who had no one to support them would try to seek a safe place, at their best friend's house or in a public shelter, rather than live alone outside during the last trimester of pregnancy, because they felt worried about the possibility of emergency labor.

"I did not want to tell anyone, so I went to live in Bangkok and worked at Klong Thom" (Lee, single, 21 years old).

Among the single women, some revealed that they did not like to tell their parents about the pregnancy because they were afraid that they would disappoint them. Hence, their parents knew their pregnancy because their physical was getting bigger.

"My mother saw my belly. At that time, it was getting big, at seven months of pregnancy. Then, she asked me whether I had menstruation. I told her that I did not. So, she went to buy a pregnancy test" (Pia, single, 14 years old, school student).

The married women preferred to consult their parents. If the relationships of the participants and the parents were more close and friendly, they tended to consult them. However, some married women revealed that they did not want to tell their parents because they already had many problems and they did not want to bother them. However, if their parents asked, they would only release some information, not all the problems.

"My mother, I did not want to consult her because she already had many problems" (Joy, married, 24 years old, factory worker).

"If my parents asked, I would tell them part of the information (not all of it)" (Air, married, 21 years old, factory worker).

After the women gained support and information from the person they consulted, it was surprising that most of them made decisions by themselves. A few cases followed their parents' decision.

"I did not consult anyone, I made decision by myself (put the baby for adoption)" (Porn, single, 18 years old).

"At that time I wanted to terminate pregnancy. My mother made decision (put the baby for adoption) because I did not know the man who made me pregnant" (Noi, single, school student, 14 years old).

3.3.3. Choosing Options
After the women with unplanned pregnancies gained information and recommendations from consulting others, there were two decision-making options, terminating the pregnancy and continuing the pregnancy. The majority needed to terminate the pregnancy, while a few cases needed to continue the pregnancy. In making the decision, both options were painful for the young people. The women who chose to terminate their pregnancy faced self-conflict and other external factors, while the women who continued their pregnancy were insecure because they were unsure how to cope with present and future situations. It was important to note that the young women would change their minds, which depended on their partners and their parents. If these significant people supported them, they tended to keep the baby to term. But if they did not care, or showed no responsibility, the young women tended to terminate

the pregnancy. The factors that influenced the choices of the young people are explained below.

1. Society and community. Most of the unplanned pregnancies were caused by premarital sex, while studying, or with abandonment by the partner. As a result, they all felt ashamed to have a belly that kept getting bigger. They were afraid that people in the community would gossip and reproach them that they were bad or promiscuous girls. In addition, their family members would be blamed. One example was a young woman named Pae, who was 16 years old. Her parents divorced when she was young. Her mother left her with her aunt, while she was working as a dressmaker in Brunei. After she finished grade 9, she quit school. She liked going out with her friends, and one night at the discotheque, she was drunk and taken away by men she did not know before. After she woke up, she found herself alone at a motel, and she realized that she had been raped. She kept it secret until the fourth month, when her aunt asked why she was getting bigger. Her aunt took her to a clinic and found that she was pregnant. She wanted to terminate the pregnancy but the doctor at the private clinic could not do as requested because her pregnancy term was over three months, so that if she wanted to do it, it was risky. So, she went to another clinic, but it was too expensive that she could not afford it.

> "I was in the fourth month of pregnancy. I was very stressed but I could eat normally. I did not want it (the baby) but I had no way out. I needed to find a new place to hide myself (to avoid gossiping by the neighbors). My neighbors' gossiped that 'I did not study but had a sexual partner instead'. I did not like them to show contempt for my mother and my family members" (Pae, single, 16 years old, out-of-school student).

The women disliked gossip because it would spread by word of mouth, with the addition of the attitudes of the ones who hastened the news. Nowadays, the relationships among people in the community were bonded weakly. Premarital sex was a subject that attacked cultural morals and norms, and therefore was considered a good subject for gossip among community members. However, if the relationships of the women with their neighbors were strong, the gossip could be very useful, because their neighbors would support them and make them feel secure and dare to disclose their troubles. The women who had support from their neighbors tended to keep their babies to term. But the situation where women gained support from their neighbors was rare. However, this is only one of several factors that affected the women's decision.

> "My neighbors did not repeat my faults; on the contrary, they supported me. They know my background and understand me. They pity me" (Fon, single, 19 years old).

Another reason that the people tended to support the women is that, at present, the situation of premarital sex is seen more often than in the past, people tend to accept it more and seem to understand the women situation. Consequently, it is important to note that increasing numbers of people view premarital sex as normal in the current situation.

> "My neighbor knew. She did not repeat my fault, instead, she said 'it is not serious. It has already happened'" (Tuk, single, 21 years old, vocational school student).

> "She was sympathetic. She said, 'at present the situation is different from the past when people would repeat your faults. Currently, there are many women like you (having premarital sex and pregnant)'" (Tuk, single, 21 years old, vocational school student).

2. Family members. If the young women lived with their parents, the parents were the most influential on the young women's choice of terminating the pregnancy or keeping the baby. Most of the parents wanted their daughters to terminate the pregnancy if they had had premarital sex; the women themselves did not want to burden their parents, as well. They felt that they could not support themselves and had no income. For the women who lived with their parents, the mother was the person who played the important role in the women's decision-making. They were the ones who took their daughters to terminate the pregnancy, because they did not want their daughters or the families to lose social status. One example was Brew, a 16-year-old school student who was living with her parents. She liked going out, and got pregnant with her boyfriend. After the pregnancy was recognized, the boyfriend disappeared. At nearly fourth months of pregnancy, her mother knew that she was pregnant. She took her to many clinics but the providers refused to perform an abortion for her because her pregnancy term was more than three months, and it would be risky. She was referred from the clinic to a shelter, to avoid gossip. After staying at the shelter, her parents decided to let her keep the baby, with their support, so that she could return to school without having to worry.

"When I knew I was pregnant, I only wanted to terminate the pregnancy. I did not want to be a burden. My father and mother are getting old" (father 50; mother 45) (Brew, single, 16 years old, school student).

3. Partner. For the women who lived away from parents or lived with their partner, the partner had the most influence on the women's decision whether to terminate the pregnancy or keep the baby. Most of the women with unplanned pregnancies wanted to terminate the pregnancy because of their partners. Many of them were faced with irresponsible men. The reasons for which their partners were influential included disappearing after having sex, using drugs, beating the women, or having another woman. One example was "On", a young woman of 20 years. She ran away from home and lived with her boyfriend. After living together for a while, her boyfriend started to use drugs and did not take responsibility for anything. She worked alone as a waitress in a restaurant to earn income to spend on the expenses of daily life. Her partner took his friends to their room and used drugs. Sometimes, he disappeared for 2-3 days after he got some money from her. After a while, she was using drugs, as well. Without using any contraceptive method, she was pregnant and tried to terminate the pregnancy by using abortifacient products, but it was not successful. One day, policemen came to their room, and all of them were arrested, but because she was pregnant, the policemen referred her to a shelter.

"He was changed after using drugs. He brought his friends to our room. Sometimes, he disappeared for 2-3 days after he got money. One day, I also was arrested after I came back from buying food" (On, single, 20 years old, waitress at a restaurant,).

Some of the young women expected their partners to come back. After their partner left them during pregnancy, some of them waited and expected their partner to come back, so they kept the baby to term waiting and hoping that one-day their partner would come back and responsible for the baby future.

"…before I needed his love, understand, and responsible. But now, the most important is responsible. I do not want him to come back and live with me. I want him to responsible for the baby. This is the only thing that I need from him" (Koi, single, 24 years old).

4. Friends. During the adolescent period, the young people tended to follow their peers. The majority of them spent more of their time among friends than with their parents. Once they faced an unplanned pregnancy, they tended to consult their friends. The majority of the young people tended to terminate their pregnancy because they wanted to avoid follow-on problems, such as quitting school, disappointed parents and relatives, no income to support the baby, being laid off, and lack of acceptance by society and the community. Most of the young people would follow their friends' advice. Moreover, some of them had friends who had experience of unplanned pregnancy and used to terminate the pregnancy. For these reasons, they tended to terminate the pregnancy.

> "While I was a student, I found many of my friends were pregnant. Sometimes, I went with them. One of my friends was pregnant but her parents did not like her partner. So, they went to an illegal abortion clinic. They used suction as an abortion method" (Koi, single, 24 years old,).

> "My friend said 'if he's no good, then get an abortion'; they told me like it was a normal event" (Nu, single, 20 years old, factory worker).

5. Women's situations. Some women were not in crisis situations when they were pregnant, including being a student, workplace policy prohibiting pregnancy, or having a new baby too soon following the previous one. These situations are explained as follows:

Student status. In the regular primary-to-high school system, married or other students are not allowed to have a baby. Any woman who fell pregnant while studying was perceived as promiscuous and would be asked to drop out of school. Consequently, young women in this situation would terminate their pregnancy. Some, who could not terminate their pregnancy, would hide themselves and/or quit from school to avoid gossip from others in the community.

> "If I keep the baby, first, I will stop studying. Second, how do I avoid disappointing my parents? If I raise the baby, I will quit school. The better way is to terminate the pregnancy. If I go to the clinic on Friday, I can rest on Saturday and Sunday" (Oil, single, 20 years old, vocational school student).

> "I wanted to terminate the pregnancy for sure. If I kept the baby, my mother would suffer dishonor. The people in the community would look down us because I was a student" (Jaw, married, 24 years old, housewife).

Quit job or laid off due to pregnancy. In many situations, the women would quit their job because of premarital sex. They would quit the job by themselves because they wanted to avoid gossip. In addition, in some workplaces, they would lay off any worker who fell pregnant, because that was their policy. Moreover, the characteristics of some occupations, such as standing all day long, were not suitable for pregnant women. In some workplaces, the policy was that they would not accept any pregnant women. If a woman was pregnant, she had to resign from the job.

One example was "Nid", who was 23 years old. She came to work in a factory in Bangkok when she was 15 years old, and had her first partner at the same age. Three years later, she had a child with him and lived with her mother-in-law up-country. She moved to work in a new textile factory, because she did not live with the first partner regularly, and later there was another man who was fond of her and became her second partner. Both partners knew about their love affairs with "Nid". Their love affairs were smooth, until one day "Nid" fell pregnant again. At the second pregnancy, she could not identify who the father was. When her belly was growing large, she quit the job because it was a regulation of the factory not to hire pregnant women. At the second pregnancy, her partners did not take any responsibility and left her alone. She was very depressed and wanted to terminate her pregnancy, but she could not afford the high cost at the fifth month of pregnancy. One of her friends recommended a shelter, so she decided to stay there.

Having the baby too soon. Some of the women did not use any contraceptive methods because they thought that the period a few months after delivery was safe. In some women, their fertility resumed very quickly, so that instead of menstruating, they fell pregnant again. This was a stressful situation for most of the women, especially the low-income women, because they needed to consider trying to get more income to save the family. If it was not possible to earn more income, they preferred to terminate the pregnancy, to forestall the problem.

One example was Jum, who was 24 years old. She had married about 3 years previously, and had a one-year-old boy, and a few-months-old baby. She told me that her husband was using drugs and did not take responsibility for the family. She used to run away from him, but her parents asked her to come back because of the children. When she knew of the second pregnancy, she tried to terminate it using abortifacient products, but it was not successful. She had no choice, only to keep the baby to term and raise it without knowing the future. With the economic crisis, their neighbors also looked down on her family because they were poor.

> "They said, 'the elder one was still young, and then it is followed by a new pregnancy; one baby grasped in a hand, the elder one walking beside, and another one in the belly'. They talked like I was a promiscuous girl" (Jum, married, 24 years old, small food vender).

6. Women's Experiences. *Having unplanned pregnancy or abortion experiences.* Some of the study participants had had experience of abortion. They tended to terminate the pregnancy because they knew the place and the procedure. They did not panic like the inexperienced ones.

Inexperience of sex and pregnancy. Some of the young women did not realize that having sexual intercourse or having sexual intercourse only once could cause pregnancy.

One example was Noi, who was a 14-year-old school student. She participated in a school camp and overnighted at the school. Someone that she did not know raped her that night. She did not realize that it could lead to pregnancy. At the sixth month of pregnancy, her body had changed, and was becoming bigger. Her mother asked her why she was getting bigger, and took her to several clinics for an abortion. All of the providers refused, and one clinic referred her to a shelter. They wanted to terminate the pregnancy but the pregnancy term exceeded the abortion criteria. Hence, they had no choice but to keep the baby to term and delivery. After delivery, they would put the baby up for adoption.

Rumors and misperceptions. Since abortion information was not openly disclosed to public, the women needed to seek information themselves. Some of them gained information by word of mouth. Some information was full of misperceptions about abortion, such as that it was a lethal procedure. One of the young women told the researcher that she heard from her friend that once a woman entered the abortion clinic, the provider would give her some kind of medicine. After she took the medicine, she would feel dizzy and lose consciousness. If the abortion was complete, but the woman still felt dizzy, the provider would take her into a field and leave her there. If she survived, it was only by good luck. If she was bleeding, she might die without anyone knowing or caring. She was told that because abortion was illegal, the providers were afraid of being caught.

"She told me that she used to go there. The provider gave her some medicine. After she took the medicine, she felt dizzy. After the abortion procedure was over, if she were awake and conscious, she would survive…but if she was unconscious or felt dizzy, the providers would take her into a field and leave her there. If she was bleeding, she would die" (Maew, married, 18 years old, housewife).

7. Access to Information. Since abortion is illegal in Thailand, women who wanted to access safe abortion places needed to search for the information themselves. They knew the places by word of mouth, but without any evidence to prove that the clinic they visited provided safe abortions. Some of them took a long time to search for abortion information. When they visited the clinic, the provider could not provide the service requested because the pregnancy term exceeded the medical criteria. For this reason, the women kept their babies to term with no choice.

Example of Rat, 22 years old, 3rd years college student, she was realized of pregnancy when it was three months of pregnancy. After, the pregnancy was confirmed, she went to drugstore and asked for menstruation inducers, and then the seller asked whether she was pregnant. She told him that she was pregnant with her boyfriend. Then he gave her the medicines to take 2 tablets two times a day. After taking the medicines from drugstore, there was noting happen. So, she sought more information towards abortion and abortifacient products from her friends. She tried several regimens by asking her friends to buy for her. At the fourth month of pregnancy, she realized that the abortifacient products would not help her. Then, at the fifth months of pregnancy she searched for an abortion clinic, when she visited the clinic, it was closed. She decided to keep the baby to term.

Some of them, after failing in their visits to the clinics, tried to terminate the pregnancy by themselves, using various abortifacient products, and/or other methods, e.g. massage, or beating the belly. They did not know or realize that there were clinics that could provide abortion services even when the pregnancy term was greater than three months. Moreover, a few cases learned that there were shelters available for pregnant women.

8. Affordable. The cost of an abortion was the major concern for the women with unplanned pregnancies. After they had obtained information and knew the cost of an abortion, some of them took time to save and borrow money from people they trusted to pay for it. When they visited the clinic with the money, the provider could not provide the requested service because the pregnancy term exceeded the medical criteria. Some of the women tried hard to save and borrow the money but it was not successful. They could not get enough money to satisfy the fee requested by the clinic. Some clinics requested for more than 10,000 Baht for cases exceeding three months' pregnancy. Many of them, after failing to have an abortion because of the high cost, just kept the baby to term even though they were not ready to have it. Some of them decided to put the baby up for adoption after delivery, whereas some of them raised the baby alone.

"The provider said 'If I want to terminate the pregnancy, it will cost 12,000 Baht'(I was at the fifth month of pregnancy)" (Joy, single, 24 years old, factory worker).

Some women could not afford the high cost of a safe abortion, or even the low cost of an unsafe abortion. One example was a married woman with her partner, who had one six-year-old child. Later, they moved to Bangkok and worked in a gasoline station. Her husband worked as a cashier, while she worked in a small supermarket in the gasoline station. One night, her husband left her, taking all the money in the cash register, which was more than ten thousand Baht. The gasoline station owner asked her to take responsibility for what her husband did, but she could not. So, she quit the job. At that time, she had been pregnant for 4 months. After her husband left, she tried to find abortion services. Her neighbors at her hometown in Isan (north-eastern Thailand) recommended her to an illegal unsafe abortion clinic, where an old lady performed the abortions. When she visited the place, the old woman examined her belly and said that the baby was already formed. She requested 3,000 Baht for the abortion. However, the woman could not afford it because she only had 500 Baht. With such a small amount of money, the provider refused her request. She returned to Bangkok and her friend recommended her to a shelter.

> "My friend took me to a house located in a remote area upcountry. I only had 500 Baht. When I arrived, an old lady examined my belly. She said 'the baby was already formed'...I told her that I had 500 Baht. She said that if I gave her 3,000 Baht (1 US$ = 35 Baht), she would do it for me. I told her that I could only afford 500 Baht. Hence, she did not do as I requested" (Pen, married, 24 years old, unemployed).

3.3.4. Compromise with Self-conflict and Finding a Rationale for Support

Not only the external and internal factors influenced the decision, as explained. In addition, the women also needed to prevail over internal self-conflicts towards terminating the pregnancy, which may be attributed to Thai norms and culture, in which women are taught to be caretakers for family members, and mothers. Society expects that any woman who falls pregnant will be a mother, without looking at their circumstances. Moreover, as Buddhists, many women have been taught that terminating pregnancy is sinful because it is the killing of an innocent life. With the negative consequences of keeping the baby to term, which were due to socio-economic and internal conflict problems, most of the women decided to terminate the pregnancy after weighing up the outcomes and the long-term effects on their lives, which would be those of mothers responsible for their babies' futures. However, some women decided to keep the baby to term. The following are the rationales, based on terminating the pregnancy and keeping the baby to term.

3.3.4.1. Rationale for Terminating the Pregnancy

Once the women decided to terminate the pregnancy, they would gain support from a person they trusted, get more relevant information, or interact with themselves to overcome their feelings towards terminating the pregnancy, which included 1) terminating a pregnancy was immoral, 2) terminating a pregnancy was risky for their life, and 3) terminating pregnancy was losing a loved one (please see figure 3.2).

Terminating a pregnancy was immoral. Most of the women understood that terminating a pregnancy was sinful, but it was more shameful to disclose premarital sex and pregnancy to society. They compromised with self-conflict by saving their parents' status and making their future come true. Moreover, some women said that they terminated their pregnancy because they did not want to be a burden on their parents, because they already had younger brothers and sisters who needed support from their parents. However, many of them felt guilty after terminating their pregnancy because they realized that it was sinful. It was difficult to delete the pain from their memories after terminating the pregnancy.

> "I felt it was sinful...sinful. I feel regretful up until now" (2 years after terminating the pregnancy) (Yam, married, 19 years old, a singer).

Many of them told the researcher that after they had successfully terminated the pregnancy, they would try their best to make their parents happy and to take care of them. After they had endured the crisis situation, they realized that their parents were passed through a hard time of taking care of them and they were the only ones who were the most sincere. This was one of the ways the women thought, to make them feel better about their sinful action.

"After the providers completed the process of abortion, I felt relieved. I am not a burden on my parents. My mother was the greatest, she really helped me" (mother took her to the abortion clinic) (Nu, single, 20 years old, factory worker).

Some of them felt that terminating the pregnancy was better than raising the baby without any future, and that the baby would feel bad because of growing up without a father like the other children. So, they made the decision that terminating the pregnancy was better than keeping the baby. One of a vocational school student, who was failing from terminating pregnancy, told that:

"If I keep the baby to term and I want to continue my education, I may not have money to raise the baby. If I want to abandon the baby later, how do I do? Should I leave the baby under the public bridge like someone did and was posted on the front page of newspaper. I felt pity for the baby. If I terminate before it formed to be a baby, it is better to leave until facing problem" (Aui, single, vocational student, 19 years old).

Terminating the pregnancy was risky to their lives. Many of the young women realized that the termination of a pregnancy was a risky process, because they would bleed, and it was very painful. Some of them heard, by word of mouth, that it could cause death because of the bleeding. However, they felt strongly about terminating the pregnancy, without being afraid of what would happen after that.

"In my heart, I did not want to terminate the pregnancy because I was scared of the bleeding and the pain. When I arrived at the clinic, I needed to do it. If I kept the baby, my family and I would be in a difficult situation. Moreover, the child would grow up without a father" (Nu, single, 20 years old, factory worker).

Some of the women felt insecure after they went to the clinic, because the setting and environment of the clinic scared them. Some of the young women said that the way to the abortion room was complicated. Moreover, the staff asked them to provide a signature to approve the provider providing treatment for the uterus instead of an abortion. This process made the women feel unhappy, because they felt that the clinic staff did not behave honestly.

"I felt insecure after the abortion process was completed. The physical appearance of the room was complicated, but the medical equipment was clean. However, I thought that they do not feel responsible for our safety because they asked us to provide a signature to approve uterine treatment instead of an abortion" (Nu, single, 20 years old, factory worker).

Termination was losing a loved one. More than half of the young women had had their first experience of pregnancy. Consequently, at the beginning of pregnancy they did not care much about the baby in the womb compare with the women who had experience of pregnancy. The longer the pregnancy period became, the more attached they felt to the baby. They needed to terminate the pregnancy because of their partner. They were irresponsible, disappearing after knowing about the pregnancy, having another woman, or forcing the woman to have an abortion.

> "He begins scolding, beating me. Then, he took me to an abortion clinic. I did not want to go but he forced me to. If I did not go, he would beat me" (Yam, married, 19 years old, singer).

3.3.4.2. Keeping the Baby to Term

A few cases among the women with unplanned pregnancies decided to keep the baby to term without attempting to terminate pregnancy. The women who decided to keep the baby to term would weigh the positives and negatives of pregnancy. They tried to adjust themselves to appreciate keeping the baby, by thinking about morality, the mother's role, and the health risks of abortion (please see figure 3.2).

The moral issue was mentioned the most by the women who had decided to keep the baby to term. The longer the pregnancy period, the more the women could adjust their attitudes, because the baby could react to them as the pregnancy term increased. So, they felt attached to the baby, especially the women who lived in the shelters, because they had a chance to care for other people's babies, and thus realized how hard a time their mothers had endured raising them. In addition, they were among other women who were in the same situation. They compared and shared their experiences with others, which made them rethink, based more on logic than the emotions.

> "We made it (the baby). It does not know anything that we did. We did it wrong and then we are going to kill it. It was wrong to kill even it was only a bloody shape, because the blood was formed from us. We made a life. If we put it up for adoption, it would be OK. But if we kill it, it is sinful" (Gay, single, 20 years old, out-of-school student).

Some of them did not want to take the risk of terminating the pregnancy because they were afraid of bleeding, which would cause death. Moreover, if there were something wrong, the provider(s) might not take responsibility for their lives.

> "Maybe the clinic might not take responsibility for my life, if I was bleeding. When I decided to get an abortion, I did not know what would happen to me" (Ple, single, 16 years old, out-of-school student).

Some of the women did not want to lose the baby even they did not plan to have the baby at the beginning. They lived with their partner happily, but one day their partner left them. They tried to survive and keep the baby to term. After the baby had delivered, the bonding between the mother and her baby became stronger.

> "I felt proud of doing the right thing in my life (keeping the baby). Life should be born and grow up. The baby did not do anything wrong. I am happy to have her because I have a friend. I feel happy... I cannot explain to you" (Dao, single, 24 years old, office employee).

Moreover, it was found that the majority of the women who did not put any effort into terminating the pregnancy lived or worked with a religious group. These religious groups provided counseling and information for the women. In addition, they referred the women with unplanned pregnancies to a shelter. However, most of the women did not need to keep the baby to term or raise the baby. Yet they could not overcome the feeling of sinfulness within the religious environment. Thus, some of them put the baby up for adoption after they learned that there was a choice of adoption available.

> "I knew sister Vienna. She's one of my relatives. She always supported me, provided counseling, and gave my baby's name…Another sister came to talk to me. Then, she referred me to a shelter" (Kai, single, 20 years old, caretaker for the elderly).

Premarital sex, or pregnancy without a responsible man, represented a shameful situation, and because of this, women would seek other ways to relieve their stress. The following are explanations of the young women's reactions towards keeping the baby to term: 1) seeking a place to hiding during the pregnancy, and 2) putting the baby up for adoption after delivery.

Seeking a place to hide. Most of the young women realized that their pregnancies were not consistent with social norms and culture. Consequently, if they were to keep the baby to term they needed to seek a place to hide themselves or go away and stay at a place where nobody knew them, because their belly was getting big. This reaction was to avoid gossip by the people they knew.

For the women whose lived or worked with the religious group after they knew about their unplanned pregnancy, they would help the women find a shelter to hide their pregnancy, because they did not want the women to terminate pregnancy.

In this study, it was found that the women knew about the shelter(s) from reading the magazine named "Cheewit Thongsue", news stories on television, and from their friends and relatives by word of mouth.

> "I decided to visit Ante-natal Care clinic at one hospital in Bangkok (pregnancy term was 5th months). I told a provider that I separated from my husband. Then the provider asked me to meet with the social worker. The social worker recommended me to come to Emergency house at Sukothai (Sukhothai Road). At that time, I thought it was located at Sukhothai province" (Lee, married, 21 years old).

> "I kept searching information about abortion and pregnancy from various magazine and found information of Emergency house at Dong Muang from Cheewit Thongsue, page 59"(Lee, married, 21 years old).

Put the baby up for adoption. Many of the young women who continued their pregnancies felt more relaxed and comfortable while they stayed at the shelter, because they were among women who had the same problems and could share and tell their stories to each other. In addition, they had more time to reconsider the choices. Since many of them were abandoned by their partners, and some of them were raped, the women tended to put their babies up for adoption after delivery. The women who decided to put their babies up for adoption would feel free after they left the shelter, but some of them missed the baby because they had a chance to raise and feed the baby before departure.

> "I definitely put the baby for adoption. If I have money like others, I may not want to do so. Moreover, I have parents who are getting old and still need my support. Also, my family is poor. If I raise the baby by myself, it might face a difficult life. Even, it is clever, but I can support only up to grade 10 or 12. If he/she lives with the adopter, she/he might have a better life" (Lee, married, 21 years old)

Actions. The help- or health-seeking patterns of the young women with unplanned pregnancies are presented in section 3.4 in more detail. The details cover the explanations of the women who decided to keep their babies to term and the women who terminated their pregnancies.

3.4. Actions: Help- or Health-Seeking Patterns of the Young Women with Unplanned Pregnancies

In Thai culture, pre-marital sex among young women is stigmatized. Thus, most of the women delayed making a decision about whom to consult to solve their problems and many of them sought help from other people (popular sector) instead of the formal healthcare system, because most of the young people perceived that the formal healthcare sector only provided physical care. When they confronted an unplanned pregnancy, which was not a physical illness, they did not visit healthcare practitioners. Once, they had made the decision to terminate the pregnancy, they sought services from folk or professional sectors when they needed more advanced services, after they had gained information from other people, in order to solve the problem. In this section, the data focus on how and why people choose a particular sector and its patterns.

The results derived are from an analysis of 45 young women with unplanned pregnancies, from both shelters and communities, using an in-depth interview technique. It was found that when the pregnancy was confirmed, most of the women would consult the "popular sector", which included their partners, friends, parents, and relatives. After they gained support and information, most of them visited drugstores for self-medication. A few cases sought help from traditional healers for abortifacient products. About one third of the women consulted the professional sector about terminating the pregnancy. A few cases managed by using their hands to beat the womb, in order to force the baby out. Some women did not put any effort into terminating the pregnancy.

Some of the women attempted using various ways to terminate the pregnancy, and if it were successful, the process of seeking help would end at that point. However, it was found that the majority of the women were not successful as planned after attempting to terminate the pregnancy. Thus, some of them would stop all efforts and continue the pregnancy to term because they had no choice. Some of them would stop because they felt guilty about hurting the baby. However, the majority of them would try other ways to solve the problem. Many of them went to private clinics, some visited drugstores/grocery stores again, to try as hard as they could to terminate the pregnancy (please see figure 3.3).

Help –or Health Seeking Patterns Model

The model of health-seeking behavior of the young women with unplanned pregnancies can be explained by using the most effort, and then explaining the patterns by which the women made decisions to solve their problems. There were four different patterns, as follows:

3.4.1. Did not Put any Effort into Terminating the Pregnancy

Once the pregnancy had been confirmed, the women in this group would consult their partner, friends, relatives, or parents, to gain information and support. All of them accessed a shelter or a place to hide their pregnancy because they got information from the people they consulted. To avoid gossip and embarrassment, the women in this group would stay in the shelter or a new place. After delivery, the majority of them raised the baby by themselves. Some of them put the baby up for adoption because of partner abandonment, study, or financial problems.

When comparing the women who consulted the popular sector (partner, friends, neighbors, relatives, or parents) and the women who did not consult the popular sector at the onset of knowing about the pregnancy, it was found that the women who consulted the popular sector were more ready to raise the baby by themselves.

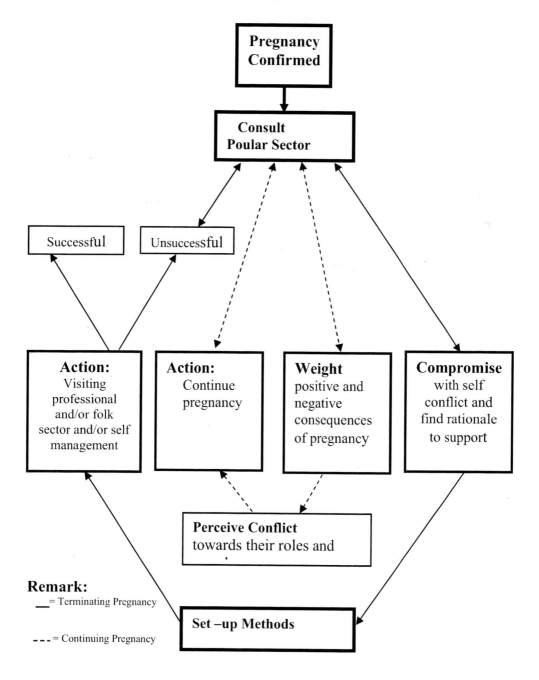

Figure 3.2. Decision Making Process among the Young Women with Unplanned Pregnancies.

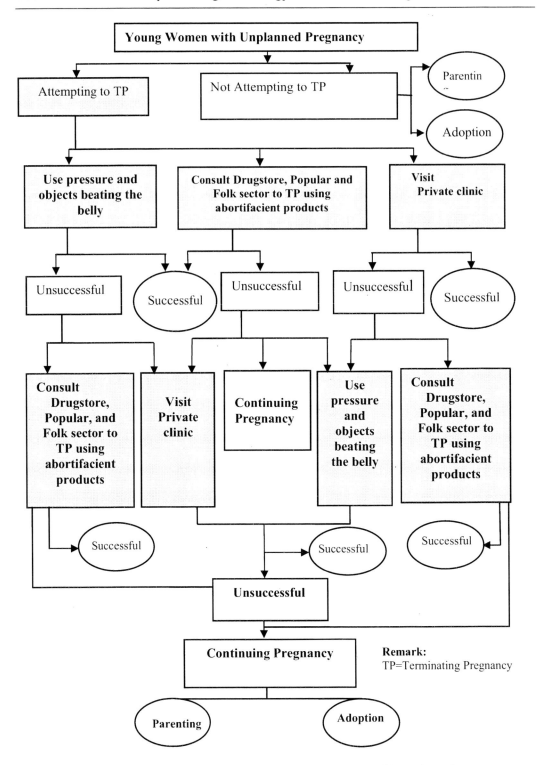

Figure 3.3. Patterns of Help- or Health-Seeking among Young Women with Unplanned Pregnancy.

Examples of Women with Unplanned Pregnancy who did not Put any Effort into Terminating the Pregnancy

Miss Gay (1) was 20 years old. She was an orphan because her parents divorced when she was about 10 years old. Her mother took her to an orphanage at Pattaya, which belonged to the Catholic Church. She never returned to visit her. She was referred to Bangkok for further study supported by the Srichumpaban Unit, which was a nuns' group. While she was studying in grade 12; she met a man who became her boyfriend later. He was a final year vocational school student. After a few months they had sex and she fell pregnant. At the onset of pregnancy, she did not realize that she was pregnant, even though she felt nauseous and liked eating sour fruits. Moreover, missing her menstruation did not make her suspect pregnancy because she had had irregular menstruation periods from the onset of puberty. When the signs and symptoms were more obvious; she decided to visit a private clinic with a friend. At the clinic, the urine pregnancy test showed positive. She was in shock and dared not to tell the sisters, who were her caretakers. Some of her friends recommended an abortion, but her best friend told her not to do it because it was a sin. She followed her close friend's advice. She told and discussed her pregnancy with her boyfriend, and moved to live with him to gain a sense of family and get support from him. When she had lived with him for 2 months, she learned that he had another girlfriend before her. They started quarreling and she was seriously beaten. She returned in deep depression and stayed at a dormitory belonging to the Catholic Church.

She planned to keep the baby to term and raise the baby herself because she did not want the baby to be an orphan like she was. Moreover, because she was a Christian, she believed that one life was valuable. She quit school and started a new class at a vocational training center that belonged to the Catholic Church. After completing the course, she intended to find a job to earn income to raise her baby.

Miss Kai (2) was 20 years old. Her mother had died when she was young. Her father, who was a public driver, had remarried. Kai lived with her step-mother and her father until she graduated in grade 12; her mother-in-law hit and beat her quite often. Before she left home to find a job, she was hit and was hurt on the head with a big piece of wood. She got a new job as a caretaker at a Catholic house for ageing people. A few months after working at the house she met a construction worker and they fell in love with each other. After two months, she unknowingly fell pregnant, until the sister who was in charge of the house asked her to visit a clinic for testing. She suspected that Kai might be pregnant because her belly was getting big. At the clinic, it was found that she was 4 months' pregnant. She was in shock. She decided to tell her boyfriend about the pregnancy. He showed no responsibility for the outcome and told her that he had a wife. Kai was very stressed and depressed. After the sister knew about her situation, she referred Kai to a shelter that also belonged to the Catholic Church.

Kai did not want to terminate the pregnancy because she received counseling from the Catholic sisters. She planned to put the baby up for adoption after delivery because she could not support or raise the baby. Without support from her parents, she could survive on a salary of only 2,500 Baht per month, and it was difficult for her to raise another baby.

3.4.2. Put Effort to Terminate Pregnancy

There were 3 patterns of help-or health seeking patterns of the young women with unplanned pregnancy who put effort to terminate pregnancy, which were explained as follows:

- **Terminating the Pregnancy Using Pressure and Objects to Beat the Belly**

The women in this situation were both single and married. Most of them had a very negative attitude towards their partner because the partners had abandoned them and had not taken responsibility. However, none of the women dared consult anyone else at the beginning. Thus, they were stressed and tried to find some relief from the stress. When they were at their utmost level of stress, they would beat their belly to make the baby out from the womb. If it were successful the women would feel relieved. The women who could not solve the problem would seek further help through consultation, to relieve their stress. However, after beating their bodies, they felt guilty and afraid that the baby would be deformed if it did not come out. Some of them visited private clinics for terminating pregnancies but the pregnancy term exceeded the medical criteria, and some of them did not visit private clinics because they had no money. So, they tried using abortifacient products, but it was not successful. Once these efforts had failed, they tried to seek a place to hide their pregnancy, to avoid gossip. After the baby was born, if the partner was not responsible, the women tended to put the baby up for adoption. However, if the partner showed responsibility, the women tended to raise the baby themselves.

Examples of Women with Unplanned Pregnancies Beating the Belly

Miss Koi (1) was 24 years old. She was the youngest of four brothers and sisters. Her father had died two years previously, and her mother had remarried. She met her boyfriend, who was a musician, while studying at a vocational school. Without the approval of her parents or relatives, she lived with him after graduation. When she fell pregnant, she decided to keep the baby because her partner promised to take responsibility for the family. While she was pregnant, her partner frequently came home late. One day, he left her to go to Bangkok, by claiming that there were more jobs in the city, but lost contact after that. At the sixth month of pregnancy, she followed him to Bangkok and found that he had another woman, who had just delivered a baby boy. She was furious and very depressed. At the seventh month of pregnancy, she delivered a premature baby girl, because she was depressed and beat the womb very often; she beat herself whenever she felt depressed.

When the researcher met and interviewed her, she had delivered a one-month-old baby girl. She had reunited with her parents and her own family and her boyfriend's family gave her support. She decided to keep and raise the baby, and was living happily with the baby.

Miss Oam (2) was 18 years old and studying at a vocational school. Her parents divorced because her father had many wives. She could not communicate with her new mother-in-law. Thus, she decided to live alone at the dormitory with her father's support. She also worked as a waitress in a restaurant in the evening after classes ended, to earn more income to support her studies. Later, she met a man who was a customer in the restaurant; they became friends, and soon had sex. She realized that she was pregnant at the fourth month of pregnancy because her friend asked her to get a pregnancy test. The test result shocked her because it was positive. She did not expect that she would be pregnant because she only had sex with him once. She contacted him and told about the pregnancy, but he showed no responsibility and told her that he had a wife. She was very distressed. She said that, at that time, she hated the baby and tried to hit her belly using her hands and beer bottles to drive the baby out of her womb. Finally, she delivered a baby girl and put her up for adoption.

When the researcher met her, the baby was already living with her new parents. She told me that she felt very sorry when she saw others holding a baby. She cried and showed the researcher the baby's picture.

- **Consult Popular and Folk Sectors, and Drugstores for Abortifacient Products**

The women in this group were both married and unmarried. Once the pregnancy was confirmed, they were unprepared to have it. So, many of them consulted their friends, relatives/parents, or their partner who was the most important. If their partners were prepared to be responsible for the baby and accept the women as his wives, the women did not terminate the pregnancy and raised the baby by themselves. However, it was found that their partners abandoned many of them. Thus, they tended to terminate their pregnancies. Since many of them had financial problems and could not afford the cost of an abortion at a clinic, they tended to manage by themselves using various abortifacient products.

The women tended to purchase abortifacient products from drugstores or grocery stores. Few of them sought abortifacient products from traditional healers. Less than half were successful, and the majority was not. The outcomes of their efforts varied greatly because of external factors, which were separate from the physical conditions of the women, including pregnancy term, abortifacient product regimen, and duration utilizing the product. Moreover, the psychological condition, the acceptance level of the baby and the relationship with the partner, were the main pressures causing the women to persist in doing as planned, or canceling the effort.

The women in this group tried as hard as they could to terminate the pregnancy with varying results, as mentioned above. After trying for a while, some of them were successful, but the majority of them were not. The women who failed to use abortifacient products successfully tended to visit private clinics, and/or hospitals to seek further services. As a last resort, some of them might beat the fetus or jump up and down on the floor, hoping that it would help to terminate the pregnancy. Once there was no choice, they decided to continue the pregnancy, and needed a place to hide themselves during the pregnancy, until delivery. After delivery, some of them decided to raise the baby by themselves, but some of them put the baby up for adoption.

However, some of the women who had information about shelters came to stay at a shelter immediately after they had failed to terminate the pregnancy using an abortifacient product. They got information about the shelters from their friends, relatives, neighbors, or printed material. The women who did not know about the shelters would persist in trying to terminate the pregnancy until they felt that there was no way left to help them.

It is important to note that the women who were seeking help/health in this pattern took a long time and used various abortifacient products regimens. Thus, when they realized that it was not successful, it was too late for them to try another solution. Also, it was found that the women who failed to terminate their pregnancies by using various abortifacient product regimens without the support of their partners, friends, relatives, or parents would put the baby up for adoption rather than raise the baby themselves. This was because of the financial aspect, which was the main problem. The women who did not have information of availability of shelters or adoption services just kept the baby to term without knowing the future. Some of them decided to give the baby to their relatives/parents as an adopter after delivery.

Examples of Women with Unplanned Pregnancies who Consulted Popular, Folk, and Professional Sectors using Abortifacient Products

Miss Pung (1) was 18 years old. She had married about 3 years previously with parental approval. She could not use contraceptive pills due to the side effects and her husband did not want to use condoms. Thus, after 3 years of living with her husband, she already had her third pregnancy. The first pregnancy occurred a few months after living together. At the second month of that pregnancy, her husband became addicted to amphetamines, so she decided to terminate the pregnancy at a private clinic, with a successful result. A few months after the abortion she had her second pregnancy. She decided to keep the baby to term and raise the baby by herself because her husband had quit amphetamine use and was back to normal. After the baby was 4 months old, she fell pregnant again. At the third pregnancy, she was worried and not ready to have the baby, because she already had one child to take care of and their family income was not stable. She had no money to buy milk powder, and the baby got only sweetened condensed milk, for which infant consumption was forbidden. With the family crisis situation, she decided to terminate the pregnancy by utilizing various abortifacient products. She went to drugstores and took 2-3 times higher doses of the products than the regular doses recommended by the providers to regulate menstruation. However, after she took the product it was not successful. Thus, she asked friends to buy the abortifacient product for her again, with the same outcome; the product could not push the fetus out. Finally, she went to see a traditional healer in the community for uterine massage but was refused.

When the researcher met her, it was her seventh month of pregnancy; she was very sad, her face showed worry and depression because she had no choices left. She still wanted to terminate the pregnancy; she asked me whether any places would agree to perform an abortion in the seventh month of pregnancy. If there were no choice, she said that she would give the baby to relatives, because she could not afford to raise another baby.

Miss Koi (2) was 21 years old. During her last years at vocational school, she ran away from home. She moved to live with her boyfriend who was also a student. She fell pregnant a few months after living together because her boyfriend did not use a condom and she was scared of using contraceptive pills because they made her get fat. So, her partner used withdrawal as a contraceptive method, but it failed. When she realized she was pregnant, it had only progressed two months. At that time, she quarreled with her boyfriend because he had another woman and he showed irresponsibility and was unconvinced that Koi was pregnant to him. Koi felt very sad and stressed, and decided to consult her friends who used to terminate pregnancies while studying. She went with her friend to an unsafe abortion place, which looked like a house. After her friend completed the process, she went to rest at her apartment with heavy bleeding for many days. She felt exhausted and looked pale. With that bad experience, Koi decided to use abortifacient products instead of the services at that house. She took one bottle of "Ya Satee" and one sachet of "Ya Tanjai" together. She felt dizzy and drunk, just like drinking alcohol. The next morning, she had heavy bleeding and a big bloody tissue mass came out that looked like a bees' nest. She told me that the big bloody tissue mass might be a baby, which had just formed. She felt scared when she saw the bloody tissue. It was difficult to make up her mind that she did not kill the baby, because she tried to compensate by thinking that it was just formed; it was just blood. She felt that terminating the pregnancy while the baby was just formed was better than terminating it when the blood had formed into a baby-like shape. After that horrible morning, she suffered from bleeding for another two months. She had heavy bleeding, which required her to use a sanitary pad every day. She was very weak and looked very pale. She went to see a doctor at a private clinic after one month of bleeding. She told the researcher that she was afraid to be blamed by the doctor if he examined her vagina, because he would know that she had undergone an unsafe abortion. However, the doctor did not blame her and he ordered iron and vitamin tablets for her to take every day.

When the researcher met her, it was nearly a year after she had the experience of terminating the unplanned pregnancy. At present, nobody in her family member was aware of her pregnancy because she kept it secret and there was no evidence, because the product of pre-marital sex had already come out and gone down the toilet.

- **Visiting the Professional Sector using Modern Medicine**

The women with unplanned pregnancies in this group were both married and unmarried. They could afford the cost of terminating a pregnancy at a private clinic. More than half were successful, while the remainder failed because the pregnancy term exceeded three months. If they wanted to terminate the pregnancy, the cost was very high, and they could not afford it. Some of them went to a clinic and changed their minds because they saw scenes of women bleeding after finishing the process and waiting to go home. Thus, they changed their minds from terminating the pregnancy to continuing the pregnancy, because of the consequences of terminating the pregnancy.

Some of the women who failed to visit a private clinic or hospital would visit drugstores or grocery stores to try again, utilizing abortifacient products, especially women who were afraid of the consequences of abortion. However, the majority of those who had experienced failure to terminate their pregnancy by visiting a private clinic or hospital, which was their first choice, kept trying.

Finally, most of the women in this group tended to raise their babies after delivery because they were more financially ready than the women who visited drugstores or grocery stores at the first attempt. The results implied that the women who visited a private clinic as their first choice were financially better off than the women who visited drugstores or grocery stores. Thus, when faced with unsuccessful termination of pregnancy, more tended to raise the baby than put it up for adoption.

Examples of common types of unplanned pregnancy, visiting the professional sector to terminate the pregnancy

Miss Yam (1) was a 19-year-old singer. Her parents worked in a massage parlor that belonged to her aunt. She became a singer after completing grade 8 because her friend asked her to quit school. By the age of 19 years, she had had three partners. At the age of 17 years, she met her first boyfriend. While living with the first boyfriend, she was beaten. A few months after living with him, she fell pregnant because she did not know about contraception. She was not ready to have a baby at all. However, she did not consider terminating the pregnancy. During her pregnancy, she was still beaten by her boyfriend. She decided to leave him and return to live with her parents. One day in the fourth month of her pregnancy, she lifted a Pepsi crate and there was heavy bleeding. She found out that it was a miscarriage after visiting a private clinic the next day. Some time later, she met her second boyfriend, and moved in to live with him. She fell pregnant again. Her second boyfriend forced her to terminate the pregnancy. He divulged that he had a wife with a 3-year-old child. He beat her and forced her to go to a clinic even though she did not want to. She could not refuse to give in to him because he beat her harder and harder. Finally, he took her to a private clinic when she was in the fourth month of pregnancy. The clinic requested 7,000 Baht but they only had 5,000 Baht. After her boyfriend negotiated, they paid 5,000 Baht. She felt very bad after completing the abortion with the second boyfriend because he showed no responsibility for her or the baby. Moreover, her parents did not like him, so they subsequently separated.

She told the researcher more about the scene at the clinic, which was still fresh in her memory even though it was nearly a year. The process began with waiting in the waiting area for registration. After that, she was called to change clothes upstairs for preparations to starting the procedure. After she had finished changing her clothes, she was asked to lie down on a bed. Her eyes were closed with big eye pads, so that she could not see anything. She was given an injection after she had lain down, without any conversation. She felt scared because she did not know what would happen next. She wanted to change her mind and go back home because her parents did not know that she would terminate the pregnancy. If they knew, they might be upset because they did not want her to do it, but she dared not to tell them because her partner forbade her. If she told her parents he would beat her. After the injection, she fell asleep a few minutes later. When she woke up, the procedure was completed. She had been asleep for about 2 hours. After she had rested for a while, they allowed her to go home without recommending anything.

When the researcher met her, she had the third partner, who was a mechanic. They were living happily together. However, she still felt bad for terminating the pregnancy. She believed that it was a sin to kill the life of a baby.

Miss Noi (2) was 14 years old. She studied in grade 8 in a school. She did not realize that she was pregnant until her mother asked, "Why are you getting fat?". She could not tell her mother what was wrong with her. Her mother decided to take her to a clinic for a check-up. They were in shock and crying when the doctor told them she was in her sixth month of pregnancy. She recalled one night in the past six months when she went camping at school, and a stranger came into her room and raped her. She kept it secret and did not divulge it to anyone. Moreover, she did not realize what the consequences would be. Her mother decided to tell her aunt and grandmother. They were all miserable. Her mother taught her that the baby was disgusting because it was not her child. Then she took her to many clinics to seek an abortion. All of the providers refused to terminate the pregnancy because her pregnancy term exceeded the medical criteria. At the last clinic, the staff recommended she stay at a shelter while she was pregnant. She felt better after staying at the shelter because she was ashamed to live in the community, and ashamed for her parents.

When the researcher met her, she was eight months pregnant. She had arrived at the shelter a few days beforehand. The researcher felt depressed, seeing a young, innocent student with a big belly. She told me that she did not see the man's face or know who he was. She and her parents decided to put the baby up for adoption after delivery.

Miss Brew (3) was 16 years old. She studied in grade 9. She lived with her parents; her mother was a housewife and her father was a guard. She liked to go out shopping with her friends. She had many friends, both boys and girls, who did the same. Later, she had sex with her boyfriend unintentionally. However, she realized that she was pregnant when she missed her menstruation for two months, because she had a regular menstruation cycle. She kept it secret from her parents, but told her close friends. Her friend warned her not to have an abortion and she agreed. At nearly fourth months of pregnancy, she had an abnormal discharge from her vagina, and told her mother about it, but did not tell her about missing her menstruation. Her mother took her to a clinic and found out that she was pregnant. She apologized to her mother and told her the truth. Her mother told her father, and instead of being angry, he asked her to keep the baby. They forgave and understood her situation. However, her mother did not want her to keep the baby because she wanted her to complete studying at school. She took her to an abortion clinic, but the providers refused because she was in her fourth month of pregnancy. They referred her to a shelter. Her mother came to visit her often at the shelter.

> "After I could not terminate pregnancy (because the pregnancy term was more than 3 months). Then, my mother called BUG 1113 and talk to a social worker at a hospital. Then

she recommended me a shelter. After that my mother took me to the shelter" (Brew, single, school student, 16 years old).

When the researcher met her, her mother was coming to see her. They decided to keep and raise the baby themselves. Brew told me that her mother would raise the baby for her while she went to school. Also, they would tell their neighbor that the baby was their nephew.

3.5. Women-Provider Interaction

Information about the interaction of the women and the providers was derived from indepth interviews during Phase I of data collection with 45 young women who had experienced unplanned pregnancy. This information on reproductive health services for young people will aid understanding of the status of services available for young people, so that gap(s) can be identified, and the health system and personnel can be strengthened, to serve the needs of the target population. When the young women made their decisions, they had to interact with themselves to find the rationale to support their decision, especially the decision to terminate the pregnancy. The first choice for the majority of the young women with unplanned pregnancies was to terminate the pregnancy. Most of the women felt that the clinic that they visited was run by professionals, providing safe abortions, because of their friends', neighbor, relatives, and parents hearsay. Once it was not successful, the women would interact with themselves and others, in order to keep the baby. Some women decided to go to an Antenatal Care Clinic for a check-up and/or try to find a place to hide their pregnancy. Premarital sex or sex among students are not socially accepted, and therefore most young students try to keep it confidential. The larger the belly gets, the more stress they feel. The following illustrate the feelings and interactions when women visit the professional sector, including drugstores, abortion clinics, Antenatal Care Clinics, and shelters. In addition, a few cases visited the folk sector or traditional healers for abortifacient products.

Interaction with Drugstore Personnel

Most of the women who purchased abortifacient products at drugstores had particular product(s) in mind, and therefore visited them in a short period of time. For this instance, they rarely had a chance to have any dialog with drugstore personnel. They felt that this service sector was convenient and comfortable for them just to walk in, unlike other health facilities where they met the providers and had to answer questions.

"At that time, I did not know about abortifcient products. Thus, I bought Ya Satree at the drugstore because it indicates that pregnant women should not use. Hence, I took 2-3 tablespoon at a time as indicated in the leaflet. But nothing had happen" (Lek, single, 23 years old)

Some of the respondents revealed that if they wanted to repeat another abortifacient regimen at the same drugstore, they would ask a friend to purchase the products for them because they were afraid that the drugstore personnel would be suspicious and ask them about the purpose of using them.

Interaction with Providers at the Abortion Clinic

Once the young women with unplanned pregnancies made the decision to terminate the pregnancy, they interacted with themselves and other persons they could trust to support the choice. If there was at least one supportive person, and they had enough money, they felt confident about terminating the pregnancy. Most of them thought that it was the best solution, because they would return to their prior status, without their parents or others knowing. Not every woman who decided to go to an abortion clinic to terminate her pregnancy was as successful as planned, due to the clinic's conditions and the women themselves. Most of the respondents who visited an abortion clinic revealed that the providers performed abortion for women who were pregnant for less than three months. If the pregnancy were over three months, the providers would refuse or refer the client to a clinic that agreed to terminate pregnancies at any term.

> "The doctor examined by belly, and asked me whether I had sex. I said yes, but only once. Then, he asked me to check for urine. It was found that I was pregnant (6 months). I told him that I was not ready to have a baby. He asked me to talk with my partner. I told him the truth that my partner did not know that I was pregnant. He warned me that it was dangerous to do abortion at this period because it was risky to my life. However, he recommended another 2 clinics but they refused to do so" (Oam, single, vocational school student, 18 years old).

However, the respondents revealed that it was very expensive, and depended on the month of pregnancy; it ranged from 8,000–20,000 Baht. With the very high cost, many respondents gave up and decided to keep the baby to term without knowing their future.

> "The provider told me that they would do it (5 months of pregnancy) but it cost 20,000 baht. At that time I had only 10,000 baht. So, I asked the provider to give me a special rate. They said the last price would be 18,000 baht" (Oil, single, vocational school student, 20 years old).

Low-priced clinics were also not well accepted by the young people. One respondent revealed that her friend recommended a clinic that charged 2,000 Baht for terminating a three-month pregnancy. She hesitated to go there because she had heard that women suffered from bleeding after visiting the clinic. However, she went to the clinic with her friend, but gave up after seeing the clinic from outside, because she was unsure that the providers would provide a safe abortion.

A Difficult Situation for Young Women Walking Into an Abortion Clinic

However, walking into an abortion clinic was a crisis situation for many young women, especially students. They felt unsure about doing as planned because of their inexperience, but they needed to confirm what the abortion clinic really looked, even though they had some information about abortion from friends and various other sources. At first, they decided definitely to terminate the pregnancy, but many of the young people were uncertain about what would happen to them. The idea that it was sinful to kill the life of the baby also made the women distressed. Some of them made a new decision after visiting the clinic, because they were not sure that their lives would be safe.

One example was a respondent who was a pregnant vocational school student. When she realized her pregnancy, she spent a few days for gathering information on abortion and collecting money. She drove a motorcycle alone to a clinic recommended by her friend, and drove around the clinic three times before entering it. She was afraid of seeing anyone she knew while visiting the clinic. Moreover, she was not sure what would happen to her once she went in.

> "I felt nervous. I drove the motorcycle around the clinic three times. The fourth time, when only a few people were passing by, I decided to stop the motorcycle and walk inside" (Oam, 18 years old, vocational school student).

Having entered the clinic, most of the young women felt shy and dared not to ask any questions. However, if the clinic provided a private place for history taking and counseling, the women would feel relaxed, warm, and comfortable enough to divulge their confidential information. If the situation were opposite, the women would feel bad and be more stressed.

> "At first, I felt shy walking into the clinic. But I thought that there are others who have the same problem as me. This made me feel better. However, I was not alone, my mom went with me" (Brew, 16 years old, secondary school student).

> "When I arrived at the clinic, I didn't know how to start. The staff at the clinic was not nice to me. She did not pay attention to me. She did not ask me about my problem or offer any service. I decided to talk to her first. That area was an open area. Luckily, there were no other people, otherwise I would not have dared to talk " (Oil, 20 years old, vocational school student).

The Scene and the Cost of the Abortion Made the Women Change Their Minds

Some of them returned from the clinic after entering because they had seen women who had just had their pregnancies terminated and they looked exhausted. This reaction implies that the women did not get counseling so that they might not have had an opportunity to explore every dimension of abortion and the other choices that were available.

> "I went to the clinic by myself. While I was waiting, after agreeing upon on the price of the abortion, I saw a few women with pale faces come out of the room after the procedure was complete. I felt bad; I was scared when I saw the blood. At that time, I was not sure about doing as planned. I told the service provider that I changed my mind. The provider said 'don't worry, it's up to you'. Then I went home and did not want to do it any more" (Porn, single, 18 years old, factory worker).

Mostly, the women returned from the clinic without terminating their pregnancy because of the high cost. If the pregnancy term exceeded three months, pregnancy termination was very expensive. Many women revealed that the clinic asked for more for than 10,000 Baht. Thus, some women returned to get more money, but some could not afford the high price and gave up and continued the pregnancy. (Please see section 4.3.3 under affordability, which provides more detail).

Women Need Counseling Before the Final Stage

Once the women met the providers, most of them needed counseling, and many women went to the clinic with the most common doubt being what would happen to them. Moreover, many women revealed that they had used abortifacient products or menstruation-regulation products during pregnancy and they were afraid that the products had affected the fetus. If the fetus had formed into a baby-like shape, most of the women would hesitate to do so. They felt guilty about doing it because it was like taking the life of their baby. Moreover, the Buddhists believed that taking lives was sinful, especially the lives of innocent babies who have done nothing wrong.

However, most of the women revealed the same story, i.e., they did not get any counseling from the providers and they dared not ask for it. However, a few clinics provided counseling when the pregnancy term exceeded three months, and the providers would refer them to other clinics or to shelters. The women were afraid to ask the providers questions addressing the issues of concern to them, because it was more difficult for them to start asking questions than to walk into the clinic. They were afraid that if they did ask, the providers might ask more questions that they did not want to answer. Hence, they were growing increasingly gloomy during the process of terminating the pregnancy. Without proper counseling before terminating the pregnancy, some women felt distressed, and this feeling would leave a black scar on their hearts forever.

> "I felt afraid. I felt it was sinful. I wanted to get out of the bed when the provider started the process and go home" (Yam, married, 19 years old).

> "After the injection, there was a pressure in the lower abdominal area. I felt that I might not survive and I was not sure that it would be successful" (Jaew, married, 24 years old). (During this conversation, the interviewee was crying. The researcher stopped the interview for a while, waiting until she felt better before starting again).

With doubts about what would happen to them and their babies, most of the women needed psychological support from the provider and their significant person, because during the pregnancy termination process, physical pain and psychological trauma commonly occur to young people.

> "The provider in my home town does not care about the clients, if you want to do it then you do it. If you are unsatisfied and do not want to do it, you go home. When I felt pain and was nervous, the provider scolded me and told me to stay still or go back home" (Pung, married, 18 years old).

In addition, one 18-year-old respondent lived in a low-income community. She believed that if a woman did not recover after terminating the pregnancy, the staff at the clinic would take her out into a field. They were afraid that if someone came and saw women who had just had their pregnancies terminated at the clinic, they would be arrested, because it is illegal to terminate pregnancies, and the owner(s) and the provider(s) would end up in jail. If the women were left in a field after the abortion, some would recover and some would die of blood loss.

> "One of my friends, who had experience of abortion, told me that the provider gave her some medicine that made her felt dizzy. During this time, if a woman felt dizzy for a long period of time, the clinic's staff would take her out into a field and leave her there. If she were lucky, she would be safe. If she had bad luck, she would die due to blood loss" (Maew, married, 18 years old, housewife).

Interaction with the Provider at the Antenatal Care Clinic

When faced with an unplanned pregnancy, most of the women wanted to terminate it. However, some young women knew only after the first trimester. Thus, this group had fewer choices than others who knew in the early months of pregnancy. As discussed earlier, terminating a pregnancy is very expensive after the first trimester. Thus, most of the women in this situation gave up and continued their pregnancy to full term. However, a few cases decided to keep the baby to term and visited the Antenatal Care Clinic (ANC) because of stigmatization. The cases who visited the ANC were less sensitive to social stigma, e.g. the married women.

Young Single Women Did Not Dare to Visit the ANC Clinic

Once the women realized that they could not terminate the pregnancy, some decided to go to the Ante Natal Care Clinic (ANC), but most of the young women did not go to the ANC clinic because they were afraid that they would meet someone they knew. Lack of money was also a main reason for many women deciding not to go to the ANC clinic. Married and out-of-school adolescents tended to go to the ANC clinic more than others.

"I visited the ANC clinic at the fourth month of pregnancy after the abortifacient products were not successful" (Tan, married, 18 years old, housewife).

Factors Deterring Young Women from Visiting the ANC Clinic

The cost of the services was not the main concern of the young people because this was their first experience of pregnancy. Some of them could utilize the thirty-Baht scheme. Their main concern was stigmatization, because some of them were students or unmarried. They were afraid that the providers would blame them or have contempt for them.

"I paid 30 Baht for services apart from the medical fee. The thirty-Baht card helped me at the time of delivery" (Lek, single, 18 years old, factory worker).

The distance from home to the ANC clinic was also an issue for concern, because many of the young women with unplanned pregnancies had separated from their partners. Moreover, most of the women lived alone. Some lived with their parents, relatives, or friends, but at the beginning, most of them hide their pregnancy from others. Consequently, they preferred to visit the clinic by themselves. For this reason, if the clinics were near their residences, it would be helpful for married women. For the unmarried women, distance was not a problem because stigmatization was the main concern.

"Far or near is a concern because I consider that it is possible for me to go alone" (Maew, married, 18 years old, housewife).

Apart from the external factors that deterred young women from seeking ANC services, the interaction with providers at the clinic was a concern. The women would have negative or positive impressions, which depended on the provider's approach. If the providers provided services with a positive attitude and approach, the young women would feel good. However, if the providers had negative attitudes towards premarital sex, they would feel bad.

"Before visiting the clinic, I thought they would ignore me. When I visited, I found that they cared because they came and asked whether the baby was hungry. I felt good" (Lek, single, 18 years old).

At the ANC clinic, if the young women received a positive service approach, they would feel warm and dare to consult the providers. Most of the women were afraid to ask questions because they did not want to be blamed by the providers. They would keep the questions to themselves and try to find the answers on their own. They might seek information from friends, relatives, and various media. With unreliable sources of information, they might get inappropriate answers.

Interaction with Friends and Providers at the Shelter

The shelter is a place where women with unplanned pregnancies can hide themselves from others. In this place, they meet other women with the same problem. They have a chance to interact with themselves, other women, and providers. Women are assigned to stay together in the big or small room depending on the design of each shelter. Some shelters have small income-generating activities for the women, such as sewing and cross-stitch. One shelter had a cooking group to generate a small income for the women. These activities made the women work together as a team, and this created a friendly atmosphere, where it was easy to get together, share experiences, and care for each other.

Sadness and Happiness Are Common at the Shelter

When many people stay together, it is common for them to quarrel. Sometimes, the women argued with one another because of stress, because many of them still had no solution to how they could manage their lives in the future. Some of them felt that they had nowhere to go and nobody supported them. In these stressful situations, some women could control their tempers, but some could not. Women stayed at the shelter for periods ranging from a few days up to many months. One case stayed at the shelter for nine months; she had nowhere to go because her parents had divorced and they had both remarried. She used to live with her mother but her father-in-law raped her. So, she ran away to seek help from the shelter. However, women who stayed for a long time got together as a group and became powerful. Thus, it was difficult for the newcomer to join and communicate with the earlier group. Sometimes, the newcomers who could not adjust themselves would suffer from isolation. Some women tried to get together with other newcomers. Thus, there was conflict at the shelter when there were larger numbers of women staying together. However, this conflict lasted for a while, and then they got together and later became friends. One respondent compared the situation to teeth and tongue, which sometimes fight and sometimes are friendly. However, some women realized that the women were different in many ways, including background, thinking, and age. This rationale made them apologize to the others.

> "I felt good at the beginning when I came here. When I stayed on longer, we started quarreling and fighting" (Tan, married, 18 years old, housewife).

> "Women who stay here are separated into groups. As a newcomer, I felt that it was difficult" (Lek, single, 23 years old).

> "It should be (Fighting with one another). Women came from different families and were staying together in the same place. They had different backgrounds, ways of thought, and age. Some were very young, some old, so they did not get along well" (Aui, 19 years old, vocational school student).

Some of the women even disclosed a conflict situation among themselves at the shelter. However, there were many positive outcomes of staying at the shelter. Many women said the same thing; that they felt better when they decided to stay there. They stayed at the shelter with other women who were in the same situation, so they could compare their situation with others that were worse than theirs. Thus, they motivated themselves into believing that they needed to fight for themselves and the baby. At the shelter, they were not alone; they had a person they could walk in and consult at any time. Moreover, the activities arranged by the providers at the shelter included a workshop for mother and baby, recreational activities, handicraft work, and other assigned group work. These activities made them feel relaxed, happy, and enjoy living with the other people. Once they became friends, they helped each other by encouraging, telling them about their experiences, sharing their knowledge, and supporting the routine activities of the shelter.

> "Sister always emphasizes every week that everyone has their own problems, so we must not let problems assail us or make us blue. Let beautiful thoughts come into our minds" (Su, single, 19 years old, babysitter).

"When I lived outside, there was social pressure because I was pregnant without a responsible partner. Living at the shelter, there are women who all have problems. We share our history and experiences. I also had a chance to ventilate by sharing my experiences. I feel better" (Ploy, single, 17 years old).

"It made me realize (by staying at the shelter) that there are other people who are in worse situations than me" (Brew, student, 16 years old).

"There are many reasons that made me feel better. Some of my friends have more serious problems. For me, I already have a solution. After I deliver, I can still raise my baby but others cannot. They need to give the baby up for adoption" (Pu, single, 21 years old, unemployed).

Encouragement and Arranging Activities Are Provider Roles

Most of the women with unplanned pregnancies who visited and stayed at the shelter had failed in the use of abortifacient products or had financial problems going to an abortion clinic. Thus, they would come and stay at the shelter, to hide until delivery. At the beginning of their stay at the shelter, some of them did not have any solution for their future. Some women were depressed, however, interaction with providers through counseling, workshops, and assigned routine activities, helped them to feel better because they started building relationships with the providers and with others. The women trusted them and felt that they could help them solve their problems. Whenever they had problems their friends could not help them solve, they would turn to the providers. In addition, group counseling helped them gradually to make them stronger by learning and sharing experiences with each other. By learning from other people's experiences, the women could reflect on themselves and understand themselves better. Once they could understand themselves, they could establish their goals and be ready to go back into the community. One example was Porn, who was an 18-year-old, single factory worker. She was alone after her parents had separated. She did not know any of her relatives. She was pregnant because a man she knew raped her. She came to stay in the shelter because her friend told her about it. At the shelter, she could make the decision to put the baby up for adoption and go back to work in the new factory. The second example was Su, who was a babysitter. She was pregnant at 19 years of age to her boyfriend without the knowledge of their parents. She decided to raise the baby but she did not know how to manage her life because her boyfriend lived in another province and she lived alone in Bangkok. Afterwards, she consulted a provider and got a better idea, which was to put the baby into the nursery provided by Ban Tantawan, which was a non-governmental organization.

"I decided (to put the baby up for adoption) while I was staying here. If I took the baby with me, how could I raise it? I have no money, which I need to pay for the costs of accommodation, milk powder, baby sitter, and daily living costs. I do not know how to earn an income to pay for these costs. Moreover, I have no experience of raising a baby. If I put the child up for adoption, the baby and I will be better off. The provider gave me information on how to raise the baby. She also asked me how I could raise the baby by myself. If I put the baby up for adoption, the baby will have a future. The providers will check the adopters before giving the child to them" (Porn, single, 18 years old, factory worker).

"First of all, I consulted my close friends, but my friends had no ideas. Then, I consulted providers regarding a temporary place for raising the baby. The providers suggested that I needed to wait in a queue" (Su, single, 19 years old, baby sitter).

DISCUSSION AND RECOMMENDATIONS

Decision-Making Process and Help – or Health-Seeking Pattherns of Young Women with Unplanned Pregnancies

As evidenced in the above discussion, the in-depth interviews indicated that once the pregnancy was confirmed, they would feel worried and seek help or consultation from the popular sector first, which included the partners, parents, and friends. After they had gained more information and interaction with themselves, their partners and/or parents, they would make the decision by themselves, which was based on their status, attitudes, relationships and the consultation outcomes. If they decided to keep the baby to term, they would not seek further service from the professional sector but might consult the popular sector to seek support. The majority who decided to terminate their pregnancies would seek further professional services, especially at drugstores, which were most popular among low-income young people seeking abortifacient products for self-terminating the pregnancy. It was popular because there would be less interaction with the providers. Few of the young people utilized government health facilities due to the abortion laws, beliefs and stigmatization that deterred the individual and the family member from seeking services there.

However, if the women failed in their use of abortifacient products, they tended to seek more efficient facilities, such as private clinics. Some of them were successful, but some were not. The unlucky women would try as hard as they could to seek ways to terminate their pregnancies until they felt that it was not possible to do as planned, and then they would abandon the attempt with no hope for the future.

Regarding the health-seeking patterns of the low-income young women with unplanned pregnancies, it was observed that the women started with simple self-medication, then moved towards more complex efforts i.e. taking higher doses or mixing abortifacient regimens, beating, jumping up and down, or visiting private clinics to terminate the pregnancy. However, because of premarital sex, which is a major cause of unplanned pregnancy, it was different from other health problems. The women's ability to seek and utilize certain help- or health-services is socially controlled by laws, regulations, culture, and norms. However, none of these factors were studied, but they do impact upon the choices of young women with unplanned pregnancies.

To examine this research question more extensively, it is important to compare the help - or health-seeking patterns among young women with unplanned pregnancies. According to Kleinman's (1980) healthcare system framework, the professional sector consists of modern medicine, while the folk sector is, in general terms, traditional medicine. The popular sector is the sector where health problem are first defined and help- or health-seeking behaviors are initiated. It is also the sector where multiple layers of factors (individual, family, society/peers, and community) interact to shape and influence these help, or health, beliefs and behaviors. Hence, the findings for help or healthcare seeking in this study are consistent with Kleinman's theoretical framework of the healthcare system.

The Characteristics of Service Facilities That Meet the Needs of Young Women with Unplanned Pregnancies

Expectations of Women with Unplanned Pregnancies of the Types and Characteristics of Services Needed

The provision of sexual and reproductive health services (SRH) to young women with unplanned pregnancies need to be sensitive to the characteristics of service provision, because values, norms, and culture control their help- or health-seeking behaviors. Thus, to have them change their utilization to the existing service interventions, they need to be involved in all of the processes of service provision. According to the in-depth interviews and observations at the shelter, unplanned pregnancy was not a physical illness; hence, women in this situation need more psychological support and counseling. While they were in a crisis situation, they had nobody to counsel them, and many of the young women mentioned that if they had got counseling they might have arrived at a better solution and pass through the crisis more smoothly. They also said that they needed shelter to hide in while their belly was getting big. Moreover, they needed support setting up with the baby as a single mother, because many of them faced an unfaithful man and were abandoned. The following are details of each type of service needed:

Counseling once pregnancy is confirmed. The in-depth interviews indicated that before knowing about the shelters, many women expressed the same view, that they had nobody to advise them how to manage when they were in trouble. If they had someone to counsel them they might have better solutions instead of living under a dark cloud. They said that telephone counseling was more convenient and comfortable for them before they came in to utilize the services. Most preferred female counselors with a friendly manner.

Shelter to hide in while the belly was getting big. During the first trimester of pregnancy, most of the women still hid their pregnancy in large clothes because their belly was not very big. However, during the second to third trimester, their belly was getting big. The in-depth interviews indicated that the bigger the belly was, the more stress the women felt. As there are a limited number of shelters throughout the country, shelter is available only in the big cities and Bangkok. Moreover, few women know about the shelters, thus, some of the young women with unplanned pregnancies ran away from their community to new places where nobody knew them. The women with bigger bellies who still lived in the community would feel embarrassed. Hence, if there were more shelters available, the women would endure less stress and could cope with their problems. Moreover, the in-depth interviews with the women in the shelters revealed that the shelter is a good place where women who have the same problem can share, support, and learn from each other's experiences. It helps them feel stronger and ready to return to their communities.

Nursery care a few months after delivery. The in-depth interview results revealed that the women who failed to terminate their pregnancies would be very worried about the baby's future, because they had no income and had been abandoned. Hence, many of them felt worried about how to manage their lives after they delivered. Many women said that they needed a place to nurse their baby at least for 3 months, so that they could earn income and set up the new life first; then they would be ready to take care of the baby. However, the results from the in-depth interviews with the social workers at the shelters revealed that the women needed to wait in a queue for a nursery room for their baby, because there were limited numbers of free nursery care services available.

Support for setting up a new family. The in-depth interviews indicated that the majority of the women had had their first unplanned pregnancy. Moreover, due to inexperience, youth, immaturity, and lack of income, many of them needed support at the beginning of setting up the new family.

Counseling to prevent recurrent unplanned pregnancies. Apart from the services and activities provided at the shelters, explained above, the in-depth interviews indicated that the women expected counseling, which was very important. If they were in a shelter, they preferred to have face-to-face counseling. The counseling would support them and prevent them from recurrent unplanned pregnancies.

The in-depth interviews of the young women with unplanned pregnancies indicated that friendly administrative processes included: 1) a private area for history taking, 2) anonymity, 3) no identity card required, 4) no need for the parents or caretakers to approve of using the service. The minimum requirement was confidentiality, to make the young women feel relaxed and comfortable to utilize the services with a good impression.

Apart from the types and characteristics of services needed, public relations and information dissemination to potential users about the services should be widely available, so that the women would have more alternatives to taking abortifacient products or visiting a private clinic to terminate the pregnancy, even when they did not want to.

Recomendations

Based on the in-depth interviews and FGDs, solutions and recommendation for various health systems emerge from this study, which are listed as follows:

Pharmacist Association, Pharmacy Association, Drugstore Club of Thailand, and Other Related Pharmacy Organizations

Local business/drugstore as a focal point for increasing access to prevention and care for young women with unplanned pregnancies. Based on the in-depth interview study of the help-or health-seeking patterns of the young women with unplanned pregnancies, most of the women did not seek help or services from the formal government healthcare system. Thus, the provision of comprehensive unplanned pregnancy prevention and care services should be established through collaboration from both private and public sectors. Drugstores should be an initial source of collaboration and referral, since the majority of the young women with unplanned pregnancies sought abortifacient products, menstruation regulators, and other essential products from this source.

The most important is that drugstore should be the best option for providing primary prevention services, education, and information for both unmarried and married youths. Information towards emergency contraception, and other related contraceptive technologies to the potential users to prevent unplanned pregnancy should be provided through this channel.

Health Department, Ministry of Public Health

Healthcare providers in all levels of health facilities need to screen for unplanned pregnancies. In the in-depth interviews with the providers of obstetric services, it was suggested that nurses or clinicians should assess young people's pregnancies, and make more detailed decisions in determining planned or unplanned pregnancies. In addition, in assessing the women decision-making on the choices for unplanned pregnancies, they should consider whether to continue or terminate the pregnancy, so that the provider can provide appropriate counseling and support, which will increase women's decision-making capacity in areas of life, sex, and pregnancy.

Establishing comprehensive sexual and reproductive health systems. Health Department should play as an umbrella's role for all organizations dealing with sexual and reproductive health (SRH) provision. The organization should collaborate by segmentation to provide a comprehensive SRH package, to make a broader contribution in delivering SRH services and preventing unplanned pregnancies among young women, such as counseling and testing for pregnancy, STI/HIV; diagnoses for abnormal vaginal discharge or menstruation; treatment and care for STI/HIV; post-abortion care; and contraceptive technologies.

Clinics or small hospitals may be better targeted to provide secondary services and care, including antenatal care, delivery, postpartum care, and well-baby care. Tertiary care, including general hospitals, university hospitals and large private hospitals that are well-equipped and have medical specialists, should provide more complex health services, including diagnosis, delivery, treatment services, and any complications or abnormal pregnancy or delivery.

Moreover, all organizations should provide couple counseling and information to prevent unwanted pregnancies in the future. Most important is that the services should ensure that all women who in different situations are effectively referred to facilities with services and encourage the use of such services. For example, youths who visit drugstore personnel for abortifacient products might be given a referral to see a counselor(s) at a women's organization or at a shelter. In this way, "friendly service" could be linked to several types of healthcare facilities.

The referral network should include drugstores, clinics, community health centers, hospitals and shelters. Moreover, the beneficiary group, the school and home, should be strengthened to network with the service facilities, so that it can be assured that women with unplanned pregnancies and other SRH problems are fully assisted. All the organizations need to work together to develop formal acceptable practice guidelines or protocols to help ensure that each organization provides specific services as indicated in the protocol and have clear criteria for referral.

Training of providers. The Health Department should provide training of service providers at all level of service facilities on delivery of gender-sensitive, gender equality, and quality of services (i.e., positive interpersonal relationship, confidentiality, privacy, in counseling and management, and referral).

Provision of emergency contraception, i.e., emergency contraceptive pills, and postcoital insertion of IUD. Based on the in-depth interviews majority of the sexual intercourse had happen by chance. So, all level of health care facilities need to provide and made available of the emergency contraception to the person who are in needed.

Strengthening counseling services, which are essential for unplanned pregnancies women. In the in-depth interviews, most of the women mentioned that they needed counseling once the pregnancy was confirmed. Counseling services should provide both hotlines and face-to-face. Moreover, it should add on male and couple counseling to their routine services, which emphasize on female. They should have specially trained personnel to provide counseling to young people about unplanned pregnancy. They should also be able to provide comprehensive counseling to respond to women's emotional and physical needs, and their other concerns related to their trouble.

Adoption services. As shown in the in-depth interviews, abortion was most popular among the young people with unplanned pregnancies. One underlying reason was that many young people did not know that an adoption agency was available. For this reason, information about this agency should be provided to women who will potential want to have an abortion, so that they have one more choice for consideration. Moreover, the government needs to support and strengthen this type of service and make it available nationwide.

Male involvement in reproductive health. The in-depth interviews indicated that the majority of unplanned pregnancies were attributable to males, so that it is important to develop programs targeting males, aiming to change their attitudes and behaviors, to be more responsible for sex and its consequences.

Involve young people in all stages of program development. It is important to involve young people in all stages of program development because they can help ensure that the programs are relevant to young people's real needs. Moreover, they can help identify communication channels, activities, and messages to other young people in meaningful ways.

Evaluation. The umbrella organization should be responsible for evaluation of all components of the program, to determine the effectiveness of preventing current and future pregnancies among young people, and expanding upon those shown to be effective.

School Masters, and Teachers

Enhancing sex education in the school by collaboration with the home. The in-depth interview and structured interview results showed that unplanned pregnancy could occur at the age of 12, or older. Even though they are at a low risk compared to those who engage in risky behavior, such as drug taking, alcohol consumption, or smoking, it is important to prepare them to make responsible decisions when the rare opportunity to have sex occurs. Life-skills decision-making regarding sex, unplanned pregnancy, its consequences and prevention, should be taught in school by collaboration with the home before completion of grade 6. Sex education should be comprehensive and consistent. This will help the young people make decisions based on rationality, responsible choices made with an awareness of the available options. Strategies for school training are as follows:

Expanding the training of teachers. Teachers who train in life skills should be trained on a regular basis in transaction and teaching techniques.

Involving young people. Since peers have more influence on sexual behaviors, the school program should promote more active involvement of young people in all stages of program development to increase the effectiveness and marketing of its activities. Feedback should be sought from the young people regarding what kinds of support would be helpful for them to prevent unplanned pregnancies, and what things the providers should keep in mind when providing services or addressing issues of sexuality. All the responses would help improve the program and increase its acceptability among young people.

Encouraging the school system to work with the home. Since parents also impact upon their children's sexual behavior, the school program should support parents developing and nurturing their children. Moreover, the school system should work with the parents to assess the developmental needs of the young people and identify programs, resources, and tools to assist them in making responsible choices. In addition, they could share information to prevent substance abuse at all levels of childhood development, because substance abuse is likely to be associated with unplanned pregnancy.

Encourage the school system to work with the community. The community environment also impacts upon the sexual and reproductive health of young people. Thus, the school system should work with community leaders to assess and develop a youth-friendly environment.

Family

Parent-child relationship. As indicated in the findings that family played important roles on unplanned pregnancy among young women. Parents are the key people who play in shaping the perceptions, beliefs, and behavior of the young people towards adolescent sexual and reproductive health. If the relationship between the young people and parents is weak, then they will turn to their peers and follow their advises. However, if the relationship is strong the young people will turn to their parents whenever they have problems.

To create a good relationship among them, parents need to change of attitude, including understanding their own sexuality in the a way that enabled them to relate positively with their children on sexuality; and understanding of sexuality and adolescent psychology, communication, and counseling skills.

Representative of Shelters

P.R. the services to the potential users. Based on the findings from in-depth interviews, there were a few young women who knew about the shelters services. Majority of them were refereed from private clinics, churches, or words of mouth. If they knew about shelters' services, it would help them released from the crisis, and had more choice.

Create shelter's image as a second home for the women. The shelters should create images as a second home for the women. Also, it should be a place for all young women who want to get information, education, counseling, and cares towards women issues.

Continue to support the women who want to raise the baby themselves. The women with unplanned pregnancies who want to raise the baby themselves need a follow-on support at least for 3 months. Due to they are young and less experience on caring the baby, thus, the shelter needs to create a systems to help support and follow-up after the women go back to their family, or community.

Create the self-help group in the shelter and continue to strengthen the network. During the women who face the same crisis are at the shelter, it is important to create a friendly environment by having them get together, and sharing experiences. Counselor at the shelter should play as a facilitator at the beginning in establishing group activities. After they are settled, the facilitators should let them manage the group by themselves.

Decision Makers, Policy Development, and Women's NGO(s)

Provision of one stop comprehensive services. The health care facilities should provide a comprehensive one-stop service for the young women with unplanned pregnancies to reduce crisis that they may encounter at the long processes.

Established youth friendly shelter nationwide. At present, all the shelter s provide services for the women at all age group. However, majority of the unplanned pregnancy women are in the adolescent stage. Thus, it is worth to create youth friendly environment and services for the young women while they are staying at the shelters.

Relief regulation in educational system. Based on the findings from in-depth interview, the main reason of terminated pregnancy was that the young women were student. So, to relief regulation in educational system would help those adolescents having more choices rather than terminating pregnancy.

Revise of business or labor rules and regulations. The business, labor rules, and regulation, which are unfair, and discriminatory, i.e., deterrence of pregnancy during employment, no paid for maternity leave need to be revised.

Revise of the abortion law. The most important in issue of unplanned pregnancy is that the abortion law, which is unfair to the women, need to be revised. Also, the law needs to decrease in restrictions for doctors to perform induce abortion and less stringent conditions than the existing one. Moreover, it should allow the women to access to induce abortion if needed. This effort will decrease risks of unsafe abortion especially those performed by "quacks" and self-management using several of abortifacient product regimens.

ACKNOWLEDGEMENTS

We would like to express our sincere gratitude and deep appreciation to all the young women in the five shelters and communities of Bangkok Thailand who patiently, candidly answered, and shared more on their grief story.

Last, we are greatly indebted our family who are always shares their love, support, and encouragement.

REFERENCES

Asian Institute for Development Communication (AIDC). (1999). "Module 1: Knowledge and Information on Adolescent Reproductive Health." Promoting Advocacy for Adolescent Reproductive and Sexual Health Through Effective Communication: A Training Program for Media Practitioners, Bangkok, Thailand, November, 1999.

Boonmongkon, P. et al. (2000). "Thai Adolescent Sexually and Reproductive Health: Implications for Developing Adolescents' Health Programs in Thailand." Center for Health Policy Studies, Faculty of Social Sciences and Humanities, Mahidol University at Salaya, Thailand.

Burack R. (1999). "Teenage Sexual Behavior: Attitudes Towards and Declared Sexual Activity." *Br J Fam Plann. Jan; 24 (4)*: 145-8.

Chuamanocharn, P. et al. "Community Drug Utilization and Health Service System Development Project: Situation of Community Drug Utilization, Problems, Obstacles and Ways to Solve Through Drugstores Services in Payao, Lampang, and Nan." Pharmaceutical Science faculty, Chiengmai University, 2000.

Ford, N., and Kittisuksathit, S. (1996). "Youth Sexuality: The Sexual Awareness, Lifestyle and Related-Health Services Needs of Young, Singles, Factory Workers in Thailand." Institute for Population and Social research, Mahidol University at Salaya.

Gray, A. and Punpuing, S. (1999). "Gender, Sexuality and Reproductive Health in Thailand." Institute for Population and Social Research. Mahidol University, Thailand.

Gramzow, R and Major, B (1999). "Abortion as Stigma: Cognitive and Emotional Implication of Concealment". *Journal of Personality and Social Psychology, v. 77 no 4*, (oct. 1999), p.735-45.

Kanchanaraj, T. et al. (2001) "Situation of Community Pharmacy Services: Problems of Drug Utilization in Khon Kaen and Udornthani and Recommendation for Promoting Rationale Drug Use in the Community" Part of Community Drug Utilization and Health Service System Development Project Phase I, Khon Kaen." Community Pharmacy Division, Pharmaceutical Science Faculty, Khon Kaen University.

Kleinman, A. (1980). "Patients and Healers in the Context of Culture: An Exploratory of the Borderland between Anthropology, Medicine and Psychiatry." Comparative studies of health care systems and medical care. London England: University of California Press Ltd.

Koetsawang, S. (1993). "Illegally Induced Abortion in Thailand." Paper Presented at IPPF SEAO Regional Programme Advisory Panel Meeting on Abortion, Bali, Indonesia, 29-30 October.

Nelson, K. (2000). "The Effect of Youth Friendly Services on Service Utilization among Youth in Lusaka, Zambia." A dissertation submitted to Tulane University in conformity with the requirements for the degree of Doctor of Public Health, New Orleans, Louisiana, USA.

Naravage W. et al. (2005). "Factors Affecting Decision Making of Low-Income Young Women with Unplanned Pregnancies in Bangkok, Thailand." *Southeast Asian J Trop Med Public Health, Vol 36*, No.3, p 775-782.

Manisha G.; Sunita B.; and Hemlata P. (1997)." Abortion Needs of Women in India: A Case Study of Rural Maharashtra." *Reproductive Health Matters, no. 9*, p.77-86.

PATH (2001). "Adolescent Health Center: Ban Wai Sai." Paper present at the Asia Pacific Conference on Reproductive Health (APCRH), Manila, Philippines, February.

Pisulbutr S. (1997). "Thai Economic Classification." *Statistics Association Journal, 23*: 20.

Punyawuthikrai, P. et al. (2001). "Community Drug Utilization and Health Service System Development Project (subproject: Bangkok)." Bangkok: Pharmaceutical Council (Thailand).

RHO (2002). Internet site: http:www.rho.org

Ratchukul S. (1998). "An Unwanted Pregnancy and Decision to Terminate Pregnancy." A dissertation submitted to Srinakarindtrawiroj University in conformity with the requirements for the degree of Doctor of Social Development, Bangkok Thailand.

Sainsbury, J. (1997). "The New Inequality-Women Workers's lives in Thailand and the Philippines." A Catholic Institute for International Relations Briefing.

Sertthapongkul, S and Phonprasert, P. (1993). "Causes of Unplanned Pregnancy and Decision Process for Abortion: A Case Study at Bangkok Private Clinic." Journal of Development Administration, Bangkok, Thailand.

Soonthorndhada, A., (1996). "Sexual Attitude and Behaviors and Contraceptive Use of Late Female Adolescents, Bangkok: A Comparative Study of Students and Factory Workers." Institute for Population and Social Research. Mahidol University, Thailand.

Warakamin, S. and Boonthai N. (2001). "Situation of Induced Abortion in Thailand." Paper Presented at the Seminar on Problems of Terminated Pregnancy, Bangkok, Thailand, 6 August, 2001.

WHO (1997). Internet site: http:www.who.int/reproductive-health/publications/MSM/97.16

UNESCO Regional Clearing House on Population Education and Communication Asia and the Pacific Regional Bureau for Education Bangkok, Thailand. (2001) "Package of Research Briefs Series 2: Adolescent Reproductive Health". December, 2001

In: Thailand: Economics, Political and Social Issues
Ed: Randle C. Zebioli

ISBN: 978-1-60456-583-6
©2009 Nova Science Publishers, Inc.

Chapter 6

YU DUAN PRACTICES: THE SIGNIFICANCE AND IMPLICATIONS FOR WOMEN'S HEALTH IN NORTHERN THAILAND

Pranee Liamputtong
School of Public Health, La Trobe University
Bundoora, Victoria, Australia 3086

ABSTRACT

In this chapter, I address traditional confinement beliefs and practices among Thai women in northern Thailand. The chapter is based on qualitative research involving in-depth interviews with 30 women in Chiang Mai province. In northern Thai culture, the period after birth is considered as the most vulnerable period of a new mother and of her life. For a period of 30 days, known as *yu duan* in northern Thailand, she is in a state of vulnerability to ill health and diseases. During this period, a new mother follows many dietary and behavioural proscriptions and prescriptions. It is clear that traditional beliefs and practices are still carried on by the women in this study. It is, therefore, imperative that these traditions need to be taken into account in providing postpartum care to Thai women. I contend that a serious consideration of traditional beliefs and practices may go a long way in improving women's birthing care in Thailand and elsewhere.

INTRODUCTION

Cross-cultural evidence has pointed to the importance of the period immediately following birth (Sich, 1981; Laderman, 1987; Chu, 1996; Cheung, 1997; Uzma et al., 1999; Lewando-Hundt et al., 2000; Liamputtong Rice, 2000; Whittaker, 2000, 2002; Liamputtong, 2007a, b). In many cultures, a new mother is perceived as vulnerable to harmful agents, natural and supernatural. Within these cultures we see numerous proscriptions and prescriptions imposing on a new mother and her newborn. Similar patterns of postpartum practices have been observed in many traditional societies (Pillsbury, 1978; Manderson,

1981; Sich, 1981; Cosminsky, 1982; Kitzinger, 1982; McCormack, 1982; Laderman, 1987; Jodan, 1993; Chu, 1996; Symonds, 1996; Townsend and Liamputtong Rice, 1996; Cheung, 1997; Liamputtong Rice, 2000; Liamputtong, 2007a, b).

Postpartum beliefs and practices among women in Thailand have also been observed. More than four decades ago, Hanks (Hanks, 1963) studied postpartum rituals including *yu fai* (lying by a fire) ritual among women in Bang Chan village, central Thailand. This was followed by a publication of a Thai scholar on confinement customs (Anuman Rajadhon, 1987). In the last three decades, some western researchers have conducted research relating to postpartum beliefs and practices in Thailand (Muecke, 1976; Mougn, 1978; Poulsen, 1983; Whittaker, 2000, 2002). Arguably, these writers suggest that postpartum beliefs and practices are beneficial to women's health care after giving birth.

In this chapter, I examine the persistence of postpartum beliefs and practices in the context of northern Thai society. In particular, I attempt to find out if women in the north still believe in and adhere to traditional practices at a time that modernisation has reached almost all sectors in the Thai society. I propose that traditional beliefs and practices have a positive impact on women's health in Thailand and these should be incorporated into women's birthing care.

METHODOLOGY

The Women

I conducted in-depth interviews with 30 Thai women who are living in Chiang Mai, Northern Thailand in 1999. Fifteen women were recruited from Chiang Mai City and fifteen from Mae Chantra sub-district (fictitious name), 49 km from the municipality of Chiang Mai. This was to ensure that women from different socio-economic backgrounds would be participants. Women from Chiang Mai City were mainly from urban and middle class backgrounds with a higher educational level, while women from Mae Chantra sub-district were from a peasant background and have lesser educational attainments and income. The majority of the women in this study have recently given birth but only a few were pregnant at the time of this study being conducted.

The theoretical sampling technique set out by Strauss (1987) was used to determine the required number of women. Accordingly, interviews shall continue until little new data is being generated. In this study, the sample was restricted to 30 as there was little new data being generated after the 30th interview. The women's socio-demographic characteristics are presented in Table 1.

Women in Chiang Mai City were firstly recruited through my personal network as well as through a snow-ball sampling technique (Gubrium and Holstein, 2001; Liamputtong and Ezzy, 2005; Liamputtong, 2007c); that is, women were asked to nominate or contact their friends or relatives who would be interested in participating in the study. Women from Mae Chantra sub-district were firstly recruited with the assistance of a health worker at Mae Chantra hospital antenatal clinic. A snow-ball sampling technique was then applied. Through these networks, all women approached agreed to participate in the study. Each woman was informed about the nature of the research and her participation. An informed consent form (in Thai) was signed once the women agreed to participate in the study.

Table 1: Demographic characteristics of Thai women, n=30

Age	
< 20	1
20-30	12
31-40	15
41-50	2
Religion	
Buddhist	30
Marital Status	
Married	28
Widowed	1
Living together	1
Length of Marriage	
1-5 ys	15
6-10 ys	7
11-15 ys	5
16+	3
Education Level	
Primary	11
Secondary	7
Diploma	4
Tertiary	8
Occupation	
Home Duties	4
Self-employed	6
Government Officials	9
Farmer	3
Casual/Part-time job	8
Number of Children	
0-1	14
2-3	15
4-6	1
Family Members in the Household	
Spouse and Children	11
Spouse Children and other Relatives	19
Family Income (in baht)	
<5,000	10
5,001-10,000	6
10,001-20,000	6
20,001-30,000	2
30,001-40,000	2
>40,001	4

Method

This chapter is based on a larger study on the cultural construction of childbearing and motherhood among women in Chiang Mai, northern Thailand. An in-depth interviewing technique was adopted to elicit information (Gubrium and Holstein, 2001; Liamputtong and Ezzy, 2005). This is an appropriate method since the goal of this study is to uncover and understand the women's subjective experiences of childbearing and motherhood. In this way, culturally relevant and sensitive care can be designed and implemented (Liamputtong and Ezzy, 2005).

The women were individually interviewed about their childbirth experiences and their background information on socio-demographic characteristics. The interviews were held in the women's homes. All interviews were conducted in Thai. Each woman was interviewed once and the interview lasted between one to two hours, depending on the participant. Women were asked several main questions and these were prompted with questions to verify their explanations such as reasons for their actions/non-actions. All interviews were tape-recorded for later transcription and analysis. The study was undertaken between December 1998 and July 1999. However, all interviews were conducted during March and April 1999. The study was approved by the Faculty of Health Sciences, La Trobe University Ethics Committee. As the study was approved by my institution, permission to conduct the study was granted by the Ethics Committee of Chiang Mai University in Thailand.

The in-depth data concerning their childbirth experiences was analyzed using a thematic analysis method guided by phenomenology (Liamputtong and Ezzy, 2005). In this study, the interview transcripts were used to interpret how women described their perceptions and experiences of traditional confinement practices in their everyday lives. The focus of my analytic approach was on identifying not only themes and patterns that the women gave their accounts of their lived experience (Liamputtong and Ezzy, 2005), but also "contradictions, ambivalence and paradoxes" (Lupton, 2000, p. 53) of their narratives, as presented in the following section. Women's explanations concerning their traditional confinement beliefs and practices are presented and their names have been changed for confidentiality. My interpretation of the data relies heavily on women's accounts given in the in-depth interviews. Due to time constraints, I could not employ other means such as extensive participant observations for data collection. Hence, I cannot claim a triangulation of information generated.

RESULTS

The Significance of *Yu Duan* Practices

In northern Thai culture, as in other cultures (Pillsbury, 1978; Manderson, 1981; Sich, 1981; Cosminsky, 1982; Kitzinger, 1982; McCormack, 1982; Laderman, 1987; Jodan, 1993; Chu, 1996; Symonds, 1996; Townsend and Liamputtong Rice, 1996; Cheung, 1997; Liamputtong Rice, 2000; Whittaker, 2000, 2002; Liamputtong, 2007a), the period after birth is considered to be the most vulnerable period of a new mother and of her life. For a period of 30 days she is vulnerable to all sorts of ill health and diseases. Hence, women believe that after giving birth they must be extremely cautious about their activities and diet. One grave consequence of not doing this is that a woman will experience *lom pid duan*; which literally means wind illness caused by doing something wrong in the postpartum month. Minor symptoms of *lom pid duan* include thinness, weakness and being easily affected by allergy. *Lom pid duan* may also be manifested as bodily aches and pains. The aches and pains may appear in later life, but they may also appear soon after the confinement period is ended. More severe symptoms manifest as dizziness and pain in the head. It is believed that these two symptoms caused by wind rising or pushing into the head and resulting in dizziness and pain. Most importantly, *lom pid duan* is embodied as symptoms of madness. And if the woman is severely affected by *lom pid duan*, she may die.

There are many aspects of the etiology of *lom pid duan*. *Lom pid duan* can be caused by bad odours from food or other things including perfume and soap. Saijai, an urban educated woman, explained:

> During *yu duan*, women must be careful about breathing in bad smells. When my mother was cooking, she would ask me to breath in *ya dom* (smelling medicine) or close my nose with a piece of cloth. She was afraid that I might become allergic to smells and hence even after I finish my *yu duan* I would have this bad smell and become dizzy whenever I smell anything and I would also vomit.

Some foods may not have bad odours, but considered *pid* (wrong to the body) also causes *lom pid duan*. This is known as *khong salaeng* in general (Liamputtong Rice, 1988; Whittaker, 2000; Liamputtong, 2007b). These foodstuffs include beef, crab, pickled vegetables and fruit, and fresh vegetables particularly green melons. Malai, a rural poor woman, told me that:

> After I came home from hospital I stayed for *yu duan* and was afraid of eating wrong food; you know *khong salaeng*, pickles stuff like that, as I was afraid that I might become mad and it would cause a stomach problem in my baby when I breast-fed her too. I only ate grilled dried fish and pork liver and some cooked vegetable with egg. If I eat wrong food I will become mad and this is what people call *lom pid duan*.

Women believed that being exposed to cold water during *yu duan* also causes *lom pid duan*. A cold shower is prohibited during *yu duan* period. Malai also explained that most often if a woman breaks this taboo, the ill symptoms would appear when she is older. She remarked:

> People told me that if you take a cold shower, when your child grows up you will have aches and pain on your legs. They say when the baby is still small you won't have these symptoms, but when you are over 40 years old that is when the symptoms will appear and this is because I have done wrong things during *yu duan*.

The Practices of *Yu Duan* Ritual

As in other cultures (Pillsbury, 1978; Manderson, 1981; Sich, 1981; McCormack, 1982; Laderman, 1987; Chu, 1996; Symonds, 1996; Cheung, 1997; Townsend and Liamputtong Rice, 1996; Liamputtong, 2007a), during *yu duan* period lasting for one entire month (*duan*), a new mother must be confined to her bedroom or home. She must wear a hat or cover her head with a piece of cloth or scarf. She must wear a long-sleeved top, long trousers and socks. All the windows and doors will be closed. This is to prevent the cold wind entering the body. Failure to do so may result in aching bones and bodily pains and other ill health in later life. As Saijai elaborated:

> During *yu duan* period, I must wear a hat and cover my head. I must wear a long-sleeved top and socks. Why do I have to do this? Well, my mother told me that the wind will get into my body easily if I don't do it. And this will cause pain in the bones. When I get older, I will get sick easily; I will be sick often.

Suriya cited the example of her sister who suffered from *lom pid duan* due to not dressing properly during *yu duan* period.

I know this very well as my sister suffers from it. When she was in *yu duan*, she did not put on her bra and she went downstairs [still within the house]. She was wearing a short-sleeved top and had a long-sleeved top over but she did not button up the long-sleeved top properly and the wind got into her chest. Even up to now [a few years past] whenever she feels the cold she will be shivering and she can't have a cold shower at all.

A head is considered more vulnerable to coldness and wind. Therefore, it must be covered at all times. Malai, a rural poor woman, explained that a new mother must cover her head with a hat or scarf at all times as failure to do so may cause pain in her head and this may further cause madness due to a prolonged head pain.

During *yu duan* period, binding of the abdomen is also practised to help the uterus recover and shrink to its normal size. This will make the abdomen flat and tight and is referred to as *mod luuk kao ou* (Anuman Rajadhon, 1987; Fuller and Jordan, 1981). Practically, the woman might use a piece of cloth to tightly tie her abdomen. This is commenced around two or three days post birth. Naree, an urban poor woman, explained:

Binding of the stomach is very good. I have had 5 children but look at my tummy, it is still flat. The binding will help *mod luuk kao ou* and this makes the tummy flat quickly. I continued to do it even after *yu duan* finished because it made me feel good when I walked. If I did not bind it, when I walked I would feel that the uterus would drop and cause stomach pain.

But some women did not wish to do this as it was too restrictive on their bodies. For others, particularly poor women, the practice became difficult. The material they used would not properly stay on their bodies and as they had to keep working, it became difficult to manage. Malai, a rural poor woman, told me that:

I did not do the binding so my tummy is still big now. Well I did do it but I did not do it all the time. It was too annoying as the cloth kept coming off. I tied it and it would stay for a while and then it would get loose and fall off. Those who have plenty of money they can buy "Stay" or other belts to wear so they could do so easier. I only used *pa kao ma* [cloth used by men in their daily routine], so it was easy to fall off.

Visitors are allowed during *yu duan*, but they should not be physically too close to a new mother. This was mainly due to their fear of smelling a bad odour. Malai, a rural woman, explained:

Visitors can come to see us during *yu duan* but they must be careful with the smell stuff. They can cause *lom pid duan* in a new mother. Like if they wear a perfume or their bodies are smelly, this will cause *lom pid duan*.

But some women mentioned that this caution was mainly due to the fear of their own bodily odour. As they did not have a proper shower for a long period, their bodies would have some unpleasant odours and these might offend their visitors.

Some women mentioned that visitors must be cautious when visiting a new mother and her newborn. Suriya, a rural poor woman, explained the custom that:

Those who come to visit us, as they know that I am still observing *yu duan*, before they come, they would have had a shower to make their body clean. As they are afraid of causing *lom pid duan* in the new mother, they must make sure that their bodies will not have bad or strong smells.

As the woman's body is vulnerable during this period, visitors might not wish to visit them if they are ill. Women remarked that most visitors would know the customs very well. Only close relatives might visit the pair during *yu duan* period. Distant relatives and friends would normally wait until the *yu duan* period ended.

Proscriptions and Prescriptions During *Yu Duan*

Cross-cultural studies have shown that there are many proscriptions and prescriptions that new mother must observe during the postpartum month (Pillsbury, 1978; Manderson, 1981; Sich, 1981; McCormack, 1982; Laderman, 1987; Chu, 1996; Symonds, 1996; Townsend and Liamputtong Rice, 1996; Cheung, 1997; Liamputtong Rice, 2000; Whittaker 2000; Liamputtong, 2007a, b). Women in this study too were told not to take any cold showers during this period, as these would cause aches and pains on the body, apart from being the main cause of *lom pid duan*. Most women mentioned that at least two weeks post birth they should not take a cold shower. Despite this prohibition, women keep the body clean by sponging with warm water. However, a strict practice is to avoid washing hair for the whole *yu duan* period. Pimpan, a rural poor woman, explained:

> I can't take a cold shower, but I can sponge my body with warm water. During *yu duan*, I can't wash my hair. Older people say that if you take a cold shower you will experience aches and pains, like pain on your back and waist. Cold water will get into your body through your skin which is opened when you give birth. The process of giving birth makes your body change to some extent and it is very vulnerable to cold water.

During *yu duan*, a new mother is also prohibited from leaving her bedroom or the house. She must stay indoors away from the wind and cold. When asked to articulate on this prohibition, most women said it was to protect a new mother from having contact with an obnoxious odour which would cause *lom pid duan*. Wilai, a rural poor woman, explained:

> We are not allowed to get out of the house as people were afraid that if I went out I might be exposed to a bad smell. If people are burning a car tire or rubbish and this thing causes a bad smell it will cause *lom pid duan*. I will become sick, dizzy and have pain in my head. Once I get this, I will have it for the rest of my life. This is serious.

Some women articulated that the prohibition was to protect the woman's body from being exposed to wind. Sumalee, an urban woman, remarked:

> We are not allowed to get outside the room and I need to be careful with being exposed to the wind. Even if it is hot I need to tolerate that. I was lucky. The *yu duan* period was in January which was not hot so it was not too bad.

However, some volunteered that the prohibition was for the mother to have a close contact with her newborn infant. Pimpilai explained her logical thinking this way:

> In my view I think the practice intends for the mother to just take care of her new baby. In the first month of life, a newborn baby has to adjust to a new life and environment as he has just emerged from her mother's body and hence the baby needs extra and careful care. If you notice, a newborn baby always jerks and this makes me think that the baby needs to be close to the mother in the first month of life and *yu duan* practice allows us to do so.

Lifting heavy objects or working too hard is prohibited. The main reason is that the uterus has not returned to its correct position and it can be damaged easily. This might appear as prolapse of the uterus, known as *huan pood*, in old age (Mougn, 1978; Whittaker, 2000). This problem seems to be more prevalent among rural poor women who have little support during the confinement period. Malai, a rural poor woman told us that:

> We are not allowed to do any heavy work during *yu dua*n as we are afraid of *huan pood*. I am very afraid of this. I have seen poor old women who have this problem. They told me that when the uterus is protruded, it is difficult to walk or to sit. I have seen it too; it is rather large, the protruded bit. They told me because they had to do hard work during *yu duan*. So I was afraid I might end up like them.

Sexual intercourse during *yu duan* is also prohibited. Apart from fear of prolapsy, the women remarked that the episiotomy wound might not have healed properly and the act of sexual intercourse would further damage it. All women mentioned that sexual prohibition extended to at least three postpartum months, as this would allow the wound to heal properly. Pimjai, a rural poor, had this to explain:

> When you give birth, of course, it is natural to have a tear and if you sleep with your husband, the wound might become worse. When you go to see a doctor, it would be so embarrassing. The doctor might say to you that your wound has not properly healed and you slept with your husband and this is why you have more wounds. I would feel so embarrassed if it happened this way, so no sex for this period. Any one should know this. If your wound is not properly healed even at the end of *yu duan* period, you should continue for another month or two.

Puerperal Dietary Practices During *Yu Duan*

Cross-cultural studies also point to the importance of postpartum diets (Wilson, 1973; Weise, 1976; Pillsbury, 1978; Sargent et al., 1983; Laderman, 1984, 1987; Fishman et al., 1988; Symonds, 1996; Townsend and Liamputtong Rice, 1996; Liamputtong Rice, 2000; Whittaker 2000; Liamputtong, 2007b). Similarly, Thai women must also adhere to certain foodstuffs during the *yu duan* period. Foodstuff producing a strong smell is particularly to be avoided. Women mentioned such food as lemongrass, spring onion, and c*ha-om* (Acacia pennata), green vegetables that are typically used in northern Thailand dishes.

Most commonly prescribed puerperal food consumed by a new mother during *yu duan* comprises steamed rice or sticky rice or grilled sticky rice called *kao chi* and grilled pork or chicken. In the first postpartum week or two weeks, a new mother only consumes dried food, as it is believed that wet food such as soup will slow down the healing of perineum. Later on, the consumption of wet food is promoted, particularly for the production of breast-milk. Regarding rice, there was an inconsistent notion among the women in this study. Among urban women, steamed jasmine scented rice, which is commonly consumed as their daily staple food, was allowed but not sticky rice. However, among rural poor women, it was believed that jasmine rice should be avoided as it has a strong odour. A common staple diet is *kao chi* (grilled sticky rice). Common dishes are grilled or fried pork. Among the poor, deep fried pork skin seems to be a common diet during *yu duan*. Chicken is prohibited as it is perceived as poisonous because it prevents a proper healing of the wound. Freshwater fish is allowed, but not catfish which is seen as poisonous. A snakehead fish is suitable as it has scales, and any other scaly fish is also allowed. Beef is considered poisonous, as it can cause *lom pid duan*. Frogs are prohibited as they cause aches and pain on the body and joints.

Seafood such as sea fish, prawns and crabs are also prohibited. Most women mentioned that food consumed during *yu duan* must be plain. No spicy stuff such as chillies and curries are allowed as they might cause *lom pid duan* and also be absorbed into breast-milk which can cause ill health in the newborn. Foods that emit strong smells such as onion, garlic, Indian spices, shrimp paste, and *cha-om* are particularly to be avoided. Fresh vegetables of any kind are also prohibited, but boiled or steamed ones are allowed. Pickled foods such as pickled bamboo shoots are particularly dangerous for a new mother during *yu duan*. Sour food is also banned. Saijai said:

> During *yu duan* I am not allowed to eat food that has a bad smell. Often we are allowed to eat grilled pork and rice, or cooked vegetables with a bit of salt. I have to eat plain food; any spicy or tasty food should not be eaten as it may cause *lom pid duan* and also it might get into our breast-milk and this can cause diarrhea in our baby too.

The food which is allowed is symbolically meant to promote breast-milk. Most commonly mentioned is a soup made up of banana flowers referred to as *kaeng plee* in the north. Banana flowers are traditionally cooked in a soup either with chicken or pork meat or by themselves. They are considered a good source of abundant breast-milk. The banana flower symbolizes fertility. There are many flowers in clusters and each flower will turn into a fruit. This is believed to contain a certain substance which helps to stimulate milk production. A banana flower also contains white sap, perceived as milk; and it is also called "*nom hua plee*" (banana flower milk). Thus banana flowers are included in mothers' diet soon after giving birth and continued. By the third month they believe that they have established their breast-milk.

Medicinal Herbs During *Yu Duan*

Commonly found in Southeast Asia (Laderman, 1987; van Esterik, 1988; Symonds, 1996; Townsend and Liamputtong Rice, 1996; Lewando-Hundt et al., 2000; Liamputtong Rice, 2000; Liamputtong, 2007a, b), medicinal herbs play a significant role in postpartum practices in northern Thai culture. A new mother must also take a herbal shower, which is prepared by boiling a bunch of herbal medicines with water until the water turns red. The herbs can be purchased in herbal shops around the town. Some of the women mentioned that this herbal water could be prepared from *bai plao* (a medicinal plant scientifically known as Grawia paniculata) and tamarind leaves. Sumalee, an urban woman, explained:

> I had a herbal shower throughout *yu duan* period. My sister-in-law's mother prepared it for me. She went to buy bunches of branches and leaves of *bai plao* tree and boiled them with water. I then showered with that herbal water once a day for the entire *yu duan* period.

Women also mentioned that this medicinal shower was used to prevent *lom pid duan*. As people might not know whether they would be affected by *lom pid duan*, it was essential to prevent it. Warunee, an urban woman, recounted:

> My mother-in-law prepared *bai plao* water for me to take a shower. She said it would make my body strong and it will prevent *lom pid duan*. *Bai plao* are leaves which contain some sort of medicine that can protect our body.

There were some variations in the women's descriptions of herbal showers. Some women mentioned that during *yu duan*, for a period of five days, once a day, a new mother must take a very hot shower prepared from boiling several kinds of medicinal leaves. The leaves mentioned commonly included tamarind leaves, betal nut, palm leaves, the leaves of banana known as *gluoy teep* in the north (similar to a finger banana), and *bai plao*. These leaves are purchased in bunches from herbal shops. One bunch can be boiled three times. It is believed that this herbal shower eradicates any poisonous substances resulting from the process of birthing and prevents bodily aches and pain.

A hot shower made from boiling of *pu loei* herb (a formal name is *Plai*, Zingiber cassumunar, yielding rhizomes that are used medicinally) is also prescribed as it improves skin complexion. *Pu loei* is usually grown in the garden and hence it is easily accessed by most women. The rhizome is sliced and dried prior to boiling in water. Ruchira, a rural poor woman, elaborated:

> I took a shower made from *nam pu loei* because it would make my skin look good. My husband went to buy the herb from the market and boiled it for me. I did it for the whole month after giving birth and stopped as soon as I finished my *yu duan* restriction.

Women mentioned that this shower would be very hot, but they must tolerate it as best as they could as the consequence of not doing so on their future health was great. Nida, an urban woman, had this to say:

> I did not take any cold showers, but only hot showers. During *yu duan* we are not allowed to be exposed to any cold stuff including water. I need to wear a long-sleeved top and pants. Even it is very hot, I need to tolerate this heat. My body must be hot so that I can sweat out poison in my body and so that I will have good health later on.

Women in rural areas in particular also drank a medicine prepared from *pu loei*, referred to as *nam pu loei*. It is drunk as warm tea for the entire *yu duan* period. It has a pleasant smell and is refreshing. Women believed it helps with digestion and prevents bloating in the mother and her newborn. If the mother drinks this medicinal tea, it can also prevent bloating in the newborn, as the herb gets into her breast-milk. Some women mentioned that *nam pu loei* also enhances breast-milk production. *Nam pu loei* is also believed to eradicate poisonous wind and blood from the body.

A few women who resided in Chiang Mai city had modified their *yu duan* medicinal drink. Nida, an urban woman, took Chinese herbs during *yu duan* period. This herbal medicine was referred to as *tai ghek ee* and purchased from Chinese herbalists. The herbal medicine is stewed with while wine and is composed of dried leaves, bark and roots of different herbs. It is usually prepared during pregnancy. Once the wine turns brown, it is ready for consumption. Women must take this herb one tablespoon once every day for the whole month. It is believed to eradicate poisonous blood from the body.

DISCUSSION AND CONCLUSION

Symonds (1991, p. 263) points out that "all birthing systems have meaning and purpose". Childbirth including the period immediately following birth is an event in which traditions are deeply involved. Childbirth is seen as "a dangerous and liminal period when a new mother and her newborn are 'in-between' world" (1991, p. 263; see also Doulas, 1966). In this liminal stage, women must be segregated from the society at large (van Gennep, 1960;

Turner, 1967; Symonds, 1991; Flood, 1994; Yao, 1994). This is clearly seen in the separation of women in their liminal stage of postpartum among Thai women in this study. As Laderman (1987, p. 174) puts it:

> The postpartum period is the liminal stage in a woman's passage through the rite of childbirth. As in all such transitional stages, the person on the threshold is in an extremely vulnerable position and must be segregated from her community.

Laderman's argument applies concisely to northern Thai beliefs. For the new mother in Thai culture, the segregation is behavioural rather than physical. Until the dangerous period is over, women are restricted in certain activities, diet and social contacts. Both mother and baby are seen as being in a "precarious state following the birth" (Fuller and Jordan, 1981, p. 46). This belief is similar to many other cultures throughout the world where the puerperium is seen as the most vulnerable period a new mother and her newborn endure (Pillsbury, 1978; Sich, 1981; Cosminsky, 1982; McCormack, 1982; Laderman, 1987; Jordan, 1993; Symonds, 1996; Townsend and Liamputtong Rice, 1996; Cheung, 1997; Liamputtong Rice et al., 1999; Whittaker, 2000; Liamputtong, 2007a, b)

In writing about childbirth in rural Korea, Sich (1981, p. 6) points out "it is considered to be extremely dangerous for the health of a mother, if the rules for post partum care are not observed as they should". The Thai see things similarly. Thai women follow many confinement practices to enhance good health (Cheung, 1997) Thai women also place an emphasis on "prevention" during confinement. This is clearly seen in many discussions with women who speak of being particularly careful about their activities and diet.

At a simple level, it may appear that Thai women are restricted somewhat by traditional practices, although women see these practices as related to their reproduction. However, on a closer examination, we see that these practices have functional purposes. This can be seen in dietary restrictions among the Thai. This practice exists to restore the health and well-being of a new mother (Pillsbury, 1978; Cheung, 1997; Whittaker, 2000, 2002; Liamputtong, 2007a, b). It may not be detrimental to the woman as has been described by many researchers who argue that dietary restrictions during the puerperium may put new mothers at risk of inadequate nutritional intake (Wilson, 1973; Weise, 1976). As Laderman (1987) suggests, restriction of certain foodstuffs tend to occur with food seen as "dangerous" and which can be removed or reduced in their diet, whereas those categorized as "safe" are those essential for life such as rice.

Lewando-Hundt et al. (2000) suggest in their work that, although seclusion during the postpartum period is associated with "ritual purity", the practices during this time are in fact beneficial to women's health. Before resuming her household duties, the avoidance of physical activities gives a new mother both adequate rest and protection from infection. Similarly, the avoidance of sexual intercourse during the first 30 days helps restore her physical health to its normal level and prevents possible further illness. Lewando-Hundt et al. (2000, p. 539) argue that: "The belief underlines the vulnerability of mother and her infant during the first 30 days and encourages the practice of mother staying at home or close to home".

Fuller and Jordan (1981, p. 49) argue that postpartum seclusion has important impacts on "the mutual adjustment of mother and child". Relieved of everyday normal activities and household chores, a new mother can give her exclusive attention to her newborn. It is at this time that a mother may learn about her baby (Lewando-Hundt et al., 2000). In addition, this seclusion ensures more successful breast-feeding as she does not have to meet the demands of other children and housework (Forman et al., 1990). The mother will put her baby on her breast whenever the baby makes a noise. When she emerges from her confinement, breast-feeding has been established, and she has learned about her newborn. The period of separation during the postpartum period may assist women to cope with childbirth better, hence enabling them to move into the motherhood state smoothly (Lewando-Hundt et al., 2000).

Childbirth, as Niehof (1988, p. 239) suggests, implies "gradual social isolation before birth, and social re-integration thereafter" for the mother. In particular with first birth, "the accompanying ritual takes on the character of a rite of passage. Interwoven in rite-of-passage symbolisms are symbols which are thought to avert danger and which point to well-being and fertility" (Niehof, 1988, p. 239). In this chapter, I have shown similar patterns of postpartum practices in Thai culture. As discussed, all rituals surrounding confinement exist to protect the woman and enhance fertility and the well-being of the woman and her newborn baby. The woman must observe many restrictions in order to avoid ill health and misfortune. During this period dietary and other behavioural changes clearly set her apart from normal community life. After 30 days of confinement, she emerges with a "clean", healthy body. She then is able to re-integrate into society and resume her social duties and chores. The new pair has survived the dangers of childbirth and a new member has joined the society (Laderman, 1987). At this stage, the process of transition of motherhood is considered complete, and the woman returns to society as a matured woman with a higher status (Davies, 1994).

Implications for Women's Health Care

Western biomedical framework treats childbirth as the split between a body and mind. There is little regard of emotional and psychological aspect of the birthing women (Laderman, 1992; Woolett and Nicholson, 1998). However, the postpartum period is the time that most mothers recover from birth and begin to take on a new role. It is during this period that most women have mixed feelings, "exciting and emotionally fraught" (Woolett and Dosanjh-Matwala, 1990, p. 178). In recent times, research has shown that postpartum period is "a time of tremendous change for women and many women experience health problems and psychosocial upheaval (Shields et al., 1997, p. 92). Sensitive and appropriate care provided for women during this vulnerable period becomes imperative.

Although modern medicine has reduced maternal and infant morbidity and mortality, it has also "disrupted the social equilibrium provided by tradition" (Steinberg, 1996, p. 1766). But as Lewando-Hundt et al. (2000, p. 530) suggest, postpartum practices function to enhance good health in a new mother and hence they should be built on to "enhance the health and health care of both the mother and infant". Korean society, for example, "has developed an emotionally stabilizing environment by structured postpartum rituals and rites that support the mother-child unit and bind them firmly into the family and the social system". (Steinberg, 1996, pp. 1765-66]. Steinberg (1996, p. 1782) states that "traditional practices have gained legitimacy over the centuries and although some practices which are seen as unsafe should not be insitutionalised, those deemed to enrich the experiences of childbearing should be retained".

As traditional beliefs and practices are still carried on by the women in this study, it is therefore imperative that these traditions need to be taken into account in providing postpartum care to women. Steinberg (1996, p. 1766] suggests, "traditions should be made an integral part of obstetric management". I contend that a serious consideration of traditional beliefs and practices may go a long way in improving women's birthing care in Thailand and elsewhere.

ACKNOWLEDGMENTS

I am grateful to all the women in northern Thailand who participated in this study. I thank the Faculty of Nursing, Chiang Mai University for assistance while the fieldwork was being conducted as part of my Outside Study Program. I am also grateful to the Faculty of Health Sciences, La Trobe University for providing financial support during her leave period. I also thank my colleagues at the Faculty of Nursing for their kind assistance during the data collection period, and Rosemary Oakes for her editing task and comments in the preparation of this paper.

REFERENCES

Anuman Rajadhon, Phya. (1987). *Some traditions of the Thai.* Bangkok, Thailand: Thai Inter-Religious Commission for Development and Sathirakoses Nagapradipa Foundation.

Cheung, N.F. (1997). Chinese zuo yuezi (sitting in for the first month of the postnatal period) in Scotland. *Midwifery*, 13, 55-65.

Chu, C. (1996). Tso yueh-tzu (sitting the month) in contemporary Taiwan. In P. Liamputtong Rice, and L. Manderson (Eds), *Maternity and reproductive health in Asian societies* (pp. 191-204). Amsterdam: Harwood Academic Publisher.

Cosminsky, S. (1982). Childbirth and change: A Guatemalan study. In C.P. MacCormack (Ed.), *Ethnography of fertility and birth* (pp. 205-229). London: Academic Press.

Davies, D. (1994). Introduction: Raising the issues. In J. Holm Ed.), Rites of passage (pp. 1-9). London: Pinter Publishers.

Douglas, M. (1966). *Purity and danger: An analysis of the concepts of pollution and taboo.* London: Routledge and Kegan Paul.

Fishman, C., Evans, R., and Jenks, E. (1988). Warm bodies, cool milk: Conflicts in postpartum food choice for Indo Chinese women in California. *Social Science and Medicine*, 26, 1125-1132.

Flood, G. (1994). Hinduism. In J. Holm (Ed.), *Rites of passage* (pp. 66-112). London: Pinter Publishers.

Forman, M.R., Lewando-Hundt, G., Towne, D., Graubard, B., Berendes, H.W., Sarov. B., and Naggan, L. (1990). The forty day rest period and infant feeding practices among Bedouin Arabs in the Negev. *Medical Anthropology*, 12, 207-216.

Fuller, N., and Jordan, B. (1981). Maya women and the end of the birthing period: Postpartum massage-and-binding in Yucatan, Mexico. *Medical Anthropology*, Winter, 35-50.

Gubrium, J.F., and Holstein, J.A. (2001) (Eds.). *Handbook of interview research.* Thousand Oaks, CA: Sage Publications.

Hanks, J.R. (1963). *Maternity and its rituals in Bang Chan.* Ithaca: Cornell Thailand Project, Cornell University Press.

Jordan, B. (1993). *Birth in four cultures: A crosscultural investigation of childbirth in Yucatan, Holland, Sweden, and the United States*, 4th edn. Prospect Heights, Illinois: Waveland Press Inc.

Kitzinger, S. (1982). The social context of birth: Some comparisons between childbirth in Jamaica and Britain. In C.P. MacCormack (Ed.), *Ethnography of fertility and birth* (pp. 181-203). London: Academic Press.

Laderman, C. (1984). Food ideology and eating behavior: Contributions from Malay studies. *Social Science and Medicine*, 19, 547-559.

Laderman, C. (1987). *Wives and midwives: Childbirth and nutrition in rural Malaysia*. Berkeley: University of California Press.

Laderman, C. (1992). Malay medicine, Malay person. In M. Nichter Eed.), *Anthropological approaches to the study of ethnomedicine* (pp. 191-205). Amsterdam: Gordon and Breach.

Lewando-Hundt, G., Beckerleg, S., Kassem, F., Jafar, A.M.A., Belmaker, I., Saad, K.A., and Shoham-Vardi, I. (2000). Women's health custom made: Building on the 40 days postpartum for Arab women. *Health Care for Women International*, 21, 529-542.

Liamputtong, P., and Ezzy, D. (2005). *Qualitative research method, 2nd edition*. Melbourne: Oxford University Press.

Liamputtong, P. (Ed.) (2007a). *Reproduction, childbearing and motherhood: A cross-cultural perspective*. New York: Nova Science Publishers.

Liamputtong, P. (2007b). *The journey of becoming a mother amongst women in northern Thailand*. Lanham, MD: Lexington Books.

Liamputtong, P. (2007c). *Researching the vulnerable: A guide to sensitive research methods*. London: Sage Publications.

Liamputtong Rice, P. (1988). *Health and sickness: The influence of Thai cultural knowledge and commonsense interpretations among Thai schoolchildren*. Melbourne: Unpublished Ph.D. thesis, Faculty of Education, Monash University.

Liamputtong Rice, P. (2000). *Hmong women and reproduction*. Westport, CT: Bergin and Garvey.

Liamputtong Rice, P., Naksook, C., and Watson, L. (1999). The experiences of postpartum hospital stay and returning home among Thai mothers in Australia. *Midwifery*, 15, 47-57.

Lupton, D. (2000). 'A love/hate relationship': The ideals and experiences of first-time mothers. *Journal of Sociology*, 36, 50-63.

MacCormack, C.P. (Ed.) (1982). *Ethnography of fertility and birth*. London: Academic Press.

Manderson, L. (1981). Roasting, smoking and dieting in response to birth: Malay confinement in cross-cultural perspectives. *Social Science and Medicine*, 15B, 509-520.

Mougn, C. (1978). An ethnography of reproduction: Changing patterns of fertility in a northern Thai village. In P.A. Stott (Ed.), *Nature and man in South East Asia* (pp. 68-106). London: School of Oriental and African Studies. University of London.

Muecke, M.A. (1976). Health care systems as socializing agents. Childbirth in north Thai and western ways. *Social Science and Medicine*, 10, 377-383.

Niehof, A. (1988). Traditional medication at pregnancy and childbirth in Madura, Indonesia. In van der Geest, S., and Whyte, S.R. Eds.), *The context of medicines in developing countries* (pp. 235-252). Dordricht: Kluwer Academic Publishers.

Pillsbury, B.L.K. (1978). 'Doing the month': Confinement and convalescence of Chinese women after childbirth. *Social Science and Medicine*, 12, 11-22.

Poulsen, A. (1983). *Pregnancy and childbirth – Its customs and rites in a north-eastern Thai village*. Copenhagen: Danish International Development Agency.

Sargent, C., Marcucci. J., and Eliston, E. (1983). Tiger bones, fire and wine: Maternity care in the Kampuchean refugee community. *Medical Anthropology*, 7, 67-79.

Shields, N., Reid, M., Cheyne, H., Turnbull, D., and Smith, L.N. (1997). Impact of midwife managed care in the postnatal period: An exploration of psychosocial outcomes. *Journal of Reproductive and Infant Psychology*, 15, 91-108.

Sich, D. (1981). Traditional concepts and customs on pregnancy, birth and post partum period in rural Korea. *Social Science and Medicine*, 15B, 65-69.

Steinberg, S. (1996). Childbearing research: A transcultural review. *Social Science and Medicine*, 43, 1765-1784.

Strauss, A.L. (1987). Qualitative analysis for social scientists. Cambridge: Cambridge University Press.

Symonds, P.V. (1991). *Cosmology and the cycle of life: Hmong views of birth, death and gender in a mountain village in northern Thailand*. Rhodes Island: Brown University.

Symonds, P.V. (1996). Journey to the land of light: Birth among Hmong women. In L. Liamputtong Rice, and L. Manderson (Eds.), *Maternity and reproductive health in Asian societies* (pp. 103-123). Amsterdam: Harwood Academic Publisher.

Townsent, K., and Liamputtong Rice, P. (1996). A baby is born in Site 2 Camp: Pregnancy, birth and confinement among Cambodian refugee women. In L. Liamputtong Rice, and L. Manderson (Eds.), *Maternity and reproductive health in Asian societies* (pp. 125-143). Amsterdam: Harwood Academic Publisher.

Turner, V. (1967). *The forest of symbols*. Ithaca: Cornell University Press.

Uzma, A., Underwood, P., Atkinson, D., and Thackrah, R. (1999). Postpartum health in a Dhaka slum. *Social Science and Medicine*, 48, 313-320.

Van Esterik, P. (1988). To strengthen and refresh: Herbal therapy in Southeast Asia. *Social Science and Medicine*, 27, 751-759.

Van Gennep, A.V. (1960). *The rites of passage*. Chicago: University of Chicago Press.

Weise, H.J.C. (1976). Maternal nutrition and traditional food behavior in Haiti. *Human Organization*, 35, 193-200.

Whittaker, A. (2002). Water serpents and staying by the fire: Markers of maturity in a northeast Thai village. In L. anderson, and P. Liamputtong (Eds.), *Coming of age in South and Southeast Asia: Youth, courtship and sexuality* (pp. 17-41). Surrey: Curzon Press.

Whittaker, A.(2000). *Intimate knowledge: Women and their health in North-east Thailand*. Sydney: Allen and Unwin.

Wilson, C.S. (1973). Food taboos of childbirth: The Malay example. *Ecology of Food and Nutri ion*, 2, 267-274.

Woolett, A., and Dosanjh-Matwala, N. (1990). Postnatal care: The attitudes and experiences of Asian women in East London. *Midwifery*, 6, 178-184.

Woolett, A., and Nicholson, P. (1998). Post-partum experiences. In C.A. Niven, and A. Walker (Eds.), *Current issue in infancy and parenthood* (pp. 88-106). Oxford: Butterworth Heinemann.

Yao, X. (1994). Chinese religions. In J. Holm (Ed.), *Rites of passage* (pp. 66-112). London: Pinter Publishers.

In: Thailand: Economics, Political and Social Issues
Ed: Randle C. Zebioli

ISBN: 978-1-60456-583-6
©2009 Nova Science Publishers, Inc.

Chapter 7

CHILDREARING PRACTICES AMONG PRIMARY CAREGIVERS OF HIV-INFECTED CHILDREN AGED 0-5 YEARS IN CHIANG MAI, THAILAND

Pimpaporn Klunklin, Prakin Suchaxaya, Chawapornpan Chanprasit and Wichit Srisuphun

INTRODUCTION

HIV has become one of the leading causes of death worldwide in the past two decades. Having no cure, HIV causes more than 13,500 new infections each day. The Joint United Nations Programme on HIV/AIDS (UNAIDS) reported that there were 2.3 millions of children living with HIV and 57,000 of these died by AIDS in 2005 (UNAIDS, 2005). In Thailand, approximately one-seventh of new infections are children. Roughly 4,000 Thai children are being infected with HIV each year. Currently, 24,662 children are living with HIV/AIDS (The Thai Working Group on HIV/AIDS Projection, 2001). Moreover, HIV epidemiology studies in Thailand found that the highest prevalence of the infection occurs in Northern Thailand (Ministry of Public Health, Thailand, 2002). This information could be used to estimate that the number of HIV-infected children would be high around this region as they contracted the disease through their parents.

Children born with HIV-infection often display physical impairments, such as a weakened immune system, which makes them vulnerable to various illnesses and opportunistic infections. Infectious causes of death that were often reported included pneumonia, diarrhea, sepsis, and fungal esophageal infections (Chearskul et al., 2002). HIV-infected children require intensive medical and emotional attention as a result of their HIV exposure. Some presented with malnutrition, lack of vaccination, delayed development, and poor hygiene (Kompayack et al., 2002). Further, research on disease progression among HIV-infected Thai children suggests that about half of the children die by the age of 5 years with an estimated 82, 74, 56, 49 and 43 percent survival rate for 1, 2, 3, 5, and 6 year olds, respectively (Chearskul et al., 2002).

HIV-infected children often lose one or both parents to AIDS. Many grow up in traumatic circumstances without the support and care of their parents as they are often moved from one home to another during the duration of their parent's illness. Therefore, grandparents, in particular, grandmothers are often left with the responsibility to serve as the child's primary caregiver (Kespichawattana and VanLandingham, 2002). A study of HIV affected children in northern Thailand indicated that the children experience psychological distress before and after a parent dies. They often express feelings of depression, sadness, loneliness, discrimination, and tend to perceive themselves negatively (Chontawan et al., 2002).

HIV-infected children are at risk of violence, exploitation, abuse, and also mistreatment by their caregivers. Poverty, insufficient food and substandard housing are other problems they face. Moreover, society often views them as a negative stereotype, thus, increasing their sense of isolation. Having a parent with HIV is perceived to be different from having a parent who is affected from other illnesses (Chontawan et al., 2002)

Childrearing is essential to promote the child's health. Many HIV-infected children have lived with the illness and its demands on their bodies most of their life. As such, they often have health problems. Therefore, greater care is needed during childrearing to prevent or control opportunistic infections. Limited research that examines different approaches to childrearing practices from a cultural perspective was available. Further, little is known about how the presence of HIV/AIDS may influence caregivers' idea about childrearing practices, and their beliefs and practices of childrearing.

The purpose of this study was to explore Thai primary caregiver's beliefs and practices about childrearing for HIV-infected children aged 0-5 years old. A focus ethnographic approach was used to examine childrearing practices of primary caregivers of those who are affected by HIV/AIDS. The study was conducted in Chiang Mai, the capital city of Northern Thailand, where culture has great influences on childrearing practices of northern Thai people.

METHODOLOGY

Data were collected from home-based ethnographic research in Chiang Mai province. Purposive sampling was used to recruit participants who had experiences with childrearing practices for HIV-infected children. Fieldwork was conducted in 6 districts of Chiang Mai between 2001-and 2002. Data were collected through participants' observations, field notes, demographic data sheet, chart reviews, semi-structure, opened-end questions, in-depth audio-tape interviews, and photographs. The weight and development of HIV-infected children were also recorded. All informants were interviewed at least twice at home. Thirty-one people were interviewed, including 16 primary caregivers, 6 village headmen, 5 village elders who had experience on childrearing, and 4 health care workers who provided health care for families with HIV-infected children. Interviews were conducted in a naturalistic setting of the participants' choice, however most chose their home environment. The interview began with an explanation to the participants that they were the experts about what it is like to care for HIV-infected children; the participants were asked to teach the researcher about their experiences. Questions included: "What are the beliefs and practices of childrearing for your HIV-infected child?" "How do you care for your HIV-infected child in everyday life?" and "Why do you care for your HIV-infected child in the way you do it?". Questions were designed to clarify and expand on a particular focus to develop an understanding of beliefs and practices regarding childrearing experiences for HIV-infected children. Field notes and participant observations were conducted in each interview.

Interviews were initially transcribed verbatim and read using a method of constant comparison (Miles and Huberman, 1994). Codes developed as themes emerged. Themes were then shared and discussed with other researchers and developed over time based on reading of old and new interviews. Interviews were coded to identify units of thought and grouped in categories. Categories were checked by listing all units of thought under each individual category and reviewed at a later time. Finally, category summaries were arranged and the results were confirmed by discussion with other expert researchers about the groups studied, including three health care workers in pediatric HIV infectious clinics and one community nurse. The summarized results were given to five participants to determine if the findings reflected their personal experiences. All participants reviewed and agreed with the results of this study.

Chiang Mai is one of the 76 provinces of Thailand. It is a second largest city and a capital city of northern region. It is divided into 22 districts, 2 minor districts, 211 sub-districts, and 1,915 villages (Provincial Office, Ministry of Public Health, 2002). Chiang Mai's population consisted of 1.6 million. More than 85% of people are Buddhist. The practice of Buddhism here has many cultural identities almost exclusively associated with Thailand and the Theravada. Many of the mystical and mythical aspects of everyday Thai *dhamma* or Buddhist practice have their roots in Hinduism, such as the symbolic characters and habits within the religion. Thais give respect to Buddhist symbols such as *chedis*, Buddhas, monk statues and spirit houses. People decorate spirit houses, seated on plinths beside buildings everywhere. These are built as residence offerings for the spirits who occupy the area, and are important for avoiding any negative influence from a displeased spirit. They demonstrate the widespread Thai belief in making merit with the many spirits that are intertwined with their Buddhist beliefs. Likewise, they place superstitious importance on wearing amulets acquired from revered temples.

Thai society, including Chiang Mai society, is based on Thai Buddhism and on the concept of "*kam kao*", which means sins or bad actions that people have done in the past. It is based on the concept of karma. The current life is a consequence of the past actions. Everyone can hope to one day reach enlightenment, but its path can be long. It may take many lives to reach it. Each time a person dies, he or she will rebirth into something else (human or other kinds), and hence, the endless cycle of existence (calls *samsara*) continues. The rebirth condition depends on his or her "karma". People believe that if they have done good deeds in their life, the next life will be better for them. On the other hand, if they have done bad deeds or "*bab*", their next life will be harsh. As the result, people believe that their current bad health is caused by "karma" or "*bab*" from the past life.

The majority of the Chiang Mai people earn a living through agriculture and agricultural related occupations. The second largest vocation is tourism and its directly and indirectly related jobs. General commerce and industry are mainly in the form of handicrafts, and of processing agricultural products.

FINDINGS

Eight grandmothers, six HIV infected mothers, a grandfather and an HIV-infected father participated actively in the study. The mother was the primary caregiver among HIV-infected children who still had their own parents, while the grandmother provided the care for those whose one or both parent died from AIDS. In one family, an HIV-infected mother had developed full-blown AIDS and the asymptomatic HIV-infected father was the primary caregiver for their 10-month old baby. In another family, the grandfather was the primary caregiver of a 3-year old boy. The primary caregivers ranged in age between 22 – 73 years old. However, most were over 60, had low education and low economic status (Table 1).

Table 1. General Information of Primary Caregivers of HIV-Infected Children

Characteristics	Mother	Father	Grandmother	Grandfather	Total (n) Percentage
Sex					
Male		1		1	(2) 12.5
Female	6		8		(14) 87.5
Age					
20-29	3				(3) 18.8
30-39	2	1			(3) 18.8
40-49	1		2		(3) 18.8
50-59			1		(1) 6.2
60-69			4	1	(5) 31.2
70-79			1		(1) 6.2
Marital status					
Married	5	1	6	1	(13) 81.2
Widow	1		2		(3) 18.8
Education					
None	1		6		(7) 43.8
Primary	4		2	1	(7) 43.8
Secondary		1			(1) 6.2
High-school	1				(1) 6.3
Occupation					
None	1	5	7	1	(14) 87.5
Work at home		1	1		(2) 12.5
HIV sero-status					
Positive	1	6			(7) 43.8
Negative			8	1	(9) 56.2

Sixteen maternal HIV infected children participated in the study including two aged 10 months, six toddlers, and eight pre-schoolers. Their average age was 33 months. Most of them experienced opportunistic infection such as diarrhea, pneumonia, skin infection, oral thrush, and upper respiratory infections. More than half suffered from HIV-related symptoms including pain, fever, hepatomegaly and failure to thrive. Six children with severe HIV symptoms died during the study. Three of them received antiretroviral therapy continuously (Table 2). Only 31.2 % reached the standardized weight for Thai children, while only one had normal development. All others were delayed in at least one developmental task.

Table 2. General Information on HIV-Infected Children participated in the study

Code	Age	Sex	Had MTCT	Had ARV	Breast Fed	HIV and living status Mother	Father	Living with Parent	Grand-parent	No. of siblings	Education
A	10	Male	Yes	No	No	+ / Alive	+ / Alive	Yes	No	None	None
B	10	Male	No	No	Yes	+ / Alive	+ / Alive	Yes	No	None	None
C	15	Male	Yes	No	No	+ / Alive	+ / Alive	Yes	No	None	None
D	18	Female	Yes *	No-Yes	No	+ / Alive	+ / Dead	Yes	Yes	2	None

Table 2. (Continued).

Code	Age	Sex	Had MTCT	Had ARV	Breast Fed	HIV and living status Mother	Father	Living with Parent	Grand-parent	No. of siblings	Education
E	26	Male	Yes	No-Yes	No	+ / Alive	+ / Dead	Yes	Yes	None	Kindergarten
F	26	Female	No	No	No	+ / Dead	+ / Dead	No	Yes	None	None
G	29	Male	No	Yes	No	+ / Dead	+ / Alive	Yes	Yes	None	None
H	33	Male	No	No	Yes	+ / Alive	+ / Alive	Yes	Yes	1	None
I	37	Male	No	No	Yes	+ / Dead	+ / Alive	No	Yes	1	None
J	41	Male	No	No	No	+ / Dead	+ / Alive	No	Yes	2	None
K	42	Female	No	No	No	+ / Alive	- / Alive	No	Yes	1 (Dead)	Kindergarten
L	42	Male	No	No	No	+ / Dead	+ / Alive	No	Yes	None	None
M	44	Female	No	Yes	No	+ / Alive	+ / Dead	No	Yes	None	None
N	50	Male	No	No	No	+ / Dead	- / Alive	No	Yes	None	None
O	56	Male	No	No	No	+ / Alive	+ / Dead	No	Yes	None	None
P	56	Male	Yes	Yes	No	+ / Alive	+ / Alive	Yes	Yes	None	Kindergarten

MTCT = Having Mother to Child Transmission (MTCT) prevention program
ARV = Having Antiretroviral Therapy continuously
+, - = Positive, Negative
Yes* = Having incomplete ARV
No-Yes = Did not have ARV at the beginning of study but had ARV later during the study period

Rearing HIV infected children who inevitably face infection and death was very difficult for the primary caregivers who knew the HIV status of the children. However, most primary caregivers took care of their infected child as well as they could because of "love", "sympathy", and "acceptance" they felt toward their children. As taught in Buddhism, the majority of primary caregivers believed that their child was infected with HIV because of their parents' sins. Due to this belief, the primary caregivers felt more pity and thus, accepted the responsibility of being their primary caregivers. One caregiver stated:

> I love my grandson so much. I have loved him for a long time and would never leave him. Even though his parent died from AIDS, I still love to care for him. I've been living with him, staying with him since he was born. I can say without shame. I feel pity to him that he was infected with bad disease but that was because of his parent ..not him. I've accepted to be his caregivers even though I know that he will die soon. I love and pity him.

Moreover, because of disease, the childrearing practices of primary caregivers of HIV infected children were associated with social stigmatization, and interpersonal relationships within the family and the community were affected. To help reduce the social stigmatization in the community, the Thai government promoted knowledge on HIV/AIDS transmission. However, negative attitudes toward victims emerged repeatedly in the interviews. One HIV-infected mother described her feelings:

> I am afraid that other people will be disgusted by my son. They are afraid of being infected by him. I stay home and never go to other's houses. They will not tell us directly that they are afraid of being infected but they talk with others. Then, others told us because they pitied us. I stay home and tell my son not to go to other's houses.

CHILDREARING PRACTICES AND INFANT CARE

Childrearing practices of primary caregivers of HIV infected children were explored. Themes identified included daily care, developmental promotion, care during illness, as well as prevention of infection.

Daily Care

The primary caregivers practised daily care for their HIV infected children, including providing nutritious foods, good hygiene, sleep and rest. These caregivers fed the infant with bottle formula on demand since they understood that breast milk was prohibited as it could pass HIV to the child. However, due to their financial situation, three HIV mothers continued to breastfeed. The primary caregivers were not concerned about weaning the child from a bottle as they believed it was better to "let the child get a bottle than to not eat". The child was introduced supplementary foods around 4-6 months, starting with mashed bananas or ground rice and continuing with pre-masticated foods such as steamed and glutinous rice. All children began to consume adult foods by age one. The majority of the caregivers used finger feeding as traditionally practised in northern Thailand, but were less concerned about hand washing before finger feeding as they believed that they did not touch any dirty thing with their fingers. Scaleless fish, beef, buffalo, were all forbidden because primary caregivers believed that these kinds of food could harm the child's health. Coconut was also considered taboo as local northern Thai people use coconut juice to ritually wash the face of the dead. Moreover, it is believed that all people with HIV die after they drink coconut juice. Consequently, primary caregivers strictly prohibited all coconut products for their children.

The need for hygiene care was significant in their infant care practices. The primary caregivers tried to manage personal hygiene care for both themselves and their HIV infected children as they understood that good hygiene could prevent opportunistic infections among the children. Primary caregivers also understood that keeping a hygienic environment was essential in order to care for HIV-infected children. Therefore, they cleaned food containers, washed clothes, exposed mattresses to the sun, mopped floors, and other hygienic practices. Further, the study also found that the primary caregivers gave concerted efforts to maintain their child's daily care.

Sleep and rest were also imperative in the child's daily care. HIV infected infants slept most of the day, while toddlers and pre-schoolers slept 10-16 hours a day. These children often slept on a mattress that was covered by a mosquito net to prevent disease from mosquitoes. It is important to note that during the evening, children often slept with their primary caregivers. However, in extended families in Chiang Mai, some HIV-infected children slept in the same bed with both primary caregivers and/or other relatives.

Developmental Promotion

Developmental promotion revealed by the primary caregivers in this study included toilet training, play, safety, and injury prevention. These activities were taught to the children as they developed. Among symptomatic HIV infected children, toilet training was not enforced when presented with severe illness. On the other hand, asymptomatic HIV-infected children started toilet training around 18 months old as did other children in the community.

Safety and injury prevention was a part of developmental support for HIV infected children. As in any family, the primary caregivers prevented injuries and accidents by keeping harmful medicines, toilet cleaners, detergents, and other poisonous substances out of reach of their HIV-infected children. Some kept these harmful agents in high drawers while others kept them on high shelves. The primary caregivers also monitored all activities of the children when they played, ate, and went outside the home. Each kept a close watch on their child to prevent them from harm.

Play was believed to be an important activity for the child's development among the primary caregivers of HIV infected children, and the caregivers provided games and toys just as they would in caring for healthy children. A great deal of concern was shown in preventing injury or infection, which sometimes led the caregiver to become over protective. Among symptomatic HIV children, outdoor activities were not allowed. Most of them played solitary games at home while some were given plastic toys or coloring books. The play activities among children with full-blown AIDS included handling toys and listening to stories being read by their caregivers.

However, 15 out of 16 HIV infected children were delayed in at least one developmental task caused by their own health or lack of developmental stimulation from the caregivers. All primary caregivers believed that when their child grew, they would develop normally without any stimulation from others. Thus, caregivers did not do any specific activity to stimulate and support their child's development.

Care During Illness

Primary caregivers had considerable experience with illnesses because their HIV infected children were frequently ill from opportunistic infections as a result of their reduced immunity. Caring for their children's illnesses was practised by using symptom management, modern care and alternative care.

Symptom management resulted from the primary caregiver's own experience as well as information gained from others in their community. General first aid was given before taking their child to the hospital. Some caregivers used traditional treatments in addition to modern medicine to treat some illnesses such as diarrhea, skin problems, and fever.

After learning of the diagnosis of HIV infection in their children, the primary caregivers allowed each treatment decision to be made by their child's doctors, and then took care to follow medical advice. The primary caregivers believed in their doctors. However, most also sought alternative therapy to treat their child in the hope that it could alleviate other symptoms. For example, herbal medicine, holy water, paying respect to spirits, and subsidence of bad *Karma* were also used. Most primary caregivers were Buddhists, and, therefore, believed that *Karma* caused bad effects on their children's health and *Karma* came from their child's past life which caused them to suffer from this fatal disease. As a result, they attempted to change the *karma* for the better by enacting rites, such as making merit, performing "*Sungkathan*," or buying the life of either a small or large animal and then letting it free. The primary caregivers tried to get hold of the load of Buddha and prayed for their children's life. They also respected monks, donated some money to support temples, practiced meditation for the aim of gaining better healthy conditions for their children. Some primary caregivers believed in supernatural powers, spirits or ghosts and therefore, set up rituals to respect them in order to prolong the life of their loved one. Moreover, they sought traditional medicine such as herbal medicine and holy water provided by monks, and believed that traditional medicine could help to improve their child's health as it came from the representative of the Buddha. Finally, they surrendered to despair if their children could not get well or died as they believed that the children's bad karma could not be resolved.

Prevention of Infection

To prevent infectious diseases, primary caregivers had their children immunized. These HIV infected children were also isolated from those with illnesses, such as respiratory infections, to prevent opportunistic infections from either occurring or reoccurring. Public areas were avoided. Some primary caregivers used disinfectants or bleach in the bathroom to kill germs such as anti-bacterial solutions. Others used 70% alcohol solution to clean their hands after touching their child's blood or other body fluids. They believed that alcohol would kill HIV since the hospital used it for cleaning the skin before injections. Bottles of alcohol were used in the home to clean contaminated clothes. Gloves were also used to prevent transmission of HIV. However, two of the primary caregivers in this study did not use any barrier to prevent cross infection from their child because they did not know their child's HIV status and they cared for their child in a normal manner.

CHILDREARING PROBLEMS

Several problems relating to childrearing practices were mentioned, and these included financial burdens and time constraints.

Financial Burdens

Primary caregivers of HIV infected children experience financial problems as they have a very low-income. As such, these caregivers were more vulnerable than those who had moderate or higher incomes. For example, a grandmother with a 3-year old HIV symptomatic boy expressed her feelings about taking care of her grandson and her own 3 children:

> He is often sick with a fever and weak. I feel so tired when I take care of him when he is sick. It causes me a lot of suffering. I must stay with him in hospital, and I must pay for transportation fee and foods. If I stay here with my husband as grandmother and grandfather, I don't lose any money. But, if I stay with him at hospital, I must pay. Even though I don't need to pay for treatment and hospital charge, I still must pay for living expense. Living at home, I can find vegetables and local foods to eat.

Time Constraint

Time constraint was another problem in rearing HIV infected children as the primary caregivers had to stay home with the child. Due to the demands of their HIV-infected child, the primary caregivers had limited control of their time. This was especially true during the terminal stage when the child's health declined rapidly. Demands on the primary caregivers' time and efforts became particularly overwhelming. A grandmother of a 4-year old symptomatic HIV-infected girl remarked:

She takes all of my time. I cannot do anything when she is sick. I have to stay with her all the time and do everything for her. I suffer a lot. This disease brings suffering not only to patients but also to caregivers. I feel so tired.

HIV infected children often stayed close to their primary caregivers, especially in the later stages of their illness. Most did not want to stay with other family members, and became upset if their primary caregivers were not visibly present. Some wanted to be held all the time, even when there were asleep. For these reasons, the primary caregivers faced severe constraints on their time and privacy.

DISCUSSION

Childrearing practices are grounded in cultural patterns and beliefs (Mayers and Evans, 1998). These practices include activities to help a child grow and develop in a healthy manner (Stromguist, 1998). However, in unhealthy children, these practices varied. In this study, the primary caregivers' practices for their HIV infected children included daily care, developmental care, illness care, and prevention of infection. Within daily care, adequate nutrition was a major concern as it is essential for the general well-being of a child. On the other hand, inadequate nutrition has severe consequences, which can lead to a wasting syndrome among children with HIV infection (Scott, 2002).

Proper hygiene care helped the HIV infected children to reduce contracting germs. Yet, among HIV-infected children with poor hygiene care, some did not acquire infections even though they remained in an unclean environment. The study suggests that opportunistic infections may relate more to the child's immune response. As instructed by health care providers, primary caregivers in the study practised hygiene care as they were concerned about prevention of infections. These practices were consistent with those recommended by UNICEF (UNICEF, 2000).

As commonly practiced within Thai culture, all of the HIV infected children slept with their primary caregivers until they were in their teens. This practice helped the primary caregivers manage their child's illness more carefully.

In Northern Thailand, the perception of health and illness, as described by primary caregivers of HIV infected children in this study, showed that they perceived HIV/AIDS as a western disease requiring their children to use modern medicine. However, the primary caregivers in this study used self-treatment by receiving advice or treatment from a relative, friend, neighborhood or self-help group. Other times, they consulted a lay person who had special experience in a particular disorder.

Since hospitals were the first place to recruit participants for this study, the primary caregivers of HIV infected children, were more likely to utilize modern medical treatment for their children. However, the primary caregivers integrated modern, traditional, and alternative medical treatments as suggested by Kleinman (1980).

In this study, the primary caregivers learned how to prevent transmission of the disease from health care providers, later sharing this knowledge with their family members. Infection control was managed by isolating children from other infectious persons, using gloves when touching the infected child's secretions, and using disinfectant to clean up spills. These results were consistent with the recommendations by AIDS Net, AIDS ACCESS, and MSF-B (2003). Knowledge of the risk of transmission of HIV led primary caregivers to develop precautions. These principles were used at home, including the use of safe practices and appropriate barrier precaution when in contact with the child's blood or body fluids (Pizzo and Wilfert, 1998). Precautions for other infections were also included in these activities to prevent opportunistic infections and infections from common childhood illnesses.

We found in this research that routine activities for childrearing of HIV infected children required extensive time especially during the final stage of their child's illness. In addition, all families faced the stress of additional financial burden as well as social stigmatization that came with caring for an HIV child. However, despite the fact that all the primary caregivers of HIV-infected children identified problems regarding childrearing practices, they still upheld their responsibility and none chose to ignore or abandon their child. Most of the primary caregivers expressed their love and care for their child. The influence of Buddhism and Thai culture seem to have helped them to accept the responsibility of caring for their child and keeping the child as the center of 'love' in the family.

IMPLICATIONS FOR PRACTICES

Observations of childrearing practices among primary caregivers of HIV infected children obtained from this study clearly reveal an integration of modern knowledge and traditional beliefs. Consequently, in order to provide care for HIV-infected children and their families, nurses and other health care providers need to develop cultural insight, respect, and appreciation for these cultural beliefs and practices in order to provide appropriate recommendations regarding childrearing practices.

Home visits are an essential service for families with HIV infected children. These visits allow opportunities to promote positive childrearing practices, assist families with decision making, maintain growth and development, practise medical adherence, monitor health conditions of the child, as well as provide resources for the family.

Community, health providers should encourage a close relationship among primary caregivers and their relatives as these relationships help primary caregivers cope with their daily problems when nurturing the HIV infected children.

REFERENCES

AIDSNet, AIDS ACESS, & MSF-B., 2003, *Caring For Children Affected by AIDS*, AIDS Net (North-East Office): Khonkaen.

Chearskul, S., Chotpitayasunondh, T., Simonds, R.J., Wanprapar, N., Waranawat, N., Punpanich, W., Chokephaibulkit, K., Mock, P.A., Neeyapun, K., Jetsawang, B., Teeraratkul, A., Supapol, W., Mastro, T.D., & Shaffer, N., 2002, 'Survival, Disease Manifestations, and Early Predictors of Disease Progression Among Children with Perinatal Human Immunodeficiency Virus Infection in Thailand', *Pediatrics*, 110(2 Pt 1):e25. Retrieved from http://pediatrics.aappublications.org/cgi/content/full/110/2/e25

Chontawan, R., Teawkul, S., Junprasit, C., Mesukho, J., Taya, N., & Leawviriyakit, N., 2002, *Prevention and Reduction of the Impact of Having HIV Infected Parents on Children: A Participatory Approach*, Research Report, Faculty of Nursing, Chiang Mai University: Chiang Mai.

Kespichawattana, J., & VanLandingham, M., 2002, *Health Impacts of Co-Residence With and Caregiving to Persons With HIV/AIDS on Older Parents in Thailand*, Research Report No. 02-527, Population Studies Center, Institute for Social Research, University of Michigan: Michigan.

Kleinman, A., 1980, *Patients and Healers in the Context of Culture*, The Regents of the University of California, University of California Press: Berkeley.

Kompayack, J., Wichitsukon, K., Wanfhun, P., & Chaisirin, N., 2002, *The Fate of Children Born to Mothers Seropositive for Human Immunodificiency Virus. Research Report*, AIDS Division, Ministry of Public Health: Bangkok, Thailand.

Miles, M.B., & Huberman, A.M., 1994, *Qualitative Data Analysis, 2nd editon*, Sage Publications: Thousand Oaks, CA.

Ministry of Public Health, Thailand, 2002, 'Situation of HIV/AIDS in Thailand'. <http://epid.moph.go.th/home_menu_2002_1.html>

Myers, R. G., & Evans, J. L., 1998, 'Childrearing Practices', in N.P. Stromquist (ed.), *Women in the Third World: An Encyclopedia of Contemporary Issue*, pp. 441-467. Garland Publishing: New York.

Pizzo, P.A., & Wilfert, C.M. (eds.) 1998, *Pediatric AIDS: The Challenge of HIV Infection in Infants, children and adolescents*, 3rd edition, Lippincott: Philadelphia.

Scott, E., 2001, 'The Potential Benefits of Infection Control Measures in the Home', *American Journal of Infection Control, 29*: 247-249.

Stromquist, N.P., 1998, *Women in the Third World: An Encyclopedia of Contemporary Issue*, Garland Publishing: New York.

The Thai Working Group on HIV/AIDS Projection, 2001, *Projections for HIV/AIDS in Thailand: 2000-2020*, Division of AIDS, Ministry of Public Health: Bangkok, Thailand.

UNAIDS, 2005, 'AIDS Epidemic Update'. <http://www.unaids.org/epi/2005>

UNICEF, 2000, 'Water, Sanitation and Hygiene Promotion'. <http://www.unicef.org/mozambique/pdfs/water_sanitation_hygiene/waterromotion.pdf>

Viddhanaphuti, C., 1999, 'A Cultural Approach to HIV/AIDS Prevention and Care', UNESCO/UNAIDS Research Project. <http://unesdoc.unesco.org/images/0012/001206/120684e.pdf>

In: Thailand: Economics, Political and Social Issues
Ed: Randle C. Zebioli

ISBN: 978-1-60456-583-6
©2009 Nova Science Publishers, Inc.

Chapter 8

CREATING SCALES TO MEASURE READING COMPREHENSION, AND ATTITUDE AND BEHAVIOUR, FOR PRATHOM (GRADE) 7 STUDENTS TAUGHT ESL THROUGH A GENRE-BASED METHOD IN THAILAND

Russell F. Waugh and Margaret H. Bowering
Edith Cowan University

Sanguansri Torok
Rajabhat University, Muban Chombung

ABSTRACT

A questionnaire involving attitudes and behaviour towards genre-based learning of English as a second language (based on text, inter-personal relations, and behavioural controls) was given to 300 prathom 7 (grade 7) students in Thailand. A Rasch analysis was performed to create a linear scale using 18 of the original 48 items (each answered in two perspectives, an ideal and an actual). These data had good reliability and validity, and supported a modified structure of attitudes and behaviour, from which valid and reliable inferences could be made. A Rasch analysis was performed on data from a separate reading comprehension test (based on three kinds of genre texts) with the same 300 prathom 7 students using 18 of an original 60 items. These data fitted the measurement model well, but had a low Index of Separation for these students. Both scales were used in an experiment described in the next chapter on genre-based teaching versus traditional teaching learning of English as a second language.

Key words: English as a second langauge, Grade 7 students, Thailand, Rasch measurement, English comprehension, attitudes, behaviour, genre-based learning

INTRODUCTION

In the new Thai educational system, English is considered the most important foreign language taught from the first grade, introduced with the National Education Act of Thailand (1999). Difficulties in learning and teaching English in Thailand are described, highlighting problems of English reading comprehension. The genre approach to teaching is introduced as a methodology that might alleviate problems in the teaching and learning of English reading comprehension that is the subject of this dissertation.

THE STRUCTURE OF THE EDUCATION SYSTEM

The basic structure of Thai education is twelve years basic education guaranteed by the Constitution of 1997 and provided free. Of this, nine years are compulsory. The National Education Act of 1999 (Office of the Educational Commission, 1999) was introduced to implement the constitutional right of Thai citizens to twelve years of free schooling. This objective is to be achieved through formal, non-formal and informal education (Office of the National Educational Commission, 1999, Section 15, p. 7). What is of concern in this thesis is the formal school system and within it the role of English as a second language.

A curriculum framework has been developed for implementation in primary grades 1-3, primary grades 4-6, secondary grades 7-9, and, finally, secondary grades 10-12, in line with Sections 27-28 of the Education Act (ibid, p.12). The new curriculum was introduced in the academic year 2002 to be implemented in all grades by 2004, a review being scheduled for 2005. This curriculum emphasises English as the most important foreign language, taught from grade 1, for all grades. The Act itself emphasises the importance of language knowledge in Section 23, point (4), where it states that education "shall give emphases to ... knowledge and skills in mathematics and languages, with emphasis on proper use of the Thai language"(Office of the National Education Commission, 1999, p. 10). Language knowledge is emphasised together with mathematics, as properly grounded in the Thai language. This is relevant to the design of this research, as will be seen later. In Basic Education, the end of elementary grades presents a natural divide from undifferentiated learning (grades 1-6) to specialised subjects starting in grade 7. Secondary education prepares learners for Higher Education in academic subjects that also feature in University entrance examinations.

Higher education in Thailand also requires that the English language be studied as a compulsory subject. Students graduating from a secondary school can take entrance examinations to colleges and universities. The Rajabhat Universities use a semester system based on credits and grades: a four-year degree requires 130-140 credits, including English language. English is compulsory in the first year of all Rajabhat institutes and, in many Rajabhat Universities, it is compulsory for further years, depending on the subject areas studied. A reading knowledge of the language will always be important for all educated persons and in particular anyone who goes on to tertiary education.

TEACHER TRAINING IN THE RAJABHAT UNIVERSITIES IN THAILAND

The Rajabhat Universities in Thailand were established primarily for teacher training. Since 1995, there have been changes both in the administration and curricula of these institutes, which are now evolving toward autonomous tertiary institutes, to serve not only the training of the teachers, but also their communities at the local and regional levels. The Office of Rajabhat Institutes Council (ORIC) is the department within the Ministry of Education responsible for overall administration of these regionally based institutes. The institutes are now responsible for full-time and in-service teacher training and also for the operation of other programs supported by government budget allocations and local resources. They also "conduct research as academic service to the general public; improve, transfer, and develop technology..." (ORIC, 1998, p. 2)

In the field of language teaching, the National Education Act of 1999 emphasises the importance of the Thai language (Office of the National Education Commission, 1999, National Education Act of B.E.2542, Section 23, points 4, 10). It also describes English as the most important foreign language taught in Thailand, when developing curricula for basic education. The study of English was recently introduced from the first grade level. Thus, there is now pressure on the Rajabhat Universities to provide more English teachers and to improve on the teaching of English at all levels. Teachers need to teach effectively and be trained in different methodologies, so that they can choose an appropriate methodology for learning and teaching situations in the classroom (Office of the National Education Commission, 1999).

ENGLISH AS A SECOND LANGUAGE IN THAILAND

Difficulties in Teaching Reading Comprehension

English language has been a compulsory subject at all levels of the Thai school system since 1996 and the communicative approach with an eclectic orientation is intended for use in teaching English at all levels of education. The most authoritative review of language teaching in Thailand is provided by Wongsathorn, Sukamolsun, Chinthammit, Ratanothayanonth, and Noparumpa (1996) who used a UNESCO survey framework to assess the system between 1966 and 1996. They concentrated specifically on establishing national economic, social, and educational profiles for Language Learning and teaching in Thailand and found that desired levels were not being achieved. A more recent review concentrating on teachers in the Metropolitan Bangkok area can be found in Vacharaskunee (2000), who identifies training and methodological problems with the system as far as English teaching is concerned. An earlier study by Promsiri, Praphal and Vijchulata (1996) addressed the problems of English teachers and the needs of in-service teacher training in a provincial upper-secondary educational region. They reviewed English teaching in a Thai secondary school district and concluded that the communicative approach, introduced in the 1990's, had not been successful due to the lack of trained teachers. Thus to overcome the problem, researchers need to be concerned with the difficulties of teaching English.

In teaching English as a second language, the emphasis is on the development of English reading skills, which are so important in a globalising world. However, because very few English teachers have high levels of English fluency, most students achieve only a low level of English proficiency. Therefore, they cannot read, write or communicate in English, at a sufficiently high standard. Vacharaskunee (2000) studied the problem of English teaching of the teachers in Metropolitan Bangkok schools, where most likely the best qualified teachers are employed. She and others found that, even in Bangkok, most students cannot effectively use English (Torut, 1994; Ministry of Education, 2000). Several research studies in the field of English reading in Thailand during the past fifteen years show that the English reading ability of secondary and even tertiary level students is low. As shown by Sawasdiwong (1992) and Vannichbutr (2000), students cannot achieve the main objectives of the syllabus, such as reading for information, comprehension, and critical reading of the texts.

Teaching reading in Thailand can be described in terms of two problems. These problems are inappropriate methodology and the lack of teaching skills (Secondary School Education Report, 1981-1985, p. 40). These areas are also mentioned by Noisaengsri (1992) and Chittawat (1995). Their studies show that, normally, teachers start to teach by introducing vocabulary items and grammatical structures. Then they let the students read aloud or repeat the sentences after the teacher. Mostly students are asked to read and translate sentence-by-sentence for the whole class, or individually. This traditional method of teaching is found to be boring and leads to negative attitudes towards learning English. Moreover, students have no chance or incentive for active learning because there is very little chance for them to use their own ideas of learning from the text. As Smith (1971) has found, reading comprehension involves the interaction between the reader's cognitive processes and the characteristics of the text. Whilst reading, the reader tries to reconstruct a message encoded by the writer for some purpose, as emphasised also by Johns (1997) when discussing genres. This means that text, purpose and context are related in reading comprehension, and the traditional method in Thailand does not allow for this. Thus, an alternative genre-based rhetorical structures method, as used in this study, could lead to better English reading comprehension achievement.

GENRE IN READING COMPREHENSION

The current study explores the use of genres to improve the teaching and learning of reading in the context of English as a second language in Thailand. A genre can be defined as a category of text type, whether spoken or written. All languages operate in a global sense on the basis of genres, since they are the expressions of intent. They perform a certain purpose whether it be narrating, reporting, arguing or defining. Any text within a particular category exhibits similar features. On that there is agreement but a basic difference exists between its supporters on whether to place the emphasis on the context, the features or the purpose.

To set the scene for a further discussion of this matter which in turn influences classroom practice, several definitions of genre will be given. First Aviva Freedman (1991, p.192), a well-known American genre scholar, gives her view that context determines the shape of genre.

"Situation, motive, substance, form-each plays a part in defining genre. But the whole is greater than and different from the sum of these parts."

A different opinion typifies the work of Frances Christie, an Australian linguist, who highlights textual features themselves. She defines genre as (Christie, 1989, p. 168).

"A text may be said to have 'genre structure' because it has an overall characteristic pattern of shape, making it identifiably different from some other genre, whose functions will of course be of a different kind."

Finally in the United Kingdom, John Swales, an influential scholar in the development of English for Special Purposes, places the stress on communicative purpose. In describing any particular academic genre, Swales indicates that both content and form are determined by the purpose of the communication. He writes (Swales, 1990, p. 58):

"A genre comprises a class of communicative events, the members of which share some set of communicative purposes. These purposes are recognised by expert members of the parent discourse community, and thereby constitute the rational for the genre. This rationale shapes the schematic structure of the discourse and influences and constrains choice of content and style."

These definitions give a basis for the discussion which follows on what approaches scholars have taken to the use of genre theory in the classroom.

North American Genre Approaches

The first of the several studies that have influenced the design of the present study, is the argument, between Fahnestock and Freedman. In the last decade three fundamental questions were raised: Can genre be taught? Would genre knowledge help second language reading? How should genre be taught? While Fahnestock (1993) supports teaching genre explicitly citing historical examples, Freedman (1993a,b) argues against explicit genre instruction and substitutes, instead, supporting socialization into genre communities, as a way to learn from practice. According to Saccardi (1996), Harris (1996) and de Graaf (1997), genre can be taught as early as elementary school level for first language instruction through a mixture of explicit teaching and socialization into genre related practices.

Fahnestock (1993) studied how various crafts are acquired, including the writing craft. In this context, she presented historical evidence that rhetorical structures, or genres, have been successfully taught throughout history as part of the art of oratory. Oratory as a craft was used by the Greeks, the Romans, and by all the scholastics of the Middle Ages. She thus finds Freedman's (1993a) arguments against the explicit teaching of crafts (including the writing craft) not valid. According to Fahnestock the explicit teaching of techniques in the writing classroom has a long tradition and should be continued.

Freedman (1993b) defended her opposition to explicit teaching of genre by recommending "learning by doing in a social context instead".

"Research showed that the least successful pedagogies are those most explicitly presented in their teaching (as a mode) and explicit teaching of grammar (as a focus). The most successful mode of instruction is environmental through socialization into discourse communities of various genres. Far from involving explication, the most successful teaching minimizes lectures and teacher-led instruction. Instead it presents structured activities that students first perform in groups and then independently. It is true that principles are taught but not through explanation. Rather, those are taught through concrete materials and problems. The working through of problems not only illustrates the principle but involves students." (Freedman, 1993b, p.280).

Rather than discarding the teaching genre, Freedman recommends teaching genres through engagement. In summary, she agrees with Aoki (2000) arguing against reducing complexity through explanations, using, instead, complexity to stimulate the students to learn, genre being acquired through exposure, not through instruction.

Another American, Coe (1994, p.157) has adopted a compromise position accepting both Fahnestock's and Freedman's arguments, that "we can find ways to use the best of both process and genre approaches to writing". His suggestion is that teachers should first assist students to develop the idea of purpose and audience among their students and then move on to highlight the formal structures of the genre, either by discovery or by instruction (Coe, 1994, 165).

The Australian Genre School

The Australian genre school, based on the work of both linguists and researchers such as Michael Halliday, Jim Martin, Joan Rothery and Frances Christie, has developed a genre-based theory of writing and writing pedagogy. In the last two decades of the last century, the belief that the teaching of genre empowers the disadvantaged to acquire both oral and written genres led to extensive research and publication. Since their approach has been used successfully with students of all ages from both first and second language backgrounds, it is seen as appropriate in this study.

Besides producing lists and samples of basic genres which are needed by the beginner learner (Deriweanka, 1990), the school is particularly noted for producing guidelines for teaching the most common factual and narrative genres (Richardson, 1994, p.127). Suggestions for the teacher in the writing classroom include describing the context and purpose, modelling the text, explaining the text organisation and language features and then setting the students to work both jointly and individually to produce new texts. Opposition to these procedures has arisen from those who prefer to work with ideas through a process approach (Sawyer & Watson, 1987, p.47) but the genre school has been strong in defence of its position that textual analysis will help students acquire basic skills and will not damage creativity. Martin, Christie and Rothery (1987, p. 76) have given this reply to their critics.

"......Year 2 students are not James Joyce.....like all individuals who learned to make meanings, Joyce learned familiar meanings first. It is these meanings that genre theorists propose to begin with in initial literacy programs. Once established, only if established, do they afford the possibility of creativity or social change."

Although genre approaches in Australia have been more common in writing than reading programs, some studies outside Australia recommend the same type of treatment in the reading class. An article by Kay and Dudley Evsans (1998, p.312) reporting on a survey of conference delegates from 10 countries which shows that a consensus exists among them that for second language speakers genre-based approaches should be adopted in reading and speaking programs as well as in those for writing. Further examples will be given later in this chapter, but those already given signal the fact that for this study it has been concluded that the ideas of the Australian Genre School are capable of being extended to the teaching of reading for elementary and secondary EFL students in Thailand.

The emphasis of the present study is on the use of genres for teaching English reading comprehension in Thailand. It is motivated by the fact that English reading comprehension achievement is still very low in Thailand, as reported by Chandavimol (1998), whose work inspired this research. She argued that language learning should be an active process of engagement. She said that students who are bored will not learn English. She claimed that through engagement, students who are convinced that they will be able to adequately comprehend English texts can become successful learners. The reason for focusing on reading according to Soranasataporn and Chuedong (1999, p. 20) is that "of the four English language skills, reading is probably used most by EFL and ESL students in an academic context..." To achieve reading objectives, Soranasataporn and Chuedong conclude that teachers should integrate reading comprehension strategies training into regular classroom events in a natural, comfortable, but explicit way. Moreover, for successful academic progress, this needs to begin at the secondary school level because English reading comprehension achievement is still very low at this stage. That is why a genre-based method could help in better English reading comprehension for young Thai students.

SIGNIFICANCE

The current study could make two important contributions. One, it has the potential to improve the measures of reading comprehension, and attitude and behaviour to ESL, by using a recently developed Rasch computer program to make the measures. This creates a linear level scale in which the difficulties of attitude and behaviour item (or reading comprehension items) are calibrated on the same scale as the person measures (attitudes and behaviour, or reading comprehension). This has not been done in Thailand before and could lead to better measurements and use of Rasch computer programs in Thailand. Two, it tests a model of attitude and behaviour towards English reading comprehension in which attitudes and behaviour are measured on the same scale, rather than measured separately and then correlated. This is a recent development in educational and psychological development and has not been attempted in Thailand before.

PURPOSE

The main purpose was to measure student self-reported attitude and behaviour, and English reading comprehension on a linear interval scale. These measures are used in both the experimental and control groups, before and after the experiment, described in the next chapter.

RESEARCH QUESTIONS

1. How can Thai student self-reported attitude and behaviour (expected beliefs and actions) to learning English using genre-based lessons be described?
2. Can a linear measure of English reading comprehension based on genre-based reading materials and five comprehension categories (inferences for main idea from purpose and context, following a sequence of events, following a sequence of ideas, locating information in the text, making inferences for word meanings) be constructed using a Rasch measurement model?
3. Can a linear measure of attitude and behaviour to ESL, based on three aspects (reading assignments as genre texts, classroom interactions, course curriculum organisation) and two perspectives (ideally, this is what should happen, and this is what really happens), be constructed using a Rasch measurement model?

LIMITATIONS

A limitation refers to the reading comprehension test design. The test was developed using both Thai and Australian input and, thus, although comprehensive, and including materials from all genres used in the research, it turned out to be too difficult for grade 7 students in Thailand. Student performances on the pre-test were poor. This limitation might turn out to be an advantage, because it means that the test can be used also for some higher grades and/or in metropolitan Bangkok, or also private schools, on a trial basis, as a follow-up to this research.

The usual limitations of self-reported questionnaires analysed by a Rasch model to develop a scale for both the attitude and behaviour measures, and also the reading comprehension test, also apply. These limitations are compounded in this case by the fact that both the questionnaires and the reading tests were administered to relatively immature seventh grade students. Thus, control for consistency must rely on both the interest of the participants and the time allowed for the tasks. The one hour time allowed for the attitude questionnaire in Thai, and then two hours for the reading comprehension test, were adequate for this purpose.

It is assumed that students give truthful and not socially-desirable or agreed answers. Every effort was made to ensure that answers were given individually, however some may still have given socially desirable answers, that might bias the results. It is very difficult to know the extent of this.

DEFINITION OF TERMS
GENRE AND ESL READING COMPREHENSION

Genre refers to the communication patterns (both oral and written) of various discourse communities. Discourse communities are groups of people united for some social purpose, whether family, business, government, academia, or other, including cultural and ethnic reasons. What they say, or write, will depend on the roles and purpose of the participants of these social groups, to achieve communicative purposes. If there are written records, the narrow definition of genre applied in reading and writing refers to the pattern of these written records necessary to achieve the communicative purpose of the writer with the particular audience within the discourse community. The reader then faces a problem: unless he or she is part of the discourse community and knows the roles of the members, he or she would have difficulties in understanding the particular written communication. This is why it is essential to teach at an early stage the pattern of communication of different discourse communities, as embodied in the genres they use to aspiring readers, especially readers of foreign languages, where familiarity with patterns of text, role, and context (Johns, 1997) is even less likely than within a particular language or culture.

Genre-Based Rhetorical Structure Method

The method of teaching English reading is based on the principle of rhetorical structures analysed by Pappas (1993) for expository texts (P) and by Hasan (1989) for narrative texts (H). The journalistic genre combines features of the above as discussed by Marin (1994). It emphasizes teaching students to experience, by themselves, the way ideas and propositions are ordered in text for a particular objective or purpose. When the students learn or understand, they will easily comprehend the main idea and supporting details.

The procedures in teaching select from the following five steps:

1. The explanation of each kind of genre-based rhetorical structure (in both Thai and English) then students practice from the text of the lesson, vocabulary learned, using the structures from exercises, as per the lesson plans;
2. Role play (personification of some inanimate categories, in explanations) for directly experiencing meanings;
3. Students do the vocabulary work individually and discuss meanings in pairs;
4. Students do group discussion on genre-based theoretical structure, applied to the text read to find the main idea, supporting ideas, and sequencing order; and
5. Students do individual text analyses and hand them in to the teacher.

Traditional Teaching Method

This is the method of teaching English reading used by most teachers in Thailand. At Rajabhat University Muban Chombung, it is the recommended practice for trainee teachers, with some recent modifications such as stressing learner-centred activities. The teaching procedure is as follows.

1. The teacher presents vocabulary items and necessary expressions in the text to students (in both Thai and English);
2. Students practice by repeating after the teacher: the whole class, groups, and individually;
3. After that students may read the whole passage silently or aloud, and do the group discussion to answer the questions orally according to the text read;
4. Then students practice reading in pairs to do vocabulary work and discuss in groups to find the main idea, supporting ideas and sequencing order; and
5. Students do the production exercises by reading the text and complete the reading comprehension exercises individually.

English Reading Comprehension: Second language readers obtain meaning from texts by actively using both lower and higher level skills to decode the smaller elements and construct the meaning and, by relating what they read to what they already know, they are able to understand the main ideas, sequence the order and obtain detailed information.

Test for English Reading Comprehension: English reading comprehension was measured by a multiple choice test. The test was based on the genre texts used in class and other similar level texts both from Thailand and Australia. The test was checked by the English staff and experts at Rajabhat Institute Muban Chombung and the researcher's supervisor. The test data was validated using other grade 7 classes at a large provincial government school (300 participants) and a Rasch analysis. Eighteen test items (out of the original sixty) were found to form a unidimensional scale covering all categories of interest in reading comprehension, based on the various genres used.

Attitude and behaviour towards learning: This concerns students' beliefs and feelings about teaching through genre-based rhetorical structures method, and through the traditional teaching method in English reading comprehension. The data was collected by a questionnaire, designed to address text, interactions, and behavioural controls.

Attitude and behaviour towards teaching: This concerns the beliefs and feelings of the participating trainee teachers on the learning experience of their students. A teachers' version of the students' questionnaire, and the trainee teachers' journals, were used by the discussion group to probe teacher's attitudes and behaviour. The questionnaires for teachers were not otherwise validated, but used in a qualitative way by the discussion group members in discussing teachers' attitudes and behaviours.

Group discussion: A discussion group is a small group made up of perhaps six to ten individuals with certain common feature characteristics, with whom a discussion can be held to focus onto a given issue or topic (Wellington, 1992, p.55). In this research, the group was used for evidence gathering and research management purposes as well as for analysing the evidence gathered to arrive at policy recommendations, extending, thus, Wellington's definition of focus groups. The current study may therefore refer to problem solving group discussions.

MODEL AND THEORETICAL FRAMEWORK

Model of ESL Reading

A global view of English reading comprehension which supports the present study is that language learning is based on interlinked meaning, as described by Harmer (2001, pp. 23-27). These interlinked meanings defined the lexical content and communication patterns of various discourse communities (Harmer, 2001, pp. 205-209). Interlinked meanings produce certain regular and fairly stable patterns of language use for communicative purposes. These are commonly known as genre (Kamberelis & Bovino, 1999; Hasan, 1989; Papas & Pettegrew, 1998; Johns, 1997). A key to successful learning of a foreign language in this view would require familiarity with the communicative purpose of various discourse communities and the resulting language use pattern of various genres. Therefore, the current research applied a model of communicative, top down (Harmer, 2001, pp. 200-202) ESL learning based on genre to English reading comprehension of grade seven students in Thailand.

The basic assumption of the present research is that, being familiar with genre features, students can comprehend texts better. A second assumption is that genre can be taught explicitly (Cope & Kalantzis, 1993, p.10) and that it can be experienced through role play (Painter, 1986). A third assumption is that better attitudes towards the reading classroom will assist in the development of English reading comprehension.

The basic reason that the Australian approach, based on the explicit teaching of genres, is expected to lead to better reading comprehension is that language is a network of meanings as represented by various genres (Barabasi, 2002, p.245). Language learning can be described as "an evolving word web" (Dorogovtsev & Mendes, 2001, pp.2603-2606), best captured in language learning by the Australian method, (based on genre derived meanings) combined with role play in the classroom. The reason this will lead to better attitudes is based on expected and actual experience of success that, then, re-inforces learning, as shown by Ajzen (1991).

In the present research, the Australian approach for implementing a genre-based method in English reading comprehension classroom learning has been adapted. The Australian approach is based on Christie et al. (1990-1992), Derewianka (1996), and Knapp (1995). This was suitably modified for grade seven students in Thailand, since all the researchers have shown that genre could be put into implementation in schools in Australia. Moreover, the Australian authors produced a guide book for lesson plans and they categorized the types of genre which need to be taught in school, since they are common to all subject areas. These categories are: factual genres and narrative genres. The current research extends this to the journalistic genre. The journalistic genre combines elements of both the above two, because reporting often follows an event order characeristic of narratives, while the genre is basically factual.

Special lesson plans for the experimental group used in the present research were constructed from narrative genres and factual genres, emphasizing recognition of genre features to help the student comprehend the text read. This is done in the lesson plans of the present research through explanation of genre features and then role play. An example can be given from the first period where the students learned the genre features of a fable. Then they could play the roles of the mouse and the bull themselves, re-enacting the fable in class.

The model used in the present study is a genre-based classroom implementation of the Australian approach to teaching English, based on changing attitude and behaviour of the learners, related to reading of texts with a social purpose (subjective norms as genres). The experience in role-play and genre features leads to developments in the classroom of English reading comprehension, based on a model by Ajzen (1991), and applied to the reading classroom.

The way students learn ESL through community language learning was made possible in the classroom by the meaning-based role play of various genres. These are introduced through a cognitive acquisition of genre features, and then social re-enacting of meaning in a role-play scene. This is what is new in the genre based rhetorical approach, used in collaborative language learning, for better reading comprehension. This is how, in theory, grade 7 students are expected to acquire better English reading comprehension.

Reading comprehension development is assumed to be dependent on three factors. Factor one is genre-based learning of text. Factor two is interpersonal attitude and interaction in the classroom. Interpersonal attitude and interactions capture the social dynamics of learning through social interactions. Factor three is behavioural controls in the learning process. Genre-based learning texts were designed to enhance students' understanding of the meaning of the vocabulary (MIW), understanding the main idea and the supporting ideas (MI), sequencing the order of the texts read, including following a series of events (FE) and following a sequence of ideas (FI) as well as locating information in the text (L). In genre based learning, understanding main ideas depends often on understanding the purpose of the text.

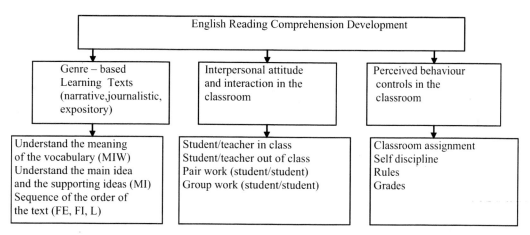

Figure 1 A model of English reading comprehension development

Source: constructed by S.Torok based on the literature review.

The way perceived behavioural controls work is similar to the organisation of traditional cooperative learning, where students are assigned procedure-based roles in classroom activities, as part of normal classroom management. In what follows details of how test items designed for genre texts of this research helped to establish whether learning objectives were achieved or not, are given.

In understanding the main idea and the supporting ideas, an English reading passage, for instance, "Land of Bikes" was taught for reading comprehension. The test item of "From Bubbles to Bottles" was used to evaluate their understanding of main ideas in test items 32 or 34 . In sequencing the order, an English reading passage about a sequence of events in "The Camping Trip" was taught for reading comprehension. "Camping Trip", and "Good-bye, Baby Bird" were used to evaluate understanding in test items 21 and 28. Also in sequencing the order, an English reading passage about a sequence of ideas in "Fresh Air to Breathe" was taught for reading comprehension . A test item on "The Singing Whales" was used to evaluate understanding of sequencing in test item 60.

For aspect one, genres as subjective norms of texts are concerned with 'meaning', 'purpose of using text', 'comprehension' and 'text for reading' in the questionnaire. For aspect two, interpersonal attitude and interactions in the classroom and the teaching of reading comprehension process are related to the interaction between students and the teacher in class, and the interaction between students and the teacher out of class, so that pair work and group work help students succeed in learning. Interpersonal attitude and interactions capture the social dynamics of learning through social interactions, as for example in a Vygotsky (1978) classroom. In aspect three, perceived behaviour controls in the learning process were classroom assignment, self discipline, rules and grades. These four perceived behavioural controls create student responsibility and support of each other. The way these perceived behavioural controls work is similar to the organisation of traditional cooperative learning, where students are assigned procedure-based roles in classroom group activities (Savova, 1985). The content taught to both groups in the experiment was based on the English Syllabus Design (Ministry of Education, 1966: 2-15).

Expected Role of Genre-Based Learning

In genre-based learning, the method of teaching English reading is based on the principle of rhetorical structure introduced by Pappas (1993) for expository texts (P) and by Hasan (1989) for narrative texts (H), and by Frederickson and Wedel (2000) for journalistic texts. It emphasizes teaching students to experience, by themselves, the way ideas and propositions are ordered in the text for a particular objective or purpose. For instance, in journalism, the headline normally gives a good idea about the communicative purpose of the news report to the audience. When the students learn or understand purpose they will easily comprehend the main idea and the supporting ideas in genre texts. There are five steps in the experimental lesson plan. First, the teacher explains the learning objective to the students to see if they understand what they have to learn. Then, the explanation of each kind of genre-based rhetorical structure (in both Thai and English), as an explicit scaffold for the students, is used. The explicit scaffold is the most important step because when the students learn, or understand the genre features, they will easily comprehend the main idea and the supporting ideas. Because of this, it can be said that genre is a vehicle that supports the students for their reading comprehension, as seen in the second step. The explicit scaffold can be likened to an actor, first studying the whole play, before playing in it.

In the second step, students do the role play to experience the meaning implicitly by personification and direct action. Students act according to their roles in each part of the story which appear in the genre features. This helps the students to understand and to comprehend the text read.

In the third step, students do the vocabulary work and discuss meanings in pairs. This helps the students feel at ease to do the work and they have more opportunity to support each other, while discussing the meaning of the vocabulary. The smart one can help the weak ones to do the work and to be able to finish the work in exercise A on time.

The fourth step is important because there is interaction among the group members. Students discuss genre features and apply this to the text to find the main idea, supporting ideas and sequencing of the order of ideas or events. In this way, students can help each other with knowledge. The group members will help each other to do exercise B. After finishing the exercise, students have their responsibility to report their work to their class.

In the fifth step, each student does his or her own work individually for text analysis in exercise C and hands it in to the teacher to see if he or she understands the genre features and could use it as a tool to help him or her to comprehend the text read. To conclude, the five steps are based on English reading comprehension development in the classroom as a learning cycle. In this way, text-related social skills, such as elaborating other's ideas, come from the interactions, including the processing and presenting of information. Genres are a tool for this and are learnt explicitly as well as through direct experience, involving role play. Current theory in ESL reading and writing focuses on the interrelationship between the reader, the writer, and the text. Grabe (1993), for instance, discussed the interactive nature of reading in which readers interact with the text, arriving at their own understanding.

In the present research, the Australian approach for implementing genre-based method in English reading comprehension classroom learning has been adapted. The approach maps out "a teaching-learning cycle....in the figure of a wheel" (see Cope & Kalantzis, 1993, p. 10).

Hoelker (2000) has also used the Australian approach as based on Christie et alia (1990-1992), Derewianka (1996) and Knapp (1995). This was suitably modified for grade seven students in Thailand, since all the authors have shown that genre could be implemented in their schools.

The lesson plans used in the present research were constructed from narrative genres and factual genres, emphasising recognition of genre features to help the student comprehend the text read. The precedent for this is Painter (1986) who explained that "the structure of genre can be highlighted by activities which concentrate attention on one element of structure at a time....". This is done in the lesson plans of the present research through explanation of genre features and then role play. The emphasis on role play is based on Richards and Rogers (1997, pp.124-125) elaborating on using it to experience genre features in the classroom through role play. The cycle is based on student interest during the teaching process. While there are many theories of language learning giving rise to creative tensions in the field of foreign language teaching (Hakuta & McLaughlin, 1996), it is the purpose of the present research to follow Bowering (1999) in introducing a particular approach to classroom based English reading comprehension development. Vygotsky's (1978) zone of proximate development implemented in the classroom through simulated genres via role-play is a major tool in this task, answering the question "can one turn the group (the class) into a knowledge building community, similar to those which presently advance each and every area of human endeavour?" (Mioduser, 2002, p.17).

To quote Bowering (1999, p. 87) "despite the change in emphasis this decade, there is still much to examine and understand about the construction of collaborative discourse particularly in content-based courses. It is these sort of contexts that what Vygotsky claims to be the overriding factor, namely of meaning shared through the blending of input and output, have not been the centre piece of collaborative language learning research to date". Blending is feedback, links established through role play in the classroom in the present research using genres, through social links and interaction among students.

A genre-based classroom implementation of the Australian approach to teaching English is based on the attitude and behaviour of the learners related to learning of texts with a social purpose (subjective norm, or genres), changing attitude and behaviour. Genres have social purpose as subjective norms, and can be understood through participatory (role-play) experience.

Expected Links between Attitude and Behaviour

It is theorised that the genre-based learning process that consists of explicit introduction of genre features and direct experience through organised, meaning-based role-play during the lessons, helps to achieve better attitude and behaviour towards learning ESL. Specifically the meaning-based roles for each genre also help to experience meaning through feedback (from for example, a Vygotskyan perspective, as discussed by Roller, 2002, Gee, 2001, Connor, 1996, Bowering, 1999, and Mioduser, 2002). In order to link ESL learning and attitude and behaviour to English reading comprehension, a reading comprehension test and an attitude and behaviour model were needed. This is supplied by Ajzen (1991) who suggested that subjective norms (involving texts in this ESL case) lead to action (behaviour); that attitudes (developed by interaction with other students) lead to intentions and, in turn, to actions; and that perceived behavioural controls (involving classroom assignments, self-discipline and rules) lead to actions.

Table 1. English reading comprehension for grade seven in Thailand.

Idea level
Inferences for main idea on purpose and context (MI)
Following a sequence of events (FE)
Following a sequence of ideas (FI)
Locating relevant information in the text (L)
Word level
making inference for word meaning (MIW) (including guessing)

Source : Modified by S. Torok from Lim Tock Keng (1994, p. 25) to suit the genre texts used in the lesson plans for this study and the level of participating grade 7 students in Thailand. The abbreviations MI, FE, FI, L and MIW relate to the classification of comprehension categories.

For the present study, what was needed was an advocacy by learners, trainee teachers, and heads of English departments, for introducing learner-centered changes into the English reading classroom in Thailand through practical interventions. Expected links between learning and attitude and behaviour were postulated to depend on an experience of success for ESL students and their trainee teachers. Achieving better reading comprehension is a success experience for the students. Similarly, introducing a methodology leading to better reading comprehension is a success experience for trainee teachers. In a dynamic framework, their self-confidence is expected to increase (Porter, 1996), through positive feedback based on a Vygotskyan classroom experience, rendering the Kennedy and Kennedy (1996) model dynamic.

MEASUREMENT

The item difficulties used in this study are discussed in terms of ordering from easy to hard, and calibrated, on the same scale as person abilities, while person abilities are ordered from low to high. Calculating item difficulties and person measures on the same scale using a Rasch measurement model will produce a linear scale. This is the reason a Rasch measurement model is used to solve measurement problems in the current study. A linear scale is better than a rank ordering and an improvement on the usual True Score Theory measures.

Problems with True Score Measurement Theory

There are at least five problems with current variable measures of attitude and behaviour based on a set of items answered with a Likert response set, and data analysed with True Score Test Theory. One, the response categories of strongly disagree, disagree, agree, and strongly agree are not ordered from low to high, as there is a discontinuity between disagree and agree. If a neutral category is used, this further complicates the construction of a linear measure because it attracts answers such as 'don't know', 'undecided', 'don't want to answer' and 'indifferent', which themselves are not part of an ordered structure, even if these answers could be separately identified. Thus it is argued that the Likert response format often does not provide a proper basis for the construction of a linear measure.

Two, it is not determined whether students agree on the difficulties of the items along the scale. There is a need to test whether students agree on the item difficulties.

In a proper linear scale, students with high, medium and low measures of ability will agree that certain items are easy and that others are hard. For instance, persons with low measures are only likely to answer the easy items positively. Persons with medium level measures are likely to answer the easy and medium difficulty items, rather than the hard items, most of the time. Persons with high measures will be likely to answer all easy, medium and hard items.

Three, item 'difficulties' are not tested for conceptual order. That is, in True Score Theory, the theoretical ordering of item 'difficulties' is not tested with the real data to create a linear scale. The Rasch model, on the other hand, tests that item difficulties are ordered.

Four, the item difficulties (from easy to hard) and the person measures (from low to high) are not calibrated on the same interval-level scale. This is a fundamental necessity in the creation of a proper linear scale.

Five, the data for many measures do not show high reliability and construct validity. In the literature, there are many measures of attitude and behaviour in classrooms where reliability is 0.7 or less and where construct validity has not been adequately tested.

Rasch Measurement and the RUMM Computer Program

Two objectives of this study were to measure two variables, (1) attitude and behaviour towards a genre-based learning of ESL reading, and (2) reading comprehension of English, on interval-level scales. One way to do this was to calibrate all the item difficulties and all the person scores on the same scale, using a Rasch measurement model (Andrich, 1988a,b; Rasch 1980/1960) with the computer program Rasch Unidimensional Measurement Models, referred to as RUMM (Andrich, Sheridan, Lyne & Luo, 2000).

Use of this Rasch measurement program ensures that only items that contribute logically and consistently to the measurement of attitude and behaviour, and to reading comprehension test, are included in the scales. Any items that do not fit on the scales in a consistent pattern with the other items are rejected.

The most likely reason for an item to be rejected is that it is not consistently measuring the variable attitude and behaviour towards genre-based learning of English, or reading comprehension. The RUMM computer program tests that items fit the model from easy to hard, and calibrates the person measures from low to high. These measures of the attitude and behaviour, and reading comprehension, are calibrated on the same scale with the item difficulties. A separate scale for the questionnaire and for the test is obtained through separate Rasch model analyses for each.

The RUMM program estimates threshold parameters to create an ordered threshold structure, in line with ordered response categories of the items. Within a four category response set (as in the present attitude and behaviour measure), there are three thresholds or boundaries, and it is necessary for these to be aligned with the order of the response categories for satisfactory discrimination or differentiation between measures. In the present study, ability measures are the students attitude and behaviour score and, at a threshold between two response categories, there are odds of 1:1 of answering in either category.

Parameter estimates are substituted back into the model and the RUMM 2010 program examines the difference between the expected values predicted from the model and the observed values, using two tests of fit. The first is the item-trait test-of-fit (a chi-square) which examines the consistency of the item parameters across the students with differing measures along the scale (see Andrich & Van Schoubroeck, 1989, pp. 479-480 for the equations). Essentially, a consensus is obtained for all item difficulties across students with differing measures along the scale. If students cannot agree on the difficulty of an item, then the item is discarded.

The second test-of-fit is the person-item interaction which examines the response patterns for students across items and for items across students. The residuals between the expected estimate and the actual value for each student-item are summed over all items for each student and over all students for each item (see Andrich & Van Schoubroeck, 1989, p. 482, for the equations). When the data fit the measurement model the fit statistics approximate a distribution with a mean near zero and a standard deviation near one. Negative values indicate a response pattern that fits the model too closely, probable because response dependencies are present (see Andrich, 1985).

After a successful fit on the linear scale, persons with high measure are likely to be able to answer the high, medium and easy items positively. Persons with medium measures are likely to be able to answer only the medium difficulty and easy items positively. Persons with low measures are likely to answer only the easy item positively. They are unlikely to be able to answer the medium and hard items positively.

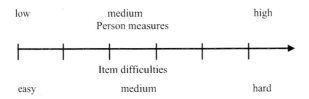

Figure 2. Idealised scale of item difficulties with person measures.

ATTITUDE AND BEHAVIOUR MEASUREMENT

A New Attitude/Behaviour Questionnaire

In the questionnaire, items are grouped under three major headings related to text, interactions, and controls, respectively, all amenable to classroom interventions by the teacher as a facilitator. The items are grouped under subheadings that are arranged according to an order of increasing difficulty, as found by a pilot group of students, not participating in the current study who were asked to respond to them. Ordering is essential for establishing a unidimensional scale as described by Waugh (2002, pp.67-68). The items were grouped under their various headings so that it would be clear to the convenience sample of 300 grade 7 students at a large provincial government school what was being asked of them. Thus all items were written in a positive sense, with an ordered response format, from easy to hard. All items were written in Thai. The questionnaire contained 48 items, each answered in two perspectives, my expectation and what actually happens (see Table 2).

Pilot Testing of the Questionnaire

In general, pilot testing involved having the questionnaire scrutinized by peers, and then administered to a sample of prospective students of the same grade level not participating either in the Rasch model analysis sample or in the experiment. Administration involved letting them do all questions, observing the time, then talking about their experience in class with their teacher.

The language of the questionnaire was simplified, so as to be understandable at the grade 7 level. All questions were retained. The total number of questions was 96 (48 times 2). The questionnaire was scrutinised again with Thai native speakers at Rajabhat University Muban Chombung. Those native speakers who were experts in testing found the questionnaire acceptable.

The Thai version was then administered by a trainee teacher teaching grade seven in another school, not the participating schools in the research. It was observed that the students took about one hour to complete the questionnaire. The trainee teacher asked the students whether they understood the questions or not, and whether they understood the difference between expectation (attitude) and actual (behaviour) in the questions.

The trainee teacher reported that in the class of 30 grade 7 students all answered the above questions affirmatively, saying that they understood the questions and that they knew the difference between what they expected to happen and what really happened in the classroom. They felt that they could, in general, do more than what they had thus far achieved in English. Moreover, for the future, they felt that they could do even better. After seeing these results, the researcher decided to use the Thai translated questionnaire without change for the Rasch model analysis with the convenience sample of 300 grade 7 students.

READING COMPREHENSION MEASUREMENT

The Reading Comprehension Test

In constructing the test, the objective was to have both comprehension categories and genre variety adequately covered in the test items. Comprehension categories included locating relevant information in the text (LI) represented by 26 test items from all three kinds of genre texts, expected to be easier with genre knowledge than without. The second comprehension category was following a sequence of events (FE), relevant mainly to the narrative genre and journalism, represented by two items. The third comprehension category was following a sequence of ideas (FI), mainly relevant to the expository/explanation genre represented by only one item. The last two comprehension categories related to main idea identification (MI) represented by 15 items, and word level inference (MIW) represented by 16 items. Classified by genre types, the same sixty items can be broken down into 21 from narrative texts, 7 from journalistic texts, 25 from explanations and another 7 undefined in terms of genre category.

There was limited opportunity to pilot test the reading comprehension test before the Rasch model analysis, there was extensive scrutiny and several revisions made to ensure quality. Only one grade 7 student of high ability took the test and completed it in one and a half hours. Later, the test was administered to the convenience sample of 300 grade 7 students, with instructions that it was a difficult test and that they should use their best guesses about the meanings of words, since they would want to do their best. Correct answers only would be counted. This may have introduced a bias for guessing, however it was judged to be both pedagogically and procedurally realistic in a competitive learning environment in Thailand. It was also ensured that students were sufficiently physically separated so that they answered the questions independently. The test turned out to be more difficult than expected. Some of the difficulty was due to design, since the comprehensive set of English reading materials included different genre texts (narrative, expository, journalistic) both from

Thailand and Australia. The test was checked by curriculum experts both from Thailand and several academics in Australia.

DATA COLLECTION AND ANALYSIS

The next step was to administer the English reading comprehension test and the attitude and behaviour questionnaire to 300 students in a large provincial primary school. These grade 7 students were representative of the grade 7 students used in the experimental and control groups. The chosen school had about twelve grade six classes of about 27 students each. This school was located in Samutsakhon Province which was about 100 kilometers from Ratchaburi, not too far from the practical teaching area of the Rajabhat University Muban Chombung.

Sample

The 300 sample of gender-mixed grade 7 students came from a large provincial secondary school which was located in Samutsakhon Province, 25 kilometers from Bangkok. The school has about 2500 students with 110 teachers. There were 102 male and 198 female students aged between 11-12 years old. Most of their parents are stallholders, sellers, and administrative officers. The chosen school was located outside the Rajabhat Institute Muban Chombung practice teaching area but close enough to have similar student abilities and characteristics to those in the experiment in Ratchaburi, which can be the representative of many other schools in Thailand. It took 2 ½ hours for the examination, including the questionnaire, for all 12 classes of grade six students from 09.00-11.30 AM. After going back to Rajabhat Institute Muban Chombung, the third year Science students collated the data which then was entered into an EXCEL computer program an saved as text in Word.

Ethics Procedure

The school principals with the regular English teachers at the school were approached (after the Edith Cowan University Ethics Committee had approved the letter of consent), and asked if they would be willing to participate in this classroom research. The statement in the letter outlined the purpose of the experiment and ensured the regular English teachers and the students of confidentiality and anonymity, with the right to refuse to participate, and to withdraw from the experiment at any time. After they had read the information and were satisfied, they were asked to sign a form of consent. Then, students signed the form of consent based on the conditions mentioned above, indicating their willingness to participate.

DATA ANALYSIS

Attitude and Behaviour, and English Reading Comprehension

Data were analysed using the Rasch Unidimensional Measurement Model (RUMM) computer program (Andrich, Sheridan, Lyne & Luo, 2000). The results are presented by tables, figures and descriptive text. The general meaning of the students' attitudes and behaviour towards reading comprehension (questionnaire) and reading comprehension (test) are discussed, and the relevant aspects are also discussed. The data on the variables attitude and behaviour towards learning English and English reading comprehension support the view that the data are valid and reliable.

Several steps were taken in order to create a proper interval level scale of students' attitude and behaviour, and English reading comprehension. First the item thresholds were checked to see that they were ordered in line with the ordering of the response categories. Only those items with ordered thresholds (indicating that the response categories for the item were answered consistently and logically) were included in the final analysis. The other items were deleted. Then, the residuals were examined. A residual is the difference between the expected item 'response' calculated according to the model and the actual item 'response' as marked by students. Residuals should be as close together as possible for a good fit but in practice are acceptable within $-2SD < x < +2SD$. The item-trait test-of-fit chi-square tests the consistency of the item parameters across the students' attitude and behaviour questionnaire, and the English reading comprehension test measures for each item, After that, the person-item trait fit was investigated to determine whether there was agreement among students as to the 'responses' of all the items along the scale. The non-performing items of students' attitude and behaviour questionnaire (60 items out of 96, determined through the steps described) and the non-performing items of English reading comprehension (42 items out of 60) were deleted from the scale, thus creating a proper scale with only items that fitted the measurement model. Variable measures were calibrated on the same scale as the item difficulties by the RUMM program.

RESULTS

Attitude and Behaviour Measure

The summary statistics of the Rasch analysis are shown in Table 2. Table 3 shows the item thresholds and person measures on the same scale. The item difficulties are ordered from easy to hard and the attitude and behaviour measures are ordered from low to high.

Reading Comprehension Measure

The summary statistics of the Rasch analysis are shown in Table 4. Figure 3 shows the person-item map of the student measure of the English reading comprehension and item difficulties on the same scale from easy to hard with the student measures ordered from low to high. Low is at the bottom of the figure (-) while high is at the top (+). Items are labelled according to comprehension categories.

Attitude and Behaviour Measure (Psychometric Characteristics)

Of the original 96 items of the attitude and behaviour measure, 60 did not fit the measurement model, in either the real or ideal aspect, and were deleted. Of the 36 items that did fit the measurement model, 18 items measured a real (or behaviour) aspect of students' attitude and behaviour (that is what really happens), and 18 items measured an expectation (or attitude) aspect of students' attitude and behaviour (that is what I expect should happen).

Together, these 36 items fitted the measurement model and the data formed an interval-level scale from which valid and reliable inferences can be made.

The item-trait test-of-fit is acceptable and supports the claim of creation of a unidimensional scale ($X^2 = 170.75$, df = 144, p = 0.06) (the null hypothesis is that there is no significant interaction between the responses to the items and the person measures along the trait). There was a reasonable consensus among students about the difficulties of the items, ordered along the scale from easy to hard. This means that students with low, medium or high measures agreed that certain items were easy, that others were of moderate difficulty, and that some others were hard. Category threshold values were ordered from low to high, which indicates that students answered the response categories consistently for the 36 items. The Index of Separability for the 36 item scale with the four response categories is 0.92. This means that the proportion of observed variance considered true is 92 percent. The overall power of tests-of-fit was rated as excellent, based on the Index of Separation.

Table 2. Summary statistics for 36 item students' attitude and behaviour measure

	Items	Students
Number	36	296
Location mean	0.00	0.69
Standard deviation	0.72	0.81
Fit statistical mean	0.18	0.32
Standard deviation	0.90	1.85
Item-trait interaction chi square = 170.75		
Probability of item-trait (p) = 0.06		
Degrees of freedom = 144		
Student Separation Index = 0.92		
Power of test-of-fit excellent (based on the Separation index)		

Notes on Table 2:
1. The item means are constrained to zero by the measurement model.
2. When the data fit the measurement model, the fit statistic approximates a distribution with a mean near zero and a SD near one (a good fit for this scale). They are reported only to 2 decimal places because the errors are to two decimal places.
3. The item-trait interaction indicates the agreement displayed with all items across all students from different locations on the scale (acceptable for this scale). That is, the items measure a unidimensional trait (just).
4. The Student Separation Index is the proportion of observed variance considered true (92%, excellent).
5. Standard errors are between 0.08 and 0.10.

There is a range of values from easiest to hardest going down from the top of each subgroup to the bottom (see Table 3). For the subgroup *interactions*, this range is -1.50 to -0.14 for the expectations perspective and -0.50 to +1.21 for actual perspective (what really happened). For the subgroup *behavioural controls*. This range is 0.45 to -0.02 for the expectations perspective and +0.25 to +1.21 for the actuals. For the subgroup genre-based learning text, the range is -1.43 to +0.44 for the expectation perspective and -0.69 to +1.81 for the actual perspective. This is intersting because it shows some overlap in the three factors, part of the same unidimensional scale.

Table 3. The final 36 items for the attitude and behaviour measure.

Item nos. Original item no.	Item nos. New item no.	My ideal expectation	This is what really happened
Subgroup: Interpersonal attitudes and interactions in the classroom			
Opportunity of interaction (student/student)			
59-60	1-2 I can have more opportunity to participate in activities among friends	-1.50	-0.50
51-52	3-4 I like to talk or study in pairs	-0.94	-0.40
49-50	5-6 I like to learn new words from friends	-0.77	-0.32
Student and teacher in class			
43-44	7-8 I like the way my teacher teaches me English reading	-0.56	-0.05
Group work (student/student)			
55-56	9-10 I like to compare different points of view found in reading with friends	-0.40	0.53
53-54	11-12 I can tell my friends whether I believe what I have read, or not	-0.35	0.55
Student and teacher out of class			
41-42	13-14 I can discuss my hobbies and my future plans with my teacher	-0.16	+0.86
39-40	15-16 I can talk to my teacher informally about news, sport, and everyday life related to my reading assignment	-0.14	+0.85
Subgroup: Perceived behavioural controls in the classroom (10 items)			
Classroom assignments			
83-84	17-18 I can study reading materials in groups with other friends	-0.45	+0.51
81-82	19-20 I can participate in class discussion	-0.37	+0.25
Self discipline			
73-74	21-22 I can use note for stories, information about my reading assignment	-0.25	+0.76
75-76	23-24 I can finish my reading tasks in time	-0.03	+0.84
37-38	25-26 I can make an appointment to see my teacher in his/her office to discuss my reading.	-0.02	+1.21
Subgroup: Genre based learning text (10 items)			
Meaning			
7-8	27-28 I like to guess the meaning of the words in the text	-0.75	0.51
Purpose of using text			
31-32	29-30 I find English reading is useful.	-1.43	-0.69
29-30	31-32 I can read English at home	-0.39	0.23
Comprehension			
15-16	33-34 I can find the causes of the problem after reading.	0.07	1.16
Text for reading			
3-4	35-36 I like reading news reports in English	0.44	1.81

Figure 3 gives the order of items with hard items on top (RHS) and easy items at the bottom RHS). How items were ordered according to their locations on the Rasch unidimensional scale is presented in Table 3 with 16 items (8 pairs) on classroom interaction, 10 items (5 pairs) on behavioural controls, and 10 items (5 pairs) on text. The difficulties of some of the items in these subgroups overlap, as seen in Table 3. As a result of the analysis, it can be concluded that the data on the variable attitude and behaviour towards learning English are valid and reliable. The 36 items are ordered in difficulty from easy to hard. The student answers are ordered from low to high, and there is a strong agreement amongst the students about the ordering of the item difficulties. There is, therefore, an expectation that valid and reliable inferences can be made from the data.

```
LOCATION         STUDENTS              ITEM DIFFICULTIES
-----------------------------------------------------------------
  4.0       HIGH MEASURES OF       |    HARD    ITEMS
            ATTITUDE/              |
            BEHAVIOUR              |
                                   |
                              X    |
  3.0                              |
                                   |
                              X    |
                              X    |
                             XX    |
  2.0                         X    |
                           XXXXX   |
                           XXXXX   |  4LNT
                        XXXXXXXXX  |
                         XXXXXXXX  |  16CCT
  1.0           XXXXXXXXXXXXXXX    |  76SDC,  38SDC
              XXXXXXXXXXXXXXXXXX   |  54.GWI, 40STOI, 42STOI
                XXXXXXXXXXXXXX     |  84RGC,  74SDC
             XXXXXXXXXXXXXXXXXX    |   3LNT,  82RGC,  56GWI
                 XXXXXXXXXXX       |  30PUT
  0.0              XXXXXXXXX       |   8GMT,  75SDC,  15CCT,  37SDC
                  XXXXXXXXXX       |  52PWI,  50PWI,  44STI,  73SDC
                    XXXXXXX        |  81RGC,  55GWI,  53GWI,  39STOI,
                                   |  60SSI,  41STOI
                     XXXXXX        |  29PUT,  43STI,  83RGC
                      XXXX         |  32PUT,   7GMT
 -1.0                  XXX         |  49PWI
                        XX         |  31PUT,  51PWI
                       XXX         |  59SSI
                         X         |
                                   |
 -2.0                              |
                                   |
        LOW   MEASURES    OF       |    EASY    ITEMS
        ATTITUDE  AND  BEHAVIOUR   |
-----------------------------------------------------------------
Each X = 2 persons
-----------------------------------------------------------------
```

Figure 3. Person-item map (attitude/behaviour measures and item difficulties on the same scale, N=296, I= 36)

Notes: odd numbers are expectation (attitude), even numbers are actual behaviour.
I = interaction, C=controls, T = text, STI = student-teacher interaction, PWI = pair-work interaction, PUT = purpose of using text, SSI = student-student interaction,
STOI = student-teacher out-of-class interaction, SDC = self discipline controls,
CCT = comprehension of causes of problems in text, GWI = group work interaction,
RGC = rules group controls, LNT = like newspaper text, GMT = guess meaning of words from text.

Reading Comprehension Measure (Psychometric Characteristics)

For the reading comprehension measure, there were 60 original items, and 42 did not fit the measurement model. That left 18 test items that did fit the measurement model. These 18 test items were about understanding the main idea, sequencing the order of ideas and events, and understanding the meaning from English reading genre texts, as well as locating information within these texts.

There was a reasonable consensus among students about the difficulties of the items, ordered along the scale from easy to hard. The item-trait test-of-fit (X^2 = 68.61, df = 72, p = 0.59) was good, supporting a unidimensional scale (the null hypothesis is that there is no significant interaction between the responses to the items and the person measures along the trait). All the data together means that students with low, medium or high measures agreed that certain items were easy, that others were of moderate difficulty, and some others were hard. The Index of Separability for the 18 item scale with the two response categories is 0.41. This means that the proportion of observed variance considered true is 41 percent. This is low and, therefore, there is room for improvement in any future use of the scale, when it should be revised. The main problem here is that some easier items and some harder items need to be added to the scale, especially easier items for these grade 7 students. The RUMM computer program rates the overall power of tests-of-fit in the categories of too low, low, good, and excellent, and in this case, it was rated a low, based on the Index of Separation. The problem here is that the errors are large in comparison to the separation of the person measures along the scale, and this means that some easier items need to be added to improve targeting.

The English reading comprehension test contained some Australian materials which were too difficult. Nevertheless, a unidimensional scale was established with the remaining items properly ordered. These could be used to compare the experimental results in the teaching experiment described in the next chapter, since the linear model fitted the data and all errors were randomly distributed. In Figure 4 the distribution of labeled test items is shown, based on the person-item distribution.

In figure 4, there are no items matching persons at either the lowest (-2.0) or the highest (1.0) end of the scale, indicating that improvements may be possible for the test if both easy items and hard items are added. In the light of the low power of test fit in Table 4, a word on errors from guessing on an admittedly hard test are in order. Errors were likely to be uniformly distributed, since there were three possible wrong guesses and only one correct answer on the multiple choice test items, rendering a wrong answer three times more likely than a correct one on any item, from pure guessing. Only correct answers were counted, with no penalty (except loss of score) for wrong guesses. Thus, even if correct guesses improved the score of some participants, there was likely to be a larger number of incorrect guesses lowering the score of most. The results for the whole convenience sample of 300 students may be slightly biased through guessing, and the variance of answers may be somewhat larger. It is unlikely that the unidimensional scale would be substantially altered with these most likely uniformly biased errors, in spite of the low power of the tests-of-fit. At 72 degrees of freedom, the total item trait chi-square of 68.6 can be considered good with a probability of 0.59, as reported in Table 4. This supports the claim of unidimensionality for the scale. When comparing two groups in the teaching experiment using the scale, the differences would remain meaningful, because only identical biases from guessing may characterise both samples (Torok, 1976, p.223-224).

Table 4. Summary statistics for 18 item English reading comprehension measure.

	Items	Students
Number	18	300
Location mean	0.00	-0.27
Standard deviation	0.49	0.67
Fit statistical mean	0.02	0.26
Standard deviation	0.85	0.71

Item-trait interaction chi square = 68.61
Probability of item-trait (p) = 0.59
Degree of freedom = 72
Student Separation Index = 0.41
Power of test-of-fit: low

Notes on Table 4
1. The item means are constrained to zero by the mesurement model.
2. When the data fit the measurement model, the fit statistic approximates a distribution with a mean near zero and a SD near one (a good fit for this scale)
3. The item-trait interaction indicates the agreement displayed with all items across all students from different locations on the scale (very good for this scale).
4. The Student Separation Index is the proportion of observed English reading comprehension variance considered true (in this scale 41% and low).

Table 4 (Continued). Individual item fit, reading comprehension test (N=300, I=18)

New No.	Old item No.	Chi Sq	Prob	Location	SE	Residual	DegFree
1	3	3.155	0.520	-0.85	0.13	0.22	282.39
2	5	0.210	0.335	0.02	0.12	1.04	282.39
3	7	8.374	0.054	0.70	0.13	2.30	282.39
4	12	1.626	0.799	0.53	0.13	0.98	282.39
5	15	2.872	0.568	0.70	0.13	1.67	282.39
6	21	3.473	0.468	-0.61	0.12	0.10	282.39
7	24	2.784	0.584	0.18	0.12	0.44	282.39
8	30	2.284	0.675	0.25	0.12	2.14	282.39
9	31	2.363	0.661	-0.10	0.12	0.97	282.39
10	32	5.025	0.266	-0.27	0.12	2.14	282.39
11	33	5.087	0.259	0.17	0.12	1.11	282.39
12	47	7.159	0.104	-1.16	0.13	-0.86	282.39
13	49	9.536	0.024	-0.07	0.12	1.24	282.39
14	50	6.137	0.167	0.19	0.12	1.19	282.39
15	56	3.693	0.434	0.39	0.13	1.08	282.39
16	58	0.878	0.926	-0.05	0.12	0.73	282.39
17	59	1.157	0.882	0.10	0.12	-0.10	282.39
18	60	2.797	0.582	-0.13	0.12	1.96	282.39

Creating Scales to Measure Reading Comprehension, and Attitude ... 175

Location	Students	Item Difficulties
2.0	High Measure Of Reading Comprehension	Hard Items
1.0	XXXX	
	XXX	MIW/E MI/N
	XXXXXXXXX	MIW/N
	XXXXXXXXXXXXX	L/E MI/E
	XX	
0.0	XXXXXXXXXXXXX	MI/E L/E L/E L/N L/E
		FI/E L/E MI/E MI/E
	XXXXXXXXXXXX	MI/E
	XXXXXXXXXXXX	
	XXXXXXXXXX	FE/N
-1.0		L/E
	XXXXXXX	MIW/E
	XXXX	
	XXXX	
-2.0		
	X	
-3.0	Low Measure Of Reading Comprehension	Easy Items

Each X = 3 Persons

Figure 4. Person measures against item difficulty map for reading comprehension test (N=300, I=18).

Notes on test item categories
MI/N = main idea identification, narrative, MI/E = main idea identification, explanation,
MIW/N = making inferences for word meanings, narrative, MIW/E = making inferences for word meanings, explanation, FI/E = following a sequence of ideas, explanation,
FE/N = following a sequence of events, narrative, L/E = locating information, explanation,
L/N = locating information, narrative.

DISCUSSION

Attitude and Behaviour

The data presented in the results indicate that a good unidimensional scale of attitude and behaviour towards ESL has been constructed. For this scale of 36 items, the errors are small and the internal reliability is very high with a separation index of 0.92 and the power of the tests-of-fit statistics is excellent. The 36 items are aligned on the scale in order of item difficulty from easy to hard as shown in Figure 4. Most students answered the easier items positively. As the items become more and more difficult on the scale, respondents needed a higher attitude and behaviour measure to answer them positively. This means that the more difficult items are answered positively only by students with high attitude and behaviour measures. Students with lower attitude and behaviour measures would not have answered the more difficult items positively. All items were harder in behaviour than in expectation (attitude), as expected. Table 3 indicates that classroom interaction items were the easiest to achieve, while behavioural control and text related items were more difficult.

Table 5. Rank order item difficulties for interactions, behavioural controls, and text

	Expectation		Actual behaviour		
Easiest	59	SSI	32	PUT	(least trouble)
	31	PUT	52	PWI	
	51	PWI	50	PWI	
	49	PWI	60	SSI	
	7	GMT	44	STI	
	43	STI	8	GMT	
	83	RGC	30	PUT	
	55	GWI	82	RGC	
	29	PUT	84	RGC	
	81	RGC	56	GWI	
	53	GWI	54	GWI	
	73	SDC	74	SDC	
	41	STOI	76	SDC	
	39	STOI	40	STOI	
	75	SDC	42	STOI	
	37	SDC	38	SDC	
	15	CCT	16	CCT	
Hardest	3	LNT	4	LNT	(most trouble)

Notes: I = Interactions, C = Behavioural controls (rules), T= Text, easiest (least trouble) items are at the top of the scale while hardest (most trouble) items are at the bottom. Labels are as in Figure 1.
STI = student-teacher interaction, PWI = pair-work interaction, PUT = purpose of using text,
SSI = student-student interaction, STOI = student-teacher out of class interaction,
SDC = self discipline controls, LNT = like newspaper text, GMT = guess meaning of words from text.

It can be seen from Table 6 that what actually happened is always harder to achieve than the expected one, a result consistent with the model used. First, easiest expectations were for interaction opportunities SSI (item 59). The corresponding behaviour item (item 60) was fourth down on the scale on the right hand side of Table 5, meaning that, in actual behaviour, some other items (32, 52, and 50) were easier. Two of these are interaction related, also (PWI) referring to pair-work interaction, while the first one (PUT) is concerned with knowing the purpose of using the text. That was found to be the easiest in behaviour and also in expectation (second down on the left hand side of Table 5), both referring to the item "I find English reading is useful".

Table 6. The final 36 items for the attitude and behaviour measure

Item Number		Mean location		Thresholds	
New	Old	(difficulty)	Lower	Middle	Upper
1	59	-1.50	-3.41	-1.34	0.26
2	60	0.30	-1.82	-0.26	1.20
3	51	-0.94	-1.98	-1.11	0.27
4	52	-0.40	-2.01	-1.15	0.97
5	49	-0.77	-1.99	-0.84	0.53
6	50	-0.32	-1.90	-0.06	1.01
7	43	-0.56	-1.84	-0.46	0.61
8	44	-0.05	-1.07	-0.05	0.97
9	55	-0.40	-1.97	-0.30	1.08
10	56	+0.53	-1.51	0.51	2.58

Table 6. (Continued).

Item Number New	Old	Mean location (difficulty)	Thresholds Lower	Middle	Upper
11	53	-0.35	-1.92	-0.30	1.17
12	54	+0.55	-1.37	0.83	2.17
13	41	-0.16	-1.53	-0.25	1.30
14	42	+0.86	-0.81	0.98	2.42
15	39	-0.14	-1.28	-0.27	1.11
16	40	+0.85	-0.37	0.87	2.05
17	83	-0.45	-1.27	-0.43	1.06
18	84	+0.51	-1.17	0.61	2.07
19	81	-0.37	-1.42	-0.40	0.70
20	82	+0.25	-1.37	0.49	1.67
21	73	-0.25	-1.75	-0.02	1.02
22	74	+0.76	-1.21	0.70	2.78
23	75	-0.03	-1.47	0.01	1.38
24	76	+0.84	-0.87	1.15	2.24
25	37	-0.02	-1.36	0.14	1.28
26	38	+1.21	-0.11	1.18	2.57
27	7	-0.75	-2.01	-0.62	0.36
28	8	+0.15	-1.20	0.01	1.65
29	31	-1.43	-2.99	-1.12	-0.20
30	32	-0.69	-1.97	-0.68	0.57
31	29	-0.39	-1.29	-0.53	0.66
32	30	+0.23	-1.32	0.28	1.72
33	15	+0.07	-1.45	0.03	1.63
34	16	+1.16	-0.89	1.28	3.08
35	3	+0.44	-1.02	0.48	1.87
36	4	+1.81	-0.04	1.96	3.49

Note: Odd numbered item difficulties (expectations) are easier than the next even numbered item difficulties (actual behaviour), as conceptualised.

It is also of interest to observe that the most difficult items are text related (15 and 3) CCT and LNT, the first one "I can find causes of the problems after reading" referring to both Narrative and Expository genres and the practical use of information while the second one "I like reading newspapers" refers to the journalistic genre where liking is not diminished by the difficulty of the text. Actually, completing reading assignments on time was easier than expected when ranked with the other items on the right hand side of the scale on Table 5 (items 75 and 76, SDC, from the behavioural controls cluster, referring to self discipline). In general, students prefer easier (less troublesome) items than harder ones, although sometimes harder items are more challenging than easy ones (eg.: reading newspapers and linking it, items 3 and 4). About behavioural controls related items, an additional observation is that these need some improvement, especially items 39, 40, 41 and 42 when these refer to interactions between students and teacher teachers out of class (STOI), presumably governed by school rules and teacher initiatives.

Reading Comprehension

Although the reading comprehension measure could be improved in terms of psychometric properties to obtain a better item separability index, the test as given was found useful for the purpose of the experimental comparisons reported in the next chapter. The psychometric properties presented here are used for evaluating reading comprehension based on the teaching of genre structures. Table 7 shows the 18 items, left after the Rasch model analysis, forming a unidimensional scale. Text item categories are given, where E stands for expository genre, N stands for narrative genre and J stands for journalistic (news report) genre. It is noted that no journalistic item survived the Rasch model analysis. The result is consistent with the Rasch model analysis of the attitude and behaviour questionnaire, where journalistic genre texts were expected to be, and were found to be, the most difficult. In spite of this, students liked reading and using text with a purpose (item 32 is on the top of the scale on the right of Table 5) as easy. It is considered that the reading comprehension data are valid and reliable and can be used for experimental comparisons, although the separability could be improved, if some easy items would be added.

Table 7. Distribution of test items according to comprehension category and genre

Categories:	MI	L	FE	FI	MIW
Item number, with genre indicator	15N 32E 49E 56E 58E 5E 59E	3E 24N 30E 33E 31E 50E	21N	60E	7E 12N 47E

Notes : N= narrative text (mainly fables), E = expository text (mainly explanations),
MI= inferences for main idea on purpose and context, FE= following a sequence of events, FI= following a sequence of ideas, L= locating relevant information in the text, MIW =making inferences for word meanings (including guessing).

Table 8. The difficulties of the final items for reading comprehnesion, from easy (-) to hard (+)

Original Item Number	New Item Number	Item Location (difficulty)	Label	Item Category
47	1	-1.16	E/MIW	Expository: making inference for word meaning including guessing (understanding the meaning).
3	2	-0.85	E/L	Expository: locating relevant information in the text (understanding the supporting idea).
21	3	-0.61	N/FE	Narrative: following a sequence of events (sequencing the order of events).
32	4	-0.27	E/MI	Expository: inferences for main idea on purpose and context (understanding the main idea).
60	5	-0.13	E/FI	Expository: following a sequence of ideas (sequencing the order of ideas).
31	6	-0.10	E/L	Expository: locating relevant information in the text (understanding the supporting idea).
49	7	-0.07	E/MI	Expository: inferences for main idea on purpose and context (understanding the main idea).
58	8	-0.05	E/MI	Expository: inferences for main idea on purpose and context (understanding the main idea).
5	9	+0.02	E/MI	Expository: inferences for main idea on purpose and context (understanding the main idea).

Table 8. (Continued).

Original Item Number	New Item Number	Item Location (difficulty)	Label	Item Category
59	10	+0.10	E/L	Expository: locating relevant information in the text (understanding the supporting idea).
33	11	+0.17	E/L	Expository: locating relevant information in the text (understanding the supporting idea).
24	12	+0.18	N/L	Narrative: locating relevant information in the text (understanding the supporting idea).
50	13	+0.19	E/L	Expository: locating relevant information in the text (understanding the supporting idea).
30	14	+0.25	E/L	Expository: locating relevant information in the text (understanding the supporting idea).
56	15	+0.39	E/MI	Expository: inferences for main idea on purpose and context (understanding the main idea).
12	16	+0.53	N/MIW	Narrative: making inference for word meaning including guessing (understanding the meaning).
7	17	+0.70	E/MIW	Expository: making inference for word meaning including guessing (understanding the meaning).
15	18	+0.70	N/MI	Narrative: inferences for main idea on purpose and context (understanding the main idea).

Note: Labels left of the slash refer to genre while right of the slash are comprehension categories as defined in Table 7.

Table 8 gives items ordered according to item difficulty on the unidimensional scale produced by the RUMM programme. Table 8 shows that psychometrically the categories MIW, L, FE, MI, FI, MIW are not really much different in difficulty, as items could be found anywhere on the unidimensional scale. From the point of view of genre learning and how it helps reading comprehension, it is seen that the two strongly genre-dependent items, namely FE (following a sequence of events mainly for narratives) and FI (following a sequence of ideas mainly in explanations) are relatively easy, while guessing (MIW) and main idea identification (MI) are relatively difficult, depending, of course, on actual text content. Based on actual text content they may appear anywhere on the scale, similarly for items related to supporting ideas and locating information (L). Thus it may be concluded that genre learning might lead to a uniform improvement of reading comprehension based on improved ability to locate information as well as understanding main ideas and supporting ideas based on location and the guessing of words. This argues for reading comprehension being an integral measure, which is difficult to be broken down into distinct components. Meanings are always interlinked. It is difficult to construct tests with a unidimensional scale that completely eliminate noise, even though giving useful insights into the difficulty for students of the analysed test items (Lim, 1994).

SUMMARY

A Rasch measurement model was used to create a scale to measure attitude and behaviour towards English reading comprehension development in the classroom. This comprised 36 items (18 expected and 18 actual corresponding to these). Each of the 36 items fits the model and are aligned together on a linear scale. The data were valid and reliable as shown by the separability index (0.92) and formed one unidimensional scale comprising three partially overlapping subgroups related to interactions, behavioural controls, and text, respectively, with increasing degree of 'difficulty'.

A reading comprehension test has been developed for this study, using various genre reading materials. A sixty item multiple choice test, (only one correct answer each item), with narrative, expository, and journalistic genre reading materials was used. A Rasch measurement model analysis yielded a unidimensional scale of 18 items that can be used to assess the English reading comprehension development of grade seven students. The reading comprehension test may need futher refinements to improve its separability index, such as possibly analysing it with higher than grade seven groups, as it was slightly too difficult for grade seven. Test items at both the lowest and highest levels of difficulty may need to be added for possible improvements.

It can be concluded that the data for the attitude and behaviour measure is valid and reliable, and that valid and reliable inferences can be made from the unidimensional scale created. The conclusion can also be drawn that a unidimensional measure for reading comprehension was created, but that its separability is low because some of the test items were too difficult for many of the students, initially (that is in pretesting), but satisfactory in the posttesting . The Rasch analysis has provided valuable understanding of the structure of the data while creating the two scales.

REFERENCES

Adams, R. J., Griffin, P. E., & Martin,L (1987). Latent trait method for measuring a dimension in second language proficiency. *Language Testing,* 4 (1), 9-27.

Ajzen, I. (1991). *Attitude, Personality and Behaviour.* Milton Keynes: Open University Press.

Alalou, A. (1999). Using student expectations and perceived needs to rethink pedagogy and curriculum: a case study. *Foreign Language Annals,* 30 (1), 27-44.

Anders, P. L. (2002). Towards understanding of the development of reading comprehension instruction across the grade levels. In Roller, C.M. (Ed.),*Comprehensive Reading Instruction Across the Grade Levels, pp.111-132*

Newark, Del.: International Reading Association.

Applebaum, B. (1995). Creating a trusting atmosphere in the language classroom. *Educational Theory,* 45 (4), 443-452.

Anderson, N. A.(1998). Providing feedback to preservice teachers of reading in field settings. *Reading Research and Instruction,* 37 (2), 123-136.

Andrich, D. (1982). Using latent trait measurement models to analyse attitudinal data: a synthesis of viewpoints. In D. Spearritt (Ed). *The improvement of measurement in education and psychology : contributions of latent trait theories,* pp.89-126. Melbourne: Australian Council for Educational Research.

Andrich, D. (1985). A latent trait model for items with response dependencies: implications for test construction and analysis. In S. E. Embreston (Ed), *Test design: developments in psychology and psychometrics*, pp. 245-275. Orlando: Academic Press.

Andrich, D. (1988a). A general form of Rasch's extended logistic model for partialcredit scoring. *Applied Masurement in Education,* 1 (4), 363-378.

Andrich, D. (1988b). *Rasch models for measurement.* Sage university paper on quantitative applications in the social sciences (SN 07/068). Newbury Park CA: Sage.

Andrich, D. and van Schoubroeck, L. (1989). The General Health Questionnaire: APsychometric analysis using latent trait theory. *Psychological Medicine*, 19, 469-485.

Andrich, D., Sheridan, B., Lyne, A., & Luo, G. (2000) RUMM 2010: A windows based item analysis program employing Rasch unidimensional measurement models Perth: Murdoch University.

Aoki, D. S. (2000). The thing never speaks for itself : Lacan and the pedagogical politics of clarity. *Harvard Educational Review*, 70 (3), 347-369.

Au, K. H. (1997). Literacy for all students: ten steps toward making a difference. *The Reading Teacher*, 51 (3), 186-194.

Au, K. & Raphael, T. E. (2000). Equity and literacy in the next millennium. *Reading Research Quarterly*, 35 (1) January / February / March, 170-188.

Ayal, E. B. (1963). Value systems and economic development in Japan and Thailand. *Journal of Social Issues*, 19, pp.35-51.

Baker, L. & Wigfield, A. (1999). Dimensions of children's motivation for reading and their relations to reading achievement. *Reading Research Quiarterly,* 34 (4), 452-477.

Bean, T.W. (2002). Text comprehension: the role of activity theory in navigating students' prior knowledge in context teaching, pp.133-147. In Roller, C.M. (Ed.). *Text comprehension: reading instruction across the grade levels.* Newark, Del: International Reading Association.

Biria, R. & Tahirian, M. H. (1994). The methodology factor in teaching ESP. *English for Specific Purposes*, 13 (1), 93-101.

Bowering, M. (2003). *Genre Based Approach and Record*, Unpublished Seminar Notes, Edith Cowan University, March.

Bowering, M.H. (1999). Collaboration and foreign language learning: A case study in a Cambodian university. Unpublished EdD thesis. Sydney: The University of Sydney.

Bowles, S., Bradly, B.A., Burnett, R.Carr Edwards, E., Font, G., Francis, M., Heron, A.H., Henderson-Smith, C., Dougherty- Stahl, K.A., McCartney, A.A., Montero, M.K., Park, M., Payne, C.R. ,Rush,L., Tauferner, D., Waldrip,P., Yoon, J.C., with Stahl, S.A.& Commeyras, M. (2001). The 1999/2000 University of Georgia Doctoral Seminar in Reading Education. *Reading Reasearch Quarterly,* 36 (1), 74-85.

Brito, M. & Nunes, C. (1992). Action research and reading difficulty. *English for Specific Purposes*, 11(1), 177-186.

Brown, K. (1994). *The Effects of teaching a specific top-level structure on the organization of written text.* Unpublished Master's Thesis, Edith Cowan University, Mt. Lawley, Perth, WA.

Brown, R. (2000). Cultural continuity and ELT teaching training. *ELT Journal,* 54 (3), 227-239.

Bunnag, S. (2002a). Retirees to be imported to give lessons. *Bangkok Post,*15 Mar, 2002.

Bunnag, S. (2002b). *Bangkok Post,* 30 Sep, 2002,p.6.

Carriedo, N., & Alonson-Tapia, J. (1996). Main idea comprehension: training teachers and effects on students. *Journal of Research in Reading*, 19 (2), 128-153.

Chandavimol, M. (1998). Reading comprehension: an active engagement or a passive experience? *PASAA* 28, pp. 31-42.

Chawhan, L. & Oliver, R. (2000). What beliefs do ESL students hold about language learning? *TESOL in Content.* 10(1), 20-26.

Chayarathee, S. (1994). *A Comparison of The Effects of The Language Experience Approach Versus the use of A Teacher's Manual of the General Education Department Supervisory Unit on the English Reading Ability and Motivation of Mathayom Suksa two Students at Omnoisoponchanupatham School, Samut Sakorn Province*. Unpublished master's thesis, Silpakorn University, Bangkok, Thailand.

Chen, T.Y. (2000). Self training for ESP through action research.*English for Specific Purposes,,* 19, 389-402.

Chittawat, H. (1995). Teaching English through communicative trends. *Mitr Krue*, 27 (29), 42-43.

Christie, F. Gray, B., Gray, P., Macken, M., Martin, J. R. & Rothery, R. (1990-1992). *Language: A Resource for Meaning* (Teachers' and Student Books), Sydney.Harcourt Brace Jovanovich.

Christie, F. (1999). *Pedagogy and the shaping of consciousness.* London: Cassell.

Clachar, A. (2000). Opposition and accomodation: an examination of Turkish Teacher's attitudes towards Western approaches to the teaching of writing. *Research in the Teaching of English*. 35, pp. 66-100.

Clark, C. & Medina (2000). How reading and writing literacy narratives affect preservice teachers' understanding of literacy, pedagogy, and multiculturalism. Journal of Teacher Education, 5 (1), 63-75.

Coe, R. (1994). Teaching genre as process in A. Freedman & Medway. (Eds), *Learning and teaching genre*, 157-190.Portsmith, NH: Heinemann.

Cohen, J. (1988). *Statistical power analysis for the behavioural sciences.* Hillsdale, NJ: Erlbaum.

Connor, N. (1996). *Contrastive Rhetoric.* Cambridge: Cambridge University Press.

Cope, B., Kalantzis, M. (1993). *The powers of Literacy: A genre Approach to Teaching Writing.* London: The Falmer Press.

Cummins, J. (1983). Language proficiency and academic achievement in Oller, J. (Ed.). *Issues in Language Testing Research.* London: Newbury House.

Cunningham, J. W. & Fitzgerald, J. (1996). Epistemology and reading. *Reading Research Quarterly*, 31 (1), 36-60.

Daisey, P., & Shroyer, M. G. (1993). Perceptions and attitudes of content and methods instructors toward a required reading course. *Journal of Reading*, 36 (8), pp.624-627.

De Graaf, R. (1997). *Differential Effects of Explicit Instruction on Second Language Acquisition (Ph.D. Thesis).* Leiden: Holland Institute of Generative Linguistics.

De Mars, C. (2001). Group differences based on IRT scores: Does the model matter? *Educational Psychological Measurement,* 61 (1), 60-70.

Derewianka, B. (1996). *Exploring the writing of genres.* Royston: United Kingdom Reading Association.

Devitt, A. J. (2000). Integrating rhetorical and literacy theories of genre. *College English*, 62 (6), 696-718.

Dorogovtsev, S.N. & Mendes, J.F.F. (2001). Language as an evolving word web. *Proceeding of the Royal Society of London*. B268, 2603-2608.

Doyle, J. A., & Brown, K. J. (1996). The effect of strategy instruction on the comprehension performance of at-risk students. *Reading Research Quarterly*, 31 (1), 62-88.

Ellis, R. (1997). *Second Language Acquisition.* London: Oxford University Press.

Fahnestock, J. (1993). Genre and rhetorical craft. *Research in the teaching of English*, 27, pp. 264-271.

Farrell, T.S.C. (2001). Concept maps to trace conceptual change in preservice English teachers. *RELC journal,32* (2), 27-43.

Feez, S. (1999). Text-based syllabus design .*TESOL in Context*, 9 (1), 11-14.

Fieg, J. (1980). *Thais and North Americans*. Yarmouth, ME: Intercultural Press.

Frager, A. M. (1993). Affective dimensions of content area reading. *Journal of Reading*, 36 (8), 616-629.

Frederickson, T., & Wedel, P. (2000). *English by Newspaper*. (9th printing). Bangkok: Bangkok Post press.

Freedman, A. (1993a). Show and tell ? The role of explicit teaching in the learning of new genre. *Research in the Teaching of English*, 27, pp.222-251.

Freedman, A. (1993b). Situating Genre: a rejoinder. *Research in the teaching of English*, 27, pp. 272-281.

Gee, J.P. (2001). Reading as situated language: A sociocognitive perspective. *Journal of Adolescent and Adult Literacy*, 44, 714-715.

Goodson, F. T. (1994). Reading and Writing across genres: textual form and social action in the high school. *Journal of Reading*, 30 (1), 6-12.

Govoni, J. M. & Feyten, C. M. (1999). Effects of the ACTFL-OPI- type training on student performance, instructional methods and classroom materials in the secondary foreign language classroom. *Foreign Language Annuals*, 32 (2),198-203.

Grabe, W. (1993). Current developments in second language reading research. In Silberstein, S. (Ed.), . *State of the Art TESOL Essays,* (pp.250-256). Bloomington, Ind: TESOL.

Grellett, F. (1981). *Developing reading skills*. Cambridge: CUP.

Griffe, D. T. (1982). *Listen and act: scenes for language learning.* Tokyo: Lingual House.

Guthrie, J. T., Schater, W., Wang, Y. Y. & Attlerbach, P. (1995). Relationship of instruction to amount of reading : an exploration of social, cognitive, and instructional connections. *Reading Research Quarterly*, 31(1), 8-25.

Guthrie, J. T., VanMeter, P., McCam, A. D., Wigfield, A., Bemsett, L Poundstone,C.C., Rice, M.E., Faibish, F.M., Hunt, B. & Mitchell, A. M. (1996). Growth of literacy engagement: changes in motivation and strategies during concept oriented reading instruction. *Reading Research Quarterly*, 31 (3), 306-332.

Hadley, C. (1998). Returning full circle: a survey of EFL syllabus design for the new Millennium, *RELC journal*. 29 (2), 51-71.

Hague, S. A., & Scott, R. (1994). Awareness of text structures; is there a match between readers and authors of second language texts ? *Foreign Language Annuals*, 27 (3), 343-363.

Hakuta, K. & Mc.Laughlin, B. (1996). *Bilingualism and second language learning: seven tensions that define the research.* In D.C. Berliner & R.C. Calfee (Eds.) Handbook of Educational Psychology(pp.603-621). New York: Macmillon.

Harmer, J. (2001). The Practice of English Language teaching. Edinburgh Gate, Harlow. Essex: Longman (Pearson Education Ltd.)

Harris, S. (1996). Bringing about change in reading instruction. *The Reading Teacher*, 49 (8), 612-618.

Hasan, R. (1989*). Linguistics, language and verbal art*. Oxford, England: Oxford University Press.

Henk, W.A., & Melnick, S. A. (1995). The reader self-perception scale (RSPS): a new tool for measuring how children feel about themselves as readers. *The Reading Teacher*, 48 (6), 470-482.

Henning, G., Hudson,T., & Turner, J. (1985). Item response theory and assumption of unidimensionality for language tests. *Language Testing*, 2 (2), 141-154.

Hoffman, J. & Pearson, P. D. (2000). Reading teacher education in the next millennium: what your grandmother's teacher didn't know that your granddaughter's teacher should. Reading Research Quarterly, 35 (1), 28-40.

Hoelker, J. (2000). Kolb: a paradigm for teacher style. *MET,* 9(3), 67-69.

Hyon, S. (1996). Genre in three traditions. *TESOL Quarterly*, 30 (4), 693-722.

Ingram, D. E., & O. Neill, S. (1999). Cross-cultural attitudes in foreign language programmes. *PASAA*, 29 December, pp.1-32.

Jetton,T. L. & Alexander, P. A.(1997). Instructional importance: what teachers value and what students learn. *Reading Research Quarterly,* 32 (3), 290-308.

Johns, A. M. (1997). *Text, Role, and Context.* Cambridge: Cambridge University Press.

Johnstone, R. (1997). Research on language learning and teaching: 1996. *Language Teacher*, 30, pp. 149-165.

Kamberelis, G., & Bovino, T.D. (1999). Cultural artifacts as scaffolds for genre development. *Reading Research Quarterly*, 34 (2), 138-170.

Kang, H. W. (1994). Helping second language readers learn from content area text through collaboration and support. *Journal of Reading*, 37 (8), 646-652.

Katib, A. (1990). The role of second language teachers. *PASAA,* 20 (1), 26-30.

Keng, L. T. (1994). Analyzing primary level reading tests using the Rasch model and classical method. *PASAA*, 24 December, pp.24-35.

Kennedy, C. & Kennedy, J. (1996). Teacher attitudes and change implementation. *System*, 24 (3), 351-360.

Knapp, P. (1989). *The report genre.* Sydney : DSP productions.

Knapp, P. (1995). The trouble with genre. *Idiom.* 29, 34-41.

Komin, S. (1990). Culture and work-related values in Thai Organizations. *International Journal of Psychology*, 25, pp.681-704.

Kletzien, S. B. (1992). Proficient and less proficient comprehenders' strategy use for different top-level structures. *Journal of Reading Behavior*, 24 (2),191-215.

Knutsen, E. (1997). Reading with a purpose-communicative reading tasks for the foreign language classroom. *Foreign Language Annals*, 30 (1), 49-57.

Krashen, S. (1993). *The power of reading.* Englewood,Cliffs: Libraries Unlimited.

Kuhlemeir, M., Van den Bergh, H., & Melse, L. (1996). Attitudes and achievements in the first year of second language instruction in Dutch secondary education. *The Modern Language journal*, 80 (4), 494-508.

Lester, J. H. (1998). Reflective interactions in secondary classroom: an impetus for enhanced learning. *Reading Research and Instruction.* 37 (4), 273-231.

Lim,T. K.(1994). Analysing primary level reading tests using the Rasch Model and classical methods. *PASAA,* 24, pp. 24-35.

Linek, M., Sturtevant, E. G., Rasinski, T. V. & Padak, N. D.(1991). Second grade urban students' attitudes to reading. *Reading is Knowledge*, pp.77-86.

Littlefair, A. (1992). Let's be positive about genre. *Reading,* 3 Nov., pp. 2-6.

Lowenberg-Ball, D. (2000). Intertwining content and pedagogy in teaching and learning to teach. *Journal of Teaching Education*, 51 (3), 241-247.

Mantle-Bromley, C. (1998). Positive attitudes and realistic beliefs : links to proficiency. *The Modern Language Journal*, 79 (3), 372-386.

Marin, R. (1994). Using newspaper in the ESL classroom. *PASAA*, 24 Dec., pp.66-73.

Matthews, S. (1993). Helping college tutors define reading and mould active learners. *Journal of Reading*, 36 (8), 636-641.

McNamara, T. (1996).*Measuring Second Language Performance.* London: Longman.

Ministry of Education. (1996). *English Syllabus Design.* Bangkok: Ministry of Education..

Ministry of Education. (2000). *Evaluation of secondary school Education*, Bangkok: Ministry of Education..

Mioduser, D. (2002). From real virtuality in Lascaux to virtual reality today –cognitive processes in the cognitive technologies. Unpublished paper.

Moje, E.B. & Handy, D. (1995). Using literacy to modify traditional assessment: alternatives for teaching and assessing content understanding. *Journal of Reading.* 38, 612-625.

Moorman, G. B., Blanton, W. E. & Mclaughlin, T. (1994). The rhetoric of whole language. *Reading Research Quarterly*, 94 (4), 309-329.

Mori, Y. (1999). Epistemological Beliefs and language learning beliefs: what do language learners believe about their learning? *Language Learning.* 49 (3), 377-415.

Morrison, T. G., & Wilcox, B. (1997). Development of teachers' theoretical orientations toward reading and pupil control ideology. *Reading Research and Instruction*, 36 (2), 141-156.

Nation, P. (1978). "What is it?" A multipurpose language teaching technique. *English Teaching Forum,* 16 (3), 20-23.

Nation, P. (1985). Opportunities for learning through the communication approach, in Das, B. K. (1985). *Communicative language teaching.* Singapore: RELC

Natraj, S. (1990). Large classes and second language instruction. *PASAA*, 20 (1), 31-34.

Nelson, J. (1990). This was an easy assignment: examining how students interpret academic writing tasks. *Research in the Teaching of English*, 24, pp.262-296.

Noel, K. (2000). Experience the theory: constructivism in pre-service teacher training preparation programs. *Theory and Practice,* 6(2), 183-196.

Noels, K. A., Kimberly, A., Pelletier, L. G., Clement, R., Vallerand, R. J., (2000). Why are you learning a second language? Motivational Orientations and self determination theory. *Language Learning*, 50 (1), 57-85.

Noisaengsri, P. (1992). *Problems in teaching English in the second school.* Unpublished, Ramkumhaeng University, Bangkok, Thailand.

O'Connell, R. (1994). Quality Teaching Resources. Lynwood, W. A.: Praxis Productions.

Office of the National Education Commission. (1999). *National Education Act of B.E. 2542*, Office of the Prime Minister, Bangkok.

Oller, J. W. (1997). On the relation between language teaching and testing. *PASAA*, 27 Dec., pp. 39-63.

Oxford, R. L. (1997). Cooperative learning, collaborative learning, and interaction: three communicative strands in the language classroom. *The Modern Language Journal,* 81 (4), 443-456.

ORIC, Ministry of Education (1998). *Strategies for Staff Development Policies and Challenges, Office of Rajabhat Institutes Council.* Bangkok: Kurusapa Press.

Painter, C. (1986). The role of learning to speak and learning to write. In C. Painter & J. Martin (Ed.). *Writing to mean: Teaching genres across the curriculum*, Sydney: ALAA, 62-97.

Pallant, J. (2001). *SPSS Survival Manual: a step by step guide to data analysis Using SPSS.* Crows Nest, NSW: Allen & Unwin

Paltridge (2001). Genre, text type and the English for Academic Purposes (EAP) classroom. *In Genre in the classroom (pp.73-90) New Jersey:* Lawrence Erlbaum.

Pappas, C. C. (1993). Is narrative "primary"? : Some insights form kindergartners' pretend readings of stories and information books. *Journal of Reading Behavior: A Journal of Literacy*, 25, pp.97-129.

Pappas, C. C., & Pettegrew, B. S. (1998). The role of genre in the psycholinguistic guessing game of reading. *Language Arts*, 75 (1), 36-44.

Parkinson, J. (2000). Acquiring scientific literacy through content and genre: a theme based language course for science students. *English for Specific Purposes*, 19, pp.369-387.

Porter, L. (1996). *Student Behaviour.* Sydney: Allen & Unwin.

Prior, P. (1995). Redefining the task: an ethnographic examination of writing and response in graduate seminars. In D. Belcher & G. Braine (Eds.) *Academic writing in a second language: Essays on research and Pedagogy*, (pp.47-62), Norwood, NJ: Ablex.

Promsiri, R., Prapphal, K., & Vijchulata, B.(1996). A survey of English teaching problems and wants in teaching training of upper-secondary English teachers in government secondary schools in educational region 12, *PASAA*, 26, Dec., pp.80-88.

Punch, K.F. (2000). *Developing Effective Research Proposals*. London: Sage

Rasch, G. (1980/1960). *Probabilistic models for intelligence and attainment tests (expanded edition, original published 1960)*. Chicago: University of Chicago Press.

Rattanavich, S. (1987). *The effects of using top-level structures instructional modules and traditional teaching method in teaching English reading to Thai students.* Singapore: RELC.

Rattanavich, S. (1999). Concentrated language encounter teaching program: ELT in the new millennium. *PASAA*, 29, pp.105-112.

Reid, J. (1987). The learning style preferences of ESL students. *TESOL Quarterly*, 21(1), 87-111.

Richards, J. & Rogers, T. (2001). *Approaches and Methods in Language Teaching*. Cambridg: Cambridge University Press.

Richardson, B. (2000). Linearity and its discontents :rethinking narrative form and ideological valence. *College English*, 62 (6), 685-695.

Richardson, P. (1998). Literacy, learning and teaching. *Educational Review*, 50 (2), 115-134.

Robles, A. (1998). Reflective learning: why and how. *MET*, 7 (1), 43-46.

Roller, C.M. (2002). *Comprehension Reading Instruction across the grade Levels* Nevark, Del: Interaction Reading Association.

Rongsa-ard, W. (1990). Needs and expectations as source of motivation. *PASAA*, 20(1), 10-25.

Saccardi, M. C. (1996). Predictable books: Gateways to a lifetime of reading. *The Reading Teacher*, 49 (7), 588-590.

Sawasdiwong, S. (1992). *Communicative approach*. Paper presented at the Teaching communicative approach conference in English class, Asia Hotel, Bangkok, Thailand, 14 September, 2000.

Savova, L. (1985). *Groupwork in EFL. Unpublished doctoral dissertation.* Sofia University, Sofia.

Secondary School Education Report (1981-1985). *Secondary School Curriculum*. Bangkok, Thailand: Ministry of Education.

Short, K. G. & Burke, C, (1996). Examining our beliefs and practices through inquiry. *Language Arts*, 73, pp.97-104.

Sinatra, R. (1991). Integrating whole language with the learning of texts structure. *Journal of Reading*, 34 (6), 424-433.

Smith, F. (1971). *Understand Reading*. New York: Holt, Rinehart and Winston.

Smith, R., & Savage, W. (1994). Challenge, skill, and motivation. *University of Hawaii Working Papers in ESL*, 12 (2), 1-25.

Soranastaporn, S. & Chuedong, M. (1999). Comparative study of reading comprehension strategies employed by ESP students. *SLLT*, 8, 20-25.

Spooren, W., Mulder, M.,&Hocken, H.(1998). The role of interest and text structure in professional reading. *Journal of Research in Reading*, 21(2), 109-120.

Stark, W. (2001). *Dialectics provide a breakthorough*. Bangkok Post, Thursday, May 24, p.11.

Stuart, C. & Thurlow, D. (2000). Making it their own: preservice teachers' experiences, beliefs, and classroom practices. *Journal of Teacher Education*, 51 (2), 113-121.

Tarone, E. & Kuehn, K. (2000). Negotiating the social service oral intake interviews: communicative needs of nonnative speakers of English. *TESOL Quarterly, 34* (1), 99-115.

Tashakkori, A. & Teddlie, C. (1998). *Mixed Methodology. Mixing Qualitative and Quantitative Approaches.* Applied Social Research Methods Series Vol.46. London: Sage.

Tiersky, E. & Hughes, R. (1996). *Morning Edition: Mastering Reading and Language skills with the Newspaper.* Lincolnwood, Ill. : National Textbook Co.

Torok, S.J. (1976). *Value Changes, Gaming, a Behavioural Approach to Guided Negotiations and Macroeconomic Planning.* Ph.D. dissertation (unpublished), Columbia University, N.Y., USA.

Torut, S. (1994). *A Comparision of Language Learning Strategies of Thai University Students in Acquiring English Proficiency.* Unpublished Ph.D. thesis,Sounthern Illinois University, Carbondale.

Vacharaskunee, S. (2000). *Target Language Avoidance by Thai Teachers of English: Thai Teachers Beliefs.* Ph.D. Dissertation (unpublished) Edith Cowan University, Perth, Western Australia.

Vanichbutr, N. (2000). Education with a heart ; *Bangkok Post,* 7 May, p.6

Vygotsky, L. (1978). *Mind in Society. The development of higher mental functions.* Translation by M. Cole, V. John-Steiner, S. Scritmer & E. Souberman (Eds. & trans.) Cambridge, MA: Harvard University Press.

Wade, S. E., Buxton, W.M. & Kelly, M. (1999). Using think-aloud to examine reader-text interest. *Reading Research Quarterly,* 34 (2), 194-216.

Waugh, R. (1999). Approaches to studying for students in higher Education: A Rasch measurement model analysis. *British Journal of Educational Psychology,* 69, 63-79.

Waugh, R. F. (2000). Self concept: multidimensional or multi-faceted, unidemensional. *Educational Research and Perspectives,* 27 (2), 75-94.

Waugh, R. F. (2001). Quality of student experiences at University. *Australian Journal of Education,* 45 (2), 183-206.

Waugh, R. F.(2002). Creating a scale to measure motivation to achieve academically: linking attitudes and behaviour using Rasch measurement. *British Journal of Educational Psychology,* 72 (1), 65-86.

Wellington, J. J.(1992). *Method and Issues of Educational Research.* University of Sheffield, Division of Education, Sheffield, U.K.

Wigfield, A. & Guthrie, J.T. (1997). Relations of childrens' motivation for reading to the amount and breadth of their reading. *Journal of Eductional Psychology,* 89, 430-432.

Williams, E. & Moran, C. (1989). Reading in a foreign language at intermediate and advanced levels with particular reference to English. *Language Teaching,* 22 (4), 217-228.

Wongsathorn, A., Sukamolsun, A., Chinhamnit, P., Ratanothayanonth, P., & Noparumpa, P. (1996). National profiles of language education: Thailand.*PASAA,* 26 (Dec), 89-100.

Wright, B. D. & Masters, G. N. (1982). *Rating Scale Analysis.* Chicago: MESA Press.

Zephir, F. (2000). Focus on form and meaning: perspectives of developing teachers and action-based research. *Foreign Language Annals,* 33 (1), 19-29.

In: Thailand: Economics, Political and Social Issues
Ed: Randle C. Zebioli

ISBN: 978-1-60456-583-6
©2009 Nova Science Publishers, Inc.

Chapter 9

COOPERATIVE LEARNING VERSUS COMMUNICATIVE THAI TEACHING OF ENGLISH AS A SECOND LANGUAGE FOR PRATHOM (GRADE) 6 STUDENTS TAUGHT IN THAILAND

Russell F. Waugh and Margaret H. Bowering
Edith Cowan University

Sutaporn Chayarathee
Rajabhat University, Muban Chombung

ABSTRACT

A controlled experiment in teaching English as a second language was implemented. The experiment involved 96 students from three primary schools in Ratchaburi, Thailand. The students from each school were randomly assigned to an experimental group (N=48) and a control group (N=48). The experimental group was taught by using cooperative learning and the control group was taught by the Thai communicative method. Great care was taken to ensure that students were treated the same in all respects, except the method of learning, in both the experimental and control groups. Pretest and posttest measures were administered and significant differences tested using ANOVA (SPSS). There were four main findings. (1) Students improved their English reading comprehension under both the cooperative learning and Thai communicative group methods of teaching. (2) Students improved their English reading comprehension under the cooperative learning method significantly more than under the Thai communicative group method. (3) Students improved their attitude and behaviour towards learning English as a second language under both the cooperative learning and Thai communicative group methods of teaching. (4) Students improved their attitude and behaviour towards learning English as a second language significantly more under the cooperative learning method than under the Thai communicative group method of teaching.

Key words: English as a second language, cooperative learning, grade 6 students, Thailand, experimental and control groups, ANOVA

INTRODUCTION

This chapter provides a description of the results of the data analysis for the reading comprehension experimental results, and the students' attitude and behaviour experimental results. The data were analysed with the SPSS computer program (Pallant, 2001), and one way ANOVA results are presented through tables and descriptive text. Tables 1 and 2 contain material relating to the research design. Tables 3, 4, 5 and 6 contain the reading comprehension results by pretest, posttest, experimental and control groups. Table 7 shows the interaction effect of the experimental and control groups for reading comprehension. Figure 1 provides the reading comprehension mean measures of the experimental and control groups in graphical format. Tables 8, 9, 10 and 11 contain the attitude and behaviour results by pretest, posttest, experimental and control groups. Table 12 shows the interaction effect of the experimental and control groups for the attitude and behaviour measures. Figure 2 provides the attitude and behaviour mean measures of the experimental and control groups in graphical format.

The two research questions related to this chapter are: (1) Do the students improve their English reading comprehension as a result of using cooperative learning compared with when they are taught using the Thai communicative method?; and (2) Do students improve their attitude and behaviour to learning English when taught by cooperative learning compared to when they are taught by the Thai communicative method? The linear scales described in the previous chapter and constructed using Rasch analysis were used as the measures in the experiment described in this chapter to answer these two research questions.

METHODOLOGY

Sample

Three schools were chosen for the experiment within the Rajabhat Institute Muban Chombung area of the trainee teacher practice. They are in the same area in Ratchaburi province and they all could be described as typical small provincial village temple schools for grade one to six students. The reason that the schools in the same area were chosen was that the researcher and the teachers were able to contact each other easily. The first area (Wat Chong Lom) which was the biggest school with 970 students in total, while the other two (Wat Phikulthong and Wat Don-Ta-Lung) were smaller with 745 and 678 students respectively in total. For Wat Chong Lom schools, there were sixty-five teachers involving six English teachers and there were three grade six classes of about twenty-five students each. In the second school, Wat Phikulthong, there were fifty-eight teachers, including five English teachers, and there were two grade six classes of about twenty students each. In Wat Don-Ta-Lung, there were fifty-five teachers, including five English teachers, and there were two grade six classes of about twenty students each.

The number of students in the seven grade six classes at Wat Chong Lom, Wat Phikulthong, and Wat Don-Ta-Lung chosen for this study was seventy-five, forty and forty, respectively. Because a smaller number of students was needed, simple random sampling was used to allocate students to the control and experimental groups within each class.

The thirty-two participants from Wat Chong Lom, Wat Phikulthong, and Wat Don-Ta-Lung were divided into two groups (in each school) by random sampling, and then they were allocated to control groups (N = 16) in each school and experimental groups (N = 16) in each school. Thus, the total for the three schools was ninety-six students.

All of the ninety-six students were twelve years old and of mixed gender. They had studied in five learning experience groups: Basic Skills Group, Life Experiences, Character Development, Work- Oriented Experiences and Special Experience (Office of the National Education Commission, 1999). English is one of the subjects which was in Basic Skills Group. The school hours were from 8.00 AM to 15.30 PM everyday, Monday to Friday.

Procedure

There were four letters asking permission to do the experiment with the Prathom 6 (grade 6) students in the three schools (Wat Chong Lom, Wat Phikulthong, and Wat Don-Ta-Lung schools). They were sent from the Dean of the Faculty of Education at Rajabhat Institute Muban Chombung. The four letters involved (1) getting three trainee teachers to be volunteers for the experiment, (2) getting permission from the students' parents/guardian, (3) getting permission from the school Principal, and (4) getting permission from the regular teacher to be part of a group discussion. In preparing three trainee teachers for the experiment, a two-day orientation seminar on practice teaching for the trainee English major teachers in the two methods of reading comprehension learning, were given. These were the Thai communicative method and the cooperative learning method.

Table 1. Planned time scheduling during the experiment.

Day Time	Mon	Tue	Wed	Thu	Fri
8.30 - 8.50	Exp	Con	Exp	Con	Training teacher meets researcher
8.50 - 9.10	Exp	Con	Exp	Con	
9.10 - 9.30	Exp	Con	Exp	Con	
9.40 - 10.00	Con	Exp	Con	Exp	
10.00 - 10.20	Con	Exp	Con	Exp	
10.20 - 10.40	Con	Exp	Con	Exp	
10.50 - 11.10					
11.10 - 13.00	Lunchtime				
13.00 - 13.20					
13.20 - 13.40					
13.40 - 14.00					
14.10 - 14.30					
14.30 - 14.50					
14.50 - 15.10					
15.10 - 15.30	remedial teaching and sport activity				

Note : Exp. means experimental group taught by cooperative learning.
Con. means control group taught by Thai communicative method.

After the orientation seminar on practice teaching, an assignment test on knowledge of the two teaching methods (cooperative learning and Thai communicative) was used, and three trainee teachers who had obtained similar high scores were chosen. This helped to ensure that the trainee teachers had similar knowledge and skills in the teaching methods, an aspect of experimental control. Next, the lesson plans for both methods of teaching were written by the researcher. The contents were about being able to understand the main ideas, sequencing the order of content, and understanding the meaning from English reading tasks using pictures. Finally, the three trainee teachers and the three English teachers from the three schools studied the whole plan of the research, another aspect of experimental control.

During the experiment, the three control groups were taught by the Thai communicative approach. The three experimental groups were taught by the cooperative learning approach. The length of the experimental study was sixteen hours. In each of the three schools, the one trainee teacher taught both the experimental and control groups. After the sixteen hours of teaching, the reading test and the questionnaire, which were the same papers as the pretests, were given as posttests, and compared with the pretests.

The Experimental Design

Thirty-two Prathom six (grade 6) students at three schools, Wat Chong Lom, Wat Phikulthong and Wat Don-Ta-Lung schools, Ratchaburi province, studying Fundamental English, were chosen. They were allocated by random sampling, with sixteen Prathom six students to each of an experimental group and a control group at each of the three schools. Thus, there were forty-eight students in three experimental groups, and another forty-eight students in three control groups, making a total of ninety-six students.

Three control groups were taught by the Thai communicative approach. Three experimental groups were taught by the cooperative learning approach. The experimental groups and the control groups were treated the same in every respect, except the steps of teaching which were different. These treatment controls are explained later in this chapter.

The length of the experimental study was sixteen hours. Before the experiment, two pretests (involving reading comprehension, and an attitude and behaviour questionnaire) were given for the three experimental groups and the three control groups. After the treatment, the reading comprehension test and the attitude and behaviour questionnaire, which were the same as the pretest, were used again as posttests to see whether the students improved in English reading comprehension, and in attitude and behaviour.

Pretests and Posttests

After the data (N = 300) were analysed with the RUMM computer program, there were 32 valid items measuring English reading comprehension, and 40 valid items measuring attitude and behaviours left. These items in the pretests and posttests (English reading test and attitude and behaviours) were from the same papers that had been used before and after the experiment (for 3 experimental groups and 3 control groups) in order to see whether expected actions had changed before and after this experiment (See Table 5 below).

Table 2 The pretest and posttest administration for the experiment

	Pretest	Posttest
Experimental groups N = 48	reading comprehension & attitude and behaviour	reading comprehension & attitude and behaviour
Control groups N = 48	reading comprehension & attitude and behaviour	reading comprehension & attitude and behaviour

For all the students in the experimental and control groups, the raw total scores, were converted to a measure on the linear Rasch scale for each measure. These measures were then used in ANOVA and t-tests, for the experimental and control groups to test for a significant difference.

Controls in the Experiment

Before the experiment, random sampling was used to allocate the students to the control and the experimental groups, so that the characteristics of the students in each group were similar. The three trainee teachers were carefully selected and monitored so that the treatment of the students was the same, except for the teaching methodology. During the experiment, the text, visual aids, assignments, activities, exercises, and material from the lesson plans were the same, except that the steps of teaching in both groups were different. This means that the assignments for the students of both groups in the lesson plans were the same. The teaching times in both the experimental group and the control group were the same, one hour, three periods per day, each. The planned time-scheduling of both the experimental and control groups were during the morning, not in the afternoon, because of possible tiredness of the students which might have affected their studying ability. In the planned time schedule, the teaching periods of both groups were taken in turn. When the experimental group was taught first, then the control group was taught later, and the next day, the control group was taught first, while the experimental group was taught later. This action was done to prevent any bias in the session times.

Trainee teachers often used Thai when the objectives of the lessons were mentioned, so that the students would understand them clearly. Trainee teachers were advised to use the same amount of Thai words in both groups and the trainee teachers were reminded of this from time-to-time. They spoke English in both groups during their teaching, but Thai words were often used during telling the objectives of the lessons. Again, an attempt was made to use the same number of Thai words in each group, and trainee teachers were reminded of this from time-to-time.

An attempt was made to limit any cooperation between students across the experimental and control groups by informing them not to do so. The researcher supervised classes in all schools at least twice a week during the experiment and met the trainee teacher for weekly journals as part of the supervisory control.

In summary, a great deal of care was taken to treat the experimental groups and the control groups the same, in every way, except for teaching methodology. Then, if there were any measured differences in reading comprehension, or in attitude and behaviour, those differences could reasonably be attributed to the different teaching method.

RESULTS FOR READING COMPREHENSION

Posttest versus Pretest Results for the Experimental Group

The students in the experimental group did significantly better on the posttest than the pretest in regards to the reading comprehension measure ($F = 53.25$, $df = 1, 94$, $p < 0.001$). This means that the reading comprehension of the students learning under the cooperative learning approach was significantly better at the end of the experiment than at the beginning. The effect size, eta squared, equals 0.65 and, under Cohen's (1988) rules, this is a large effect.

Table 3. One way ANOVA: Statistics for the reading comprehension experiment measure by pretest and posttest for the experimental group (N= 48)

	PRETEST	POSTTEST
EXPERIMENTAL GROUP	$\overline{X}$ = -0.95 SD = 0.63 CI = 0.68 SE = 0.09 N = 48	$\overline{X}$ = +0.89 SD = 0.74 CI = 1.10 SE = 0.11 N = 48

Note 1. CI = confidence interval.
2. SE = standard error of the measure of attitude and behaviour towards reading comprehension.
3. $\overline{X}$ = mean, SD = standard deviation.

Posttest versus Pretest Results for the Control Group

The students in the control group did significantly better on the posttest than the pretest in regards to reading comprehension in English (F = 53.25, df = 1, 94, p < 0.001). This means that the reading comprehension of the students learning under the Thai communicative approach was significantly better at the end of the teaching period than at the beginning. Eta squared is 0.38, a large effect size.

Table 4. Statistics for the reading comprehension measure by pretest and posttest for the control group

	PRETEST	POSTTEST
CONTROL GROUP	$\overline{X}$ = -0.88 SD = 0.49 CI = -0.25 SE = 0.07 N = 48	$\overline{X}$ = -0.08 SD = 0.56 CI = 0.08 SE = 0.08 N = 48

Note 1. CI = confidence interval.
2. SE = standard error of the measure of reading comprehension.
3. $\overline{X}$ = mean, SD = standard deviation.

Pretest versus Pretest Results for the Experimental versus the Control Group

The students in the experimental group were not significantly better than those in the control group in regards to reading comprehension in English (F = .40, df = 1, 94, p = .53), as measured for reading comprehension at the beginning of the experiment.

Table 5. One way ANOVA: The reading comprehension pretest results for the experimental group versus the control groups

	Sum of Squares	df	Mean Square	F	Signif.
Between groups	0.13	1	0.13	0.40	p = 0.53
Within groups	30.33	94	0.32		
Total	30.46	95			

Posttest versus Posttest Results for the Experimental versus the Control Group

The students in the experimental group were significantly better than those in the control group (F = 53.23, df 1, 94, p < 0.001) at the end of the experiment. The conclusion is that the students' reading comprehension under the cooperative learning method was significantly better at the end of the experiment than those taught by the Thai communicative method. Eta squared is 0.38, a large effect size.

Table 6. One way ANOVA: The reading comprehension posttest results for the experimental group versus the control groups

	Sum of Squares	df	Mean Square	F	Signif.
Between groups	22.84	1	22.84	53.23	p<0.001
Within groups	40.34	94	0.43		
Total	63.18	95			

Interaction Effect

Table 5 indicates that there is a significant difference between the experimental and the control group. The conclusion is that the experimental group achieved better than the control group after being given the treatment. There is a larger effect in cooperative learning than the Thai communicative method so, in technical terms, there was an interaction between them.

Table 7. The reading comprehension interaction effect of the experimental versus the control groups

Source	Type III Sum of Squares	df	Mean Square	F	Sig.	Partial Eta Squared
Intercept	12.561	1	12.561	22.961	.000	.196
VAR00001	9.779	1	9.779	17.874	.000	.160
Error	51.425	94	.547			

Figure 1 shows the mean of reading comprehension measures by experimental/control groups and pretest/posttest. The first line represents the control group, the other represents the experimental group. Both lines increased but the control group line slowly increased while the experimental group line rapidly increased. This means that the experimental method exerts a significantly larger effect than the control method on reading comprehension.

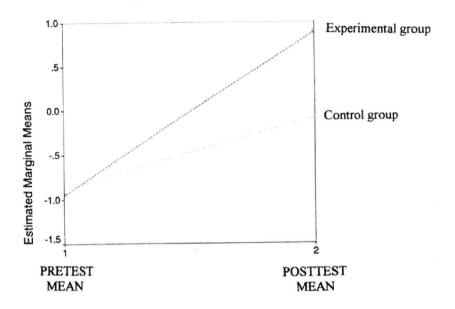

Figure 1. Graph of reading comprehension means (Pretest/posttest v experimental and control groups).

ATTITUDE AND BEHAVIOUR MEASURE

Posttest versus Pretest Results for the Experimental Group

Table 8. Statistics for the attitude and behaviour measure by pretest and posttest, the experimental group (n=48)

	PRETEST	POSTTEST
EXPERIMENTAL GROUP	$\overline{X}$ = 1.46 SD = 0.54 CI = 2.65 SE = 0.07 N = 48	$\overline{X}$ = 2.87 SD = 0.78 CI = 3.10 SE = 0.11 N = 48

Note 1. CI = confidence interval.
2. SE = standard error of the measure of attitude and behaviour towards reading comprehension.
3. $\overline{X}$ = mean, SD = standard deviation.

Students in the experimental group did significantly better on the posttest than the pretest for the experimental group in regards to attitude and behaviour towards learning English (F = 56.85, df = 1, 94, p <0.001). This means that the attitude and behaviour of students learning English as a second language under the cooperative learning method was significantly better at the end of the teaching experiment than at the beginning. The effect size, eta squared, equals 0.52 and, under Cohen's (1988) rules, this is a large effect.

Posttest versus Pretest Results for the Control Group

The students in the control group did significantly better on the posttest than the pretest for the control group, in regards to attitude and behaviour towards learning English (F = 56.85, df = 1, p < 0.001). This means the attitude and behaviour of students learning English as a second language under the Thai communicative method was significantly better at the end of the teaching than at the beginning. The effect size, eta squared, equals 0.53 and under Cohen's (1988) rules, this is a large effect.

Table 9. Statistics for the attitude and behaviour measure by pretest and posttest for the control group (N=48)

	PRETEST	POSTTEST
CONTROL GROUP	$\overline{X}$ = 0.98 SD = 0.33 CI = 1.72 SE = 0.05 N = 48	$\overline{X}$ = 1.87 SD = 0.50 CI = 2.01 SE = 0.07 N = 48

Note 1. CI = confidence interval.
2. SE = standard error of the measure of attitude and behaviour towards reading comprehension.
3. $\overline{X}$ = mean, SD = standard deviation.

Pretest versus Pretest Results for the Experimental versus the Control Group

The students in the experimental group were significantly better than those in the control group (F = 27.48, df 1, 94, p < 0.001), before the experiment was begun, as measured by the attitude and behaviour questionnaire. Eta squared is 0.23, a large effect size.

Table 10. One way ANOVA : The students' attitude and behaviour questionnaire pretest results for the experimental versus the control group

	Sum of Squares	df	Mean Square	F	Signif.
Between Groups	5.48	1	5.48	27.48	p< 0.001
Within Groups	18.75	94	0.20		
Total	24.23	95			

Posttest versus Posttest Results for the Experimental versus the Control Group

The students in the experimental group were significantly better than those in the control group (F = 56.85, df =1, 94, p < 0.001). Eta squared is 0.38, a large effect size. The conclusion is that the students' attitude and behaviour towards reading comprehension for the experimental group was better than the students' attitude and behaviour for the control group, at the end of the experiment.

Table 11. One way ANOVA: The Students' attitude and behaviour questionnaire posttest results for the experimental versus to control group

	Sum of Squares	df	Mean Square	F	Signif.
Between groups	24.40	1	24.40	56.85	p< 0.001
Within groups	40.35	94	0.43		
Total	64.75	95			

Interaction Effect

Table 10 indicates that there is a significant interaction effect between the experimental and the control groups. The conclusion is that both the experimental group and the control group improved their attitude and behaviour after their respective teaching methods (cooperative learning and Thai communicative teaching of ESL) but the experimental group improved significantly more than the control group.

Table 12. The attitude and behaviour questionnaire interaction effect between the experimental and control groups

Source	Type III Sum of Squares	df	Mean Square	F	Sig.	Partial Eta Squared
Intercept	617.624	1	617.624	1427.803	.000	.938
VAR00001	26.507	1	26.507	61.279	.000	.395
Error	40.662	94	.433			

In *Figure 2*, the bottom line represents the control group, and the other represents the experimental group. Both lines increased with the experimental group line increasing more than the control group line. This means the students have responded significantly more to the cooperative learning method than the Thai communicative teaching method, as measured by their attitude and behaviour.

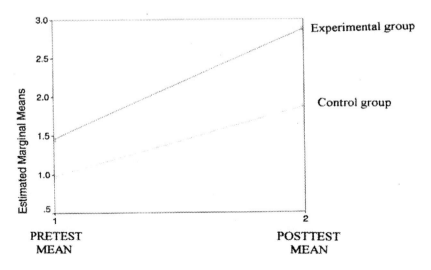

Figure 2. Graph of attitude and behaviour towards reading comprehension means by pretest and posttest for experimental and control groups.

SUMMARY OF RESULTS

Reading Comprehension Measure

1. Students improved their reading comprehension in English as a second language under both the cooperative learning and Thai communicative methods of teaching.
2. Students improved their reading comprehension in English as a second language under the cooperative learning method significantly more than under the Thai communicative method.

Attitude and Behaviour Measure

3. Students improved their attitude and behaviour towards learning English as a second language under both the cooperative learning and Thai communicative methods of the teaching.
4. Students improved their attitude and behaviour towards learning English as a second language significantly more under the cooperative learning method than the Thai communicative method of teaching.

REFERENCES

Cohen, J. (1988). *Statistical power analysis for the behavioural sciences.* New York: Lawrence Erlbaum.

Pallant, J. (2001). *SPSS Survival Manual: a step by step guide to data analysis using SPSS.* Crows Nest, NSW: Allen & Unwin.

INDEX

A

abdomen, 128
abdominal, 110
abortion, 61, 62, 63, 65, 66, 67, 68, 69, 71, 72, 73, 74, 75, 79, 83, 84, 90, 91, 92, 93, 95, 96, 97, 101, 103, 104, 105, 106, 107, 108, 109, 110, 113, 114, 117, 119
academic, 42, 56, 152, 153, 154, 156, 182, 185
academic progress, 156
academics, 168
acceptance, 143
access, 8, 17, 35, 37, 40, 44, 46, 53, 54, 62, 63, 64, 65, 67, 74, 93, 116, 119
accidents, 145
accommodation, 58, 113
accountability, 30
accounting, 6, 19, 27, 46
achievement, 154, 156, 181, 182
action research, 182
activities, 126, 133
activity theory, 181
acute, 38
Adams, 180
additives, 39
adjustment, 22, 133
administration, 2, 5, 6, 36, 37, 47, 51, 52, 53, 54, 55, 57, 58, 59, 152, 192
administrative, 49, 116, 168
adolescence, 75, 76
adolescents, 62, 63, 64, 65, 111, 119, 149
adoption, 54
adult, 3, 144
adult population, 3
adulthood, 64, 66, 71
adults, 63, 65
advertising, 47
advocacy, 164
affect, 56
affiliates, 35
Afghanistan, 8, 52, 53
Africa, 56, 57, 60
afternoon, 193

age, 2, 28, 48, 62, 63, 67, 69, 71, 75, 76, 83, 87, 91, 105, 112, 113, 118, 119, 130, 136, 137, 139, 141, 142, 144, 186, 187
ageing, 101
agent, 47
agents, 16, 17, 123, 136, 145
agricultural, 2, 7, 8, 36, 37, 38, 41, 48, 49, 141
agricultural commodities, 7, 8
agricultural exports, 37
agriculture, 6, 7, 36, 39, 141
aid, 30, 52, 95, 107, 129, 145
AIDS, 3, 8, 63, 139, 140, 141, 143, 145, 147, 148, 149
air, 47
aircraft, 55
Al Qaeda, 52, 54
alcohol, 36, 47, 81, 104, 118, 146
alcohol consumption, 118
alienation, 58
aliens, 46
allergic, 127
allergy, 126
allies, 51, 52, 53
alternative, 61, 65, 145, 147, 154
alternatives, 21, 116, 185
ambivalence, 126
amendments, 6, 41, 42, 43, 48
amphetamine, 104
amphetamines, 81, 104
Amsterdam, 135, 136, 137
anal, 126
anatomy, 64
animals, 37
ANOVA, 189, 190, 192, 194, 195, 197, 198
anthropology, 135, 136
anti-bacterial, 146
antiretroviral, 142
anti-terrorism, 53, 59
anxiety, 78, 87
apples, 37
application, 30, 36, 38, 39, 43

Arabs, 135
arbitration, 40
argument, 17, 18, 19, 30, 57, 59, 133, 155
armed forces, 9, 58
arrest, 7
ASEAN, 2, 5, 8, 25, 29, 36, 37, 52, 54, 55, 56, 57, 59, 60
Asia, 2, 3, 4, 5, 8, 11, 14, 17, 18, 19, 30, 31, 32, 51, 52, 53, 55, 56, 57, 58, 60, 121, 131, 136, 137, 186
Asia-Pacific Economic Cooperation, 5
Asian, 4, 5, 6, 11, 12, 15, 16, 17, 18, 19, 20, 21, 22, 26, 29, 30, 31, 32, 52, 54, 56, 57, 60, 120, 121, 135, 137
Asian countries, 11, 12, 15, 16, 17, 18, 19, 21, 22, 26, 29, 30, 52, 54, 56, 57
assessment, 39, 71, 185
assets, 27, 45, 49, 53
assignment, 162, 171, 185, 191
Association of Southeast Asian Nations, 5
associations, 21
assumptions, 49
asymptomatic, 141, 144
atmosphere, 70, 75, 112, 180
attacks, 23, 51, 52, 54, 55, 56, 58
attention, 29, 30, 57, 66, 109, 133, 139, 163
attitude, 156, 157, 160, 161, 163, 164, 165, 167, 168, 169, 170, 171, 172, 175, 176, 178, 180, 189, 190, 192, 193, 194, 196, 197, 198, 199
attitudes, 22, 28, 29, 59, 65, 70, 72, 73, 77, 80, 89, 96, 111, 114, 118, 137, 143, 151, 154, 156, 159, 160, 163, 168, 171, 182, 184, 187
attorneys, 45
attractiveness, 57
audio, 140
auditing, 17, 27
Australia, 8, 56, 57, 123, 136, 156, 159, 160, 168, 187
authority, 4, 5, 43, 49, 59, 80
automobiles, 2, 36
automotive, 36, 38, 48
automotive sector, 38, 48
autonomous, 152
availability, 41, 49, 103
averaging, 6
aviation, 49
avoidance, 133
awareness, 56, 64, 118
axis of evil, 53

B

babies, 89, 93, 94, 96, 97, 98, 105, 109, 110
background information, 126
backwardness, 19
bacterial, 146
Bahrain, 57
balance sheet, 25

Bali, 52, 120
bananas, 144
bandwidth, 44
Bangladesh, 57
bank account, 42
bank debt, 22
bankers, 14, 17
banking, 8, 11, 26, 27, 28, 30, 46, 48
bankruptcy, 15, 20, 25, 28
banks, 13, 15, 16, 17, 19, 21, 22, 23, 24, 25, 46
barrier, 46, 65, 146, 147
barriers, 8
beating, 90, 93, 96, 102, 114
beef, 37, 127, 144
beer, 36, 102
behavior, 42, 64, 66, 67, 78, 81, 98, 118, 135, 137
behaviour, 151, 156, 157, 159, 160, 161, 163, 164, 165, 167, 168, 169, 170, 171, 172, 175, 176, 177, 178, 180, 187, 189, 190, 192, 193, 194, 196, 197, 198, 199
behavioural controls, x, 151, 159, 161, 162, 164, 170, 171, 172, 176, 177, 180
behaviours, 159, 192
Beijing, 54, 55
beliefs, 66, 72, 114, 118, 123, 124, 126, 133, 134, 140, 141, 147, 148, 157, 159, 181, 184, 185, 186
benefits, 41, 54, 56
beverages, 36
bias, 40, 158, 167, 193
bilateral, 8, 38, 47, 54, 55, 56
bilateral trade, 55
Bin Laden, 52
binding, 128, 135
biology, 64
biomedical, 134
biotechnology, 39
birth, 62, 64, 67, 71, 72, 123, 124, 126, 128, 129, 130, 131, 132, 133, 134, 135, 136, 137
birth control, 64
birthing women, 134
births, 62
black, 110
blame, 75, 77, 104, 111
bleeding, 83, 92, 93, 95, 96, 104, 105, 108
blends, 5
blood, 63, 96, 104, 109, 110, 132, 146, 147
blood supply, 63
body, 127, 128, 129, 130, 131, 132, 134, 146, 147
body fluid, 146, 147
boiling, 131, 132
bomb, 54
bonding, 96
bonds, 19
borrowers, 23, 30
borrowing, 15
bottleneck, 16
boys, 63, 106
breast, 127, 130, 131, 132, 133, 144

Index

breast, 142, 143
breast milk, 144
breast-feeding, 133
breathing, 127
Britain, 135
British, 3, 187
broadband, 44
brokerage, 46
brothers, 64, 94, 102
bubble, 17, 18
bubbles, 161
Buddha, 145
Buddhism, 3, 141, 143, 148
Buddhist, 1, 28, 58, 125, 141
buildings, 12, 141
bureaucracy, 38
bureaucratic elite, 4
Burma, 3, 8, 9
burning, 129
Bush administration, 51, 52, 53, 54, 55
business, 15, 16, 17, 18, 19, 21, 23, 24, 25, 26, 27, 38, 45, 46, 47, 48, 52, 56, 116, 119, 158
business environment, 16, 18, 19, 45

C

cabinet members, 27
cable operators, 43
California, 120, 135, 136, 149
Cambodia, 5, 8, 54
Cambodian, 137, 181
campaigns, 15, 24, 29
candidates, 5
capacity, 9, 44, 45, 64, 116
capital, 3, 7, 13, 14, 17, 18, 19, 20, 21, 22, 30, 31, 46, 140, 141
capital account, 14
capital markets, 19
capitalism, 16, 30
caregiver, 140, 141, 143, 145
caregivers, 140, 141, 142, 143, 144, 145, 146, 147, 148
caretaker, 5, 97, 101
carrier, 55
cartel, 22
case study, 69, 180, 181
cast, 26, 59
catalyst, 19, 54
category a, 141, 178
catfish, 130
Catholic, 101, 121
causality, 18
cement, 2
central bank, 12, 21, 23
Central Bank, 46
Central Intelligence Agency (CIA), 54, 60
certificate, 38
certification, 39, 43

certifications, 39
chaebols, 15, 21, 25
channels, 57, 118
character, 134
chemical, 39, 54
chemical weapons, 54
chemicals, 2, 7, 9
cherries, 37
chi, 130
Chicago, 6, 137, 186, 187
chicken, 130, 131
child abuse, 29
childbearing, 125, 134, 136
childbirth, 126, 133, 134, 135, 136, 137
childhood, 64, 71, 118, 148
childrearing, 140, 143, 146, 148
children, 64, 92, 95, 118, 119, 128, 133, 139, 140, 141, 142, 143, 144, 145, 146, 147, 148, 149, 181, 183
China, 2, 3, 7, 15, 17, 18, 29, 51, 54, 55, 57
Chinese, 2, 13, 18, 19, 22, 23, 25, 27, 29, 31, 54, 55, 56, 132, 135, 136, 137
Chinese women, 135, 136
citizens, 30, 45, 53, 152
citrus, 36
civil liberties, 35
civil servant, 6
civil servants, 6
civil society, 6, 59
civilian, 4, 59
classes, 28, 102, 159, 168, 185, 190, 193
classical, 184
classification, 164
classroom, 153, 154, 155, 156, 157, 160, 161, 162, 163, 164, 166, 167, 168, 171, 172, 176, 180, 183, 184, 185, 186
classroom events, 156
classroom management, 161
classroom practice, 154, 186
classrooms, 165
cleaning, 146
clients, 110
clinical, 63
clinicians, 116
clinics, 61, 79, 85, 90, 92, 93, 98, 102, 103, 106, 107, 108, 109, 111, 114, 117, 119, 141
closure, 22
clothing, 38, 43
clouds, 53
clusters, 131
Co, 2, 5, 8, 31, 32, 42, 54, 56, 57, 148, 187
coalitions, 17
coatings, 39
coconut, 144
coding, 73
coffee, 36
cognitive, 154, 160, 183, 184
cognitive process, 154, 184
Cold War, 18, 51

collaboration, 72, 116, 118, 181, 184
colleges, 152
colonialism, 3
colonization, 4
Columbia University, 187
combat, 49, 52, 53
combined effect, 37
commerce, 48, 49, 141
commercial, 25, 35, 41, 42, 46, 48, 63
commercial bank, 25, 46
commodities, 7, 8, 39, 40
communication, 56, 64, 81, 118, 119, 154, 158, 159, 185
Communist Party, 2
communities, 3, 53, 56, 57, 58, 61, 65, 69, 70, 72, 75, 78, 79, 87, 98, 115. 120, 152, 155, 158, 160
community, 2, 38, 48, 51, 55, 70, 72, 75, 77, 78, 85, 87, 89, 91, 104, 106, 110, 113, 114, 115, 117, 118, 119, 133, 134, 136, 141, 143, 144, 145, 154, 158, 160, 163
competition, 19, 40, 45, 46, 49
competitiveness, 18
competitor, 18
compilation, 3
complementary, 56
complex, 132
complexity, 28, 39, 155
compliance, 39, 41, 43, 47
complications, 53, 61, 62, 63, 117
components, 58, 66, 72, 118, 179
composite, 23
composition, 38
comprehension, 151, 152, 153, 154, 156, 157, 159, 160, 161, 162, 163, 164, 165, 167, 168, 169, 172, 173, 174, 175, 177, 178, 179, 180, 181, 182, 186, 189, 190, 191, 192, 193, 194, 195, 196, 197, 198, 199
computer, 48, 70, 156, 165, 168, 173, 190, 192
computers, 2, 7, 48
concentrates, 69
conception, 64
concrete, 155
condom, 104
condoms, 80, 84, 104
conduct, 126
confidence, 4, 7, 18, 20, 21, 22, 52, 56, 59, 164, 194, 196, 197
confidence interval, 194, 196, 197
confidentiality, 61, 73, 74, 116, 117, 126, 168
configuration, 55
confinement, 123, 124, 126, 130, 133, 134, 136, 137
conflict, 20, 29, 54, 85, 88, 94, 112
conformity, 43, 121
confrontation, 54, 55
Confucian, 16, 31
confusion, 17, 20
consciousness, 64, 92, 182

consensus, 18, 57, 156, 166, 170, 173
consent, 73, 74, 124, 168
consequence, 126, 132
conspiracy, 16, 18
Constitution, 2, 49, 152
constitutional, 1, 4, 5, 8, 35, 152
constraints, 126, 146, 147
construct validity, 165
construction, 8, 13, 22, 23, 25, 39, 46, 101, 125, 163, 164, 180
construction materials, 39
consultants, 46
consulting, 16, 67, 68, 85, 88
consumer goods, 39
consumers, 7
consumption, 22, 27, 30, 104, 118, 130, 132
contempt, 89, 111
content analysis, 61, 69, 73
context, 57, 124, 136
continuing, 88, 105, 144
continuity, 181
contraceptives, 64, 65, 80
contractions, 11
contracts, 40, 45, 49
control, 6, 12, 16, 23, 43, 45, 47, 49, 55, 58, 64, 73, 81, 82, 112, 115, 140, 146, 147, 157, 168, 176, 185, 189, 190, 191, 192, 193, 194, 195, 196, 197, 198
control group, 157, 168, 189, 190, 191, 192, 193, 194, 195, 196, 197, 198
controlled, 54, 82, 114, 189
conversion, 45
conviction, 41, 42
cooking, 23, 111, 127
cooperative learning, 161, 162, 189, 190, 191, 192, 193, 195, 196, 198, 199
cooperative learning method, 189, 191, 195, 196, 198, 199
coordination, 14, 57, 58
Copenhagen, 136
coping, 20
copyright, 41, 43
corn, 2, 7, 37
corporate governance, 16, 20, 21, 25
corporate restructuring, 25, 27
corporations, 12, 13, 17, 25, 26, 27
corruption, 4, 24, 41, 49
costs, 30, 37, 47, 113
Council of Ministers, 56
counsel, 115
counseling, 96, 97, 101, 109, 113, 115, 116, 117, 119
counterfeit, 41, 42
counterfeiting, 41
counter-terror, 55
country of origin, 40
Court of Appeals, 5
courts, 5, 42
covering, 61, 69, 159

crab, 127
cracking, 56, 59
creativity, 7, 156
credit, 18, 21, 22, 23, 41
credit creation, 22
credit rating, 18
creditors, 15
crime, 9, 29, 41, 42, 49, 62
crimes, 42, 51
criminal activity, 9
criminal behavior, 42
criminals, 27
critical period, 64
criticism, 24, 53
cronyism, 24
cross-cultural, 136
crude oil, 7
crying, 84, 106, 110
cultivation, 3
cultural, 8, 41, 51, 54, 56, 58, 66, 89, 123, 125, 129, 130, 136, 140, 141, 147, 148, 158, 184
cultural beliefs, 148
cultural identities, 141
cultural perspective, 136, 140
culture, 2, 27, 28, 66, 68, 71, 72, 75, 77, 87, 94, 97, 98, 114, 115, 123, 126, 131, 133, 134, 140, 147, 148, 158
cultures, 123, 126, 127, 133, 135
currency, 11, 14, 15, 18, 19, 20, 21, 23, 24, 29, 30, 54
current account, 13, 22
current account deficit, 22
curriculum, 152, 157, 168, 180, 185
customers, 47, 84
cyber crime, 49, 51

D

Daewoo, 23, 25
daily care, 144, 147
daily living, 113
dairy, 48
damage, 130
danger, 8, 69, 134, 135
data analysis, 73, 74, 185, 190, 199
data base, 7
data collection, 61, 69, 71, 72, 73, 74, 107, 126, 135
data processing, 73
death, 58, 62, 63, 95, 96, 137, 139, 143
deaths, 53, 58
debt, 7, 12, 13, 15, 16, 25, 26, 27
debts, 12, 22, 24
decision makers, 66, 69
decision making, 61, 66, 67, 68, 71, 148
decision-making process, 61, 66, 67, 71, 74, 85
decisions, 19, 39, 62, 72, 79, 87, 88, 98, 107, 116, 118

deep-sea, 7, 52
defects, 16
defense, 9
deficit, 12, 13, 15, 35
deficits, 19, 22
definition, 43, 71, 85, 158, 159
deflation, 54
degree, 18, 24, 25, 29, 52, 87, 121, 152, 180
degrees of freedom, 173
delays, 27, 39, 40
delivery, 9, 47, 66, 77, 78, 79, 85, 92, 93, 97, 98, 101, 103, 105, 106, 111, 113, 115, 117
demand, 4, 6, 7, 19, 45, 144
democracy, 4, 5, 25, 35
Democrat, 59
democratic elections, 5
Democratic Party, 4, 24
democratisation, 15, 25, 28, 30
demographic, 71, 72, 74, 124, 126, 140
demographic characteristics, 71, 72, 74, 124, 126
demographic data, 140
Department of Agriculture, 39
deposits, 21, 22
depreciation, 18, 19, 21, 24
depressed, 82, 84, 92, 101, 102, 106, 113
depression, 22, 101, 104, 140
deregulation, 12, 13, 15, 16, 17, 18
destruction, 53
detergents, 145
deterrence, 119
developed countries, 21
developing countries, 17, 31, 48, 62, 63, 136
development, 135, 136
Development Assistance, 56
developmental care, 147
developmental promotion, 144
deviation, 166, 170, 174, 194, 196, 197
diarrhea, 131, 139, 142, 145
dictatorship, 25
diet, 126, 130, 131, 133
dietary, 123, 133, 134
dieting, 136
diets, 130
differentiation, 165
digestion, 132
direct action, 162
direct investment, 19, 35, 56
disability, 62, 63
disappointment, 87
disaster, 21
discipline, 18, 162, 164, 171, 172, 176, 177
disclosure, 39, 42
discomfort, 53
discontinuity, 164
discounts, 27, 47
discourse, 154, 155, 158, 160, 163
discrimination, 58, 140, 165
discriminatory, 119
disease progression, ix, 139

disenchantment, 53
disorder, 147
disputes, 25, 42
distress, 63, 140
distribution, 43, 49, 166, 170, 173, 174
diversity, 3
divorce, 6
dizziness, 126
doctor, 89, 104, 106, 108, 130
doctors, 69, 72, 119, 145
domestic credit, 21
domestic demand, 6, 7
domestic economy, 56
domestic markets, 21
donor, 20, 30
doors, 22, 127
draft, 14, 42, 43, 47
dream, 83
drinking, 104
drought, 6
drug addict, 81
drug trafficking, 9, 56
drugs, 42, 49, 81, 87, 90, 92
drugs [medicines], 131, 136
dry, 36
duration, 39, 103, 139
duties, 36, 37, 38, 133, 134

E

early warning, 26
ears, 1
East Asia, 11, 15, 16, 17, 18, 19, 21, 22, 26, 29, 30, 31, 32, 60, 136
East Timor, 8
eating, 101, 127, 135
eating behavior, 135
economic, 4, 6, 7, 8, 11, 12, 14, 15, 16, 17, 18, 19, 20, 21, 22, 23, 24, 25, 26, 27, 28, 29, 30, 36, 46, 51, 54, 56, 57, 79, 84, 92, 94, 124, 141, 153, 181
economic assistance, 8
economic behaviour, 19
economic boom, 19
economic cooperation, 56, 57
economic crisis, 11, 15, 18, 19, 20, 25, 84, 92
economic development, 7, 11, 12, 14, 15, 17, 30, 181
economic growth, 4, 6, 7, 12, 17, 54
economic growth rate, 12
economic indicator, 22
economic integration, 19
economic policy, 6
economic problem, 79, 84
economic reform, 24
economic stability, 22, 24
economic status, 141
economic systems, 29
economics, 24, 25
economies, 12, 16, 17, 18, 19, 21, 22, 25, 26, 30
economy, 6, 7, 11, 12, 13, 14, 15, 16, 17, 19, 20, 22, 23, 25, 26, 30, 37, 45, 56
education, 3, 8, 9, 29, 64, 75, 76, 81, 85, 95, 116, 118, 119, 121, 125, 136, 142, 143, 152, 153, 154, 162, 181, 182, 183, 184, 185, 186, 187, 191
educational attainment, 124
educational profiles, 153
educational system, 119, 152
egg, 127
Egypt, 57
elderly, 97
elders, 140
election, 24, 25, 59
electrical, 2, 7, 36, 39
electricity, 7
electronic, 7, 18, 48, 49
electronics, 2, 7, 22, 36
elementary, 152, 155, 156
elementary (primary) school, 155, 168, 189
elementary school, 155
embezzlement, 25
emergence, 51
emission, 40
emotion, 63
emotional, 117, 134, 139
emotions, 64, 81, 96
employees, 7
employers, 80
employment, 48, 119
empowered, 39
encouragement, 6, 120
energy, 8
engagement, 53, 54, 155, 156, 181, 183
engineering, 46
engines, 15, 37
England, 120, 183
English, 1, 77, 78, 151, 152, 153, 154, 156, 157, 158, 159, 160, 161, 162, 163, 164, 165, 167, 168, 169, 171, 172, 173, 174, 176, 180, 181, 182, 183, 184, 185, 186, 187, 189, 190, 191, 192, 193, 194, 196, 197, 199
English as a second language, 151, 152, 153, 154, 189, 196, 197, 199
English comprehension, 151
English for Specific Purposes, 181, 182, 185
English Language, 183
English Reading Comprehension, 159, 164, 168
enterprise, 6, 46
enthusiasm, 27
environment, 5, 16, 18, 19, 45, 48, 52, 74, 81, 95, 97, 118, 119, 129, 134, 140, 144, 147, 167
environmental, 8, 71, 72, 155
environmental factors, 71, 72
epidemic, 3, 63
epidemiology, 139
episiotomy, 130

equality, 117
equilibrium, 14, 19, 134
equipment, 8, 23, 36, 39, 95
equity, 25, 27, 45, 46, 47
ESL learning, 160, 163
esophageal, 139
ethical, 74
ethics, 74
etiology, 127
Europe, 7, 8, 19, 52
European, 3, 4, 9, 14, 21, 31, 32
European Union, 9
evening, 102, 144
everyday life, 140
evidence, 16, 17, 24, 63, 93, 105, 123, 155, 159
evil, 53
examinations, 42, 152
exchange rate, 12, 13, 14, 16, 17, 19, 21, 22, 23, 49
exchange rates, 13, 14, 49
excise tax, 36, 38
excuse, 16, 20
exercise, 9, 162
expansions, 17
expenditures, 3, 26, 84
expert, 141, 154
experts, 71, 140, 159, 167, 168
exploitation, 48, 140
export subsidies, 41
exporter, 7
exports, 2, 6, 7, 9, 15, 18, 21, 23, 27, 35, 36, 37, 38, 40
exposure, 62, 139, 155
externalities, 31
eye, 106
eyes, 56, 106

F

facilitators, 119
failure, 17, 20, 59, 105, 128, 142
failure to thrive, 142
faith, 58
family, 3, 6, 8, 13, 20, 23, 25, 27, 62, 63, 64, 65, 66, 68, 70, 72, 74, 75, 77, 79, 81, 82, 83, 84, 87, 89, 92, 94, 95, 97, 101, 102, 104, 114, 115, 118, 119, 120, 125, 134, 141, 143, 145, 147, 148, 158
family conflict, 62
family income, 70, 72, 104
family life, 79, 82
family members, 66, 75, 77, 89, 94, 147
family planning, 3, 8, 64, 65
Far East, 22, 24, 27, 31
farm, 37
farmers, 24
fat, 81, 87, 104, 106
faults, 89

FDA approval, 40, 42
fear, 128, 130
February, 4, 6, 8, 17, 28, 32, 55, 59, 60, 121, 181
fee, 93, 111, 146
feedback, 163, 164, 180
feeding, 133, 135, 144
feelings, 68, 70, 71, 75, 79, 94, 107, 134, 140, 143, 146, 159
fees, 37, 38, 44, 47
females, 64, 65
fertility, 92, 131, 134, 135, 136
fertilizers, 2
fetus, 68, 86, 103, 104, 109
fever, 142, 145, 146
fighters, 52
finance, 9, 17, 26, 35
financial crisis, 4, 6, 7, 22, 37, 46, 51, 57
financial institution, 12, 15, 16, 17, 18, 19, 26, 27, 30, 53
financial liberalisation, 11, 12, 15
financial problems, 79, 98, 103, 113, 146
financial sector, 7, 11, 21, 29, 46
financial soundness, 25
financial stability, 29
financial support, 81, 135
financial system, 18, 23, 30
financing, 41
fines, 47, 62
fire, 124, 136, 137
firearms, 58
firms, 6, 15, 35, 40, 44, 45, 46, 47, 49
first aid, 145
first language, 155
First World, 21
first-time, 136
fish, 2, 7, 37, 127, 130, 144
flight, 20
floating, 12, 13, 20, 21
focus group, 74, 75, 78, 87, 159
focus groups, 159
focusing, 16, 17, 18, 42, 156
food, 7, 23, 36, 37, 38, 39, 90, 92, 127, 130, 131, 133, 135, 137, 140, 144
Food and Drug Administration, 39
food products, 36, 37, 39
food safety, 39
foodstuffs, 23, 127, 130, 133
footwear, 2
Ford, 65, 120
foreign banks, 23
foreign direct investment, 19, 35, 56
foreign exchange, 11, 12, 13, 15, 16, 18, 20, 21, 22, 23, 26, 29
foreign exchange market, 11
foreign firms, 46
foreign investment, 6, 7, 11, 12, 20, 22, 24, 29, 44, 48
foreign language, 152, 153, 158, 160, 163, 181, 183, 184, 187

Foreign Military Financing, 9
foreign nation, 45
foreign nationals, 45
foreign policy, 8, 56
foreign producer, 40
foreigners, 24
forestry, 37
framing, 25
France, 1
free trade, 8, 20, 54
free trade agreement, 8
free trade area, 54
freedom, 47, 64, 82, 170, 173, 174
Friday, 91, 191
friends, 62, 63, 65, 77, 78, 79, 83, 86, 87, 89, 90, 91, 92, 93, 97, 98, 99, 101, 102, 103, 104, 106, 107, 108, 110, 111, 112, 113, 114, 124, 129
fruit, 127, 131
fruits, 36, 39, 101
frustration, 58
fuel, 17, 36
functional, 133
Fundamental English, 192
funds, 13, 16, 18, 19, 20, 22, 29, 30, 42, 46, 49
fungal, 139
furniture, 7
futures, 17, 94

G

games, 17, 19, 145
gas, 2, 39, 49
gasoline, 36, 93
gauge, 59
gender, 28, 64, 117, 137, 168, 191
gender equality, 117
gender-sensitive, 117
General Agreement on Trade in Services, 47
general election, 5, 24, 25, 59
General Health Questionnaire, 181
generation, 6, 7, 44
genre, 151, 152, 154, 155, 156, 157, 158, 159, 160, 161, 162, 163, 164, 165, 167, 170, 173, 177, 178, 179, 180, 182, 183, 184, 185
genre-based learning, 151, 161, 162, 163, 165, 170
genre-based learning process, 163
Georgia, 181
gestures, 53
girls, 63, 74, 89, 106
global trade, 54
gloves, 147
goals, 113
goods and services, 6, 18
gossip, 81, 89, 90, 91, 97, 98, 102
governance, 20, 21, 25

government, 2, 3, 4, 5, 6, 7, 12, 13, 15, 16, 17, 20, 21, 22, 23, 24, 25, 26, 27, 35, 36, 37, 38, 39, 40, 41, 42, 43, 45, 46, 47, 48, 49, 51, 52, 53, 54, 55, 56, 57, 58, 59, 62, 65, 68, 69, 80, 84, 85, 114, 116, 117, 125, 143, 153, 158, 159, 166, 186
government budget, 153
government expenditure, 3
government policy, 47
government procurement, 40
government-to-government, 41
grades, 75, 152, 157, 162
grandparents, 139
grapes, 36
greed, 13, 20, 22
Greeks, 155
grief, 120
Gross Domestic Product (GDP), 2, 6, 12, 13, 14, 15, 18, 22, 23, 26
ground-based, 47
group activities, 119, 162
group work, 112, 161, 172
groups, 1, 2, 3, 19, 25, 27, 44, 52, 53, 57, 59, 62, 71, 80, 96, 112, 141, 155, 157, 158, 159, 162, 168, 171, 173, 180, 189, 190, 191, 192, 193, 194, 195, 196, 198
growth, 1, 2, 3, 4, 6, 7, 12, 14, 16, 17, 18, 21, 23, 26, 43, 45, 47, 54, 148
growth rate, 1, 2, 6, 12, 18, 23, 26
Guantanamo, 52
guardian, 191
guerrilla, 58
guessing, 164, 167, 173, 178, 179, 185
guidance, 61
guidelines, 21, 39, 47, 53, 70, 71, 73, 74, 117, 156
guilt, 83
guilty, 94, 98, 102, 109
Gulf War, 52

H

Haiti, 137
handling, 59, 145
hands, 16, 26, 30, 98, 102, 146, 162
hanging, 136
harm, 144, 145
harmful, 64, 123, 145
Harvard, 181, 187
hate, 136
Hawaii, 186
hazards, 15, 17, 21
head, 2, 4, 101, 126, 127, 128, 129
healing, 72, 130
health, 3, 8, 20, 29, 43, 61, 62, 64, 65, 66, 67, 68, 69, 70, 71, 74, 75, 80, 81, 84, 85, 96, 97, 98, 101, 103, 107, 114, 115, 116, 117, 118, 119, 120, 121, 123, 124, 126, 127, 131, 132, 133,

134, 135, 136, 137, 140, 141, 144, 145, 146, 147, 148
health care, 64, 65, 66, 67, 68, 117, 119, 120, 124, 134, 140, 141, 147, 148
health care system, 66, 120
health care workers, 140, 141
health education, 3, 8, 81
health problems, 62, 65, 66, 114, 134, 140
health services, 65, 66, 67, 68, 107, 115, 117
healthcare, 47, 65, 72, 98, 114, 116, 117
heart, 95, 187
heat, 132
heavy, 130
hedge funds, 18
hegemony, 18, 20, 30
hemisphere, 37
hepatomegaly, 142
herbal, 131, 132, 145
herbal medicine, 131, 132, 145
herbalists, 132
herbs, 131, 132
heroin, 9
high risk, 63
high school, 58, 85, 91, 183
high scores, 191
higher education, 124
hip, 117
hips, 15
HIV/AIDS, 3, 8, 62, 63, 117, 139, 140, 141, 142, 143, 144, 145, 146, 147, 148, 149
HIV infection, 3, 139, 145, 147
Hmong, 2, 136, 137
holistic, 66
Holland, 135, 182
homes, 82, 126
homogeneous, 2
Hong Kong, 17, 22
hospital, 47, 62, 63, 83, 97, 105, 106, 124, 127, 136, 145, 146
hospital beds, 63
hospitalization, 63
hospitals, 47, 49, 61, 85, 103, 117, 147
house, 5, 24, 53, 121, 182, 183
household, 133
households, 28
housing, 140
human, 17, 24, 51, 56, 58, 74, 141, 163
human rights, 58
humanitarian, 53, 56
husband, 87, 92, 93, 97, 103, 130, 132, 146
hygiene, 139, 144, 147, 149
hygienic, 144
hypothesis, 18, 170, 173
Hyundai, 25

I

ice, 73

id, 13, 16, 18, 21, 23, 28, 32, 77, 81, 91, 92, 96, 101, 103, 106, 110, 128, 194, 197
identification, 167, 175, 179
identity, 3, 5, 58, 64, 65, 116
ideology, 25, 135, 185
Illinois, 135, 187
illness care, 147
images, 119, 149
immigration, 29, 53
immune response, 147
immune system, 139
immunity, 145
impairments, 139
implementation, 39, 41, 152, 160, 163, 184
imports, 2, 7, 9, 19, 22, 35, 36, 37, 39, 40
inactive, 12
incentive, 38, 154
incentives, 39
inclusion, 42, 53, 71, 73, 75
income, 2, 7, 14, 28, 61, 67, 69, 70, 71, 72, 75, 83, 84, 86, 90, 91, 92, 101, 102, 104, 110, 111, 113, 114, 115, 116, 124, 125, 146
incomes, 28, 70, 84, 146
independence, 8, 23, 25, 55
India, 51, 54, 55, 56, 57, 59, 121
Indian, 54, 55, 56, 57, 60, 131
Indian Ocean, 54, 56, 57
indicators, 13, 14, 18, 22, 23, 67
indigenous, 29, 48
Indonesia, 8, 11, 12, 13, 14, 15, 16, 17, 18, 20, 21, 22, 23, 24, 25, 26, 27, 28, 29, 31, 32, 52, 57, 59, 120, 136
industrial, 38
industrialisation, 11, 12
industry, 16, 36, 37, 39, 42, 43, 44, 53, 141
inefficiency, 17
inequality, 30, 65
infancy, 137
infant, 129, 133, 134, 135
infant care, 144
infant feeding practices, 135
infants, 144
Infants, 149
infection, 133, 139, 142, 143, 144, 145, 146, 147
infections, 3, 139, 140, 142, 144, 145, 146, 147, 148
infectious, 141, 146, 147
infectious disease, 146
inferences, 151, 157, 170, 172, 175, 178, 179, 180
inflation, 12, 13, 14, 22, 23, 28
influence, 136
informal sector, 71, 72
informed consent, 124
infrastructure, 49
infringement, 41, 43
injection, 80, 106, 110
injections, 146
injuries, 145

injury, 144, 145
injustice, 58
insertion, 117
insight, 148
instabilities, 16
instability, 11, 15, 19, 24, 25, 26, 27, 30
institutionalisation, 29
institutions, 4, 12, 15, 16, 17, 19, 26, 27, 30, 42, 46, 53, 66, 72
instruction, 155, 180, 181, 182, 183, 184, 185
instructional methods, 183
instructors, 182
instruments, 18, 55, 56, 71
integrated circuits, 2, 7
integration, 19, 134, 148
intellectual property, 42, 43
intelligence, 58, 186
intentions, 163
interaction, 66, 68, 70, 71, 85, 107, 111, 113, 114, 154, 161, 162, 163, 166, 170, 171, 172, 173, 174, 176, 185, 190, 195, 198
Interaction, 66, 68, 107, 110, 111, 186, 195, 198
interaction effect, 190, 198
interaction process, 85
interactions, 71, 77, 107, 157, 159, 161, 162, 166, 170, 171, 176, 177, 180, 184
interdependence, 12, 30
interest, 157, 159, 163, 177, 186, 187
interest rates, 20, 21, 23
internal consistency, 73
international, 4, 8, 9, 11, 12, 13, 14, 15, 16, 17, 18, 19, 21, 22, 23, 26, 27, 29, 30, 38, 43, 44, 45, 47, 48, 51, 52, 55, 56, 58, 59
international financial institutions, 16
international markets, 9, 15, 18
International Military Education and Training, 9
International Monetary Fund, 11
international standards, 43
international terrorism, 52
internationalism, 25
Internet, 44, 48, 64, 121
interpersonal attitude, 161
interpersonal relations, 64, 66, 117, 143
interpersonal relationships, 64, 66, 143
interpretation, 49, 126
interval, 157, 165, 169, 170, 194, 196, 197
interview, 57, 61, 69, 70, 71, 73, 74, 79, 85, 98, 110, 115, 116, 118, 119, 124, 126, 135, 140
interviews, 70, 73, 74, 75, 85, 87, 107, 114, 115, 116, 117, 119, 123, 124, 126, 140, 143, 187
intimidation, 41
Investigations, 42
investigative, 42
investment, 6, 7, 8, 9, 11, 12, 17, 18, 19, 20, 22, 24, 30, 35, 42, 44, 47, 48, 54, 56
investors, 6, 7, 9, 12, 13, 16, 18, 19, 20, 21, 23, 26, 27, 30, 45, 48
Iran, 54, 57
Iraq, 8, 53

iron, 2, 7, 104
Islamic, 5, 23, 52, 59
isolation, 112, 134, 140
issues, 135
item parameters, 165, 169

J

Jamaica, 135
January, 4, 22, 24, 31, 41, 42, 45, 48, 53, 58, 59, 60, 129, 181
Japan, 2, 4, 7, 8, 9, 15, 19, 21, 29, 31, 37, 51, 54, 55, 56, 57, 60, 181
Japanese, 4, 16, 18, 31, 37, 39, 55, 56, 60
Java, 22
jewelry, 2, 7
jobs, 23, 28, 102, 141
joints, 130
Jordan, 128, 133, 135
journalism, 162, 167
judge, 15
judges, 5, 77
judiciary, 5
Jung, 20, 25, 27
jurisdiction, 5
justice, 52

K

Kashmir, 54
Kenya, 56, 57
Keynes, 180
Keynesian, 22
killing, 94
kindergartners, 185
King, 2, 3, 4, 5, 6, 49
knowledge, 136, 137, 143, 147, 148
Korea, 8, 11, 12, 13, 14, 15, 16, 17, 19, 20, 21, 22, 23, 24, 25, 26, 27, 28, 29, 31, 32, 54, 55, 57, 133, 136
Korean, 14, 15, 16, 17, 20, 21, 23, 24, 25, 26, 28, 31, 32, 55, 134
Korean government, 15, 17, 24, 25

L

labeling, 39
labor, 2, 6, 7, 42, 69, 88, 119
labor force, 2, 7, 69
labour, 15, 18, 27, 28, 54
labour market, 28
land, 1, 47, 48, 137
language, 1, 2, 40, 151, 152, 153, 154, 155, 156, 158, 159, 160, 163, 167, 180, 181, 183, 184, 185, 186, 187, 189, 196, 197, 199
language proficiency, 180

Index

language skills, 156
Laos, 5, 8, 9, 54
large-scale, 9, 64
later life, 126, 127
Latin America, 30
law, 3, 9, 35, 42, 43, 44, 45, 46, 47, 48, 49, 58, 62, 65, 66, 69, 82, 83, 91, 101, 102, 112, 119, 131
law enforcement, 9, 42, 43
laws, 5, 39, 114
lead, 2, 41, 59, 62, 64, 69, 86, 92, 147, 154, 156, 160, 163, 179
leadership, 2, 5, 17, 23, 24, 25, 51, 58
leaks, 41
learners, 152, 156, 160, 163, 164, 184, 185
learning, 113, 145, 151, 152, 153, 154, 155, 156, 157, 159, 160, 161, 162, 163, 164, 165, 167, 169, 170, 171, 172, 179, 181, 183, 184, 185, 186, 189, 190, 191, 192, 193, 194, 195, 196, 197, 198, 199
learning environment, 167
learning process, 161, 162, 163
legislation, 39, 41, 42, 48, 49
legislative, 5, 43
lemongrass, 130
lenders, 12
lending, 15, 17, 21
lesson plan, 158, 160, 162, 163, 164, 191, 193
letters of credit, 23
liberal, 17, 30
liberalisation, 11, 12, 15, 16, 17, 18, 27, 54
liberalization, 44, 47
license fee, 37, 44
licenses, 36, 37, 38, 42, 44, 45, 46
licensing, 38, 42, 44
life experiences, 66
lifestyle, 82
life-threatening, viii, 61
lifetime, 64, 186
light, 137
limitation, 13, 37, 157
limitations, 157
linear, 151, 156, 157, 164, 165, 166, 173, 180, 190, 192
linear model, 173
linguistically, 3
linkage, 42
links, 58, 163, 164, 184
liquidity, 11, 16, 19, 21
liquidity trap, 21
listening, 145
literacy, 156, 181, 182, 183, 185
literature, 71, 161, 165
liver, 127
loans, 11, 15, 20, 21, 22, 25, 26, 27, 29, 41, 46
location, 19, 74, 176, 177, 179
logistics, 73
London, 120, 135, 136, 137, 182, 184, 186, 187
loneliness, 140

long period, 49, 62, 110, 128
long-distance, 45
long-term, 15, 29, 30, 56, 58, 94
loopholes, 43, 57
Los Angeles, 6
losses, 43
Louisiana, 121
love, 82, 90, 91, 101, 120, 136, 143, 148
low power, 173
low risk, 118
lower prices, 23
low-income, 61, 69, 70, 71, 75, 92, 110, 114, 146
lying, 124

M

machinery, 2
machines, 23, 38, 43, 46
macroeconomic, 13, 14, 15, 16, 23
macroeconomic management, 16
maintenance, 8, 9, 74
Malaysia, 1, 7, 8, 11, 13, 29, 52, 55, 57, 59, 136
males, 63, 117
malicious, 58
malnutrition, 139
management, 4, 12, 16, 17, 27, 29, 36, 40, 44, 46, 62, 72, 117, 119, 134, 145, 159, 161
mandates, 3
mangosteen, 36
manpower, 11
manufacturing, 6, 7, 18, 22, 23, 35, 38, 39
marital status, 65
market, 7, 11, 12, 14, 15, 17, 18, 19, 20, 21, 22, 23, 24, 27, 28, 35, 37, 41, 45, 46, 49, 132
market access, 35, 37
market economy, 17
market value, 28, 45
marketing, 118
markets, 2, 6, 7, 8, 9, 15, 18, 19, 20, 21, 26, 28, 40, 41, 45
marriage, 6, 52, 62, 77, 87
married women, 75, 77, 80, 81, 82, 84, 88, 110, 111
Mars, 182
martial law, 35, 58
maternal, 134, 142
mathematics, 152
matrix, 72
Mauritius, 56, 57
Maya, 135
meanings, 77, 156, 157, 158, 159, 160, 162, 167, 175, 178
measurement, 151, 157, 164, 165, 166, 169, 170, 173, 174, 180, 181, 187
measures, 36, 37, 38, 44, 48, 52, 56, 156, 157, 164, 165, 166, 169, 170, 172, 173, 175, 189, 190, 192, 195
meat, 37, 131

media, 40, 43, 47, 111
median, 63
medical care, 120
medical services, 47
medication, 61, 62, 63, 79, 98, 114, 136
medicinal, 131, 132
medicine, 72, 92, 93, 110, 114, 127, 131, 132, 134, 136, 145, 147
meditation, 145
melons, 127
membership, 15, 57
memory, 74, 105
men, 63, 64, 75, 77, 78, 81, 89, 90, 128
menstruation, 65, 85, 86, 88, 93, 101, 104, 106, 109, 116, 117
merchandise, 9, 49
messages, 118
metallurgy, 3
methamphetamine, 9
methodology, 152, 153, 154, 164, 181, 193
Mexico, 21, 135
Middle Ages, 155
middle class, 23, 28, 30, 124
Middle East, 2
midwives, 136
military, 2, 4, 5, 8, 25, 35, 51, 52, 53, 55, 58
military government, 4
milk, 37, 48, 104, 113, 130, 131, 132, 135, 144
millennium, 183
minerals, 38
Ministry of Education, 153, 162, 184, 185, 186
minority, 2
miscarriage, 105
misleading, 38
missiles, 55
mixing, 114
mobile phone, 45
mobile telephony, 44
mobility, 30
models, 66, 67, 180, 181, 186
modernisation, 124
modules, 186
momentum, 54
monetary policy, 20
money, 12, 17, 19, 20, 30, 80, 82, 83, 84, 86, 90, 93, 95, 97, 102, 104, 107, 108, 109, 110, 113, 128, 145, 146
monks, 145
monopoly, 22, 49
monsoon, 1
moon, 16, 32
moral hazard, 15, 17, 21
morality, 96
morals, 89
moratorium, 15
morbidity, 134
morning, 80, 104, 193
mortality, 1, 134
mortality rate, 1

mosquitoes, 144
motherhood, 125, 134, 136
mothers, 75, 77, 94, 96, 131, 133, 134, 136, 141, 144
motivation, 181, 183, 186, 187
motorcycles, 36, 38, 40
mouse, 160
mouth, 89, 92, 93, 95, 97, 119
movement, 7, 47, 58, 86
Mozambique, 57
multiculturalism, 182
multidimensional, 187
multilateral, 5, 8, 56, 57
Muslim, 1, 52, 53, 58
Muslims, 2, 5, 53, 58
mutual, 133
Myanmar, 54, 57

N

narcotics, 9
narratives, 126, 160, 179, 182
nation, 3, 4, 9, 29
national, 5, 13, 14, 15, 22, 23, 24, 26, 30, 31, 39, 48, 49, 52, 55, 56, 58, 153
national debt, 15
national identity, 5
national interests, 55
national product, 14, 26
national security, 52
National Security Council, 52
nationalism, 24, 25
NATO, 8, 53
natural, 2, 6, 11, 20, 48, 80, 123, 130, 152, 156
natural gas, 2
natural resources, vii, 6, 11, 20, 48
nausea, 80
needs, 55, 129
negative attitudes, 65, 77, 111, 143, 154
negative consequences, 94
negative relation, 78
negativity, 16, 17
neglect, 29
negligence, 17
neoliberal, 20, 30
neoliberalism, 30
neomercantilism, 12, 30
network, 44, 54, 57, 72, 117, 119, 124, 160
networks, 124
New Jersey, 185
New Orleans, 121
New World, 60
New York, 6, 32, 136, 149, 183, 186, 199
newspapers, 177
noise, 133, 179
non-citizen, 45
non-violent, 5, 53, 55
normal, 89, 91, 104, 128, 133, 134, 142, 146, 161

normal development, 142
norms, 66, 73, 87, 89, 94, 97, 114, 115, 160, 161, 163
North America, 7, 155, 183
North Korea, 54, 55
Northeast, 31, 57
Northeast Asia, 31, 57
Norway, 45
novelty, 42
nuclear, 54, 55
null hypothesis, 170, 173
nurse, 115, 141
nurses, 72, 116, 148
nutrition, 136, 137, 147

O

obligation, 4, 48
obligations, 36, 38, 42, 48
observations, 115, 126, 140
offal, 37
oil, 7, 23, 36, 57
old age, 130
Oman, 56, 57
omission, 24
onion, 130, 131
open economy, 16
open markets, 6
operator, 44
opium, 9
opposition, 4, 15, 20, 59, 155
opposition parties, 4, 59
optical, 41, 43
oral, 80, 83, 84, 142, 155, 158, 187
oral contraceptives, 80
organ, 52
organization, 3, 39, 62, 113, 117, 118, 181
Organization of American States (OAS), 8
organizations, 5, 8, 62, 116, 117
organized crime, 42
orientation, 153, 191
Osama bin Laden, 52
other cultures, 126, 127, 133
oversight, 43, 44
ownership, 45, 47

P

Pacific, 27, 51, 52, 55, 56, 57, 58, 60, 121
pain, 20, 83, 94, 95, 110, 126, 127, 128, 129, 130, 132, 142
Pakistan, 54, 55, 57
Pakistani, 54, 55
paper, 31, 32, 36, 73, 120, 121, 135, 181, 184, 186
paralysis, 23
paramedics, 72

parenthood, 137
parenting, 66, 67, 68, 70, 71, 72, 74
parents, 61, 62, 64, 75, 76, 77, 78, 79, 81, 82, 83, 84, 87, 88, 89, 90, 91, 92, 94, 95, 97, 98, 99, 101, 102, 103, 105, 106, 107, 108, 111, 112, 113, 114, 116, 118, 119, 139, 141, 143, 168, 191
Paris, 42
Parkinson, 185
Parliament, 4, 8, 39, 41, 46
participant observation, 126, 140
participation, 124
partnership, 54, 55
partnerships, 57
party system, 2
passenger, 37, 38
passive, 56, 181
patients, 147
Peace Corps, 8
peacekeeping, 8
pears, 37
pedagogical, 181
pedagogies, 155
pedagogy, 155, 180, 182, 184
pediatric, 141
peer, 81, 82
peers, 61, 64, 66, 72, 77, 80, 82, 83, 87, 91, 114, 118, 166
penalties, 42, 43, 47, 49
penalty, 62, 173
per capita income, 14
perception, 66, 147, 183
perceptions, 49, 70, 118, 126
performance, 6, 7, 26, 182, 183
perineum, 130
periodic, 39
permit, 46, 71, 73
Persian Gulf, 57
personal, 64, 67, 124, 141, 144, 151
personal history, 67
personal hygiene, 144
personal relations, 151
perspective, 58, 140
Perth, 181, 187
pesticide, 84
pesticides, 2
petroleum, 2, 6, 9, 38, 49
pharmaceutical, 38, 39, 49
phenomenology, 126
Philadelphia, 149
Philippines, 8, 52, 59, 121
philosophy, 30
phone, 45
photographs, 140
physical health, 133
physiology, 64
pineapples, 7
piracy, 41, 43
pirated, 41, 42

planning, 3, 8, 45, 59, 64, 65
plastic, 7, 145
plastic products, 7
play, 17, 19, 27, 30, 56, 116, 118, 119, 131, 144, 145, 158, 160, 162, 163
pneumonia, 139, 142
poison, 132
poisonous, 130, 132, 145
police, 41, 42, 43, 84
policymakers, 51, 55
political, 3, 4, 5, 7, 8, 11, 12, 15, 24, 25, 27, 30, 49, 51, 52, 53, 54, 55, 57, 58, 59, 73, 74
political instability, 24
political leaders, 15
political parties, 4, 25
political stability, 25
political uncertainty, 7
politicians, 27
politics, 4, 24, 25, 59, 181
pollution, 135
poor, 11, 28, 30, 44, 92, 97, 127, 128, 129, 130, 132, 139, 147, 157
population, 1, 2, 3, 5, 20, 52, 57, 70, 74, 107, 141
population growth, 1, 3
pork, 37, 127, 130, 131
pornography, 64
portfolio, 15, 28
portfolio investment, 15
positive attitudes, 29, 73
positive feedback, 164
positive relation, 78
positive relationship, 78
post-Cold War, 18, 51
postnatal, 135, 136
postpartum, 117, 123, 124, 126, 129, 130, 131, 133, 134, 135, 136
postpartum, 124, 135, 137
postpartum period, 133, 134
poultry, 37
poverty, 28
powder, 37, 104, 113
power, 3, 4, 5, 6, 12, 25, 29, 30, 40, 55, 65, 66, 170, 173, 175, 182, 184, 199
power generation, 6
powers, 4, 5, 14, 18, 19, 28, 43, 49, 56, 145, 182
predicate, 42
preferential treatment, 22
pregnancy, 61, 62, 63, 64, 65, 66, 67, 68, 69, 70, 71, 72, 73, 74, 75, 77, 78, 79, 80, 81, 82, 83, 84, 85, 86, 87, 88, 89, 90, 91, 92, 93, 94, 95, 96, 97, 98, 99, 101, 102, 103, 104, 105, 106, 107, 108, 109, 110, 111, 114, 115, 116, 117, 118, 119, 132, 136
pregnancy test, 65, 85, 86, 88, 101, 102
pregnant, 62, 63, 77, 79, 80, 81, 82, 83, 84, 85, 86, 87, 88, 89, 90, 91, 92, 93, 94, 101, 102, 104, 105, 106, 107, 108, 113, 124
pregnant women, 81, 91, 92, 93, 107
preparation, 42, 135, 185

preparedness, 78
preservice teachers, 180, 182, 186
president, 16, 23
President Bush, 53
pressure, 51, 53, 61, 81, 82, 83, 110, 113, 153
prestige, 13
prevention, 64, 116, 118, 133, 143, 144, 145, 147
prevention of infection, 144, 147
price ceiling, 49
price index, 23
price stability, 20
prices, 18, 21, 23, 30, 44, 49
primary, 152, 168, 184, 185, 189
primary care, 140, 141, 143, 144, 145, 146, 147, 148
primary caregivers, 140, 141, 143, 144, 145, 146, 147, 148
primary school, 168, 189
priming, 23
principal, 191
printing, 36, 183
prior knowledge, 181
privacy, 74, 75, 117, 147
private, 5, 6, 7, 12, 13, 16, 22, 27, 35, 40, 45, 47, 49, 56, 61, 65, 69, 79, 80, 84, 85, 86, 89, 98, 101, 102, 103, 104, 105, 109, 114, 116, 117, 119, 157
private banks, 13, 22
private investment, 7
private sector, 6, 7, 40, 49, 56
privatization, 6, 44, 45
probability, 173
probe, 72, 159
problem solving, 159
procedures, 38, 39, 40, 42, 43, 49, 54, 62, 156, 158
producers, 37, 40, 43
production, 6, 7, 9, 15, 19, 26, 36, 38, 42, 43, 130, 131, 132, 159
production networks, 19
productivity, 7, 14
professions, 48
profit, 49
profits, 15, 27
program, 3, 8, 9, 18, 23, 30, 39, 41, 49, 62, 68, 118, 143, 156, 165, 168, 169, 173, 181, 186, 190, 192
programming, 8
prolapse, 130
proliferation, 55
promote, 24, 48, 57, 118, 131, 140, 148
property, 42, 43, 58
prosperity, 56
protection, 17, 41, 42, 43, 49, 74, 133
protectionism, 24
protocol, 117
protocols, 117
psychological, 62, 63, 64, 103, 110, 115, 134, 140, 157

psychological development, 157
psychological distress, 63, 140
psychology, 119, 180
psychometric properties, 177
psychosocial, 62, 66, 67, 71, 72, 134, 136
psychosocial factors, 67, 71, 72
puberty, 64, 86, 101
public, 3, 7, 26, 27, 40, 42, 44, 55, 56, 58, 65, 70, 84, 88, 92, 95, 101, 116, 153
public corporations, 26, 27
public education, 3
public goods, 55, 56
public health, 3, 42, 65
public relations, 116
public sector, 7, 116
publishers, 43
puerperium, 133
pulses, 36
punishment, 27
pupil, 185
purchasing power, 14
Pyongyang, 55

Q

Qatar, 57
qualitative research, 61, 72, 123, 136
quality control, 73
quality of service, 44, 117
quarantine, 39
questionnaire, 151, 157, 159, 161, 165, 166, 167, 168, 169, 178, 192, 197, 198
questionnaires, 157, 159
quotas, 37

R

radio, 40, 44
random, 190, 192, 193
range, 1, 9, 16, 22, 36, 38, 42, 170
rape, 62
Rasch analysis, 151, 159, 169, 180, 190
Rasch measurement, 151, 157, 164, 165, 180, 187
Rasch measurement model, 157, 164, 165, 180, 187
Rasch Unidimensional Measurement Model (RUMM), 165, 168, 169, 173, 179, 181, 192
Rasch Unidimensional Measurement Models, 165
rat, 37
ratings, 20, 33
rationality, 118
raw material, 21, 36, 38
reading, 97, 140, 151, 152, 153, 154, 155, 156, 157, 158, 159, 160, 161, 162, 163, 164, 165, 167, 168, 169, 171, 173, 174, 175, 176, 177, 178, 179, 180, 181, 182, 183, 184, 185, 186, 187, 189, 190, 191, 192, 193, 194, 195, 196, 197, 198, 199
reading comprehension, 151, 152, 154, 156, 157, 158, 159, 160, 161, 162, 163, 164, 165, 167, 168, 169, 173, 174, 175, 177, 179, 180, 186, 189, 190, 191, 192, 193, 194, 195, 196, 197, 198, 199
reading comprehension test, 151, 157, 163, 165, 167, 168, 169, 173, 174, 175, 180, 192
reading skills, 153, 183
real estate, 15, 17, 18, 26
real wage, 28
realism, 30
reality, 184
reasoning, 18
reception, 57
recognition, 3, 160, 163
reconciliation, 59
reconstruction, 8, 53
recovery, 6, 7, 22, 23, 24, 26, 27, 29
recreational, 112
recruiting, 69, 73, 74
reduction, 37, 38
redundancy, 44
reflection, 3, 26
reforms, 4, 12
refuge, 19, 22
refugee, 136, 137
regional, 1, 7, 8, 9, 17, 20, 29, 30, 51, 56, 57, 59, 152
regional cooperation, 29, 57
regional policy, 51
regular, 81, 91, 104, 106, 118, 156, 160, 168, 191
regulation, 17, 45, 69, 91, 109, 119
regulations, 6, 39, 40, 41, 43, 46, 47, 49, 114, 119
regulators, 116
regulatory framework, 44
regulatory requirements, 38
rehabilitation, 53
relationship, 8, 17, 24, 52, 56, 64, 66, 67, 77, 78, 81, 82, 103, 117, 118, 119, 136, 148
relationships, 27, 29, 54, 64, 66, 72, 78, 83, 88, 89, 113, 114, 143, 148
relatives, 62, 78, 79, 81, 82, 83, 85, 86, 87, 91, 97, 98, 99, 102, 103, 104, 107, 111, 113, 124, 129, 144, 148
reliability, 71, 151, 165, 175
religion, 3, 141
religions, 3, 137
religious, 3, 51, 54, 58, 96, 97
religious groups, 96
reparation, 21
reproduction, 133, 136
reproductive age, 63
reputation, 41, 58, 64
research, 12, 61, 65, 66, 67, 69, 70, 71, 72, 73, 74, 114, 120, 123, 124, 134, 135, 136, 139, 140, 148, 152, 153, 155, 156, 157, 159, 160,

161, 163, 167, 168, 181, 182, 183, 186, 187, 190, 191
research design, 190
researchers, 71, 72, 124, 133, 140, 153, 155, 160
reservation, 52
reserves, 15
residuals, 166, 169
resistance, 6, 27, 28, 45, 55
resource allocation, 24
resources, 2, 6, 11, 20, 42, 48, 62, 63, 64, 65, 118, 148, 153
respiratory, 142, 146
response, 136
response format, 164, 166
restaurant, 36, 84, 90, 102
restoration, 22, 27
restructuring, 7, 20, 21, 25, 27, 28, 30, 36
retail, 41, 43, 46, 47, 49
returns, 24, 134
revenue, 39, 45
rhetoric, 185
rhizome, 132
rice, 2, 3, 7, 23, 27, 37, 41, 49, 130, 131, 133, 144
Rice, 123, 126, 127, 129, 130, 131, 133, 135, 136, 137
rights, 53, 58
risk, 19, 20, 21, 39, 40, 47, 56, 62, 63, 64, 96, 118, 133, 140, 147, 182
risk assessment, 39
risks, 17, 96, 119
robustness, 15
Royal Society, 182
rubber, 2, 7
rules of origin, 38
rural, 2, 8, 127, 128, 129, 130, 132, 133, 136
rural areas, 132
rural development, 8
Russia, 55
Russian, 55, 59
rust, 59

S

sadness, 140
safeguard, 26
safety, 19, 28, 39, 40, 49, 95, 144
salary, 80, 84, 101
sales, 8, 35, 37, 38, 41
salt, 131
sample, 70, 71, 72, 74, 75, 124, 166, 167, 168, 173
sampling, 124, 140, 190, 192, 193
sanitation, 149
satellite, 44, 45
satellite service, 44, 45
saturation, 74
Saturday, 91
savings, 14, 83

scaffold, 162
scaffolds, 184
scheduling, 191, 193
school, 2, 12, 58, 62, 63, 64, 65, 69, 78, 81, 82, 83, 85, 86, 87, 88, 89, 90, 91, 92, 95, 96, 101, 102, 104, 105, 106, 107, 108, 109, 111, 112, 117, 118, 142, 152, 153, 155, 156, 157, 159, 160, 163, 166, 167, 168, 177, 183, 184, 185, 186, 189, 190, 191, 192, 193
schooling, 152
science, 8, 185
scientific, 35, 72, 185
scientists, 137
scores, 165, 182, 191, 192
search, 42, 93
searches, 64
searching, 97
second language, 1, 151, 152, 153, 154, 155, 156, 180, 183, 184, 185, 186, 189, 196, 197, 199
second language (ESL), 151, 152, 153, 154, 155, 156, 157, 158, 159, 160, 162, 163, 164, 165, 175, 180, 181, 183, 184, 185, 186, 189, 196, 197, 198, 199
Second World War, 4, 5
secondary education, 153, 184
secondary school, 152, 153, 156, 168, 184, 186
secret, 53, 83, 84, 87, 89, 105, 106
secrets, 39
securities, 46
security, 8, 51, 52, 53, 54, 55, 56, 58, 59
Security Council, 52
seeds, 41
segmentation, 117
segregation, 28, 133
seizures, 9
selecting, 71
self, 87, 94, 125, 147, 171, 182, 187
self-confidence, 164
self-discipline, 164
self-help, 119, 147
self-identity, 64
self-management, 62, 119
self-report, 157
Senate, 5, 24
sentences, 42, 62, 154
separability index, 177, 180
separation, 58, 133, 134, 173, 175
sepsis, ix, 139
sequencing, 158, 159, 161, 162, 173, 178, 191
series, 4, 18, 55, 70, 161
service provider, 68, 71, 109, 117
services, 6, 9, 18, 35, 38, 44, 45, 46, 47, 49, 62, 65, 66, 67, 68, 70, 71, 72, 80, 83, 93, 94, 98, 103, 104, 107, 111, 114, 115, 116, 117, 118, 119
sex, 63, 64, 68, 71, 72, 73, 75, 77, 78, 79, 80, 81, 82, 83, 84, 85, 87, 89, 90, 91, 92, 94, 97, 98, 101, 102, 105, 106, 107, 108, 111, 114, 116, 118, 130

Index

sexual, 130, 133
sexual activity, 62
sexual behavior, 64, 118
sexual health, 64, 65, 75, 81
sexual intercourse, 63, 81, 84, 92, 117, 130, 133
sexual risk behavior, 64
sexuality, 64, 68, 71, 73, 74, 75, 77, 118, 119, 137
Seychelles, 57
shame, 143
shape, 96, 104, 109, 114, 154
shaping, 118, 182
shares, 26, 30, 46, 47, 120
sharing, 45, 112, 113, 119, 147
shelter, 19, 72, 78, 79, 83, 84, 88, 90, 92, 94, 96, 97, 98, 101, 103, 106, 107, 111, 112, 113, 115, 116, 117, 119
shipping, 46
shock, 19, 21, 83, 87, 101, 106
shocks, 18, 26
short period, 11, 107
short run, 19
shortage, 7, 17, 21, 44
short-term, 12, 13, 15, 26, 57, 62
shrimp, 7, 131
shy, 109
siblings, 142, 143
side effects, 64, 80, 83, 103
sign, 16, 74, 85, 168
signs, 12, 16, 22, 23, 27, 82, 84, 85, 101
similarity, 71
simple random sampling, 190
Singapore, 2, 8, 9, 17, 22, 31, 45, 52, 54, 55, 56, 57, 60, 185, 186
sites, 64, 73
skills, 4, 71, 73, 118, 119, 152, 153, 154, 156, 159, 162, 183, 187, 191
skin, 129, 130, 132, 142, 145, 146
sleep, 130, 144
smoking, 118, 136
smuggling, 9
social, 3, 23, 24, 27, 28, 29, 30, 51, 58, 62, 64, 65, 66, 68, 69, 70, 72, 75, 81, 83, 87, 90, 97, 106, 110, 113, 115, 133, 134, 135, 137, 143, 148, 153, 155, 156, 158, 160, 161, 162, 163, 181, 183, 187
social change, 156
social context, 135, 155
social development, 29
social group, 27, 158
social isolation, 134
social network, 72
social norms, 87, 97
social problems, 28, 30
social safety nets, 28
social sciences, 181
social services, 68, 70
social skills, 162
social status, 90

social stigmatization, 143, 148
social work, 69, 72, 75, 83, 97, 106, 115
social workers, 69, 72, 115
socialism, 25
socialization, 155
socializing agent, 136
socially, 18, 30, 75, 77, 78, 87, 107, 114, 157
society, 6, 11, 16, 24, 27, 29, 56, 59, 66, 75, 77, 78, 91, 94, 114, 124, 132, 134, 140, 141
soft drinks, 75
soil, 52
solidarity, 57
solutions, 56, 115, 116, 146
South Africa, 56, 57
South Asia, 55, 57
South Korea, 8, 11, 57
Southeast Asia, 2, 3, 4, 5, 8, 11, 14, 15, 16, 18, 19, 32, 52, 53, 54, 55, 56, 57, 60, 121, 131, 137
soybeans, 2, 37
specialists, 63, 117
spectrum, 44
spectrum management, 44
speculation, 54
speed, 42, 47
spices, 131
spills, 147
Sri Lanka, 57
stability, 5, 8, 15, 18, 20, 22, 23, 24, 25, 29, 30, 53, 54, 55, 59
stages, 49, 118, 133, 147
standard deviation, 166, 194, 196, 197
standard error, 170, 194, 196, 197
standard of living, 57
standards, 15, 36, 37, 39, 40, 43, 74
state enterprises, 40
state-owned, 6, 40, 44, 45
state-owned enterprises, 6, 40, 45
statistics, 15, 18, 28, 166, 169, 170, 174, 175
steel, 2, 7, 15, 21
stereotype, 140
stigma, 110
stigmatization, 68, 71, 79, 110, 111, 114, 143, 148
stigmatized, 63, 98
stimulus, 6, 36
stock, 16, 18, 19, 22, 23, 26, 35
stock markets, 19, 26
stock price, 18, 23
stomach, 127, 128
strain, 7
strategic, 18, 19, 54, 55, 57
strategies, 17, 66, 156, 183, 186
strategy use, 184
strength, 30
stress, 15, 97, 102, 107, 112, 115, 148, 154
strikes, 15, 28
structuralism, 12, 30
Student Satisfaction Inventory (SSI), 172, 176

students, 17, 23, 25, 65, 77, 82, 91, 107, 108, 111, 151, 153, 154, 155, 156, 157, 158, 159, 160, 161, 162, 163, 164, 165, 166, 167, 168, 169, 170, 172, 173, 174, 175, 177, 178, 179, 180, 181, 182, 184, 185, 186, 187, 189, 190, 191, 192, 193, 194, 195, 196, 197, 198
study, 123, 124, 125, 126, 129, 130, 133, 134, 135, 136
subgroups, 172, 180
subjective, 125, 160, 161, 163
subjective experience, 125
subscribers, 45
subsidies, 41
substance abuse, 118
substances, 132, 145
substitutes, 155
suffering, 83, 146, 147
sugar, 7, 23, 27, 49
sugarcane, 2
Suharto, 13, 17, 20, 22, 25
suicide, 84
summaries, 141
Sunday, 91
superiority, 52
supernatural, 123, 145
superstitious, 141
supervision, 17, 26, 44, 64
supervisor, 159
suppliers, 2, 37, 40, 47, 49, 55
supply, 19, 40, 47, 63
suppression, 63
Supreme Court, 5
surplus, 15, 19
surprise, 52, 58
survival, 139
survival rate, 139
suspects, 58
sweat, 132
Sweden, 135
Switzerland, 21
Sydney, 137
symbolic, 53, 141
symbols, 66, 134, 137, 141
sympathetic, 89
sympathy, 143
symptom, 145
symptoms, 82, 84, 85, 101, 126, 127, 142, 145
syndrome, 147
synthesis, 180
systems, 11, 21, 26, 27, 29, 66, 116, 119, 120, 132, 136, 181

T

Taiwan, 9, 55, 135
Taliban, 52
tangible, 55
tantalum, 2
Tanzania, 57
target population, 107
targets, 22, 23
tariff, 35, 36, 37, 38
tariff rates, 36, 37, 38
tariffs, 35, 37, 38
tax collection, 26
tax increase, 20
taxes, 30, 36, 37, 38
tea, 132
teacher training, 8, 152, 153, 185
teachers, 64, 68, 77, 118, 152, 153, 154, 155, 156, 158, 159, 164, 168, 177, 180, 181, 182, 184, 185, 186, 187, 190, 191, 193
teaching, 118, 151, 152, 153, 154, 155, 156, 158, 159, 160, 161, 162, 163, 167, 168, 173, 178, 181, 182, 183, 184, 185, 186, 189, 191, 192, 193, 194, 196, 197, 198, 199
teaching process, 163
technological, 7, 19
technology, 7, 8, 40, 54, 153
teens, 147
teeth, 112
telecommunication, 44, 49
telecommunications, 4, 6, 24, 44, 45
telecommunications policy, 44
telecommunications services, 44, 45
telephone, 44, 115
telephony, 44
television, 47, 97
tension, 55, 87
territorial, 58
territory, 41, 58
terrorism, 51, 52, 53, 54, 55, 56, 58, 59
terrorist, 52, 53, 56, 58
terrorist attack, 52, 56, 58
terrorist groups, 52, 53
terrorists, 52, 58
tertiary education, 152
test data, 159
test items, 159, 161, 167, 173, 178, 179, 180
Texas, 1
text analysis, 162
textile, 38, 91
textiles, 2, 38
theoretical, 12, 30, 66, 67, 74, 114, 124, 158, 165, 185
theory, 66, 71, 74, 154, 155, 160, 162, 181, 183, 185
therapy, 137, 142, 145
thinking, 57, 77, 78, 81, 87, 96, 104, 112, 129
third party, 20
Third World, 31, 149
threat, 3, 43, 51, 53, 54, 55
threatened, 5, 23
threatening, 61
threats, 15, 18, 51, 52, 55, 56
threshold, 42, 133, 165, 170
thresholds, 165, 169

thrush, 142
timber, 2
time, 3, 8, 11, 17, 23, 28, 39, 40, 42, 44, 45, 46, 51, 53, 58, 62, 63, 64, 71, 74, 75, 78, 79, 80, 81, 82, 83, 84, 88, 91, 93, 94, 95, 96, 97, 102, 103, 104, 105, 107, 108, 109, 110, 111, 112, 124, 125, 126, 128, 133, 134, 136, 140, 141, 143, 146, 147, 148, 153, 157, 162, 163, 165, 167, 168, 171, 177, 191, 193
time constraints, 126, 146
timetable, 6
tissue, 104
toddlers, 142, 144
toilet training, 144
Tokyo, 55, 60, 183
top-down, 58
total government expenditures, 3
tourism, 2, 24, 32, 53, 141
toys, 7, 43, 145
trade, 6, 8, 11, 12, 13, 14, 15, 19, 20, 21, 22, 26, 27, 28, 35, 37, 39, 41, 42, 46, 48, 54, 55, 57
trade agreement, 8
trade deficit, 12, 15, 19, 35
trade union, 28
trademarks, 44
trade-off, 27
Trade-Related Investment Measures (TRIMS), 48
trading, 7, 9, 23, 54
trading partners, 7
tradition, 3, 134, 155
traditional, 123, 124, 126, 133, 134, 136, 137
traditional healers, 65, 72, 98, 103, 107
traditional practices, 124, 133, 134
traditions, 123, 132, 134, 135
traffic, 40
trafficking in persons, 8
training, 8, 52, 71, 72, 73, 101, 117, 118, 144, 152, 153, 156, 181, 182, 183, 185, 186
training programs, 8
trans, 187
transactions, 17, 20, 25, 30, 40, 48
transcription, 70, 73, 126
transcripts, 74, 126
transfer, 49, 153
transition, 64, 66, 71, 134
translation, 71
transmission, 143, 146, 147
transnational, 41, 51, 56
transparency, 19, 20, 21, 25, 39, 40, 42, 47, 49
transparent, 18, 36, 37, 40, 49
transport, 46, 47
transportation, 6, 7, 48, 146
trauma, 66, 110
Treasury, 14, 15, 19, 30, 53
Treasury Department, 15, 53
treaties, 8, 43
trial, 157
triangulation, 126
tribes, 2

trucking, 47
trucks, 38
True Score Theory, 164, 165
trust, 59, 70, 72, 75, 85, 107
tsunami, 6, 7
tungsten, 2

U

U.S. Agency for International Development, 8
U.S. dollar, 7, 24
U.S. military, 8
uncertainty, 7, 18, 19, 45, 46, 49
undifferentiated, 152
unemployment, 11, 14, 20, 28, 78
unemployment rate, 14, 28
uniform, 179
unions, 6, 15, 27, 29
United Arab Emirates, 57
United Kingdom, 3, 57, 154, 182
United Nations, 9, 139
United States, 3, 5, 6, 7, 8, 9, 29, 35, 37, 38, 40, 41, 42, 47, 48, 135
United States (US), 135
universities, 152
university, 181
University of Sydney, 181
unmarried women, 62, 73, 84, 111
unplanned pregnancies, 61, 62, 63, 65, 66, 67, 68, 69, 70, 71, 72, 73, 74, 75, 77, 79, 80, 82, 85, 87, 88, 89, 90, 93, 96, 97, 98, 105, 107, 111, 113, 114, 115, 116, 117, 118, 119
upper respiratory infection, 142
urban, 2, 28, 124, 127, 128, 129, 130, 131, 132, 184
urban population, 2
urbanization, 78
urine, 82, 85, 86, 101, 108
Uruguay, 36
Uruguay Round, 36
users, 43, 44, 64, 116, 119
uterus, 95, 128, 130

V

vaccination, 139
vagina, 104, 106
vaginal, 117
valence, 186
validity, 70, 71, 151, 165
value-added tax (VAT), 36
values, 21, 28, 39, 64, 73, 115, 165, 166, 170, 184
variable, 164, 165, 172
variables, 51, 66, 67, 165, 169
variance, 170, 173, 174
vegetables, 36, 39, 127, 130, 131, 146

vehicles, 2, 7, 37, 38, 39
vein, 18
victims, 11, 18, 143
Victoria, 123
Vietnam, 5, 8, 54
Vietnamese, 2
village, 124, 136, 137, 140, 190
violence, 4, 6, 51, 53, 58, 59, 81, 140
violent, 5, 23, 53, 55, 56, 58
virtual reality, 184
visa, 53
visible, 19, 27
visual, 193
vocabulary, 154, 158, 159, 161, 162
vocational, 25, 65, 82, 86, 89, 91, 95, 101, 102, 104, 108, 109, 112
vocational training, 101
vomiting, 80
voters, 5
vulnerability, 19, 52, 64, 123, 133
Vygotsky, 161, 163, 187

W

wages, 15, 18, 80
walking, 92, 108, 109
war, 53
War on Terror, 51, 52, 53
warehousing, 42
warfare, 58
warning systems, 26
Washington, 6, 18, 31, 32, 53, 55, 60
Washington Post, 60
water, 127, 129, 131, 132, 145, 149
Watson, 136, 156
weakness, 126
weapons, 53, 54
weapons of mass destruction, 53
wear, 127, 128, 132
web, 160, 182
welfare, 29
well-being, 56, 77, 133, 134, 147
wet, 3, 130
White House, 53
wholesale, 35
wind, 126, 127, 128, 129, 132
windows, 127, 181

wine, 36, 132, 136
Wisconsin, 6
withdrawal, 16, 19, 53, 80, 104
wives, 81, 102, 103
women, 56, 61, 62, 63, 64, 65, 66, 67, 68, 69, 70, 71, 72, 73, 74, 75, 77, 78, 79, 80, 81, 82, 83, 84, 85, 86, 87, 88, 89, 90, 91, 92, 93, 94, 95, 96, 97, 98, 99, 101, 102, 103, 105, 107, 108, 109, 110, 111, 112, 113, 114, 115, 116, 117, 118, 119, 120, 123, 124, 125, 126, 127, 128, 129, 130, 131, 132, 133, 134, 135, 136, 137
wood, 7, 101
wood products, 7
word level inference (MIW), 161, 164, 167, 175, 178, 179
word meanings, 157, 175, 178
word of mouth, 89, 92, 93, 95, 97
work, 130, 133
workers, 7, 18, 27, 28, 63, 69, 72, 84, 115, 140, 141
workforce, 3
working groups, 57
workplace, 91
World Bank, 16, 18, 19, 20, 22, 26, 32, 44
World Intellectual Property Organization (WIPO), 43
World Trade Organization, 7, 54
World War, 4, 5, 8, 21
worry, 78, 79, 90, 104, 109
writing, 24, 44, 133, 155, 156, 158, 162, 182, 185, 186
writing tasks, 185
written records, 158

Y

Yemen, 57
young women, 61, 62, 64, 65, 66, 67, 68, 69, 70, 71, 72, 73, 74, 75, 77, 78, 79, 80, 81, 82, 83, 85, 86, 88, 90, 91, 92, 95, 97, 98, 101, 107, 108, 109, 110, 111, 114, 115, 116, 117, 118, 119, 120

Z

zone of proximate development, 163